CompTIA Network+®
Certification Practice Exams

(Exam N10-005)

Robb H. Tracy

New York Chicago San Francisco Lisbon London Madrid
Mexico City Milan New Delhi San Juan Seoul Singapore Sydney Toronto

The McGraw·Hill Companies

Cataloging-in-Publication Data is on file with the Library of Congress

McGraw-Hill books are available at special quantity discounts to use as premiums and sales promotions, or for use in corporate training programs. To contact a representative, please e-mail us at bulksales@mcgraw-hill.com.

CompTIA Network+® Certification Practice Exams (Exam N10-005)

1234567890   QFR QFR   1098765432

ISBN: Book p/n 978-0-07-178878-6 and CD p/n 978-0-07-178879-3
of set 978-0-07-178881-6

MHID: Book p/n 0-07-178878-6 and CD p/n 0-07-178879-4
of set 0-07-178881-6

Sponsoring Editor Meghan Riley Manfre	**Technical Editor** Daniel Lachance	**Production Supervisor** Jim Kussow
Editorial Supervisor Jody McKenzie	**Copy Editor** Lisa Theobald	**Composition** Cenveo Publisher Services
Project Manager Ridhi Mathur, Cenveo Publisher Services	**Proofreader** Carol Shields	**Illustration** Cenveo Publisher Services
Acquisitions Coordinator Stephanie Evans	**Indexer** Jack Lewis	**Art Director, Cover** Jeff Weeks

This book is dedicated to all the individuals who have made a difference in my life. To my Dad, for instilling in me a love of teaching and of all things mechanical. To my Mom, for teaching me the value of hard work and devotion. To my mentor, Dennis Simmons, for teaching me to strive for excellence in all I do. To my wife and best friend, for supporting and loving me through the process of writing this book.

ABOUT THE AUTHOR

Robb H. Tracy, CNA, CNE, CNI, A+, Network+, Linux+, has been a professional technology instructor and courseware developer since 1996. He has designed and implemented technical training products and curricula for major hardware and software vendors including Novell, Micron Technology, TestOut, Messaging Architects, Caselle, Motorola, Cymphonix, and NextPage. Robb previously served on CompTIA's Network+ Advisory Committee, where he helped define the objectives that make up the CompTIA Network+ certification. He is a co-founder of Nebo Technical Institute, Inc., a leading provider of information technology training and consulting. Robb is the author of *Novell Certified Linux Engineer (Novell CLE) Study Guide* (Novell Press, 2005), *Novell Certified Linux Engineer 9 (CLE 9) Study Guide* (Novell Press, 2006), *Linux+ Certification Study Guide* (McGraw-Hill, 2008), and *LPIC-1/CompTIA Linux+ Certification All-in-One Exam Guide* (McGraw-Hill, 2011). Robb was also a contributing author to *SUSE Linux 10 Unleashed* (Sams Publishing, 2006).

About the Technical Editor

Daniel Lachance, MCITP, MCTS, CNI, IBM Certified Instructor, CompTIA A+, CompTIA Network+, CompTIA Security+, is a technical trainer for Global Knowledge and has delivered classroom training in a wide variety of products for the past 17 years. Throughout his career, he has also developed custom applications and planned, implemented, troubleshot, and documented various network configurations.

About LearnKey

LearnKey provides self-paced learning content and multimedia delivery solutions to enhance personal skills and business productivity. LearnKey claims the largest library of rich streaming-media training content that engages learners in dynamic media-rich instruction complete with video clips, audio, full motion graphics, and animated illustrations. LearnKey can be found on the Web at www.LearnKey.com.

CompTIA Network+

The CompTIA Network+ certification ensures that the successful candidate has the important knowledge and skills necessary to manage, maintain, troubleshoot, install, operate and configure basic network infrastructure, describe networking technologies, basic design principles, and adhere to wiring standards and use testing tools.

It Pays to Get Certified

In a digital world, digital literacy is an essential survival skill. Certification proves you have the knowledge and skill to solve business problems in virtually any business environment. Certifications are highly valued credentials that qualify you for jobs, increased compensation, and promotion.

CompTIA Network+ certification is held by many IT staffers across many organizations. 21% of IT staff within a random sampling of U.S. organizations within a cross section of industry verticals hold CompTIA Network+ certification.

- The CompTIA Network+ credential—proves knowledge of networking features and functions and is the leading vendor-neutral certification for networking professionals.

- Starting Salary—the average starting salary of network engineers can be up to $70,000.

- Career Pathway—CompTIA Network+ is the first step in starting a networking career, and is recognized by Microsoft as part of their MS program. Other corporations, such as Novell, Cisco and HP also recognize CompTIA Network+ as part of their certification tracks.

- More than 325,000—individuals worldwide are CompTIA Network+ certified.

- Mandated/Recommended by organizations worldwide—Apple, Cisco, HP, Ricoh, the U.S. State Department, and U.S. government contractors such as EDS, General Dynamics, and Northrop Grumman recommend or mandate CompTIA Network+.

How Certification Helps Your Career

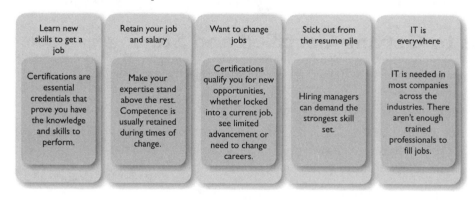

Learn new skills to get a job	Retain your job and salary	Want to change jobs	Stick out from the resume pile	IT is everywhere
Certifications are essential credentials that prove you have the knowledge and skills to perform.	Make your expertise stand above the rest. Competence is usually retained during times of change.	Certifications qualify you for new opportunities, whether locked into a current job, see limited advancement or need to change careers.	Hiring managers can demand the strongest skill set.	IT is needed in most companies across the industries. There aren't enough trained professionals to fill jobs.

CompTIA Career Pathway

CompTIA offers a number of credentials that form a foundation for your career in technology and that allow you to pursue specific areas of concentration. Depending on the path you choose, CompTIA certifications help you build upon your skills and knowledge, supporting learning throughout your career.

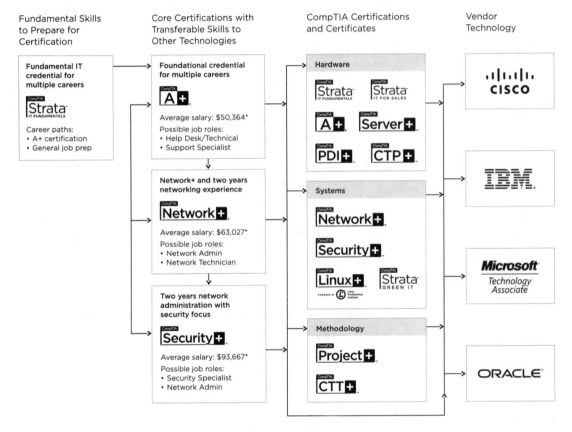

*Source: *Computerworld* Salary Survey 2010—U.S. salaries only

Steps to Getting Certified and Staying Certified

1. **Review exam objectives.** Review the certification objectives to make sure you know what is covered in the exam:
   www.comptia.org/certifications/testprep/examobjectives.aspx

2. **Practice for the exam.** After you have studied for the certification, take a free assessment and sample test to get an idea what type of questions might be on the exam:
   www.comptia.org/certifications/testprep/practicetests.aspx

3. **Purchase an exam voucher.** Purchase exam vouchers on the CompTIA Marketplace, which is located at www.comptiastore.com

4. **Take the test!** Select a certification exam provider, and schedule a time to take your exam. You can find exam providers at the following link: www.comptia.org/certifications/testprep/testingcenters.aspx

5. **Stay Certified!** Continuing education is required. Effective January 1, 2011, CompTIA Network+ certifications are valid for three years from the date of certification. There are a number of ways the certification can be renewed. For more information go to: http://certification.comptia.org/getCertified/steps_to_certification/stayCertified.aspx

Join the Professional Community

The free online IT Pro Community provides valuable content to students and professionals. Join the IT Pro Community:

http://itpro.comptia.org

Career IT job resources include:

- Where to start in IT
- Career assessments
- Salary trends
- U.S. job board

Join the IT Pro Community and get access to:

- Forums on networking, security, computing, and cutting-edge technologies
- Access to blogs written by industry experts
- Current information on cutting edge technologies
- Access to various industry resource links and articles related to IT and IT careers

AUTHORIZED

Content Seal of Quality

This courseware bears the seal of CompTIA Approved Quality Content. This seal signifies this content covers 100 percent of the exam objectives and implements important instructional design principles. CompTIA recommends multiple learning tools to help increase coverage of the learning objectives.

Why CompTIA?

- **Global recognition** CompTIA is recognized globally as the leading IT nonprofit trade association and has enormous credibility. Plus, CompTIA's certifications are vendor-neutral and offer proof of foundational knowledge that translates across technologies.

- **Valued by hiring managers** Hiring managers value CompTIA certification because it is vendor- and technology-independent validation of your technical skills.

- **Recommended or required by government and businesses** Many government organizations and corporations (for example, Dell, Sharp, Ricoh, the U.S. Department of Defense, and many more) either recommend or require technical staff to be CompTIA certified.

- **Three CompTIA certifications ranked in the top 10** In a study by DICE of 17,000 technology professionals, certifications helped command higher salaries at all experience levels.

How to Obtain More Information

- **Visit CompTIA online** Go to www.comptia.org to learn more about getting CompTIA certified.
- **Contact CompTIA** Please call 866-835-8020, ext. 5 or e-mail questions@comptia.org.
- **Join the IT Pro Community** Go to http://itpro.comptia.org to join the IT community to get relevant career information.
- **Connect with CompTIA** Find us on Facebook, LinkedIn, Twitter, and YouTube.

CAQC Disclaimer

The logo of the CompTIA Approved Quality Curriculum (CAQC) program and the status of this or other training material as "Approved" under the CompTIA Approved Quality Curriculum program signifies that, in CompTIA's opinion, such training material covers the content of CompTIA's related certification exam.

The contents of this training material were created for the CompTIA Network+ exam covering CompTIA certification objectives that were current as of the date of publication.

CompTIA has not reviewed or approved the accuracy of the contents of this training material and specifically disclaims any warranties of merchantability or fitness for a particular purpose. CompTIA makes no guarantee concerning the success of persons using any such "Approved" or other training material in order to prepare for any CompTIA certification exam.

CONTENTS

The purpose of this book is to prepare you for the CompTIA Network+ exam (Exam N10-005) as well as for your work in the network administration field. Whether you are an experienced IT professional or a newcomer to the industry, this book has been developed to serve as a comprehensive review that will prepare you for all topics covered on the exam.

Inside this Book

Within this book you will find practice exam questions that mirror the actual exam questions in content, style, tone, format, and difficulty. For each question, you will find an explanation for both the correct *and* incorrect answers, allowing you to test the information you know and learn the information you don't know.

In Every Chapter

This book is organized for efficiency so that you can make the most of the time you spend studying. Take a look at what you'll find in every chapter:

- **Certification Objectives**   Every chapter begins with these objectives, which are the vendor-provided exam objectives covered in the chapter.
- **Practice Exam Questions**   From 15 to 30 unique questions are included in every chapter. By answering these questions you will test your knowledge while familiarizing yourself with the format of the actual exam questions.
- **Quick Answer Key**   The key follows the questions and allows you to check your answers.
- **In-Depth Answers**   At the end of every chapter, these provide the opportunity to learn not only why one answer choice is correct but why the others are not.

Pre-Assessment Test

This book features a pre-assessment test as Appendix A. The pre-assessment test will gauge your areas of strength and weakness and allow you to tailor your studies based on your needs. It is recommended that you take this pre-assessment test before beginning Chapter 1.

Practice Exams

Of the 700-plus questions included with this book, 300 are organized into three practice exams. Each practice exam comprises a set of questions identical in number to the questions in the actual certification exam. Each practice exam also simulates the composition of the actual exam, with the number of questions per domain analogous to the actual exam. One practice exam is included within the book as Appendix B and the other two exams are included in simulated test engine software.

Objective Map

Following the introduction, you will find an Objective Map. This map has been constructed in the form of a table to allow you to reference the official certification exam objectives, the chapter in which each objective is covered, and the specific questions pertaining to each objective.

On the CD

Included on the CD-ROM, you will find one practice exam and a link to an additional exam available for download with free registration. For more information on the CD-ROM, please see Appendix C, "About the CD."

How to Use this Book

This book was developed and written in conjunction with the *CompTIA Network+ Certification Study Guide, Fifth Edition (Exam N10-005)*, by Glen E. Clarke. The order the objectives are covered in both books is identical, as are the chapter titles. These books were designed to work together as a comprehensive program for self-study, but both books are discrete and complete test prep guides.

Strategies for Use

There are a variety of ways in which this book can be used, whether in tandem with the *Study Guide* or on its own.

With the Study Guide   Taking a chapter-by-chapter approach, you can opt to read a *Study Guide* chapter and then practice what you have learned with the questions in the corresponding *Practice Exams* chapter, alternating between books throughout your course of study. If you choose this method, you will have five complete practice exams to take at the end of your studies.

If you opt for this approach, you can begin by taking the pre-assessment test included as Appendix A in this book. The pre-assessment test will gauge your level of competency in each of the different exam domains and highlight those domains in which you excel and those in which you would benefit from additional review. Knowing this information at the outset of your studies will allow you to check your progress and allot your study time based on your needs.

The Practice Exams Book on Its Own   Whether you are using this book after you have read the *Study Guide* or you're using it on its own, one course of study is to begin with the pre-assessment test. Armed with the knowledge of your levels of expertise by exam domain, you can use the Objective Map to tailor the order in which you review the objectives and practice exam questions.

Or, if you prefer, you can work through this book cover to cover. You have the option to begin with Chapter 1 and work through all of the chapters and exam topics in the order they are presented. If you opt for this method, you can use the pre-assessment test for additional review and use the three practice exams as the final step in your exam preparation.

ACKNOWLEDGMENTS

The title page of this book lists Robb H. Tracy as its author. However, this attribution is deceiving. By no means was this a one-person job. Behind every book is a team of individuals who rarely get the credit they deserve. They are the unsung heroes who make sure the job gets done.

First, I would also like to acknowledge the efforts of the production team behind this book. These folks were the glue that kept everything together. Thanks to Meghan Riley Manfre for giving me the opportunity to write this book. I appreciate your confidence in me! Thanks to Stephanie Evans for managing the development process. No matter the time of day, Steph was always there with the information I needed. Thanks, Steph! Thanks also to Ridhi Mathur for helping me through the final review process. Her experienced eyes are the reason this book looks good.

Finally, a huge thank you to Dan Lachance. Dan reviewed each and every test question in this book for technical accuracy. His efforts kept me honest and were absolutely invaluable, dramatically increasing the overall quality of this title. Dan spent many late nights testing the lab exercises in this book, ensuring that you have a successful experience. Thanks, Dan!

INTRODUCTION

The CompTIA Network+ exam is a vendor-neutral exam that validates your network administration skills. The CompTIA Network+ exam expects you to be familiar with the following topics:

- Network security
- Network technologies and devices
- Network media types and topologies
- Network management practices and tools

The folks at CompTIA suggest that you have some computer-related experience under your belt before embarking on the Network+ training and certification process. They recommend (but do not require) you do the following before taking your Network+ exam:

- *Complete your CompTIA A+ certification.* This will provide you with a strong background in PC hardware concepts and management tasks.
- *Gain nine months of experience supporting or managing computer networks.* This will provide you with real-world experience that helps ensure you can walk the walk as well as talk the talk. If this isn't possible, CompTIA recommends you have nine months of equivalent academic training.

The CompTIA Network+ exam consists of 100 questions. You will have 90 minutes to complete the exam. The highest score you can achieve on the Network+ exam is 900. To pass, you must post a score of 720 or better.

Please note the ratio between exam questions and completion time. If you do the math, you'll see that you have less than 1 minute to complete each question. Don't get hung up on the difficult items. If you take excessive time solving a particularly difficult question, you may eventually identify the correct answer; however, you also could torpedo the rest of your exam. If you get stuck, go on to the next item. When you're done, come back to the difficult questions and spend the remaining time you have working on them.

The CompTIA Network+ exam consists of five domains (categories). CompTIA represents the relative importance of each domain within the body of knowledge required for an entry-level IT professional taking this exam. The domains covered and their relative weights are listed here:

- 1.0 Network Technologies: 21 percent
- 2.0 Network Installation and Configuration: 23 percent
- 3.0 Network Media and Topologies: 17 percent
- 4.0 Network Management: 20 percent
- 5.0 Network Security: 19 percent

As of January 1, 2011, your CompTIA Network+ certification is valid for 3 years from the date you are certified, after which you must take the most current version of the exam to keep your certification. Detailed information regarding the CompTIA Network+ certification and exam is available at www.comptia.org.

Exam N10-005

Official Objective	Chapter	Question Numbers
1.0 Networking Concepts		
1.1 Compare the layers of the OSI and TCP/IP models.	2, 4	Chapter 2: 8, 9, 11, 12, 13, 14 Chapter 4: 1, 2, 5, 6
1.2 Classify how applications, devices, and protocols relate to the OSI model layers.	2, 3	Chapter 2: 1, 2, 3, 4, 5, 6, 7, 10, 15, 16, 17, 18, 19, 20, 21, 22, 23, 24, 25, 26 Chapter 3: 1, 2, 5, 6, 7, 9, 18, 19, 20, 21, 22, 23, 24, 32
1.3 Explain the purpose and properties of IP addressing.	4, 7	Chapter 4: 7, 8, 9, 10, 11, 12, 13, 14, 16, 17, 18, 19, 20, 21 Chapter 7: 1, 2, 3, 4, 5, 6
1.4 Explain the purpose and properties of routing and switching.	3, 6, 7	Chapter 3: 8, 10, 11, 12, 13, 14, 15 Chapter 6: 5, 11 Chapter 7: 7, 11, 12, 13, 14, 15, 16, 17, 18, 19
1.5 Identify common TCP and UDP default ports.	4	15, 28, 29, 30
1.6 Explain the function of common networking protocols.	4, 5	Chapter 4: 3, 4, 22, 23, 24, 25, 26, 27 Chapter 5: 19, 20, 21
1.7 Summarize DNS concepts and its components.	8	1, 2, 3, 4, 5, 6, 7, 8, 9, 10

Official Objective	Chapter	Question Numbers
1.8 Given a scenario, implement the following network troubleshooting methodology: identify the problem; establish a theory of probable cause; test the theory to determine cause; establish a plan of action to resolve the problem and identify potential effects; implement the solution or escalate as necessary; implement the solution or escalate as necessary; verify full system functionality and, if applicable, implement preventative measures; and document findings, actions, and outcomes.	15	1, 2, 3, 4, 5, 6
1.9 Identify virtual network components.	3	17, 31, 34
2.0 Network Installation and Configuration		
2.1 Given a scenario, install and configure routers and switches.	6, 7, 8	Chapter 6: 1, 2, 3, 4, 5, 6, 7, 8, 9, 10 Chapter 7: 8, 9, 10, 20 Chapter 8: 16, 17, 18
2.2 Given a scenario, install and configure a wireless network.	9	1, 2, 3, 5
2.3 Explain the purpose and properties of DHCP.	8	6, 11, 12, 13, 14, 15
2.4 Given a scenario, troubleshoot common wireless problems.	9	7, 14, 15, 16
2.5 Given a scenario, troubleshoot common router and switch problems.	6	12, 13, 14, 15, 16, 17, 18
2.6 Given a set of requirements, plan and implement a basic SOHO network.	12	1, 2, 3, 4, 5, 6, 7, 8, 9, 10, 11, 12, 13, 14, 15, 16, 17, 18, 19, 20, 21, 22
3.0 Network Media and Topologies		
3.1 Categorize standard media types and associated properties.	1, 3	Chapter 1: 7, 8, 10, 12, 21, 22, 23, 25, 26, 27, 28 Chapter 3: 3, 4, 25
3.2 Categorize standard connector types based on network media.	1, 3	Chapter 1: 6, 9, 24, 29, 30, 31 Chapter 3: 27, 28
3.3 Compare and contrast different wireless standards.	9	4, 6, 17, 18
3.4 Categorize WAN technology types and properties.	10, 11	Chapter 10: 1, 2, 3 Chapter 11: 1, 2, 3, 4, 5, 6, 7, 8, 9, 10, 11, 12, 13, 14, 15, 16, 17, 18
3.5 Describe different network topologies.	1	1, 2, 3, 4, 5, 15, 16, 17, 20

(continued)

Official Objective	Chapter	Question Numbers
3.6 Given a scenario, troubleshoot common physical connectivity problems.	15	7, 8, 9, 11
3.7 Compare and contrast different LAN technologies.	1, 3	Chapter 1: 11, 13, 14, 18, 19 Chapter 3: 13, 14
3.8 Identify components of wiring distribution.	3	26, 29, 30
4.0 Network Management		
4.1 Explain the purpose and features of various network appliances.	3	16, 17, 33
4.2 Given a scenario, use appropriate hardware tools to troubleshoot connectivity issues	15	10, 12, 13, 16
4.3 Given a scenario, use appropriate software tools to troubleshoot connectivity issues.	5, 15	Chapter 5: 1, 2, 3, 4, 5, 6, 7, 8, 9, 10, 11, 12, 13, 14, 15, 16, 17, 18, 22, 23, 24, 25, 26, 27 Chapter 15: 14, 15
4.4 Given a scenario, use the appropriate network monitoring resource to analyze traffic.	13	11, 12, 13, 14, 15, 16, 17, 18, 19, 20
4.5 Describe the purpose of configuration management documentation.	13	1, 2, 3, 4, 5, 6, 7, 8, 9, 10
4.6 Explain different methods and rationales for network performance optimization.	15	17, 18, 19, 20
5.0 Network Security		
5.1 Given a scenario, implement appropriate wireless security measures.	9	8, 9, 10, 13, 19
5.2 Explain the methods of network access security.	10	4, 5, 6, 7, 8, 9, 10, 11, 12, 13, 14, 15, 16, 17, 18, 19, 20
5.3 Explain methods of user authentication.	14	10, 11, 12, 13, 14, 15, 16, 17
5.4 Explain common threats, vulnerabilities, and mitigation techniques.	9, 14	Chapter 9: 11, 12, 20 Chapter 14: 1, 2, 3, 4, 5, 6, 7, 8, 9, 28
5.5 Given a scenario, install and configure a basic firewall.	14	18, 19, 20, 21, 22, 23
5.6 Categorize different types of network security appliances and methods.	14	24, 25, 26, 27, 29

1

Basic Network Concepts

QUESTIONS

To manage a computer network effectively, you must have a solid understanding of the infrastructure on which it works. Many different types of cabling have been commonly used over the years to build networks. You need to be familiar with the various media types and how the cables are physically run. Media connectors are used to connect the network cabling to network devices, such as network interface cards, hubs, switches, and routers. You need to be able to identify these connectors by sight. Many different LAN technologies have also been implemented in computer networks over the years. You need to be familiar with how each technology works along with its limitations in terms of transmission distance and speed. Finally, you need a basic level of familiarity with wiring distribution components.

1. You manage a network within an office suite composed of three Windows 7 workstations configured to work together in a workgroup. Each system is connected to the same network switch using Gigabit Ethernet network interfaces and drop cables. What type of network is this? (Choose two.)
   A. Local area network
   B. Wide area network
   C. Metropolitan area network
   D. Client/server network
   E. Peer-to-peer network

2. Which of the following are characteristics of a client/server network? (Choose three.)
   A. Each host maintains its own set of user accounts that must be kept synchronized with each other.
   B. All hosts on the network can use a common set of user and group accounts stored on a dedicated host for authentication.
   C. Printers and data folders on each network host are shared with other network hosts.
   D. Files are stored on and shared from a dedicated host on the network.
   E. All network hosts running a version of Windows are configured to be members of the same workgroup.
   F. All network hosts running a version of Windows are configured to be members of the same domain.

3. You are responsible for managing a 10Base-2 Ethernet network. The hosts on this network are connected together by a single run of coaxial cable, from system to system to system, with terminators on each end. The network does not use a hub or switch. What type of physical topology does this network use?
   A. Ring
   B. Star
   C. Bus
   D. Mesh

4. You are working with a Token Ring network, which uses token passing from host to host to control access to the network media. The network uses twisted-pair wires to connect each network host to a multistation access unit (MSAU), which manages the passing of the token. What type of physical topology does this network use?
    A. Ring
    B. Star
    C. Bus
    D. Mesh

5. You need to copy files from one Windows 7 laptop to a second one. To do this, you configured both workstations to connect to each other using an ad-hoc wireless infrastructure. What type of topology is used by this network?
    A. Wireless star
    B. Point-to-multipoint
    C. Wireless ring
    D. Point-to-point

6. Which type of connector is typically used to connect thinnet (RG-58) coaxial cabling to a network interface card?
    A. BNC
    B. AUI
    C. RJ-11
    D. RJ-45

7. A client has hired you to implement a Gigabit Ethernet network using unshielded twisted-pair cabling. Which category of cable can you use? (Choose two.)
    A. Category 2
    B. Category 3
    C. Category 5
    D. Category 5e
    E. Category 6

8. You are making a straight-through Gigabit Ethernet drop cable using UTP and RJ-45 connectors that will be used to connect a desktop system to your network switch. Which pin on the switch should be connected to the TX+ pin on the host's network interface board?
    A. TX+
    B. TX-
    C. RX+
    D. RX-

9. You are making a 568B UTP crossover cable that will be used to cascade two switches on an Ethernet network. You've attached an RJ-45 connector to one end of the cable and inserted the white with orange stripe wire into pin 1 of the connector. The orange wire has been inserted into pin 2 of the connector. Which wire should be inserted into pin 1 of the RJ-45 connector on the other end of the cable?

   A. White with green stripe

   B. Green

   C. White with orange stripe

   D. Orange

10. Which of the following is true about singlemode fiber-optic network cabling?

    A. The central core is composed of braided plastic or glass fibers.

    B. The central core is smaller than that of multimode fiber-optic cabling.

    C. It transmits multiple rays of light concurrently.

    D. It doesn't support segment lengths as long as those supported by multimode fiber-optic cabling.

11. Which media access method is used by twisted-pair Ethernet networks?

    A. CSMA/CD

    B. CSMA/CA

    C. Token passing

    D. OFDMA

12. Which network signaling method uses digital signals and consumes the entire available bandwidth of the network media as a single transmission channel?

    A. Broadband

    B. Wideband

    C. Ultra-wideband

    D. Baseband

13. You are planning the implementation of a new Ethernet network. The layout of the office complex will require some runs between workstations and the network switches to be up to 90 meters long. In addition, the client has requested that the network be capable of Gigabit or faster data transfers. Which Ethernet standards could you consider using in your implementation plan? (Choose two.)

    A. 10Base-5

    B. 10Base-T

    C. 1000Base-CX

    D. 1000Base-T

    E. Fast Ethernet

14. Which Ethernet standards use fiber-optic cabling? (Choose two.)
- **A.** 10GBase-SR
- **B.** 100Base-TX
- **C.** 1000Base-CX
- **D.** 10Base-FL
- **E.** 10Base-5

15. Which device is used as a central connecting point in a Token Ring network wired with UTP in a physical star topology?
- **A.** Bridge
- **B.** Multistation access unit
- **C.** Switch
- **D.** Hub

16. Which network service is employed by network operating systems such as Microsoft Windows Server 2008 and Novell Open Enterprise Server to store user accounts and manage access to network resources?
- **A.** Directory Services
- **B.** Network Information Services (NIS)
- **C.** Group policies
- **D.** Windows Internet Name Service (WINS)

17. Which terms refer to the ability to split a Novell eDirectory database into smaller logical portions that are copied redundantly to various servers in the network? (Choose two.)
- **A.** Partitioning
- **B.** Synchronization
- **C.** Replication
- **D.** Compartmentalization
- **E.** Redirection

18. You are developing an implementation plan for a network in a startup financial services firm. They are very concerned about security and have asked you to implement the most secure network media available. Which should you choose?
- **A.** 802.11g wireless
- **B.** 1000Base-TX
- **C.** 10Base-5
- **D.** 1000Base-SX

19. Which response best describes how token passing works?

   A. The transmitting host checks the wire to see if it is in use. If so, it will wait to transmit; if not, the host will transmit.

   B. The transmitting host checks the wire to see if it is in use. Then it sends a dummy transmission to see if it collides with any other data.

   C. If a collision is detected, each host will wait a variable length of time before retransmitting.

   D. The transmitting host waits until a circulating empty packet is free. When it is, the host grabs it and is allowed to transmit.

20. Which of the following are disadvantages of using a physical star topology when implementing a network that uses copper wiring? (Choose two.)

   A. The cabling used in a star topology is usually more expensive than that used in bus topologies.

   B. A star topology requires more cabling than bus and ring topologies.

   C. The cabling used with most physical star topologies is somewhat rigid and inflexible.

   D. If one computer fails or the cable link is broken, the entire network could go down.

   E. Failure of the central connecting point results in the failure of all hosts connected to it.

21. Which type of cable is used by networks that still use thinnet cabling?

   A. RG-58

   B. RG-8

   C. Category 3

   D. Category 5e

22. When using a straight-through UTP cable in an Ethernet network, which pin in the jack on the hub or switch should be connected to the RX- pin in the jack on the network interface card?

   A. TX+

   B. TX-

   C. RX-

   D. RX+

23. You are creating a straight-through Ethernet UTP cable for connecting a network host to your network switch. Assuming you are using 568B standards, which wire should be connected to pin 3 on both ends of the cable?

   A. White with orange stripe

   B. Blue

   C. White with green stripe

   D. Orange

24. Which connector is used to connect coaxial cabling for cable TV to your television set?
   A. LC
   B. F-type
   C. AUI
   D. BNC

25. Which standard defines specifications for a hot-swappable electrical interface that converts fiber-optic Gigabit Ethernet to copper wiring?
   A. GBIC
   B. 568B
   C. 568A
   D. IEEE 802.3z

26. When creating a T1 crossover cable, which of the following describes the correct way in which the pins should be crossed over?
   A. Pins 1, 2, 3, and 4 are connected to pins 4, 3, 2, and 1.
   B. Pins 1, 2, 4, and 5 are connected to pins 4, 3, 1, and 2.
   C. Pins 1, 2, 3, and 4 are connected to pins 4, 5, 1, and 2.
   D. Pins 1, 2, 4, and 5 are connected to pins 4, 5, 1, and 2.

27. What frequency range is used by broadband over powerline (BPL) to piggy-back digital network signals though standard AC electrical distribution wiring?
   A. 1.6 to 80 MHz
   B. 50 to 100 MHz
   C. 110 to 220 MHz
   D. 230 to 300 MHz

28. Which network connectors can be used with fiber-optic cabling? (Choose three.)
   A. RJ-48
   B. RJ-45
   C. BNC
   D. ST
   E. SC
   F. MT-RJ

29. Which connector on a PC can be used to establish a point-to-point serial connection? (Choose two.)
   A. MT-RJ
   B. F-type
   C. RS-232
   D. IEEE 1394

30. Which type of network typically uses shielded twisted-pair (STP) cabling?
   A. Token Ring
   B. 10Base-T
   C. 10Base-5
   D. 10GBase-T

31. You need to connect your 1000Base-FX network switch to a singlemode fiber-optic backbone. Which type of media converter should you use?
   A. Singlemode fiber to UTP
   B. Multimode fiber to UTP
   C. Multimode fiber to coaxial
   D. Singlemode fiber to multimode fiber

32. Which networking technology creates virtual links between two remote network end points by prefixing packets with a header containing one or more labels?
   A. ATM
   B. Ethernet
   C. MPLS
   D. Frame Relay

33. Which 10 Gigabit Ethernet standards encapsulate Ethernet data within SDH/SONET frames, allowing Ethernet equipment to work with SDH/SONET networking equipment? (Choose three.)
   A. 10GBase-SW
   B. 10GBase-LRM
   C. 10GBase-LW
   D. 10GBase-ER
   E. 10GBase-EW
   F. 10GBase-LX4

34. Which technology groups multiple physical network interfaces into a single virtual interface, distributing the networking I/O load between the interfaces?
   A. Bonding
   B. Multiplexing
   C. Inverse multiplexing
   D. Port mirroring

QUICK ANSWER KEY

1.	A, E	13.	C, D	25.	A
2.	B, D, F	14.	A, D	26.	D
3.	C	15.	B	27.	A
4.	B	16.	A	28.	D, E, F
5.	D	17.	A, C	29.	C, D
6.	A	18.	D	30.	A
7.	D, E	19.	D	31.	D
8.	C	20.	B, E	32.	C
9.	A	21.	A	33.	A, C, E
10.	B	22.	B	34.	A
11.	A	23.	C		
12.	D	24.	B		

IN-DEPTH ANSWERS

1. You manage a network within an office suite composed of three Windows 7 workstations configured to work together in a workgroup. Each system is connected to the same network switch using Gigabit Ethernet network interfaces and drop cables. What type of network is this? (Choose two.)

   A.   Local area network

   B.   Wide area network

   C.   Metropolitan area network

   D.   Client/server network

   E.   Peer-to-peer network

   ☑   **A and E.** Because all three workstations are connected to the same network switch, they all are connected to the same network segment without routing and are considered a local area network (LAN). In addition, because all three systems are running workstation operating systems in a Microsoft Windows workgroup without a server, the network can be classified as a peer-to-peer network.

   ☒   **B, C,** and **D** are incorrect. **B** is incorrect because the network in this scenario is composed of a single segment without a router and all of the systems are located in the same geographical location. **C** is incorrect because all of the systems are located in the same geographical location. **D** is incorrect because all three hosts are running a Windows workstation operating system in a workgroup configuration. No system is designated to fill the server role in the network, so this cannot be classified as a client/server network.

2. Which of the following are characteristics of a client/server network? (Choose three.)

   A.   Each host maintains its own set of user accounts that must be kept synchronized with each other.

   B.   All hosts on the network can use a common set of user and group accounts stored on a dedicated host for authentication.

   C.   Printers and data folders on each network host are shared with other network hosts.

   D.   Files are stored on and shared from a dedicated host on the network.

   E.   All network hosts running a version of Windows are configured to be members of the same workgroup.

   F.   All network hosts running a version of Windows are configured to be members of the same domain.

☑ **B, D,** and **F.** In a client/server network, all hosts on the network can use a common set of user and group accounts stored on a dedicated host for authentication (such as a domain controller). In addition, shared files are stored on a dedicated host (a file server). If the network is composed of Windows hosts, they can be configured to be members of the same domain, allowing them to share resources and a common set of user accounts.

☒ **A, C,** and **E** are incorrect. **A** is incorrect because a client-server network typically uses a common set of user accounts in a domain or directory service. **C** is incorrect because printers and folders on each network host are not typically shared with other network hosts in a client/server network. **E** is incorrect because Windows workgroups are typically configured only in a peer-to-peer network.

3. You are responsible for managing a 10Base-2 Ethernet network. The hosts on this network are connected together by a single run of coaxial cable, from system to system to system, with terminators on each end. The network does not use a hub or switch. What type of physical topology does this network use?

A. Ring

B. Star

C. Bus

D. Mesh

☑ **C.** Because all of the hosts are connected to the same physical network cable segment and don't use a central connecting point (such as a hub or switch), this network uses a physical bus topology.

☒ **A, B,** and **D** are incorrect. **A** is incorrect because a physical ring topology would require the network media to be connected in a ring without terminators on each end. **B** is incorrect because a physical star topology would require each host to have its own network cable and all would interconnect using a central hub or switch. **D** is incorrect because a physical mesh topology would require a dedicated link from each host to every other host on the network.

4. You are working with a Token Ring network, which uses token passing from host to host to control access to the network media. The network uses twisted-pair wires to connect each network host to a multistation access unit (MSAU), which manages the passing of the token. What type of physical topology does this network use?

A. Ring

B. Star

C. Bus

D. Mesh

☑ **B.** Even though this network uses a *logical* ring topology (token passing), it is wired as a *physical* star. Each host has its own network cable that connects it to a central connection point (the MSAU).

☒ **A, C,** and **D** are incorrect. **A** is incorrect because this network is physically wired as a star, even though a Token Ring network operates logically as a ring. **C** is incorrect because a bus topology would require all of the hosts to connect to the same network cable segment, which isn't the case in this scenario. **D** is incorrect because a physical mesh topology would require a dedicated link be established from each host to every other host on the network.

5. You need to copy files from one Windows 7 laptop to a second one. To do this, you configured both workstations to connect to each other using an ad-hoc wireless infrastructure. What type of topology is used by this network?

A. Wireless star

B. Point-to-multipoint

C. Wireless ring

D. Point-to-point

☑ **D.** An ad-hoc wireless network connects network hosts together without the use of a wireless access point. As such, the two laptops in this scenario are connected directly to each other, creating a point-to-point network.

☒ **A, B,** and **C** are incorrect. **A** is incorrect because a wireless star network would require the use of a wireless access point. **B** is incorrect because a point-to-multipoint network would also require the use of a wireless access point. **C** is incorrect because a wireless ring network would require data to be passed from host to host until it reached the correct destination host.

6. Which type of connector is typically used to connect thinnet (RG-58) coaxial cabling to a network interface card?

    A. BNC

    B. AUI

    C. RJ-11

    D. RJ-45

    ☑ **A.** A BNC connector is typically used to connect a host's network interface card to an RG-58 coaxial cable segment. For example, it is the type of connector used to connect a workstation to a 10Base-2 Ethernet network that uses RG-58 coaxial cabling.

    ☒ **B, C,** and **D** are incorrect. **B** is incorrect because an AUI connector is typically used to connect thicknet (RG-8) coaxial cable to a network interface board. **C** is incorrect because RJ-11 connectors are used for telephone jacks, not network connections. **D** is incorrect because RJ-45 connectors are used to connect unshielded twisted pair cables to a network interface boards.

7. A client has hired you to implement a Gigabit Ethernet network using unshielded twisted-pair cabling. Which category of cable can you use? (Choose two.)

    A. Category 2

    B. Category 3

    C. Category 5

    D. Category 5e

    E. Category 6

    ☑ **D** and **E.** Because Gigabit Ethernet runs at 1000 Mbps, you must use Category 5e or Category 6 UTP to transfer data reliably at full speed.

    ☒ **A, B,** and **C** are incorrect. **A** is incorrect because CAT 2 UTP is rated only to 4 Mbps and unlikely to be used in a modern network. **B** is incorrect because CAT 3 UTP is rated only to 10 Mbps. **C** is incorrect because CAT 5 UTP is rated only to 100 Mbps.

8. You are making a straight-through Gigabit Ethernet drop cable using UTP and RJ-45 connectors that will be used to connect a desktop system to your network switch. Which pin on the switch should be connected to the TX+ pin on the host's network interface board?

    A. TX+

    B. TX-

    C. RX+

    D. RX-

☑ **C.** In a straight-through UTP cable, the TX+ pin on the network interface card should be connected to the RX+ pin on the switch (and vice-versa).

☒ **A, B,** and **D** are incorrect. **A** is incorrect because the RX+ pin on the switch is connected to the TX+ pin on the network board. **B** is incorrect because the TX- pin on the switch is connected to the RX- pin on the network board. **D** is incorrect because the RX- pin on the switch is connected TX- pin on the network board.

9. You are making a 568B UTP crossover cable that will be used to cascade two switches on an Ethernet network. You've attached an RJ-45 connector to one end of the cable and inserted the white with orange stripe wire into pin 1 of the connector. The orange wire has been inserted into pin 2 of the connector. Which wire should be inserted into pin 1 of the RJ-45 connector on the other end of the cable?

   A. White with green stripe

   B. Green

   C. White with orange stripe

   D. Orange

☑ **A.** 568B specifications for a UTP crossover cable require that the white with green stripe wire be inserted into pin 1 of one connector if the white with orange wire has been inserted into pin 1 of the connector on the other end of the cable.

☒ **B, C,** and **D** are incorrect. **B** is incorrect because the green wire on the opposite end should be connected to pin 2. **C** is incorrect because the white with orange strip wire should be connected to pin 3 on the opposite end. **D** is incorrect because the orange wire should be connected to pin 6 on the opposite end.

10. Which of the following is true about singlemode fiber-optic network cabling?

    A. The central core is composed of braided plastic or glass fibers.

    B. The central core is smaller than that of multimode fiber-optic cabling.

    C. It transmits multiple rays of light concurrently.

    D. It doesn't support segment lengths as long as those supported by multimode fiber-optic cabling.

☑ **B.** Singlemode fiber-optic cabling transmits a single ray (or mode) of light through glass or plastic fiber. It supports longer transmission distances than multimode fiber-optic cable and is also more expensive. It also has a central core that is much smaller than that of multimode fiber-optic cabling.

☒ **A, C,** and **D** are incorrect. **A** is incorrect because the central core of singlemode fiber-optic cabling is not braided. **C** is incorrect because singlemode fiber-optic cabling transmits a single ray (or mode) of light through glass or plastic fiber. **D** is incorrect because singlemode fiber-optic cabling supports longer transmission distances than multimode fiber-optic cable and is also more expensive.

11. Which media access method is used by twisted-pair Ethernet networks?

A. CSMA/CD

B. CSMA/CA

C. Token passing

D. OFDMA

☑ **A.** Twisted-pair Ethernet networks use Collision Sense Multiple Access with Collision Detection (CSMA/CD) to regulate how multiple network hosts use the same network medium and to detect errors (collisions) that occur when two hosts try to transmit simultaneously.

☒ **B, C,** and **D** are incorrect. **B** is incorrect because CSMA/CA is not used by wired Ethernet networks, but is instead used by WiFi (802.11) wireless networks. **C** is incorrect because token passing is used by Token Ring and FDDI networks, not Ethernet networks. **D** is incorrect because OFDMA is used only in WiMAX (802.16) wireless networks.

12. Which network signaling method uses digital signals and consumes the entire available bandwidth of the network media as a single transmission channel?

A. Broadband

B. Wideband

C. Ultra-wideband

D. Baseband

☑ **D.** Baseband signaling uses digital signals and treats the entire bandwidth of the network media as a single transmission channel, unlike broadband signaling which divides the bandwidth of the network media into multiple channels. As a result, baseband signaling allows only one signal at a time on the network medium.

☒ **A, B,** and **C** are incorrect. **A** is incorrect because broadband signaling uses only a portion of the available media bandwidth (allowing multiple transmissions simultaneously). **B** is incorrect because wideband is a signaling technology used with wireless (radio) technologies. **C** is incorrect because ultra-wideband is also used with wireless (radio) technologies.

13. You are planning the implementation of a new Ethernet network. The layout of the office complex will require some runs between workstations and the network switches to be up to 90 meters long. In addition, the client has requested that the network be capable of Gigabit or faster data transfers. Which Ethernet standards could you consider using in your implementation plan? (Choose two.)

A. 10Base-5

B. 10Base-T

C. 1000Base-CX

D. 1000Base-T

E. Fast Ethernet

☑ **C** and **D.** Both 1000Base-CX and 1000Base-T are capable of transferring data at 1000 Mbps.

☒ **A, B,** and **E** are incorrect. **A** is incorrect because 10Base-5 is an older Ethernet standard that is limited to 10 Mbps transfers. **B** is incorrect because 10Base-T is also limited to 10 Mbps transfers. **E** is incorrect because Fast Ethernet standards are limited to 100 Mbps data transfers.

14. Which Ethernet standards use fiber-optic cabling? (Choose two.)

A. 10GBase-SR

B. 100Base-TX

C. 1000Base-CX

D. 10Base-FL

E. 10Base-5

☑ **A** and **D.** Both the newer 10GBase-SR and the older 10Base-FL Ethernet standards employ fiber-optic cabling.

☒ **B, C**, and **E** are incorrect. **B** is incorrect because100Base-TX uses UTP copper cabling. **C** is incorrect because1000Base-CX uses coaxial copper cabling. **E** is incorrect because10Base-5 also uses coaxial copper cabling.

15. Which device is used as a central connecting point in a Token Ring network wired with UTP in a physical star topology?

A. Bridge

B. Multistation access unit

C. Switch

D. Hub

☑ **B.** A Token Ring network that is wired with UTP in a physical star topology uses a multistation access unit (MSAU) as a central connecting point for all hosts.

☒ **A, C**, and **D** are incorrect. **A** is incorrect because bridges are used to connect two network segments together. **C** is incorrect because switches are used in Ethernet networks, which use CSMA/CD for media access control instead of token passing. **D** is incorrect because hubs are also used in Ethernet networks, which use CSMA/CD for media access control instead of token passing.

16. Which network service is employed by network operating systems such as Microsoft Windows Server 2008 and Novell Open Enterprise Server to store user accounts and manage access to network resources?

A. Directory Services

B. Network Information Services (NIS)

C. Group policies

D. Windows Internet Name Service (WINS)

☑ **A.** Directory services is a service used on Microsoft Windows, Novell Open Enterprise Server, and even Linux servers to store user accounts and manage access to network resources (such as shared folders).

☒ **B, C,** and **D** are incorrect. **B** is incorrect because, while NIS is used by Linux systems to share user accounts among multiple systems, it isn't a true directory service and it isn't commonly implemented on Microsoft or Novell servers. **C** is incorrect because group policies are used on Windows servers to define policies applied to users or machines, but they aren't used on Novell servers. **D** is incorrect because WINS is a basic network name resolution service used by NetBIOS hosts.

17. Which terms refer to the ability to split a Novell eDirectory database into smaller logical portions that are copied redundantly to various servers in the network? (Choose two.)

   A. Partitioning

   B. Synchronization

   C. Replication

   D. Compartmentalization

   E. Redirection

☑ **A** and **C.** Partitioning the eDirectory database involves dividing it up into logical "chunks." Replication occurs when you place copies of these partitions on multiple network servers.

☒ **B, D,** and **E** are incorrect. **B** is incorrect because synchronization refers to the process of keeping replicas up to date, such as when updates from a master copy of a partition are copied to its replicas. However, it does not refer to the process of partitioning and placing replicas. **D** is incorrect because compartmentalization is not a directory services-related term. **E** is incorrect because redirection refers to the process used by network clients to redirect requests for network resources to a server instead of the local operating system.

18. You are developing an implementation plan for a network in a startup financial services firm. They are very concerned about security and have asked you to implement the most secure network media available. Which should you choose?

   A. 802.11g wireless

   B. 1000Base-TX

   C. 10Base-5

   D. 1000Base-SX

☑ **D.** 1000Base-SX networks use fiber-optic cabling, which is the most immune to eavesdropping of the choices listed.

☒ **A, B,** and **C** are incorrect. **A** is incorrect because wireless networks can transmit information outside of your physical facility and are considered the least secure type of network, even with encryption enabled. **B** is incorrect because 1000Base-TX uses copper wiring and is less immune to eavesdropping than fiber-optic cable. **C** is incorrect because 10Base-5 also uses copper wiring and is less immune to eavesdropping than fiber-optic cable.

19. Which response best describes how token passing works?

   A. The transmitting host checks the wire to see if it is in use. If so, it will wait to transmit; if not, the host will transmit.

   B. The transmitting host checks the wire to see if it is in use. Then it sends a dummy transmission to see if it collides with any other data.

   C. If a collision is detected, each host will wait a variable length of time before retransmitting.

   D. The transmitting host waits until a circulating empty packet is free. When it is, the host grabs it and is allowed to transmit.

☑ **D.** With token passing, an empty packet (the token) circulates around the ring. To place data on the wire, a host must first wait for the token. Once a host has the token and it is free of data, the host can place its data on the wire. Because there is only one token and a host needs to have it to transmit, it is impossible to have collisions in a token-passing environment.

☒ **A, B,** and **C** are incorrect. **A** and **C** are incorrect because they both describe how the CSMA/CD media access scheme works. **B** is incorrect because it describes how the CSMA/CA media access scheme works.

20. Which of the following are disadvantages of using a physical star topology when implementing a network that uses copper wiring? (Choose two.)

   A. The cabling used in a star topology is usually more expensive than that used in bus topologies.

   B. A star topology requires more cabling than bus and ring topologies.

   C. The cabling used with most physical star topologies is somewhat rigid and inflexible.

   D. If one computer fails or the cable link is broken, the entire network could go down.

   E. Failure of the central connecting point results in the failure of all hosts connected to it.

☑ **B and E.** A physical star topology typically requires more cabling than bus and ring topologies because each host requires its own dedicated cable. In addition, the failure of the central hub or switch will result in the failure of all the network hosts connected to it.

☒ **A, C, and D are incorrect. A** is incorrect because the UTP cabling used in a physical star topology is typically less expensive than that used in other topologies. **C** is incorrect because UTP also tends to be much more flexible than fiber-optic or coaxial cabling. **D** is incorrect because each host has its own cable in a star topology. Therefore, the failure of one cable does not affect any other host on the network.

21. Which type of cable is used by networks that still use thinnet cabling?

A. RG-58

B. RG-8

C. Category 3

D. Category 5e

☑ **A.** Thinnet uses RG-58 coaxial cabling. This is typically used with older 10Base-2 networks.

☒ **B, C, and D are incorrect. B** is incorrect because RG-8 coaxial cabling is used with thicknet networks, such as older 10Base-5 implementations. **C** and **D** are incorrect because Category 3 and 5e UTP cabling are used with physical star Ethernet networks that use UTP and are not used in thinnet networks.

22. When using a straight-through UTP cable in an Ethernet network, which pin in the jack on the hub or switch should be connected to the RX- pin in the jack on the network interface card?

A. TX+

B. TX-

C. RX-

D. RX+

☑ **B.** The RX- pin in the jack on the network interface card should be connected to the TX- pin in the jack on the hub or switch.

☒ **A, C, and D are incorrect. A** is incorrect because the TX+ pin on the hub/switch should be connected to the RX+ pin on the network card. **C** is incorrect because the RX- pin on the hub/switch should be connected to the TX- pin on the network card. **D** is incorrect because the RX+ pin on the hub/switch should be connected to the TX+ pin on the network card.

23. You are creating a straight-through Ethernet UTP cable for connecting a network host to your network switch. Assuming you are using 568B standards, which wire should be connected to pin 3 on both ends of the cable?

   A. White with orange stripe

   B. Blue

   C. White with green stripe

   D. Orange

> ☑ **C.** When using the 568B wiring scheme to create a straight-through Ethernet cable, the white with green striped wire should be connected to pin 3 on both ends of the cable.
>
> ☒ **A, B,** and **D** are incorrect. **A** is incorrect because the white with orange wire should be connected to pin 1. **B** is incorrect because the blue wire should be connected to pin 4. **D** is incorrect because the orange wire should be connected to pin 2.

24. Which connector is used to connect coaxial cabling for cable TV to your television set?

   A. LC

   B. F-type

   C. AUI

   D. BNC

> ☑ **B.** The F-type connector is used to connect coaxial cabling for cable TV to your television set.
>
> ☒ **A, C,** and **D** are incorrect. **A** is incorrect because the LC connector is used with fiber-optic cabling. **C** and **D** are incorrect because the AUI and BNC connectors are used with coaxial network cabling.

25. Which standard defines specifications for a hot-swappable electrical interface that converts fiber-optic Gigabit Ethernet to copper wiring?

   A. GBIC

   B. 568B

   C. 568A

   D. IEEE 802.3z

☑   **A.** The gigabit interface converter (GBIC) is a standard for transceivers commonly used with Gigabit Ethernet that offers a standard interface that can support physical media such as copper and optical fiber.

☒   **B, C,** and **D** are incorrect. **B** and **C** are incorrect because 568A and 568B define standards for straight-through and crossover copper Ethernet cables. **D** is incorrect because IEEE 802.3z defines Gigabit Ethernet that runs over fiber-optic cabling or coaxial cabling.

26. When creating a T1 crossover cable, which of the following describes the correct way in which the pins should be crossed over?

    A. Pins 1, 2, 3, and 4 are connected to pins 4, 3, 2, and 1.

    B. Pins 1, 2, 4, and 5 are connected to pins 4, 3, 1, and 2.

    C. Pins 1, 2, 3, and 4 are connected to pins 4, 5, 1, and 2.

    D. Pins 1, 2, 4, and 5 are connected to pins 4, 5, 1, and 2.

☑   **D.** T1 cabling follows T568B standards, so a T1 crossover cable should connect pins 1, 2, 4, and 5 to pins 4, 5, 1, and 2.

☒   **A, B,** and **C** are incorrect. **A** is incorrect because it does not connect the TX+/- pins to the RX+/- pins, so the transmit signals will never reach the reception pins. **B** is incorrect because it also fails to connect the TX+/- pins to the RX+/- pins. **C** is incorrect because it also does not connect the TX+/- pins to the RX+/- pins.

27. What frequency range is used by broadband over powerline (BPL) to piggy-back digital network signals though standard AC electrical distribution wiring?

    A. 1.6 to 80 MHz

    B. 50 to 100 MHz

    C. 110 to 220 MHz

    D. 230 to 300 MHz

☑   **A.** Broadband over powerline (BPL) uses the 1.6 to 80 MHz frequency range to piggy-back digital network signals though standard AC electrical distribution wiring.

☒   **B, C,** and **D** are incorrect. **B** is incorrect because standard AC wiring has limited ability to carry high-frequency signals and the frequency range 50 to 100 MHz exceeds the maximum frequency supported by such wiring. **C** is incorrect because the 110 to 220 MHz frequency range also exceeds the maximum frequency supported by AC wiring. **D** is incorrect because the 230 to 300 MHz frequency range also exceeds the maximum frequency supported by AC wiring.

28. Which network connectors can be used with fiber-optic cabling? (Choose three.)

    A. RJ-48

    B. RJ-45

    C. BNC

    D. ST

    E. SC

    F. MT-RJ

> ☑ **D, E**, and **F.** ST, SC, and MT-RJ connectors are designed to transmit light instead of electricity and are used to connect fiber-optic cabling to fiber-optic devices.
>
> ☒ **A, B**, and **C** are incorrect. **A** is incorrect because RJ-48 connectors are used with T1 and ISDN copper network cabling. **B** is incorrect because RJ-45 connectors are used with UTP copper network cabling. **C** is incorrect because BNC connectors are used with coaxial copper network cabling.

29. Which connector on a PC can be used to establish a point-to-point serial connection? (Choose two.)

    A. MT-RJ

    B. F-type

    C. RS-232

    D. IEEE 1394

> ☑ **C** and **D.** The RS-232 connection can be used to establish a point-to-point serial connection between two computer systems. You can also use USB and FireWire (IEEE 1394) connectors to establish a serial point-to-point connection between computers.
>
> ☒ **A** and **B** are incorrect. **A** is incorrect because MT-RJ connectors are used with fiber-optic cabling and aren't typically used to establish serial point-to-point connections between computers. **B** is incorrect because F-type connectors are used with coaxial cable TV connections and aren't used for computer network connections.

30. Which type of network typically uses shielded twisted-pair (STP) cabling?

    A. Token Ring

    B. 10Base-T

    C. 10Base-5

    D. 10GBase-T

☑ **A.** Many Token Ring implementations use IBM Type-1 shielded twisted-pair (STP) network cabling. The extra shielding within the cable helps protect it from external electromagnetic interference (EMI) and can be used in deployments where environmental EMI would disrupt communications on unshielded twisted-pair (UTP) cabling.

☒ **B, C,** and **D** are incorrect. **B** is incorrect because 10Base-T specifies the use of UTP. **C** is incorrect because 10Base-5 uses RG-8 coaxial cabling. **D** is incorrect because 10GBase-T uses Category 6a UTP.

31. You need to connect your 1000Base-FX network switch to a singlemode fiber-optic backbone. Which type of media converter should you use?

A. Singlemode fiber to UTP

B. Multimode fiber to UTP

C. Multimode fiber to coaxial

D. Singlemode fiber to multimode fiber

☑ **D.** 1000Base-FX networks use multimode fiber-optic cabling. Therefore, to connect your 1000Base-FX switch to a singlemode fiber backbone, you must use a media converter to switch from multimode to singlemode fiber. Remember that singlemode fiber uses a single ray of light (a mode) while multimode fiber uses multiple rays of light (modes) simultaneously.

☒ **A, B,** and **C** are incorrect. **A** and **B** are incorrect because 1000Base-FX networks use multimode fiber-optic cabling, not copper UTP. **C** is incorrect because 1000Base-FX networks do not use coaxial cabling.

32. Which networking technology creates virtual links between two remote network end points by prefixing packets with a header containing one or more labels?

A. ATM

B. Ethernet

C. MPLS

D. Frame Relay

☑ **C.** Multiprotocol Label Switching (MPLS) creates virtual links between two remote network end points by prefixing packets with a header containing one or more labels. With MPLS, routing is determined by the contents of each packet's label. This allows you to create an endpoint-to-endpoint virtual circuit across a variety of network media. For example, some Cisco hardware uses MPLS to establish a virtual private network (VPN) between remote sites.

☒ **A, B,** and **D** are incorrect. **A** and **D** are incorrect because MPLS is a successor to both ATM and Frame Relay technologies, which served a similar endpoint-to-endpoint connectivity function back in the 1980s and 1990s. **B** is incorrect because Ethernet networking doesn't use packet labels or virtual endpoint-to-endpoint connections.

33. Which 10 Gigabit Ethernet standards encapsulate Ethernet data within SDH/SONET frames, allowing Ethernet equipment to work with SDH/SONET networking equipment? (Choose three.)

- A. 10GBase-SW
- B. 10GBase-LRM
- C. 10GBase-LW
- D. 10GBase-ER
- E. 10GBase-EW
- F. 10GBase-LX4

☑ **A, C,** and **E.** 10GBase-SW, 10GBase-LW, and 10GBase-EW are 10 Gigabit Ethernet standards that encapsulate Ethernet data within SDH/SONET frames. This allows 10 Gigabit Ethernet equipment to work with networking equipment designed to carry SDH/SONET frames.

☒ **B, D,** and **F** are incorrect. **B** and **D** are incorrect because 10GBase-LRM and 10GBase-ER are fiber-optic Ethernet standards that use multimode cabling. **F** is incorrect because 10GBase-LX4 is also a fiber-optic Ethernet standard that uses two pairs of legacy multimode cabling to provide 10 Gigabit Ethernet speeds.

34. Which technology groups multiple physical network interfaces into a single virtual interface, distributing the networking I/O load between the interfaces?

- A. Bonding
- B. Multiplexing
- C. Inverse multiplexing
- D. Port mirroring

☑ **A.** Bonding allows you to group multiple network adapters together and have them behave as if they were a single network interface. A single IP address is assigned to the bonded interface. The network I/O load is balanced between the network boards in a manner similar to the way striping works in a RAID 0 hard disk array.

☒ **B, C,** and **D** are incorrect. **B** is incorrect because multiplexing combines multiple data streams into a single signal on a shared medium. **C** is incorrect because inverse multiplexing is the opposite of traditional multiplexing, dividing one signal among multiple transmission channels. **D** is incorrect because port mirroring allows a network switch to send a copy of data that reaches certain ports to a monitored port, allowing the administrator to monitor network traffic.

2

Network Protocols and Standards

CERTIFICATION OBJECTIVES

❑   1.1   Compare the layers of the OSI and TCP/IP models.

❑   1.2   Classify how applications, devices, and protocols relate to the OSI model layers.

QUESTIONS

The OSI reference model was designed by delegates from major computer and telecom companies in 1983, with an original goal of designing a network communications model that was modular and that would allow products from different vendors to interoperate. They developed a model that divides the network communication process between two hosts into layers. These layers break down the communication process into general tasks. Information flows down through the layers on one side, is transmitted on the network medium, and then flows up the layers on the other side. For your Network+ exam, you need to be familiar with the seven layers of the OSI model and how different protocols and network devices relate to this model.

1. You are designing a network implementation for a client with multiple geographic locations separated by WAN links. Routers must be used to provide interconnectivity between the network segments separated by the WAN. You need to specify which network protocols will be used to enable communications between hosts. Which network protocols are nonroutable and should be avoided in this scenario? (Choose two.)
    - A. IP
    - B. NetBIOS
    - C. IPX
    - D. AppleTalk
    - E. NetBEUI

2. You are implementing Linux workstations on a network that uses Windows Server 2008 server systems. You need to configure the workstations to communicate with the servers. Which application layer protocol can be used in conjunction with NetBIOS at the session layer and TCP/IP at the transport and network layers to enable communications?
    - A. SMB
    - B. SSH
    - C. LDAP
    - D. NTP

3. Which NetBIOS mode is used for connectionless communications?
    - A. Datagram
    - B. Session
    - C. Routed
    - D. Acknowledged

4. You are configuring the IPX protocol on a network server. During the configuration process, you are prompted to enter an IPX network ID. Which of the following are valid IPX network IDs that you could assign to this host? (Choose two.)
   A. N0BADBEEF
   B. 00BADBEEF
   C. 0BGE3321
   D. 055556EF
   E. 0BADBEEF

5. You manage an Ethernet network on which Windows 7 hosts need to use the IPX protocol provided by the Novell Client to communicate with legacy NetWare servers. You need to determine a common frame type that all hosts on the network can use. Which of the following are valid IPX frame types from which you could select? (Choose two.)
   A. ETHERNET_IP
   B. 802.2
   C. 802.5
   D. ETHERNET_II
   E. ETHERNET_APPLETALK

6. Which transport layer protocols are connection-oriented, requiring acknowledgments from the recipient of a network transmission? (Choose two.)
   A. UDP
   B. IPX
   C. SPX
   D. IP
   E. TCP

7. Which protocols are application layer protocols? (Choose two.)
   A. DHCP
   B. UDP
   C. SNMP
   D. RPC
   E. SDP

8. Which layer of the OSI model ensures the data being sent from the sender is formatted correctly so it can be interpreted correctly by the recipient system?
   A. Application
   B. Presentation
   C. Session
   D. Transport

9. Which functions are provided by the transport layer of the OSI model? (Choose two.)
- **A.** Ensuring that data on the sending system is formatted correctly for the recipient system
- **B.** Establishing, managing, and terminating communications between the sender and recipient
- **C.** Managing segment sequencing
- **D.** Creating TCP and UDP ports for the IP protocol
- **E.** Managing logical addressing information for network hosts

10. Which of the following are functions of the Logical Link Control (LLC) sublayer of the data link layer in the OSI model? (Choose two.)
- **A.** Retransmits missing or corrupted frames
- **B.** Transmits electrical signals between hosts
- **C.** Provides an interface with the network layer
- **D.** Provides for the routing of the data
- **E.** Determines the next network point to which a packet should be forwarded toward its destination

11. Which layer of the OSI model defines rules for accessing the network media?
- **A.** Physical
- **B.** Data link
- **C.** Network
- **D.** Transport

12. Using network monitoring software, you've identified a system on your network using an unfamiliar MAC address. You need to gather information to help you identify this potentially rogue host. Which part of a MAC address uniquely identifies the organization that manufactured the device to which the address has been assigned?
- **A.** The first octet
- **B.** The first two octets
- **C.** The last three octets
- **D.** The first three octets

13. You are designing a network implementation for a small business client. For security and data throughput reasons, they want to implement 1000 Mbps networking using fiber-optic cabling. Which IEEE project standard defines Gigabit Ethernet over fiber-optic cabling?
- **A.** 802.2
- **B.** 802.5
- **C.** 802.3z
- **D.** 802.3ab

14. You've just been hired by an organization to manage its Token Ring network. Your past experience has been primarily with Ethernet networks and you now need to familiarize yourself with Token Ring networks. Which IEEE project standard should you consult to do this?

- A. 802.2
- B. 802.3
- C. 802.5
- D. 802.11

15. A client has hired you to implement a new wireless network. The organization already uses a wireless telephone system that utilizes the 5.8 GHz frequency range. To prevent conflicts, you need to implement a wireless network that uses frequency ranges from 2.4 GHz to 2.4835 GHz. Which IEEE project standard defines wireless networking using this range at a maximum data rate of 54 Mbps?

- A. 802.11a
- B. 802.11b
- C. 802.11g
- D. 802.11n

16. Which IEEE project standard defines 100 Mbps Ethernet networking?

- A. 802.3u
- B. 802.ae
- C. 802.3z
- D. 802.3ab

17. You've been hired by a small business to manage its legacy Ethernet network. Upon inspection, you notice that the existing network uses coaxial cable. Which 802.3 specifications use this type of cabling? (Choose two.)

- A. 10Base-2
- B. 10Base-5
- C. 10Base-T
- D. 10Base-FL
- E. 1000Base-LX

18. You are responsible for managing a legacy 10Base-2 Ethernet network. The network is composed of five network segments that are connected together using four repeaters. What is the maximum number of segments in this network that can be populated with network hosts?

- A. Two
- B. Three
- C. Four
- D. Five

19. Which protocols are transport layer protocols? (Choose two.)
    A. IP
    B. IPX
    C. UDP
    D. SMTP
    E. SPX

20. You are designing a new network that will employ one Windows Server 2008 server system and twenty Windows 7 workstations. You need to assign NetBIOS computer names to each host on the network. Which of the following are valid computer names that you could use? (Choose two.)
    A. FS1
    B. WORKGROUPSERVER12
    C. WORKSTATION:1
    D. WS19
    E. WS1*1

21. Using network monitoring software, you've noticed an unfamiliar new host on your network. The NetBIOS computer name for the host is ROGUE11. Upon analyzing each octet of the computer name, you notice that the last byte contains the ASCII characters **00**. What kind of system is this?
    A. A domain controller
    B. A primary domain controller (PDC)
    C. A master browser
    D. A workstation

22. You've opened a web browser on your workstation and have entered a URL in the Location field. Which layer of the OSI model initiates the HTTP request to the web server?
    A. Application
    B. Presentation
    C. Session
    D. Transport

23. You are copying a file from your workstation to a file server on the network. Which layer of the OSI model is responsible for physically addressing the data prior to placing those signals on the network medium?
    A. Transport
    B. Network
    C. Data link
    D. Physical

24. Your computer system is in the process of establishing a TCP-based connection at the transport layer of the OSI model with another network host. Your computer has just sent a TCP SYN message to initiate the connection. If the destination host successfully receives the TCP SYN message, what message will it send back to your computer in response?

   A. TCP SYN

   B. TCP SYN/ACK

   C. TCP ACK

   D. TCP ACCEPT

25. You need to assign an IP address to a Windows 7 workstation on your network. Which of the following is a valid IPv4 address that you could use?

   A. 192.168.1.255

   B. 192.168.1.0

   C. 192.168.1.257

   D. 192.168.1.254

26. Which protocols are network layer protocols in the OSI model? (Choose two.)

   A. HTTP

   B. IP

   C. TCP

   D. UDP

   E. IPX

27. Which layer of the OSI model manages logical addressing for network hosts?

   A. Session

   B. Transport

   C. Network

   D. Data link

QUICK ANSWER KEY

1.	B, E	10.	A, C	19.	C, E
2.	A	11.	B	20.	A, D
3.	A	12.	D	21.	D
4.	D, E	13.	C	22.	A
5.	B, D	14.	C	23.	C
6.	C, E	15.	C	24.	B
7.	A, C	16.	A	25.	D
8.	B	17.	A, B	26.	B, E
9.	C, D	18.	B	27.	C

IN-DEPTH ANSWERS

I. You are designing a network implementation for a client with multiple geographic locations separated by WAN links. Routers must be used to provide interconnectivity between the network segments separated by the WAN. You need to specify which network protocols will be used to enable communications between hosts. Which network protocols are nonroutable and should be avoided in this scenario? (Choose two.)

A. IP
B. NetBIOS
C. IPX
D. AppleTalk
E. NetBEUI

☑ **B and E.** The NetBIOS and NetBEUI protocols are LAN protocols and can't be natively routed to different networks. However, together they can be piggybacked with other routable protocols, such as IP, to enable internetworking.

☒ **A, C,** and **D** are incorrect. **A** is incorrect because IP is a routable protocol. In fact, NetBIOS and NetBEUI are frequently used together with IP to enable internetworking. **C** is incorrect because the IPX protocol is a routable protocol. **D** is incorrect because the AppleTalk protocol is also a routable protocol.

2. You are implementing Linux workstations on a network that uses Windows Server 2008 server systems. You need to configure the workstations to communicate with the servers. Which application layer protocol can be used in conjunction with NetBIOS at the session layer and TCP/IP at the transport and network layers to enable communications?

A. SMB
B. SSH
C. LDAP
D. NTP

☑ **A.** The Server Message Block (SMB) protocol can be used in conjunction with NetBIOS at the session layer and TCP/IP at the transport and network layers to enable Windows-compatible networking on operating systems such as Linux and Mac OS.

☒ **B, C,** and **D** are incorrect. **B** is incorrect because the SSH protocol is used to establish remote access to Linux systems. **C** is incorrect because LDAP is used to provide access to information stored in directory services such as Novell eDirectory or Microsoft Active Directory. **D** is incorrect because NTP is used to synchronize time between network hosts.

3. Which NetBIOS mode is used for connectionless communications?
   A. Datagram
   B. Session
   C. Routed
   D. Acknowledged

   ☑ **A.** In Datagram mode, a connection is not established and data is sent from the sender to the receiver without acknowledgments. In addition to NetBIOS, the IP protocol in connectionless mode is also frequently said to use "datagrams" instead of "packets."

   ☒ **B, C,** and **D** are incorrect. **B** is incorrect because in Session mode, the NetBIOS protocol uses connection-oriented communications where data sent to the recipient is acknowledged by the recipient. **C** and **D** are not valid NetBIOS communication modes.

4. You are configuring the IPX protocol on a network server. During the configuration process, you are prompted to enter an IPX network ID. Which of the following are valid IPX network IDs that you could assign to this host? (Choose two.)
   A. N0BADBEEF
   B. 00BADBEEF
   C. 0BGE3321
   D. 055556EF
   E. 0BADBEEF

   ☑ **D** and **E.** A valid IPX network ID is composed of eight hexadecimal characters. Therefore, 055556EF and 0BADBEEF are valid IPX network IDs that could be assigned to an IPX host.

   ☒ **A, B,** and **C** are incorrect. **A** is incorrect because N0BADBEEF uses an invalid hexadecimal character (N) and is nine characters (which is one character too long). **B** is incorrect because 00BADBEEF is also one character too long. **C** is incorrect because 0BGE3321 uses an invalid hexadecimal character (G).

5. You manage an Ethernet network on which Windows 7 hosts need to use the IPX protocol provided by the Novell Client to communicate with legacy NetWare servers. You need to determine a common frame type that all hosts on the network can use. Which of the following are valid IPX frame types from which you could select? (Choose two.)
   A. ETHERNET_IP
   B. 802.2
   C. 802.5
   D. ETHERNET_II
   E. ETHERNET_APPLETALK

☑ **B** and **D.** 802.2 and ETHERNET_II are valid IPX frame types on an Ethernet network. Although Windows 7 does not provide native IPX support, installing the Novell Client on the workstations would allow you to configure IPX and select the appropriate frame type for the network.

☒ **A, C,** and **E** are incorrect. **A** is incorrect because ETHERNET_IP is not a valid IPX frame type. **C** is incorrect because 802.5 is the IEEE specification for Token Ring networks. **E** is incorrect because ETHERNET_APPLETALK is not a valid IPX frame type.

6. Which transport layer protocols are connection-oriented, requiring acknowledgments from the recipient of a network transmission? (Choose two.)
   A. UDP
   B. IPX
   C. SPX
   D. IP
   E. TCP

☑ **C** and **E.** The SPX and TCP protocols reside at the transport layer of the OSI model and are considered to be connection-oriented because they require the recipient of a network transmission to acknowledge receipt of the data, ensuring that it arrived correctly and intact.

☒ **A, B,** and **D** are incorrect. **A** is incorrect because UDP sends transmissions unacknowledged. **B** and **D** are incorrect because the IPX and IP protocols reside at the network layer, not the transport layer, and are concerned primarily with routing data.

7. Which protocols are application layer protocols? (Choose two.)
   A. DHCP
   B. UDP
   C. SNMP
   D. RPC
   E. SDP

☑ **A** and **C.** DHCP and SNMP are both application layer protocols.

☒ **B, D,** and **E** are incorrect. **B** is incorrect because UDP is a transport layer protocol. **D** and **E** are incorrect because RPC and SDP are both session layer protocols.

8. Which layer of the OSI model ensures the data being sent from the sender is formatted correctly so it can be interpreted correctly by the recipient system?
   A. Application
   B. Presentation
   C. Session
   D. Transport

   ☑ **B.** The presentation layer of the OSI model ensures the data it receives from the application layer on the sending system is formatted correctly so it can be interpreted correctly by the application layer protocol on the recipient system.

   ☒ **A, C,** and **D** are incorrect. **A** is incorrect because the application layer provides services such as web or FTP servers. **C** is incorrect because the session layer manages the dialog between the sender and recipient. **D** is incorrect because the transport layer manages segment sequencing.

9. Which functions are provided by the transport layer of the OSI model? (Choose two.)
   A. Ensuring that data on the sending system is formatted correctly for the recipient system
   B. Establishing, managing, and terminating communications between the sender and recipient
   C. Managing segment sequencing
   D. Creating TCP and UDP ports for the IP protocol
   E. Managing logical addressing information for network hosts

   ☑ **C** and **D.** The transport layer has many functions. For example, it manages segment sequencing between the sender and the recipient. It also creates ports for the TCP and UDP protocols.

   ☒ **A, B,** and **E** are incorrect. **A** is incorrect because formatting data is the responsibility of the presentation layer. **B** is incorrect because managing communications is the job of the session layer. **E** is incorrect because managing logical addressing is the job of the network layer.

10. Which of the following are functions of the Logical Link Control (LLC) sublayer of the data link layer in the OSI model? (Choose two.)
    A. Retransmits missing or corrupted frames
    B. Transmits electrical signals between hosts
    C. Provides an interface with the network layer
    D. Provides for the routing of the data
    E. Determines the next network point to which a packet should be forwarded toward its destination

☑ **A and C.** Two of the functions performed by the LLC sublayer of the data link layer of the OSI model are to retransmit missing or corrupted frames and to provide an interface with the network layer using Service Access Points (SAPs).

☒ **B, D, and E** are not correct. **B** is incorrect because transmitting electrical signals between hosts is the function of the physical layer. **D** and **E** are incorrect because routing is the function of the network layer.

11. Which layer of the OSI model defines rules for accessing the network media?
   A. Physical
   B. Data link
   C. Network
   D. Transport

☑ **B.** The Media Access Control sublayer of the data link layer defines rules for hosts that need to access the network media. Access control schemes such as CSMA/CD, CSMA/CA, and token passing are defined here.

☒ **A, C, and D** are incorrect. **A** is incorrect because the physical layer defines how electrical signals are sent on the network medium. **C** is incorrect because the network layer provides for the routing of data between networks. **D** is incorrect because the transport layer manages segment sequencing and service addresses (such as IP ports).

12. Using network monitoring software, you've identified a system on your network using an unfamiliar MAC address. You need to gather information to help you identify this potentially rogue host. Which part of a MAC address uniquely identifies the organization that manufactured the device to which the address has been assigned?
   A. The first octet
   B. The first two octets
   C. The last three octets
   D. The first three octets

☑ **D.** The first three octets of a MAC address uniquely identify the organization that manufactured the device to which the address has been assigned. These three octets are referred to as the Organizationally Unique Identifier (OUI).

☒ **A, B, and C** are incorrect. **A** and **B** are incorrect because the first and second octets are only part of the OUI. The first three octets of the MAC address together compose the OUI and must be globally unique. **C** is incorrect because the last three octets of a MAC address (or five octets in the case of a EUI-64 MAC addresss) can be assigned by the manufacturer in any manner desired and aren't required to be globally unique.

13. You are designing a network implementation for a small business client. For security and data throughput reasons, they want to implement 1000 Mbps networking using fiber-optic cabling. Which IEEE project standard defines Gigabit Ethernet over fiber-optic cabling?

    A. 802.2

    B. 802.5

    C. 802.3z

    D. 802.3ab

    ☑ **C.** The 802.3z IEEE project standard defines Gigabit Ethernet over fiber-optic cabling or coaxial cabling in the 1000Base-X, 1000Base-T, and 1000Base-CX specifications.

    ☒ **A, B,** and **D** are incorrect. **A** is incorrect because the 802.2 standard defines the Logical Link Control sublayer of the data link layer of the OSI model. **B** is incorrect because the 802.5 standard defines the token passing media access method used by Token Ring networks. **D** is incorrect because the 802.3ab standard defines Gigabit Ethernet over twisted-pair cabling.

14. You've just been hired by an organization to manage its Token Ring network. Your past experience has been primarily with Ethernet networks and you now need to familiarize yourself with Token Ring networks. Which IEEE project standard should you consult to do this?

    A. 802.2

    B. 802.3

    C. 802.5

    D. 802.11

    ☑ **C.** The 802.5 IEEE project standard defines standards for Token Ring networks. Specifically, it defines the token passing media access method used by Token Ring.

    ☒ **A, B,** and **D** are incorrect. **A** is incorrect because the 802.2 standard defines the Logical Link Control sublayer of the data link layer of the OSI model. **B** is incorrect because the 802.3 standard defines Ethernet networking. **D** is incorrect because 802.11 defines wireless networking.

15. A client has hired you to implement a new wireless network. The organization already uses a wireless telephone system that utilizes the 5.8 GHz frequency range. To prevent conflicts, you need to implement a wireless network that uses frequency ranges from 2.4 GHz to 2.4835 GHz. Which IEEE project standard defines wireless networking using this range at a maximum data rate of 54 Mbps?

    A. 802.11a

    B. 802.11b

    C. 802.11g

    D. 802.11n

> ☑ **C.** The 802.11g IEEE project standard defines wireless networking using frequency ranges of 2.4 GHz to 2.4835 GHz at a maximum speed of 54 Mbps. If signal quality is poor or if older 802.11b hardware is used, this standard also allows the data rate to be bumped down.
>
> ☒ **A, B,** and **D** are incorrect. **A** is incorrect because the 802.11a standard transfers data at 54 Mbps, but it uses frequencies ranging from 5.725 GHz to 5.850 GHz. **B** is incorrect because the 802.11b standard uses frequency ranges of 2.4 GHz to 2.4835 GHz, but only transfers data at 11 Mbps. **D** is incorrect because the 802.11n standard transfers data at 5 GHz or 2.4 GHz and increases data transfer rates to 100 Mbps or more.

16. Which IEEE project standard defines 100 Mbps Ethernet networking?

    A. 802.3u

    B. 802.ae

    C. 802.3z

    D. 802.3ab

> ☑ **A.** The 802.3u project standard defines 100 Mbps (sometimes called Fast) Ethernet networking using inexpensive Category 5 twisted pair wiring.
>
> ☒ **B, C,** and **D** are incorrect. **B** is incorrect because the 802.3ae standard defines 10-Gigabit Ethernet networking. **C** is incorrect because the 802.3z standard defines Gigabit Ethernet over fiber-optic cabling or coaxial cabling. **D** is incorrect because the 802.3ab standard defines Gigabit Ethernet over twisted-pair cabling.

17. You've been hired by a small business to manage its legacy Ethernet network. Upon inspection, you notice that the existing network uses coaxial cable. Which 802.3 specifications use this type of cabling? (Choose two.)

    A. 10Base-2

    B. 10Base-5

    C. 10Base-T

    D. 10Base-FL

    E. 1000Base-LX

☑ **A** and **B.** The 10Base-2 and 10Base-5 standards utilize coaxial cabling. 1000Base-CX also uses a type of coaxial cabling called "Twinax."

☒ **C, D,** and **E** are incorrect. **C** is incorrect because 10Base-T uses UTP wiring. **D** and **E** are incorrect because 10Base-FL and 1000Base-LX both utilize fiber-optic cabling.

18. You are responsible for managing a legacy 10Base-2 Ethernet network. The network is composed of five network segments that are connected together using four repeaters. What is the maximum number of segments in this network that can be populated with network hosts?
   A. Two
   B. Three
   C. Four
   D. Five

☑ **B.** 10Base-2 (and 10Base-5) networks follow the 5-4-3 rule, which specifies that the network can be composed of five total network segments joined by four repeaters, but only three of the five network segments can be populated with hosts.

☒ **A, C,** and **D** are incorrect. **A** is incorrect because the 5-4-3 rule specifies that a 10Base-2 network can be composed of five total network segments joined by four repeaters with a maximum of three of those network segments populated with hosts. In this example, three of the five networks can have network hosts connected to them. The other two must be unpopulated. **C** and **D** are incorrect for the same reason.

19. Which protocols are transport layer protocols? (Choose two.)
   A. IP
   B. IPX
   C. UDP
   D. SMTP
   E. SPX

☑ **C** and **E.** The UDP and SPX protocols are transport layer protocols in the OSI model.

☒ **A, B,** and **D** are incorrect. **A** and **B** are incorrect because the IP and IPX protocols are network layer protocols. **D** is incorrect because the SMTP protocol is an application layer protocol.

20. You are designing a new network that will employ one Windows Server 2008 server system and twenty Windows 7 workstations. You need to assign NetBIOS computer names to each host on the network. Which of the following are valid computer names that you could use? (Choose two.)

A. FS1

B. WORKGROUPSERVER12

C. WORKSTATION:1

D. WS19

E. WS1*1

☑ **A** and **D.** NetBIOS computer names on a Microsoft network can have a maximum of 16 characters (each characters is composed of 1 byte of data). However, the last character is reserved for the name suffix and can't be used. Therefore, the maximum length allowed in this scenario is 15 characters. Computer names may not use characters such as ":", "*", "?", or "|". Therefore, FS1 and WS19 are both valid NetBIOS computer names.

☒ **B, C,** and **E** are incorrect. **B** is incorrect because the name is longer than 15 characters. **C** and **E** are incorrect because they use illegal characters ("*" and ":").

21. Using network monitoring software, you've noticed an unfamiliar new host on your network. The NetBIOS computer name for the host is ROGUE11. Upon analyzing each octet of the computer name, you notice that the last byte contains the ASCII characters 00. What kind of system is this?

A. A domain controller

B. A primary domain controller (PDC)

C. A master browser

D. A workstation

☑ **D.** NetBIOS computer names on a Microsoft network can have a maximum of 16 characters with the last character reserved for the name suffix, which identifies the type of system. In this scenario, the ASCII characters 00 in the name suffix identify the host as a workstation.

☒ **A, B,** and **C** are incorrect. **A** is incorrect because a domain controller would have a name suffix of 1C. **B** is incorrect because a PDC would have a name suffix of 1B. **C** is incorrect because a master browser would have a name suffix of 1D.

22. You've opened a web browser on your workstation and have entered a URL in the Location field. Which layer of the OSI model initiates the HTTP request to the web server?
    A. Application
    B. Presentation
    C. Session
    D. Transport

    > ☑ **A.** The application layer of the OSI model is responsible for initiating the HTTP request in this example. HTTP is an application layer protocol and, in this scenario, initiates the HTTP GET request that requests the resources specified in the URL from the web server.
    >
    > ☒ **B, C,** and **D** are incorrect. **B** is incorrect because the presentation layer is responsible only for formatting the information. It doesn't initiate network requests. **C** is incorrect because the session layer is only concerned with managing network sessions between hosts. **D** is incorrect because the transport layer is responsible for breaking data into packets and ensuring delivery.

23. You are copying a file from your workstation to a file server on the network. Which layer of the OSI model is responsible for physically addressing the data prior to placing those signals on the network medium?
    A. Transport
    B. Network
    C. Data link
    D. Physical

    > ☑ **C.** The data link layer of the OSI model is responsible for physically addressing the data prior to converting it into electrical signals and placing it on the network medium. Physical addressing at the data link layer is done by forming the data into frames and assigning a destination and source MAC address to each one.
    >
    > ☒ **A, B,** and **D** are incorrect. **A** is incorrect because the transport layer is responsible for breaking data into packets and ensuring delivery. It doesn't manage physical addressing. **B** is incorrect because the network layer concerned with logical addressing, such as IP addresses. **D** is incorrect because the physical layer is responsible for actually transmitting the data as electrical signals on the network medium.

24. Your computer system is in the process of establishing a TCP-based connection at the transport layer of the OSI model with another network host. Your computer has just sent a TCP SYN message to initiate the connection. If the destination host successfully receives the TCP SYN message, what message will it send back to your computer in response?

A. TCP SYN

B. TCP SYN/ACK

C. TCP ACK

D. TCP ACCEPT

☑ **B.** After the source system sends a TCP SYN message to the destination system when establishing a TCP connection, the destination system responds with a TCP SYN/ACK message. If it is successfully received by the originating host, it will respond back with a TCP ACK message to finish establishing the connection.

☒ **A, C,** and **D** are incorrect. **A** is incorrect because TCP at transport layer sends a TCP SYN to a network host to initiate a new connection. **C** is incorrect because a TCP ACK message is sent from the originating host to the destination host only after the destination host has responded with a TCP SYN/ACK message. **D** is incorrect because there is no such thing as a TCP ACCEPT message.

25. You need to assign an IP address to a Windows 7 workstation on your network. Which of the following is a valid IPv4 address that you could use?

A. 192.168.1.255

B. 192.168.1.0

C. 192.168.1.257

D. 192.168.1.254

☑ **D.** A valid IPv4 address is composed of four 8-bit octets. Therefore, the maximum decimal value that can be assigned to any octet in an IP address is 255 (the decimal equivalent of the binary number 11111111). However, the value 255 is reserved for broadcasts and 0 is reserved for network addresses. Accordingly, only 192.168.1.254 is a valid IPv4 address in the list of addresses in this question.

☒ **A, B,** and **C** are incorrect. **A** is incorrect because 192.168.1.255 is a broadcast address that can't be assigned to a network host. **B** is incorrect because 192.168.1.0 is a network address that can't be assigned to a network host. **C** is incorrect because 257 is an invalid number for an 8-bit octet.

26. Which protocols are network layer protocols in the OSI model? (Choose two.)
   A. HTTP
   B. IP
   C. TCP
   D. UDP
   E. IPX

☑ **B** and **E.** The IP and IPX protocols function at the network layer of the OSI model. As such, they are concerned with logical addressing and routing data between networks.

☒ **A, C,** and **D** are incorrect. **A** is incorrect because HTTP is an application layer protocol. **C** and **D** are incorrect because TCP and UDP are both transport layer protocols.

27. Which layer of the OSI model manages logical addressing for network hosts?
   A. Session
   B. Transport
   C. Network
   D. Data link

☑ **C.** The network layer of the OSI model is concerned with logical addressing of network hosts and routing data between networks. IP and IPX addresses are examples of logical addresses managed by the network layer of the OSI model.

☒ **A, B,** and **D** are incorrect. **A** is incorrect because the session layer is only concerned with managing network sessions between hosts. **B** is incorrect because the transport layer is responsible for breaking data into packets and ensuring delivery. **D** is incorrect because the data link layer manages physical addresses and media access rules.

3

Networking Components

QUESTIONS

In the previous chapter, the questions discussed how network protocols relate to the various layers within the OSI model. In this chapter, the questions pertain to how the networking hardware in a network also maps to specific layers in the OSI model. Understanding this relationship is critical, because it determines how the hardware in the network operates. It even determines how broadcasts and collisions affect the hosts in the network.

For your Network+ exam, you need to be very familiar with how a network is physically implemented. You should understand how wiring is run through a building and what type of wire should be used where. The Network+ exam also expects you to understand how wiring is distributed throughout a building. Included in this process is how wiring from an external telecom provider interfaces with the wiring owned by an organization. The Network+ exam will also expect you to understand the role and function of various network devices such as switches, routers, proxy servers, and content filters.

In addition, the Network+ exam now includes virtual networking concepts. With virtualization, a hypervisor is used to create virtual network components, including virtual network segments, virtual switches, and virtual machines. You should be familiar with the different types of hardware virtualization available as well as the network devices that can be virtualized.

1. You are working with a legacy 10Base-5 network interface card. Where is the transceiver for this board located?
    A. It runs on the computer itself as a software driver.
    B. It's a chip on the network interface card.
    C. It's a chip on the system motherboard.
    D. It's external to the board, plugging into an AUI port on the network interface card.

2. In which layers of the OSI model does an Ethernet network interface card operate? (Choose two.)
    A. Physical
    B. Data link
    C. Network
    D. Transport
    E. Session

3. You need to install a network interface card into a server PC system. The server will be used to provide file sharing services for network clients, and the network card must provide the fastest I/O throughput possible. Which type of network card would provide the best performance in this scenario?
    A. ISA
    B. PCI

C. PCI-X

D. PCIe

4. Which network card setting configures the interface to send and receive data at the same time?

 A. Simplex

 B. Half duplex

 C. Full duplex

 D. Time-division duplexing

5. Which of the following are valid 48-bit MAC addresses? (Choose two.)

 A. 44:87:FC:E2:E5:D3:H0

 B. 44-87-FC-E2-E5-G3

 C. 44-87-FC-E2-E5

 D. 44:87:AA:E2:E5:D3

 E. 44-87-FC-E2-E5-D2

6. After entering the **ipconfig /all** command at the command prompt of a Windows Server 2008 system, you see that the following 48-bit MAC address has been assigned to your server's network board: 3F-6B-AA-E2-25-13. What is the manufacturer ID contained in this MAC address?

 A. 3F-6B

 B. 3F-6B-AA

 C. AA-E2

 D. E2-25-13

7. Which of the following is a valid EUI-64 MAC address?

 A. 44:87:BB:E3:E5:D3

 B. 00-00-D8-EF-1B-AD-BE-EF

 C. 00:00:1B:EF:0B:AD

 D. 00-50-56-C0-00-01-AC

8. A network in a dentist's office suite comprises five systems connected by three cascaded Ethernet hubs. One host is a Linux server (FS1), the rest are Windows 7 workstations (WS1, WS2, WS3, and WS4). FS1, WS1, and WS2 are connected to the first hub, WS3 is connected to the second hub, and WS4 is connected to the third hub. If a user on WS1 sends a request for a service to the FS1 server, which hosts will receive a copy of the Ethernet frames that make up the request?

 A. WS1 and FS1 only

 B. FS1 only

 C. WS1, WS2, and FS1 only

 D. All hosts connected to all hubs

9. You need to expand an existing Token Ring network to accommodate additional network hosts by adding a second MSAU to the ring. What should you do? (Choose two.)

    A. Connect the ring out port from the new MSAU to the ring in port on the existing MSAU.

    B. Set an open port on the existing MSAU to "Cascade."

    C. Connect the cascaded port on the existing MSAU to an available port on the new MSAU.

    D. Connect an open port on the existing MSAU to an open port on the new MSAU with a crossover cable.

    E. Connect the ring in port from the new MSAU to the ring out port on the existing MSAU.

10. You manage networks for an educational institution that has three separate Ethernet networks, one for each wing of the building. You want to connect these three networks together, but you're concerned about overwhelming all three segments with excessive traffic. Which devices could you use to connect all three networks together, but still manage traffic such that frames addressed to hosts on the same local segment remain on that segment while frames addressed to hosts on a different segment are forwarded? (Choose two.)

    A. Hub

    B. Switch

    C. Repeater

    D. Bridge

11. You are working with a 24-port, layer 2 switch and want to use it to create three separate VLANs. How does this kind of switch manage VLAN traffic?

    A. Specific physical ports on the switch can be assigned to VLANs you define.

    B. The MAC addresses of the systems connected to the switch are assigned to VLANs you define.

    C. VLAN membership is based on the network layer logical address of individual network packets.

    D. Layer 2 switches can't be used to create VLANs.

12. Which VLAN feature provided on most switches allows you to connect multiple switches together and assign one port to carry VLAN traffic to the other switch?

    A. Spanning Tree Protocol

    B. Port mirroring

    C. Trunking

    D. Port authentication

13. A 24-port switch has been configured with three separate VLANs. The FS1 Server as well as workstations WS1, WS2, and WS3 are associated with the first VLAN on the switch. The FS2 server as well as workstations WS4, WS5, and WS6 are associated with the second VLAN.

The FS3 server as well as workstations WS7, WS8, and WS9 are associated with the third VLAN. If WS6 sends a network broadcast, which hosts will receive it? (Choose two.)

A. FS1

B. FS2

C. FS3

D. WS1, WS2, WS3

E. WS4, WS5, WS6

14. You manage a network for a small architectural consulting firm. The network is composed of three Ethernet switches that have been cascaded together. Two VLANs have been created: one for the firm's president, treasurer, and administrative assistants and one for architectural development work. FS1, WS1, and WS2 are connected to Switch1; WS3, WS4, and FS2 are connected to Switch2; and WS5, WS6, and WS7 are connected to Switch3. FS1, WS1, WS2, and WS3 are members of the first VLAN, while WS4, FS2, WS5, WS6, and WS7 are members of the second VLAN. What is the collision domain for the FS1 host?

A. The network port to which the FS1 server is connected on the switch

B. All hosts connected to Switch1

C. All hosts connected to Switch1, Switch2, and Switch3

D. All hosts that are members of the first VLAN

15. What mechanism do routers use to determine where data addressed to a host not residing on the local network should be sent?

A. The port on the network switch to which the sending host is connected

B. The MAC address of the destination host

C. The MAC address of the transmitting host

D. The logical network address of the destination host

16. Which network appliance can be deployed as an intermediary that manages requests from clients seeking resources from servers?

A. Load balancer

B. Proxy server

C. Content filter

D. Gateway

17. You are implementing a network for an elementary school. The school administration is concerned that young students might gain access to inappropriate content through the network's Internet connection. What should you do? (Choose two.)

A. Implement a NaaS

B. Configure a proxy server

C. Implement a content filter

D. Use SaaS

E. Install a line driver

18. Which technologies require a 64-bit EUI-64 MAC address instead of the more common 48-bit MAC-48 or EUI-48 MAC addresses? (Choose two.)

    A. IPv4

    B. IPv6

    C. 802.11 wireless

    D. 802.5 Token Ring

    E. IEEE 1394

19. Which of the following hardware devices operates at only the physical layer in the OSI model?

    A. Firewall

    B. Router

    C. Switch

    D. Hub

20. You are responsible for managing network traffic on your organization's Ethernet network. You know that the data link layer of the OSI model processes data in the form of frames. You need to monitor which network hosts are sending and receiving the most network traffic. What information is contained within a frame that could you use for this analysis? (Choose two.)

    A. Destination MAC address

    B. Source IP address

    C. Destination IP address

    D. Quality of Service (QoS) priority level

    E. CRC check fields

21. In addition to monitoring network frames, you also need to manage traffic on your network from a logical addressing perspective. What information is contained in the IP header of an IPv4 packet? (Choose two.)

    A. Source MAC address

    B. Identification tag

    C. Time to live (TTL)

    D. Destination MAC address

    E. Preamble

22. At which layer of the OSI model do switches operate? (Choose two.)

    A. Physical

    B. Data link

    C. Network

    D. Transport

23. At what layers of the OSI model does a multilayer switch operate? (Choose two.)
- **A.** Application
- **B.** Data link
- **C.** Network
- **D.** Transport
- **E.** Session

24. At which layer of the OSI model do bridges operate?
- **A.** Physical
- **B.** Data link
- **C.** Network
- **D.** Transport

25. What plastics are commonly used to create fire-retardant plenum network cabling? (Choose two.)
- **A.** Low-smoke PVC
- **B.** Fluorinated ethylene polymer (FEP)
- **C.** Polymethyl methacrylate
- **D.** Polyethylene
- **E.** Polypropylene

26. Which term refers to a signal distribution frame for connecting internal telephony or network equipment inside your facility to external cables and subscriber carrier equipment?
- **A.** IDF
- **B.** MDF
- **C.** Demarc
- **D.** Demarc extension

27. You are installing a patch panel and need to attach wires to the terminators located in the rear of the panel. According to the TIA/EIA-568-B specification, what standards can be used when connecting individual wires to specific pins in the terminator for horizontal cables? (Choose two.)
- **A.** T568A
- **B.** T568B
- **C.** 570-A
- **D.** 607
- **E.** 569-A

28. Which type of punch down block would be most appropriate for use with a Fast Ethernet network?
    A. 66
    B. 110
    C. 220
    D. 115

29. Which technology allows an organization to connect to a very high-speed T1 or T3 WAN connection from the telephone company?
    A. PSTN modem
    B. BRI ISDN
    C. ADSL
    D. CSU/DSU

30. Which type of network interface device is typically used with T1 lines and provides features such as signal conversion, loopback, and diagnostics?
    A. Telephone network interface (TNI)
    B. Network interface unit (NIU)
    C. Smartjack
    D. Optical network terminal (ONT)

31. You are designing a server and desktop virtualization strategy for your organization and need to select a hypervisor for the deployment. A key decision in this process is determining the type of hardware virtualization you want to implement. You're concerned that some of the operating systems you need to install within virtual machines are not hypervisor-aware. Which type of hardware virtualization would be the best choice in this scenario?
    A. Paravirtualization
    B. Partial virtualization
    C. Full virtualization
    D. Hardware-assisted virtualization

32. Which of the following is an encryption device that functions at the data link layer of the OSI model?
    A. EEG
    B. Firewall
    C. Proxy
    D. Multilayer switch

33. Your organization currently employs several hundred salespeople who spend much of their time traveling. They frequently need to access information on Linux servers in your company's home office. To provide secure remote access for these users, you have decided to implement a virtual private network (VPN) with a VPN concentrator. Which encryption method is typically used in by the concentrator in this configuration?

    A. Internet Protocol Security (IPSec)

    B. Kerberos

    C. Remote Authentication Dial In User Service (RADIUS)

    D. Data Encryption Standard (DES)

34. You are designing a network and telecom implementation for a new small business on a tight budget. The organization has 15 employees in a small rented office suite. The employees will need phone services such as call routing, voicemail, automated greetings, conference calling, and automatic routing of incoming calls to the first available employee. What should you do to accomplish this?

    A. Implement a virtual switch.

    B. Implement virtual desktops.

    C. Implement a hardware PBX.

    D. Implement a virtual PBX.

QUICK ANSWER KEY

I.	D	13.	B, E	25.	A, B
2.	A, B	14.	A	26.	B
3.	D	15.	D	27.	A, B
4.	C	16.	B	28.	B
5.	D, E	17.	B, C	29.	D
6.	B	18.	B, E	30.	C
7.	B	19.	D	31.	C
8.	D	20.	A, E	32.	A
9.	A, E	21.	B, C	33.	A
10.	B, D	22.	A, B	34.	D
II.	B	23.	B, C		
12.	C	24.	B		

IN-DEPTH ANSWERS

1. You are working with a legacy 10Base-5 network interface card. Where is the transceiver for this board located?
   A. It runs on the computer itself as a software driver.
   B. It's a chip on the network interface card.
   C. It's a chip on the system motherboard.
   D. It's external to the board, plugging into an AUI port on the network interface card.

   ☑ **D.** 10Base-5 network interface cards use an external transceiver that plugs into an AUI port on the network interface card.

   ☒ **A, B,** and **C** are incorrect. **A** is incorrect because a physical transceiver is required for a network board to transmit electrical signals on the network medium. **B** is true for Ethernet networks that use twisted-pair wiring, but it isn't correct for the coaxial cabling used by 10Base-5. **C** is also true for twisted-pair Ethernet network boards integrated into the system motherboard, but isn't correct for 10Base-5 network boards that use an external transceiver.

2. In which layers of the OSI model does an Ethernet network interface card operate? (Choose two.)
   A. Physical
   B. Data link
   C. Network
   D. Transport
   E. Session

   ☑ **A** and **B.** Modern network interface cards operate at the physical layer because they are responsible for transmitting electrical signals on the network medium. They also operate at the data link layer because they have a MAC address assigned that is used by data link layer protocols to identify the host uniquely on the network.

   ☒ **C, D,** and **E** are incorrect. **C** is incorrect because network interface cards don't operate at the network layer of the OSI model. **D** is incorrect because network interface cards don't operate at the transport layer of the OSI model. **E** is incorrect because network interface cards don't operate at the session layer of the OSI model.

3. You need to install a network interface card into a server PC system. The server will be used to provide file sharing services for network clients, and the network card must provide the fastest I/O throughput possible. Which type of network card would provide the best performance in this scenario?

   A. ISA
   B. PCI
   C. PCI-X
   D. PCIe

   ☑ **D.** A PCI Express (PCIe) network board would provide the fastest I/O throughput of the options listed. PCIe is different from earlier expansion bus standards in that it uses a dedicated high-speed serial point-to-point connection for each PCIe device instead of shared bus. This reduces contention and increases overall throughput.

   ☒ **A, B,** and **C** are incorrect. **A** is incorrect because legacy ISA network boards use a very narrow, very slow expansion bus and would be a poor choice. **B** and **C** are incorrect because PCI and PCI-X network boards both still use a shared parallel bus that is wide but relatively slow in comparison to the dedicated high-speed serial point-to-point connections used by PCIe devices.

4. Which network card setting configures the interface to send and receive data at the same time?

   A. Simplex
   B. Half duplex
   C. Full duplex
   D. Time-division duplexing

   ☑ **C.** When set to full duplex, a network interface card can send and receive data at the same time.

   ☒ **A, B,** and **D** are incorrect. **A** is incorrect because simplex communications are unidirectional, comparable to listening to a radio station. **B** is incorrect because half-duplex communications allow bidirectional communications, but the card would not be able to send and receive at the same time. Half-duplex communications are analogous to using a two-way radio to communicate—you can receive only when you aren't transmitting. **D** is incorrect because time-division duplexing is a scheme used to emulate full-duplex communications on a half-duplex communication channel.

5. Which of the following are valid 48-bit MAC addresses? (Choose two.)

   A. 44:87:FC:E2:E5:D3:H0

   B. 44-87-FC-E2-E5-G3

   C. 44-87-FC-E2-E5

   D. 44:87:AA:E2:E5:D3

   E. 44-87-FC-E2-E5-D2

   ☑ **D and E.** 44:87:AA:E2:E5:D3 and 44-87-FC-E2-E5-D2 are valid 48-bit MAC addresses. Each of the six 8-bit octets is represented by a two-character hexadecimal number.

   ☒ **A, B,** and **C** are incorrect. **A** is incorrect because it is 56-bits long and uses an invalid hexadecimal number in the last octet (H0). **B** is incorrect because it uses an invalid hexadecimal number in the last octet (G3). **C** is incorrect because it is only 40-bits long.

6. After entering the **ipconfig /all** command at the command prompt of a Windows Server 2008 system, you see that the following 48-bit MAC address has been assigned to your server's network board: 3F-6B-AA-E2-25-13. What is the manufacturer ID contained in this MAC address?

   A. 3F-6B

   B. 3F-6B-AA

   C. AA-E2

   D. E2-25-13

   ☑ **B.** The first three octets of any MAC address (48-bit or 64-bit) make up the Organizationally Unique Identifier (OUI) and are unique to the manufacturer that made the network board. No manufacturer is allowed to use any other manufacturer's OUI.

   ☒ **A, C,** and **D** are incorrect. **A** doesn't include the third octet of the OUI. **C** includes only one of the three octets included in the OUI. **D** includes the last three octets of the MAC address, which are assigned by the device manufacturer in any manner it wants.

7. Which of the following is a valid EUI-64 MAC address?

   A. 44:87:BB:E3:E5:D3

   B. 00-00-D8-EF-1B-AD-BE-EF

   C. 00:00:1B:EF:0B:AD

   D. 00-50-56-C0-00-01-AC

☑ **B.** 00-00-D8-EF-1B-AD-BE-EF is an example of an EUI-64 MAC address. EUI-64 MAC addresses are 64-bits long instead of 48 and are, therefore, composed of 8 octets represented with hexadecimal numbers.

☒ **A, C, and D** are incorrect. **A** and **C** are only 48-bits long (although they are both valid 48-bit MAC addresses). **D** is 56-bits long and is not a valid 48- or 64-bit MAC address.

8. A network in a dentist's office suite comprises five systems connected by three cascaded Ethernet hubs. One host is a Linux server (FS1), the rest are Windows 7 workstations (WS1, WS2, WS3, and WS4). FS1, WS1, and WS2 are connected to the first hub, WS3 is connected to the second hub, and WS4 is connected to the third hub. If a user on WS1 sends a request for a service to the FS1 server, which hosts will receive a copy of the Ethernet frames that make up the request?

A. WS1 and FS1 only
B. FS1 only
C. WS1, WS2, and FS1 only
D. All hosts connected to all hubs

☑ **D.** An Ethernet hub sends a copy of all frames transmitted to all hosts connected to the hub. If multiple hubs are cascaded, every host connected to every hub will receive a copy of all transmitted frames. Therefore, a request sent from WS1 to FS1 will be sent to all hosts on this network. However, only the host to which the frames are addressed will accept and process them. All other hosts to which the frames are not addressed will ignore and drop them.

☒ **A, B, and C** are incorrect. **A** is incorrect because all hosts connected to the hub will receive a copy of all frames transmitted. **B** and **C** are also incorrect because all hosts connected to the hub will receive a copy of all frames transmitted.

9. You need to expand an existing Token Ring network to accommodate additional network hosts by adding a second MSAU to the ring. What should you do? (Choose two.)

A. Connect the ring out port from the new MSAU to the ring in port on the existing MSAU.
B. Set an open port on the existing MSAU to "Cascade."
C. Connect the cascaded port on the existing MSAU to an available port on the new MSAU.
D. Connect an open port on the existing MSAU to an open port on the new MSAU with a crossover cable.
E. Connect the ring in port from the new MSAU to the ring out port on the existing MSAU.

☑ **A** and **E.** To uplink two Token Ring MSAUs together into a single ring, you need to connect the ring out port from the new MSAU to the ring in port on the existing MSAU and connect the ring in port from the new MSAU to the ring out port on the existing MSAU.

☒ **B, C,** and **D** are incorrect. **B** is incorrect because it is used to cascade Ethernet switches or hubs and is not applicable to Token Ring MSAUs. **C** and **D** are incorrect because they are also steps used to cascade Ethernet switches or hubs and are not applicable to Token Ring MSAUs.

10. You manage networks for an educational institution that has three separate Ethernet networks, one for each wing of the building. You want to connect these three networks together, but you're concerned about overwhelming all three segments with excessive traffic. Which devices could you use to connect all three networks together, but still manage traffic such that frames addressed to hosts on the same local segment remain on that segment while frames addressed to hosts on a different segment are forwarded? (Choose two.)

    A. Hub
    B. Switch
    C. Repeater
    D. Bridge

☑ **B** and **D.** Switches and bridges are data link layer devices and can manage traffic based on the MAC addresses contained within Ethernet frames. For example, a bridge can learn which hosts are connected to each segment. If a frame is addressed to a host on the same LAN segment, the bridge won't forward it to the other connected segments. If a frame is addressed to a host on a different segment, the bridge will forward it to just that segment.

☒ **A,** and **C** are incorrect. **A** is incorrect because hubs are physical layer devices and forward all frames to all connected hosts, thus increasing the likelihood of excess traffic and collisions. **C** is incorrect because repeaters are also physical layer devices and forward all frames to all connected hosts, thus increasing the likelihood of excess traffic and collisions.

11. You are working with a 24-port, layer 2 switch and want to use it to create three separate VLANs. How does this kind of switch manage VLAN traffic?

    A. Specific physical ports on the switch can be assigned to VLANs you define.
    B. The MAC addresses of the systems connected to the switch are assigned to VLANs you define.

C. VLAN membership is based on the network layer logical address of individual network packets.

D. Layer 2 switches can't be used to create VLANs.

☑ **B.** A layer 2 switch uses the MAC addresses of the systems connected to the switch to define VLANs. In essence, VLAN membership is based on a system's MAC address, not on the switch port to which it is connected.

☒ **A, C,** and **D** are not correct. **A** is incorrect because layer 1 switches assign specific ports to VLANs. **C** is incorrect because layer 3 switches base VLAN membership on the network layer logical address of individual network packets, not on physical hosts or physical ports. **D** is incorrect because both layer 2 and layer 3 switches can be used to create VLANs, just in different ways.

12. Which VLAN feature provided on most switches allows you to connect multiple switches together and assign one port to carry VLAN traffic to the other switch?

A. Spanning Tree Protocol

B. Port mirroring

C. Trunking

D. Port authentication

☑ **C.** Trunking is a feature available on some switches that allows you to connect two (or more) switches together and assign one port as a trunk port. The trunk port is used to carry VLAN traffic to the other switch.

☒ **A, B,** and **D** are incorrect. **A** is incorrect because the Spanning Tree Protocol is used by switches to prevent switching loops that could occur if multiple switches were wired together incorrectly. **B** is incorrect because port mirroring allows the switch to send a copy of data that reaches certain ports to a monitored port, which allows you as the administrator to monitor network traffic. **D** is incorrect because port authentication allows you to restrict hosts that are allowed to connect to a specific port by their MAC address.

13. A 24-port switch has been configured with three separate VLANs. The FS1 Server as well as workstations WS1, WS2, and WS3 are associated with the first VLAN on the switch. The FS2 server as well as workstations WS4, WS5, and WS6 are associated with the second VLAN. The

FS3 server as well as workstations WS7, WS8, and WS9 are associated with the third VLAN. If WS6 sends a network broadcast, which hosts will receive it? (Choose two.)

A. FS1

B. FS2

C. FS3

D. WS1, WS2, WS3

E. WS4, WS5, WS6

☑ **B** and **E.** Because FS2, WS4, WS5, and WS6 are members of the same VLAN, they are members of the same broadcast domain.

☒ **A, C,** and **D** are incorrect. **A** is incorrect because FS1 is a member of different VLAN and therefore not a member of the same broadcast domain. **C** and **D** are incorrect because FS3, WS1, WS2, and WS3 are also members of different VLANs and are, therefore, not members of the same broadcast domain.

14. You manage a network for a small architectural consulting firm. The network is composed of three Ethernet switches that have been cascaded together. Two VLANs have been created: one for the firm's president, treasurer, and administrative assistants and one for architectural development work. FS1, WS1, and WS2 are connected to Switch1; WS3, WS4, and FS2 are connected to Switch2; and WS5, WS6, and WS7 are connected to Switch3. FS1, WS1, WS2, and WS3 are members of the first VLAN, while WS4, FS2, WS5, WS6, and WS7 are members of the second VLAN. What is the collision domain for the FS1 host?

A. The network port to which the FS1 server is connected on the switch

B. All hosts connected to Switch1

C. All hosts connected to Switch1, Switch2, and Switch3

D. All hosts that are members of the first VLAN

☑ **A.** Because this network uses Ethernet switches, the collision domain for each host is limited to its own port on the switch. If this network used hubs instead of switches, the collision domain would be all cascaded hubs.

☒ **B, C,** and **D** are incorrect. **B** would be correct if the network used hubs instead of switches and if they weren't cascaded. However, because switches are used, this choice is incorrect. **C** would also be correct if the network used hubs instead of switches. Again, switches are in use, so this answer choice is incorrect. **D** is incorrect because it identifies the broadcast domain instead of the collision domain.

15. What mechanism do routers use to determine where data addressed to a host not residing on the local network should be sent?
    A. The port on the network switch to which the sending host is connected
    B. The MAC address of the destination host
    C. The MAC address of the transmitting host
    D. The logical network address of the destination host

    ☑ **D.** Because routers are network layer devices, they use the logical network address of the destination host (such as its IP address) to determine where data should be forwarded. Routers do not evaluate traffic based on physical ports or MAC addresses.

    ☒ **A, B,** and **C** are incorrect. **A** is incorrect because it specifies a physical layer mechanism. **B** and **C** are incorrect because they specify data link layer mechanisms.

16. Which network appliance can be deployed as an intermediary that manages requests from clients seeking resources from servers?
    A. Load balancer
    B. Proxy server
    C. Content filter
    D. Gateway

    ☑ **B.** A proxy server acts as an intermediary for clients requests seeking resources from other servers, such as a web server.

    ☒ **A, C,** and **D** are incorrect. **A** is incorrect because a load balancer manages processing loads between two or more servers. **C** is incorrect because a content filter inspects incoming and/or outgoing data according to rules the administrator defines. **D** is incorrect because a gateway appliance provides routing functionality for a network segment.

17. You are implementing a network for an elementary school. The school administration is concerned that young students might gain access to inappropriate content through the network's Internet connection. What should you do? (Choose two.)
    A. Implement a NaaS
    B. Configure a proxy server
    C. Implement a content filter
    D. Use SaaS
    E. Install a line driver

☑ **B** and **C.** You can use a proxy server and/or a content filter appliance to control access to content on the Internet in this scenario. The proxy server can be used to control access to web sites. The content filter can inspect incoming content and filter it based on rules you specify.

☒ **A, D,** and **E** are incorrect. **A** and **D** are incorrect because Network as a Service (NaaS) and Software as a Service (SaaS) are cloud computing technologies. **E** is incorrect because a line driver can be used in baseband networks to increase transmission distance by amplifying electrical signals.

18. Which technologies require a 64-bit EUI-64 MAC address instead of the more common 48-bit MAC-48 or EUI-48 MAC addresses? (Choose two.)

    A. IPv4

    B. IPv6

    C. 802.11 wireless

    D. 802.5 Token Ring

    E. IEEE 1394

☑ **B** and **E.** IPv6 and IEEE 1394 (FireWire) require 64-bit MAC addresses instead of the older 48-bit MAC addresses. IPv6 uses a host's MAC address to determine the IPv6 address that will be assigned to the host. If a host has only a 48-bit MAC address, algorithms have been implemented in IPv6 to dynamically convert the 48-bit address to a 64-bit address.

☒ **A, C,** and **D** are incorrect. **A** is incorrect because IPv4 uses 48-bit MAC addresses. **C** is incorrect because 802.11 wireless also uses 48-bit MAC addresses. **D** is incorrect because 802.5 Token Ring uses 48-bit MAC addresses as well.

19. Which of the following hardware devices operates at only the physical layer in the OSI model?

    A. Firewall

    B. Router

    C. Switch

    D. Hub

☑ **D.** Hubs are physical layer devices in the OSI model. They do not operate at any higher layers.

☒ **A, B,** and **C** are incorrect. **A** is incorrect because firewalls reside at the network, transport, and application layers of the OSI model (depending upon the type of firewall). For example, packet filtering firewalls operate at the network and transport layers while stateful firewalls operate at the transport layer. **B** is incorrect because routers operate at the network layer. **C** is incorrect because switches operate at both the physical and data link layers.

20. You are responsible for managing network traffic on your organization's Ethernet network. You know that the data link layer of the OSI model processes data in the form of frames. You need to monitor which network hosts are sending and receiving the most network traffic. What information is contained within a frame that could you use for this analysis? (Choose two.)
    A. Destination MAC address
    B. Source IP address
    C. Destination IP address
    D. Quality of Service (QoS) priority level
    E. CRC check fields

☑ **A** and **E.** Frames processed at the data link layer are composed of the preamble, recipient (destination) MAC address, sender MAC address, length, data, pad, and CRC fields. In this scenario, you could analyze network frames being transmitted on the network to determine which hosts are sending and receiving the most traffic.

☒ **B, C,** and **D** are incorrect. **B** and **C** are incorrect because the data link layer isn't concerned with logical addressing (that is the function of the network layer), so a frame isn't addressed using IP addresses. **D** is incorrect because a QoS priority level is also assigned by higher layers of the OSI model.

21. In addition to monitoring network frames, you also need to manage traffic on your network from a logical addressing perspective. What information is contained in the IP header of an IPv4 packet? (Choose two.)
    A. Source MAC address
    B. Identification tag
    C. Time to live (TTL)
    D. Destination MAC address
    E. Preamble

  ☑ **B** and **C.** The identification tag field and the TTL field are included in the IP header of an IPv4 packet. The identification tag is used to help reconstruct the packet after fragmentation. The TTL field specifies the number of router hops the packet is allowed to pass before it is discarded. For example, a packet with a TTL of 16 will be allowed to cross 16 routers before it is discarded.

  ☒ **A, D**, and **E** are incorrect. **A** and **D** are incorrect because the source MAC address and the destination MAC address are fields within a frame at the data link layer. **E** is incorrect because the preamble field is also part of a frame at the data link layer.

22. At which layer of the OSI model do switches operate? (Choose two.)
  A. Physical
  B. Data link
  C. Network
  D. Transport

  ☑ **A** and **B.** Because switches transmit electrical signals on the network medium, they are considered to operate at the physical layer. However, because switches can also manage network traffic using the MAC addresses of the hosts connected to the switch, they also operate at the data link layer of the OSI model.

  ☒ **C** and **D** are incorrect. **C** and **D** are incorrect because a network switch manages network traffic based on MAC addresses of network hosts. Therefore, they don't operate at the network or transport layer of the OSI model. However, be aware that a multilayer switch adds network layer functionality and provides network routing capabilities.

23. At what layers of the OSI model does a multilayer switch operate? (Choose two.)
  A. Application
  B. Data link
  C. Network
  D. Transport
  E. Session

  ☑ **B** and **C.** Multilayer switches operate at layers 2 and 3 of the OSI model. They provide the functionality of both a switch (at the data link layer) and a router (at the network layer).

  ☒ **A, D**, and **E** are incorrect. **A** is incorrect because multilayer switches do not operate at the application layer of the OSI model. **D** is incorrect because multilayer switches do not operate at the transport layer of the OSI model. **E** is incorrect because multilayer switches do not operate at the session layer of the OSI model.

24. At which layer of the OSI model do bridges operate?
   A. Physical
   B. Data link
   C. Network
   D. Transport

> ☑ **B.** A bridge is used to connect multiple network segments at the data link layer of the OSI model. It memorizes the MAC addresses of the network hosts on both sides of the bridge to determine which frames should be forwarded and which should not.
>
> ☒ **A, C,** and **D** are incorrect. **A** is incorrect because bridges work with MAC addresses and do not operate at the physical layer of the OSI model. **C** is incorrect because bridges do not operate at the network layer of the OSI model. **D** is also incorrect because bridges do not operate at the transport layer of the OSI model.

25. What plastics are commonly used to create fire-retardant plenum network cabling? (Choose two.)
   A. Low-smoke PVC
   B. Fluorinated ethylene polymer (FEP)
   C. Polymethyl methacrylate
   D. Polyethylene
   E. Polypropylene

> ☑ **A** and **B.** Low-smoke PVC and fluorinated ethylene polymer (FEP) are commonly used to create fire-retardant plenum network cabling. Both of these plastics resist combustion and do not emit harmful vapors when heated.
>
> ☒ **C, D,** and **E** are incorrect. **C** is incorrect because Polymethyl methacrylate is used as a glass substitute, not for the sheathing of network cable. **D** and **E** are incorrect because polyethylene and polypropylene are not fire-retardant and are not used to make plenum network cabling.

26. Which term refers to a signal distribution frame for connecting internal telephony or network equipment inside your facility to external cables and subscriber carrier equipment?
   A. IDF
   B. MDF
   C. Demarc
   D. Demarc extension

☑ **B.** A main distribution frame (MDF) is a signal distribution frame for connecting your internal network or telephony equipment to external cabling and subscriber carrier equipment.

☒ **A, C,** and **D** are incorrect. **A** is incorrect because intermediate distribution frame (IDF) is a frame that serves as a distribution point for cables from the MDF. **C** and **D** are incorrect because the term Demarc refers to the demarcation point at which the telecom network ends and connects with your organization's wiring.

27. You are installing a patch panel and need to attach wires to the terminators located in the rear of the panel. According to the TIA/EIA-568-B specification, what standards can be used when connecting individual wires to specific pins in the terminator for horizontal cables? (Choose two.)

A. T568A
B. T568B
C. 570-A
D. 607
E. 569-A

☑ **A** and **B.** According to the TIA/EIA-568-B specification, the T568A and T568B wiring standards can be used when connecting individual wires to specific pins in the patch panel terminator for horizontal cables. Although both standards can be used, the TIA/EIA-568-B specification defines the T568A wiring scheme as the preferred standard.

☒ **C, D,** and **E** are incorrect. **C** is incorrect because the 570-A standard in the TIA/EIA-568-B specification specifies standards for residential cabling. **D** is incorrect because the 607 standard specifies standards for grounding telecom cabling and equipment. **E** is incorrect because the 569-A standard defines how to implement pathways and spaces for network cabling.

28. Which type of punch down block would be most appropriate for use with a Fast Ethernet network?

A. 66
B. 110
C. 220
D. 115

☑ **B.** 110 punch down blocks are used for modern Ethernet networks. They can be used with Fast Ethernet networks because they are rated for CAT 5 (and better) UTP cabling.

☒ **A, C,** and **D** are incorrect. **A** is incorrect because 66 punch down blocks are not rated for CAT 5 cabling and are usually used for telephone wiring only. **C** and **D** are incorrect because there is no such thing as 220 or 115 punch down blocks.

29. Which technology allows an organization to connect to a very high-speed T1 or T3 WAN connection from the telephone company?
    A. PSTN modem
    B. BRI ISDN
    C. ADSL
    D. CSU/DSU

☑ **D.** A channel service unit/data service unit (CSU/DSU) is either one device or a pair of devices that allows you to connect to a high-speed T1 or T3 WAN connection provided by a telecom provider. The CSU is implemented within your organization and connects to the DSU unit managed by the provider to establish the WAN link.

☒ **A, B,** and **C** are incorrect. **A** is incorrect because a public switched telephone network (PSTN) modem is used to establish a slow point-to-point connection with an ISP over standard telephone lines. **B** is incorrect because basic rate interface (BRI) Integrated Services Digital Network (ISDN) establishes a relatively slow ISDN 128 Kbps connection that is made up of two 64 Kbps B channels and one 16 Kbps control D channel. **C** is incorrect because ADSL uses a DSL gateway device to establish digital data transmission over the wires of the local telephone network.

30. Which type of network interface device is typically used with T1 lines and provides features such as signal conversion, loopback, and diagnostics?
    A. Telephone network interface (TNI)
    B. Network interface unit (NIU)
    C. Smartjack
    D. Optical network terminal (ONT)

☑ **C.** A Smartjack is a type of network interface device (NID) that is typically used with T1 lines and provides features such as signal conversion, loopback, and diagnostics. Smartjacks can even include alarm functionality that can warn the communications provider when errors are occurring.

☒ **A, B,** and **D** are incorrect. **A** and **B** are incorrect because TNIs and NIUs are typically used with less complex telecom connections, such as telephone service. They do not provide advanced functionality such as diagnostics or loopback. **D** is incorrect because ONT interfaces are used with fiber-optic lines, not electrical T1 connections.

31. You are designing a server and desktop virtualization strategy for your organization and need to select a hypervisor for the deployment. A key decision in this process is determining the type of hardware virtualization you want to implement. You're concerned that some of the operating systems you need to install within virtual machines are not hypervisor-aware. Which type of hardware virtualization would be the best choice in this scenario?

A. Paravirtualization

B. Partial virtualization

C. Full virtualization

D. Hardware-assisted virtualization

☑ **C.** Full virtualization would be best in this scenario. With full virtualization, the hypervisor simulates a complete virtual computer system. This allows guest operating systems designed to run on physical hardware to run within a virtual machine using virtual hardware without modification.

☒ **A, B,** and **D** are incorrect. **A** and **B** are incorrect because paravirtualization and partial virtualization simulate little or no virtual hardware for the virtual machine. Guest operating systems and applications must be specially modified before they will run in these environments. **D** is incorrect because hardware-assisted virtualization specifies the use of virtualization technology (VT)–enabled processors to improve the overall performance of guests running in virtual machines.

32. Which of the following is an encryption device that functions at the data link layer of the OSI model?

A. EEG

B. Firewall

C. Proxy

D. Multilayer switch

☑ **A.** An Enterprise Encryption Gateway (EEG) is a network encryption device that functions at the data link layer of the OSI model. An EEG is used to authenticate wireless clients before they access the wireless media and to encrypt the data they transmit.

☒ **B, C,** and **D** are incorrect. **B** is incorrect because a firewall is used to prevent or allow network traffic based on the rules you define. **C** is incorrect because a proxy server mediates requests from clients seeking resources from a server (such as a web server on the Internet). **D** is incorrect because a multilayer switch provides switching functions at the data link layer and routing functions at the network layer.

33. Your organization currently employs several hundred salespeople who spend much of their time traveling. They frequently need to access information on Linux servers in your company's home office. To provide secure remote access for these users, you have decided to implement a virtual private network (VPN) with a VPN concentrator. Which encryption method is typically used in by the concentrator in this configuration?
    A. Internet Protocol Security (IPSec)
    B. Kerberos
    C. Remote Authentication Dial In User Service (RADIUS)
    D. Data Encryption Standard (DES)

☑ **A.** The Internet Protocol Security (IPSec) protocol is typically used to encrypt remote access sessions with a VPN concentrator. This configuration allows the remote salespersons to connect to your home office network securely over the Internet.

☒ **B, C,** and **D** are incorrect. **B** and **C** are incorrect because Kerberos and RADIUS can be used to authenticate remote users through the VPN concentrator, but they can't encrypt data. **D** is incorrect because DES is an older (and weaker) encryption standard that is unlikely to be used in a modern VPN solution.

34. You are designing a network and telecom implementation for a new small business on a tight budget. The organization has 15 employees in a small rented office suite. The employees will need phone services such as call routing, voicemail, automated greetings, conference calling, and automatic routing of incoming calls to the first available employee. What should you do to accomplish this?
    A. Implement a virtual switch.
    B. Implement virtual desktops.
    C. Implement a hardware PBX.
    D. Implement a virtual PBX.

☑ **D.** A virtual (sometimes called "hosted") PBX allows you to provide full PBX functionality for an organization at a much lower cost. Most virtual PBX providers offer phone services associated with hardware PBX systems, such as call routing, voicemail, automated greetings, conference calling, and automatic routing of incoming calls.

☒ **A, B**, and **C** are incorrect. **A** is incorrect because virtual switches are usually implemented within a hypervisor (such as VMWare ESX) to provide virtual networking for virtual machines. Port groups within the virtual switch can be mapped to specific physical network interfaces in the hypervisor hardware. **B** is incorrect because virtual desktops provide users with a desktop environment on low-end hardware from a central terminal server or hypervisor. **C** is incorrect because a hardware PBX would be much more expensive than a hosted PBX solution.

4

TCP/IP
Fundamentals

QUESTIONS

To manage an IP network effectively, you need to be familiar with how the TCP/IP protocol suite works. In Chapters 2 and 3, you were tested on how network protocols and hardware relate to the various layers in the OSI model. In this chapter, you'll learn how network protocols relate to an alternative networking model called the TCP/IP model. Instead of the seven layers of the OSI model, the TCP/IP model is composed of only four layers: application, transport, Internet, and network interface (also called the link layer). Unlike the OSI model, which includes specification for network hardware, the TCP/IP model is focused on protocols and is designed to be independent of the network hardware in use.

This chapter will introduce you to the various network protocols implemented at each layer of the TCP/IP model. It will also introduce you to the concept of IP ports, which are implemented at the transport layer of the TCP/IP model by the User Datagram Protocol (UDP) and Transmission Control Protocol (TCP) protocols. Ports allow a host with only one IP address to run multiple services, each assigned a different port on the same address.

1. Which transport protocols are used at the transport layer of the TCP/IP model? (Choose two.)
   A. User Datagram Protocol
   B. Routing Information Protocol
   C. Address Resolution Protocol
   D. Transmission Control Protocol
   E. Internet Control Message Protocol

2. What functionality does the IP protocol provide at the Internet layer of the TCP/IP model? (Choose two.)
   A. Ensuring that data reaches its destination by retransmitting any packets that are lost or corrupted
   B. Resolving logical addresses into physical addresses
   C. Sharing network status and error information
   D. Decrementing the TTL of network packets as they cross routers
   E. Providing logical addressing

3. You need to use a network troubleshooting utility to test communications between Windows 7 and Windows Server 2008 network hosts. Which tools use the ICMP protocol to do this? (Choose two.)
   A. arp
   B. dig
   C. tracert
   D. ipconfig
   E. ping

4. You are developing an application that will deliver streaming video from surveillance cameras to mobile data terminals in fire engines. Which protocol in the TCP/IP model would be the best choice to transport the data?
   A. UDP
   B. TCP
   C. ICMP
   D. IPsec

5. Which layer of the TCP/IP model receives packets from upper layers and encapsulates them in a frame prior to transmitting them on the network medium? (Choose two.)
   A. Application
   B. Network interface
   C. Transport
   D. Internet
   E. Link

6. Which protocols function at the application layer of the TCP/IP model? (Choose two.)
   A. ARP
   B. NTP
   C. ICMP
   D. SNMP
   E. IGMP

7. You need to determine the binary equivalent of the IPv4 address 192.168.1.1. Which of the following is the correct binary version of this IP address?
   A. 11000000. 10101000.00000001.00000001
   B. 00001010.00000000.00000000.00000001
   C. 10101100. 00010001. 00010001.00000011
   D. 11000000. 00001010.00000001.00000001

8. Your desktop PC running Windows 7 has an IP address of 172.17.8.3 assigned to it with a subnet mask of 255.255.0.0. What is the IP address of your network segment?
   A. 172.17.8.0
   B. 172.17.0.0
   C. 172.17.8.3
   D. 172.0.0.0

9. Your Linux workstation has an IP address of 192.168.1.25 assigned with a subnet mask of 255.255.255.0. It also has a DNS server address of 137.65.1.10 and a default gateway router address of 192.168.1.254 assigned. Your workstation needs to send a file to a server that has an IP address of 192.168.2.1 and a subnet mask of 255.255.255.0 assigned. Where will the packets be sent next?
   A. Directly to the server
   B. To the DNS server
   C. To the default gateway router
   D. Because of the difference in network addresses, the workstation can't connect to the server

10. Your Windows 7 workstation has an IP address of 192.168.1.35 assigned with a subnet mask of 255.255.255.0. It also has a DNS server address of 192.168.1.1 and a default gateway router address of 192.168.1.254 assigned. Your workstation is a member of the mycorp.com domain. The domain controller's address is 192.168.1.3. Your workstation needs to connect to a web server using the HTTP protocol. The web server has an IP address of 192.168.1.2 and a subnet mask of 255.255.255.0 assigned. Where will the packets be sent next?
   A. Directly to the web server
   B. To the domain controller
   C. To the default gateway router
   D. Because of the difference in network addresses, the workstation can't connect directly to the server.

11. What is the default subnet mask for an IP address of 172.17.8.2?
   A. 255.0.0.0
   B. 255.255.0.0
   C. 255.255.255.0
   D. 255.255.255.255

12. Your Linux workstation has an IP address of 00001010.00000000.00000000.01000001 (binary) assigned to it. Which class of IP addresses does this address fall within?
   A. Class A
   B. Class B
   C. Class C
   D. Class D

13. Your Windows 7 workstation has an IP address of 11001101.00000000.00000000.00000001 (binary) assigned to it. Which class of IP addresses does this address fall within?
   A. Class A
   B. Class B
   C. Class C
   D. Class D

14. Your Class C network currently has IP addresses 192.168.1.1 through 192.168.1.254 assigned to various workstations and servers using the default Class C subnet mask (255.255.255.0). A new employee has been hired and you need to provision her with a Windows 7 desktop workstation. Which IP address could you assign to this system?

   A. 192.168.1.0

   B. 192.168.1.255

   C. 192.168.2.1

   D. No addresses are available for this system on this network.

15. Your Linux workstation is configured to use DHCP for IP addressing. When the network interface is initialized during the boot process, it requests IP address configuration information from your DHCP server. Which message is sent first by your workstation as it requests an IP address?

   A. DHCPDISCOVER

   B. DHCPOFFER

   C. DHCPREQUEST

   D. DHCPACK

16. You are configuring an IP-based network service that will be distributed among multiple servers in your network. To keep the service running correctly, the servers must be able to locate each other and then share status, error, and synchronization information. Which type of network communications provides the most efficient way to do this?

   A. Unicasts

   B. Broadcasts

   C. Multicasts

   D. This type of communication isn't possible on an IP network.

17. You are implementing a Network Address Translation router on your network to translate private IP addresses into a single registered IP address to enable Internet access. Which private IP address ranges could you choose to implement on your network with this router? (Choose two.)

   A. 137.65.1.1–137.65.2.254

   B. 207.0.0.1–207.0.0.254

   C. 10.0.0.1–10.0.100.254

   D. 172.17.8.1–172.17.9.254

   E. 127.0.0.1–127.0.0.254

18. Consider the following IP address that uses CIDR notation: 17.17.8.5/22. Which of the following subnet masks corresponds to the CIDR prefix used in this address?

   A. 255.0.0.0

   B. 255.255.0.0

   C. 255.255.252.0

   D. 255.255.255.0

19. Which of the following are valid IPv6 addresses? (Choose two.)
    A. bab3:b834:45a3:0000:0000:762e:0270:5554
    B. fe80:207:e9ff:feaf:8c5e
    C. 35HC:FA77:4898:DAFC:200C:FBBC:A007:8973
    D. fe80:207:e9ff:feaf:8c5e:0bad
    E. 35BC:FA77:4898:DAFC:200C:FBBC:A007:8973

20. The network interface board in your server has the following MAC address: 00:07:E9:AF:8C:5E. Which part of this address identifies the manufacturer that made the network board?
    A. 00
    B. AF:8C:5E
    C. E9:AF:8C
    D. 00:07:E9

21. Which block of addresses is defined for use with Automatic Private IP Addressing (APIPA)?
    A. 10.0.0.0/8
    B. 169.254.0.0/16
    C. 192.168.1.0/24
    D. 172.16.0.0/16

22. Which application layer protocol is used to copy files between network hosts using the UDP protocol?
    A. FTP
    B. TFTP
    C. NTP
    D. SCP

23. You are using a web browser on your laptop to access the http://www.mycorp.com web page. The TCP/IP suite on your laptop has been configured to use a DNS server with an IP address of 137.65.1.254 for name resolution. Your laptop sends a name resolution request for www.mycorp .com to this DNS server; however, this server isn't authoritative for this domain and doesn't have a record that can be used to resolve this domain name into an IP address. What happens next?
    A. The DNS server sends a request to a DNS root server for the IP address of a DNS server that is authoritative for the mydom.com domain.
    B. The DNS server contacts the DNS server that is authoritative for the mydom.com domain.
    C. Your laptop sends a request to a root-level DNS server for the IP address of a DNS server that is authoritative for the mydom.com domain.
    D. An error message is displayed in the web browser indicating it can't connect to the web server.

24. Which protocols are used by web browsers and web servers to transfer HTML documents? (Choose two.)
   A. IGMP
   B. SSH
   C. HTTP
   D. HTTPS
   E. RTP

25. You need to access the console of a Linux server in the data center remotely from your laptop at home to fix an issue that is preventing a database service from functioning properly. Which protocol would be the best choice for accomplishing this?
   A. SSH
   B. Telnet
   C. FTP
   D. SNMP

26. You want to configure your e-mail client software such that it downloads only message headers instead of the entire message. You also want to leave all messages on the mail server after they are downloaded to the client, and you want to be able to create folders on the mail server so you can organize your messages by the project to which they relate. Which mail protocol should you use to accomplish this?
   A. POP3
   B. SMTP
   C. SSH
   D. IMAP4

27. Which network protocols are commonly used to implement Voice over IP (VoIP) communications? (Choose two.)
   A. HTTP
   B. RTP
   C. SNMP
   D. TLS
   E. SIP

28. You have just implemented the PureFTPd service on your Linux server to enable users to use FTP to upload and download files. Which ports do you need to open in the server's firewall to allow this traffic? (Choose two.)

    A. 20

    B. 53

    C. 22

    D. 21

    E. 23

29. You have just implemented the Apache Web Server on a Linux server to provide an intranet site for your organization. Which ports should you open in the server's firewall to allow web traffic through? (Choose two.)

    A. 3389

    B. 67

    C. 68

    D. 80

    E. 443

30. You have just enabled the imap and pop3 daemons on a Linux server running the postfix MTA daemon to provide e-mail services for your organization. Which ports should you open in the server's firewall to allow e-mail traffic through? (Choose three.)

    A. 25

    B. 143

    C. 123

    D. 110

    E. 119

QUICK ANSWER KEY

1.	A, D	11.	B	21.	B
2.	D, E	12.	A	22.	B
3.	C, E	13.	C	23.	A
4.	A	14.	D	24.	C, D
5.	B, E	15.	A	25.	A
6.	B, D	16.	C	26.	D
7.	A	17.	C, D	27.	B, E
8.	B	18.	C	28.	A, D
9.	C	19.	A, E	29.	D, E
10.	A	20.	D	30.	A, B, D

IN-DEPTH ANSWERS

1. Which transport protocols are used at the transport layer of the TCP/IP model? (Choose two.)
   A. User Datagram Protocol
   B. Routing Information Protocol
   C. Address Resolution Protocol
   D. Transmission Control Protocol
   E. Internet Control Message Protocol

   ☑ **A** and **D**. The User Datagram Protocol and the Transmission Control Protocol are the two transport protocols used at the transport layer of the TCP/IP model. TCP is used for connection-oriented (acknowledged) delivery of data. UDP is used for connectionless (unacknowledged) delivery of data.

   ☒ **B, C,** and **E** are incorrect. **B** is incorrect because RIP is not a transport protocol. **C** is incorrect because ARP is also not a transport protocol. It is instead used to resolve IP addresses into MAC addresses and functions at the link layer of the TCP/IP model. **E** is incorrect because ICMP is used to transmit status or error messages, not network data. It functions at the Internet layer of the TCP/IP model.

2. What functionality does the IP protocol provide at the Internet layer of the TCP/IP model? (Choose two.)
   A. Ensuring that data reaches its destination by retransmitting any packets that are lost or corrupted
   B. Resolving logical addresses into physical addresses
   C. Sharing network status and error information
   D. Decrementing the TTL of network packets as they cross routers
   E. Providing logical addressing

   ☑ **D** and **E**. The IP protocol at the Internet layer of the TCP/IP model is responsible for logical addressing of network hosts. It's also responsible for decrementing the TTL (time to live) field of network packets as they cross routers to prevent packets from endlessly looping through the network.

⊠ **A, B,** and **C** are incorrect. **A** is incorrect because ensuring data delivery is a function of the TCP protocol at the transport layer of the TCP/IP model. **B** is incorrect because resolving logical IP addresses into physical hardware addresses is the function of the ARP protocol at the Internet layer of the TCP/IP model. **C** is incorrect because transmitting status and error messages is the responsibility of the ICMP protocol also at the Internet layer of the TCP/IP model.

3. You need to use a network troubleshooting utility to test communications between Windows 7 and Windows Server 2008 network hosts. Which tools use the ICMP protocol to do this? (Choose two.)

    A. arp
    B. dig
    C. tracert
    D. ipconfig
    E. ping

    ☑ **C** and **E.** The **tracert** and **ping** commands use the ICMP protocol to test network communications between hosts. The **ping** command is provided on most operating systems and functions by sending ICMP echo request packets to the target host, which responds with an ICMP echo response packet. The **tracert** command (**traceroute** on Linux) sends ICMP echo request packets to each router a packet crosses as it is transmitted to the target host. Each router responds with an ICMP echo response, allowing you to see the path a packet takes through the network.

    ⊠ **A, B,** and **D** are incorrect. **A** is incorrect because the **arp** command uses the ARP protocol and is used to resolve IP addresses into hardware addresses. **B** is incorrect because the **dig** command is used on Linux systems to view DNS record information from a DNS server. **D** is incorrect because ipconfig is a Windows system utility used to manage IP addresses.

4. You are developing an application that will deliver streaming video from surveillance cameras to mobile data terminals in fire engines. Which protocol in the TCP/IP model would be the best choice to transport the data?

    A. UDP
    B. TCP
    C. ICMP
    D. IPsec

☑ **A.** The UDP protocol would be the best transport protocol for transmitting streaming video. UDP doesn't require acknowledgment of the data sent and thus works best in situations where latency must be low, but a certain amount of lost data can be tolerated. In this situation, losing a frame or two of streamed video would be worth the decreased latency provided by UDP.

☒ **B, C,** and **D** are incorrect. **B** is incorrect because TCP requires acknowledgment of each packet sent, which increases network overhead significantly. **C** is incorrect because ICMP is not really a transport protocol that can carry data. It's designed to work only with error and status messages. **D** is incorrect because IPsec is a security protocol that can be used to secure a connection. It doesn't provide a means of streaming data.

5. Which layer of the TCP/IP model receives packets from upper layers and encapsulates them in a frame prior to transmitting them on the network medium? (Choose two.)
   A. Application
   B. Network interface
   C. Transport
   D. Internet
   E. Link

☑ **B and E.** The lowest layer of the TCP/IP model has two names: The network interface layer or the link layer. Either usage is correct. The job of the network interface (or link) layer is to encapsulate packets received from the Internet layer of the model into network frames, which are then transmitted on the network medium.

☒ **A, C,** and **D** are incorrect. **A** is incorrect because the application layer of the TCP/IP model resides at the top layer. Its job is to interface with the applications running on the system (such as a web browser or web server) that need to send or receive data on the network. **C** and **D** are incorrect because the transport and Internet layers manage data in the form of packets. These two layers prepare the data to transmitted and send it to the network interface (or link) layer for actual transmission on the network.

6. Which protocols function at the application layer of the TCP/IP model? (Choose two.)
   A. ARP
   B. NTP
   C. ICMP
   D. SNMP
   E. IGMP

☑ **B** and **D.** The NTP and SNMP protocols function at the application layer of the TCP/IP model. The NTP protocol is used to synchronize time between network hosts. The SNMP protocol is used to monitor network hosts.

☒ **A, C,** and **E** are incorrect. **A** is incorrect because ARP functions at the link layer of the TCP/IP model. It resolves logical IP addresses into hardware MAC addresses. **C** is incorrect because ICMP is an Internet layer protocol and is used to transmit status along with error messages. **E** is incorrect because IGMP is also an Internet layer protocol used for multicast communications.

7. You need to determine the binary equivalent of the IPv4 address 192.168.1.1. Which of the following is the correct binary version of this IP address?
   A. 11000000. 10101000.00000001.00000001
   B. 00001010.00000000.00000000.00000001
   C. 10101100. 00010001. 00010001.00000011
   D. 11000000. 00001010.00000001.00000001

☑ **A.** 11000000. 10101000.00000001.00000001 is the binary equivalent of 192.168.1.1. Working right to left, the binary bits in each 8-bit octet have decimal equivalent values of 1, 2, 4, 8, 16, 32, 64, and 128. Therefore the binary number 11000000 has a decimal value of 128+64, which equals 192. The binary number 10101000 has a decimal value of 128+32+8, which equals 168.

☒ **B, C,** and **D** are incorrect. **B** is incorrect because its decimal equivalent would be 10.0.0.1. **C** is incorrect because its decimal equivalent would be 172.17.17.3. **D** is incorrect because its decimal equivalent would be 192.10.1.1.

8. Your desktop PC running Windows 7 has an IP address of 172.17.8.3 assigned to it with a subnet mask of 255.255.0.0. What is the IP address of your network segment?
   A. 172.17.8.0
   B. 172.17.0.0
   C. 172.17.8.3
   D. 172.0.0.0

☑ **B.** Assigning a subnet mask of 255.255.0.0 to a host with an IP address of 172.17.8.3 specifies a network address of 172.17.0.0. Each bit assigned a binary value of 1 in the subnet mask indicates the corresponding bit in the associated IP address is assigned to the network address. Each bit assigned a binary value of 0 in the subnet mask indicates the corresponding bit in the associated IP address is assigned to the host address. In this example, the subnet mask is 11111111.11111111.00000000.00000000, which means the first two octets in the IP address (172.17) are the network portion of the address while the last two octets (8.3) are the host portion.

☒ **A, C, and D** are incorrect. **A** is incorrect because the third octet of the IP address (8) should be part of the host address, not the network address. **C** is incorrect because it specifies all four octets are assigned to the network address. **D** is incorrect because the second octet of the IP address should be assigned to the network address, not the host portion of the address.

9. Your Linux workstation has an IP address of 192.168.1.25 assigned with a subnet mask of 255.255.255.0. It also has a DNS server address of 137.65.1.10 and a default gateway router address of 192.168.1.254 assigned. Your workstation needs to send a file to a server that has an IP address of 192.168.2.1 and a subnet mask of 255.255.255.0 assigned. Where will the packets be sent next?

A. Directly to the server
B. To the DNS server
C. To the default gateway router
D. Because of the difference in network addresses, the workstation can't connect to the server

☑ **C.** The server and the workstation reside on networks with different addresses assigned. The network address of the workstation is 192.168.1.0. The network address of the server is 192.168.2.0. Because the network address of the destination system is different from the network address of the source system, the packets for the file transfer will be sent to the default gateway router. This system will determine the best route to get the packets to the correct network segment and destination host.

☒ **A, B, and D** are incorrect. **A** is incorrect because the workstation and the server reside on different logical networks. Therefore, packets from the source system can't be sent directly to the target system. **B** is incorrect because the DNS server is used only if a hostname needs to be resolved to an IP address. It is not used to route packets. **D** is partially true. The workstation can't connect directly to the server because of the difference in network addresses. However, using a default gateway router can enable communications between the two systems.

10. Your Windows 7 workstation has an IP address of 192.168.1.35 assigned with a subnet mask of 255.255.255.0. It also has a DNS server address of 192.168.1.1 and a default gateway router address of 192.168.1.254 assigned. Your workstation is a member of the mycorp.com domain. The domain controller's address is 192.168.1.3. Your workstation needs to connect to a web server using the HTTP protocol. The web server has an IP address of 192.168.1.2 and a subnet mask of 255.255.255.0 assigned. Where will the packets be sent next?

- A. Directly to the web server
- B. To the domain controller
- C. To the default gateway router
- D. Because of the difference in network addresses, the workstation can't connect directly to the server.

☑ **A.** Because the workstation and the web server reside on the same logical network (192.168.1.0), packets are sent directly to the server and aren't redirected through a default gateway router.

☒ **B, C,** and **D** are incorrect. **B** is incorrect because domain controllers are used for authentication. They aren't used to route packets. **C** is incorrect because the two hosts reside on the same logical network. Packets can be sent directly to the server without being redirected through a default gateway. **D** is incorrect because there is no difference in the logical network addresses of the two hosts.

11. What is the default subnet mask for an IP address of 172.17.8.2?
- A. 255.0.0.0
- B. 255.255.0.0
- C. 255.255.255.0
- D. 255.255.255.255

☑ **B.** 172.17.8.2 is a Class B IP address. Therefore, the default subnet mask for this address is 255.255.0.0.

☒ **A, C,** and **D** are not correct. **A** is incorrect because 255.0.0.0 is the default subnet mask for a Class A IP address. **C** is incorrect because 255.255.255.0 is the default subnet mask for a Class C IP address. **D** is incorrect because a subnet mask of 255.255.255.255 would use all the bits of the IP address for the network address, leaving no bits available for the host portion of the address.

12. Your Linux workstation has an IP address of 00001010.00000000.00000000.01000001 (binary) assigned to it. Which class of IP addresses does this address fall within?
    A. Class A
    B. Class B
    C. Class C
    D. Class D

> ☑ **A.** The decimal equivalent of 00001010.00000000.00000000.01000001 is 10.0.0.65. Therefore, this IP address is a Class A address. The binary value of the first octet of a Class A address always begins with a 0.
>
> ☒ **B, C,** and **D** are incorrect. **B** is incorrect because the first octet of a Class B IP address must be within the range of 128 to 191. **C** is incorrect because the first octet of a Class C IP address must be within the range of 192 to 223. **D** is incorrect because Class D addresses are reserved for multicasts and are in the range of 224.0.0.0 to 239.255.255.255.

13. Your Windows 7 workstation has an IP address of 11001101.00000000.00000000.00000001 (binary) assigned to it. Which class of IP addresses does this address fall within?
    A. Class A
    B. Class B
    C. Class C
    D. Class D

> ☑ **C.** The decimal equivalent of 11001101.00000000.00000000.00000001 is 205.0.0.1. Therefore, this IP address is a Class C address. The binary value of the first octet of a Class C address always begins with a 110.
>
> ☒ **A, B,** and **D** are incorrect. **A** is incorrect because the first octet of a Class A IP address must be within the range of 1 to 126. **B** is incorrect because the first octet of a Class B IP address must be within the range of 128 to 191. **D** is incorrect because Class D addresses are reserved for multicasts and are in the range of 224.0.0.0 to 239.255.255.255.

14. Your Class C network currently has IP addresses 192.168.1.1 through 192.168.1.254 assigned to various workstations and servers using the default Class C subnet mask (255.255.255.0). A new employee has been hired and you need to provision her with a Windows 7 desktop workstation. Which IP address could you assign to this system?
    A. 192.168.1.0
    B. 192.168.1.255

C. 192.168.2.1

D. No addresses are available for this system on this network.

☑ **D.** Using the default Class C subnet mask of 255.255.255.0, all available host addresses (192.168.1.1 through 192.168.1.254) have already been assigned. To add another workstation, you could either migrate to a Class B IP address range or implement a DHCP server that dynamically assigns and releases addresses as needed.

☒ **A, B**, and **C** are incorrect. **A** is incorrect because 192.168.1.0 is a reserved address assigned to the network segment in this scenario. **B** is incorrect because 192.168.1.255 is also a reserved address used for broadcast messages on this network. **C** is incorrect because 192.168.2.1 is on a different logical network (192.168.2.0) when using a subnet mask of 255.255.255.0 and won't be able to communicate with hosts on the 192.168.1.0 network without a router.

15. Your Linux workstation is configured to use DHCP for IP addressing. When the network interface is initialized during the boot process, it requests IP address configuration information from your DHCP server. Which message is sent first by your workstation as it requests an IP address?

A. DHCPDISCOVER

B. DHCPOFFER

C. DHCPREQUEST

D. DHCPACK

☑ **A.** A system that needs to request IP address configuration information from a DHCP server begins the process by broadcasting a DHCPDISCOVER message on the network to locate all available DHCP servers. It's important to remember that these messages are broadcasts and won't be forwarded by default by most routers. Hence, you will need a DHCP server or a system running a DHCP forwarding agent on each network segment where hosts are configured to use DHCP addressing.

☒ **B, C**, and **D** are incorrect. **B** is incorrect because the DHCPOFFER message is sent from a DHCP server to the requesting host containing proposed IP address configuration information. **C** is incorrect because a DHCPREQUEST message is sent from the host back to the DHCP server that it has accepted the DHCPOFFER. It also informs any other DHCP servers that they can retract their offers. **D** is incorrect because a DHCPACK message is sent from the DHCP server to the requesting host to confirm the acceptance of the IP address offer and to initiate the DHCP lease.

16. You are configuring an IP-based network service that will be distributed among multiple servers in your network. To keep the service running correctly, the servers must be able to locate each other and then share status, error, and synchronization information. Which type of network communications provides the most efficient way to do this?

    A. Unicasts

    B. Broadcasts

    C. Multicasts

    D. This type of communication isn't possible on an IP network.

    ☑ **C.** Multicasting would provide a very efficient way for the servers to locate each other and to share information. Each server subscribed to the multicast address would receive a copy of the information being shared. This would allow a server to send a message to all other servers in the multicast group with just one network transmission.

    ☒ **A, B,** and **D** are incorrect. **A** is incorrect because using unicasts would require a separate copy of each message be sent to each server, which would be slower and use more network bandwidth than multicasting. **B** is incorrect because broadcasting would send a copy of a message to all network hosts, not just the servers that need it. Again, this would increase network traffic. **D** is incorrect because multicasting provides a very efficient way to share information with a specific group of network hosts.

17. You are implementing a Network Address Translation router on your network to translate private IP addresses into a single registered IP address to enable Internet access. Which private IP address ranges could you choose to implement on your network with this router? (Choose two.)

    A. 137.65.1.1–137.65.2.254

    B. 207.0.0.1–207.0.0.254

    C. 10.0.0.1–10.0.100.254

    D. 172.17.8.1–172.17.9.254

    E. 127.0.0.1–127.0.0.254

    ☑ **C and D.** The 10.0.0.1–10.0.100.254 and 172.17.8.1–172.17.9.254 IP address ranges fall within the defined private IP addresses (10.0.0.0–10.255.255.255, 172.16.0.0–172.31.255.255, and 192.168.0.0–192.168.255.255). Because these private IP addresses are nonroutable, they must first be converted into registered IP addresses using a NAT router before they can be used on a public network such as the Internet.

☒ **A, B,** and **E** are incorrect. **A** and **B** are incorrect because the 137.65.1.1–137.65.2.254 and 207.0.0.1–207.0.0.254 address ranges contain public (nonprivate) IP addresses that have probably been registered with another organization. Although you could technically use them behind a NAT router, it's not a best practice. **E** is incorrect because the 127.0.0.1 address is reserved for the localhost loopback address.

18. Consider the following IP address that uses CIDR notation: 17.17.8.5/22. Which of the following subnet masks corresponds to the CIDR prefix used in this address?
    A. 255.0.0.0
    B. 255.255.0.0
    C. 255.255.252.0
    D. 255.255.255.0

☑ **C.** A CIDR IP address of 172.17.8.5/22 specifies a 22-bit prefix length. The subnet mask for this address is therefore 22-bits long (11111111.11111111.11111100.00000000). In decimal notation, this would be a subnet mask of 255.255.252.0.

☒ **A, B,** and **D** are incorrect. **A** is incorrect because it specifies an 8-bit subnet mask. **B** is incorrect because it specifies a 16-bit subnet mask. **C** is incorrect because it specifies a 24-bit subnet mask.

19. Which of the following are valid IPv6 addresses? (Choose two.)
    A. bab3:b834:45a3:0000:0000:762e:0270:5554
    B. fe80:207:e9ff:feaf:8c5e
    C. 35HC:FA77:4898:DAFC:200C:FBBC:A007:8973
    D. fe80:207:e9ff:feaf:8c5e:0bad
    E. 35BC:FA77:4898:DAFC:200C:FBBC:A007:8973

☑ **A** and **E.** IPv6 addresses are composed of eight, 4-character hexadecimal numbers, separated by colons instead of periods. Therefore, bab3:b834:45a3:0000:0000:762e:0270:5554 and 35BC:FA77:4898:DAFC:200C:FBBC:A007:8973 are valid IPv6 addresses.

☒ **B, C,** and **D** are incorrect. **B** and **D** are incorrect because they are too short. **C** is incorrect because it uses an invalid hexadecimal number (35HC). Remember that a hexadecimal number uses the numbers 0–9 and the letters A–F.

20. The network interface board in your server has the following MAC address: 00:07:E9:AF:8C:5E. Which part of this address identifies the manufacturer that made the network board?

    A. 00

    B. AF:8C:5E

    C. E9:AF:8C

    D. 00:07:E9

☑ **D.** The first three octets of a MAC address uniquely identify the organization that manufactured the device to which the address has been assigned. These three octets are referred to as the Organizationally Unique Identifier (OUI). In this example, 00:07:E9 identifies Intel as the manufacturer of the network board.

☒ **A, B,** and **C** are incorrect. **A** is incorrect because it references only the first octet of the OUI. **B** is incorrect because it references the octets that are unique to the specific network board. **C** is incorrect because it references part of the OUI and part of the host address.

---

21. Which block of addresses is defined for use with Automatic Private IP Addressing (APIPA)?

    A. 10.0.0.0/8

    B. 169.254.0.0/16

    C. 192.168.1.0/24

    D. 172.16.0.0/16

☑ **B.** APIPA is a feature built into many operating systems, such as Microsoft Windows, that enables a host to assign itself an IP address automatically if the DHCP server is unreachable. The host automatically assigns itself an IP address from the range of 169.254.0.0 to 169.254.255.255. This range has been reserved for APIPA. The host will send an ARP on the local network segment to verify that the APIPA address it wants to assign itself isn't already in use.

☒ **A, C,** and **D** are incorrect. **A** is incorrect because 10.0.0.0/8 is defined as a Class A private IP address and is not used for APIPA. **C** is incorrect because 192.168.1.0/24 is defined as a Class C private IP address and is not used for APIPA. **D** is incorrect because 172.16.0.0./16 is defined as a Class B private IP address and is not used for APIPA.

22. Which application layer protocol is used to copy files between network hosts using the UDP protocol?

A. FTP

B. TFTP

C. NTP

D. SCP

☑ **B.** Trivial File Transfer Protocol (TFTP) is a simple file transfer protocol used to copy files between network hosts. It does not support listing directory contents, nor does it use authentication. TFTP uses UDP as the transport protocol instead of TCP, which is used by the FTP protocol.

☒ **A, C, and D** are incorrect. **A** is incorrect because the FTP protocol uses the TCP protocol instead of UDP to copy files between network hosts. **C** is incorrect because the NTP protocol is used to synchronize time among network hosts. **D** is incorrect because SCP also uses TCP to copy files between hosts instead of UDP.

23. You are using a web browser on your laptop to access the http://www.mycorp.com web page. The TCP/IP suite on your laptop has been configured to use a DNS server with an IP address of 137.65.1.254 for name resolution. Your laptop sends a name resolution request for www.mycorp .com to this DNS server; however, this server isn't authoritative for this domain and doesn't have a record that can be used to resolve this domain name into an IP address. What happens next?

A. The DNS server sends a request to a DNS root server for the IP address of a DNS server that is authoritative for the mydom.com domain.

B. The DNS server contacts the DNS server that is authoritative for the mydom.com domain.

C. Your laptop sends a request to a root-level DNS server for the IP address of a DNS server that is authoritative for the mydom.com domain.

D. An error message is displayed in the web browser indicating it can't connect to the web server.

☑ **A.** If the DNS server doesn't have a record for the domain name requested, it sends a request to a DNS root server for the IP address of a DNS server that is authoritative for the domain where the record resides. After going through this process, most DNS servers will cache the record for the domain name such that the next time it's requested by a client, it can respond directly without having to contact a root-level DNS server and the authoritative DNS server for the domain.

☒ **B, C,** and **D** are incorrect. **B** is incorrect because the DNS server must first identify the IP address of the DNS server that is authoritative for the requested domain name. **C** is incorrect because the DNS server, not the client system, is responsible for contacting a root-level DNS server. **D** is incorrect because an error message will be displayed in the browser only if the DNS server that is authoritative for the domain requested doesn't have a record for the specified domain name.

24. Which protocols are used by web browsers and web servers to transfer HTML documents? (Choose two.)

A. IGMP
B. SSH
C. HTTP
D. HTTPS
E. RTP

☑ **C** and **D.** The HTTP protocol is used to transfer HTML documents from the web server to the web browser using an unsecure communication channel. The HTTPS protocol accomplishes the same task, but uses encryption to scramble the contents of the transmission to prevent eavesdropping.

☒ **A, B,** and **E** are incorrect. **A** is incorrect because the IGMP protocol is used by network hosts and routers to define multicast group membership. **B** is incorrect because the SSH protocol is used to establish remote access sessions with network hosts. **E** is incorrect because the RTP protocol is used to transfer streaming media over IP networks.

25. You need to access the console of a Linux server in the data center remotely from your laptop at home to fix an issue that is preventing a database service from functioning properly. Which protocol would be the best choice for accomplishing this?

A. SSH
B. Telnet
C. FTP
D. SNMP

☑ **A.** Because the connection will be established over an untrusted network (the Internet) in this scenario, you should use a remote access protocol that encrypts data as it is being transferred over the network medium. In this case, the Secure Shell protocol (SSH) would be the best choice.

☒ **B, C,** and **D** are incorrect. **B** is incorrect because the Telnet protocol, while it does provide remote access to Linux systems, does not encrypt data. Using Telnet in this scenario would expose usernames, passwords, and all data being transferred between the server and the laptop to network packet sniffers. **C** is incorrect because the FTP protocol would only provide access to the file system of the server, and it also fails to encrypt data being transferred between the client and the server. **D** is incorrect because SNMP is used to gather status information from network hosts. It can't be used to access them remotely.

26. You want to configure your e-mail client software such that it downloads only message headers instead of the entire message. You also want to leave all messages on the mail server after they are downloaded to the client, and you want to be able to create folders on the mail server so you can organize your messages by the project to which they relate. Which mail protocol should you use to accomplish this?

A. POP3

B. SMTP

C. SSH

D. IMAP4

☑ **D.** The IMAP4 mail protocol can download message headers instead of the entire message. It can also be configured to leave all messages on the mail server after they are downloaded to the client. This would allow you to access your messages using e-mail clients on different workstations. IMAP4 also allows you to create folders on the mail server so you can organize your messages.

☒ **A, B,** and **C** are incorrect. **A** is incorrect because the POP3 protocol will download only entire messages from the mail server. It also doesn't support the creation of folders on the mail server. **B** is incorrect because the SMTP protocol supports only the sending of messages from the client to the mail server. It can't be used to download messages. **C** is incorrect because the SSH protocol can't be used to download messages directly from a mail server. However, it can be used to establish an encrypted tunnel between the client and the mail server to prevent messages from being sniffed as they are downloaded using POP3 or IMAP4.

27. Which network protocols are commonly used to implement Voice over IP (VoIP) communications? (Choose two.)

A. HTTP

B. RTP

C. SNMP

D. TLS

E. SIP

☑ **B** and **E.** The Real-time Transport Protocol (RTP) and the Session Initiation Protocol (SIP) are commonly used to implement VoIP communications over IP networks. Other protocols are also used for some VoIP implementations such as the Session Description Protocol (SDP) and the IP Multimedia Subsystem (IMS) protocol.

☒ **A, C,** and **D** are incorrect. **A** is incorrect because HTTP is used to transfer files from a web server to a client web browser. **C** is incorrect because the SNMP protocol is used to monitor network hosts and send alerts when something goes wrong. **D** is incorrect because TLS is a security protocol that uses asymmetric encryption to scramble the contents of network transmission to prevent sniffing. It should be noted, however, that TLS is frequently used with VoIP such as SIP to encrypt the data being transmitted during a VoIP session.

28. You have just implemented the PureFTPd service on your Linux server to enable users to use FTP to upload and download files. Which ports do you need to open in the server's firewall to allow this traffic? (Choose two.)

A. 20

B. 53

C. 22

D. 21

E. 23

☑ **A** and **D.** The FTP protocol uses port 20 to transfer data between the client and the server. It also uses port 21 for a control connection that is used to manage the FTP session. In this scenario, both ports must be opened in the server's firewall for the FTP service to work.

☒ **B, C,** and **E** are incorrect. **B** is incorrect because port 53 is used by DNS servers to handle name resolution requests. **C** is incorrect because port 22 is used by the SSH protocol to establish secure remote access sessions. **E** is incorrect because port 23 is used by the Telnet protocol to establish unencrypted remote access sessions.

29. You have just implemented the Apache Web Server on a Linux server to provide an intranet site for your organization. Which ports should you open in the server's firewall to allow web traffic through? (Choose two.)
 A. 3389
 B. 67
 C. 68
 D. 80
 E. 443

☑ **D** and **E.** The HTTP protocol is used by web servers and web browsers to transfer clear-text (unencrypted) data on port 80. It also uses port 443 for secure data that has been encrypted using the TLS/SSL protocols.

☒ **A, B,** and **C** are incorrect. **A** is incorrect because port 3389 is used by the Remote Desktop Protocol (RDP). RDP is used by Windows server operating systems to provide remote desktop access to client systems over an IP network. **B** and **C** are incorrect because ports 67 and 68 are used by the DHCP protocol. Port 67 is used to send data from the DHCP client to the server, and port 68 is used by the server to send data to the client.

30. You have just enabled the imap and pop3 daemons on a Linux server running the postfix MTA daemon to provide e-mail services for your organization. Which ports should you open in the server's firewall to allow e-mail traffic through? (Choose three.)
 A. 25
 B. 143
 C. 123
 D. 110
 E. 119

☑ **A, B,** and **D.** The postfix MTA is an SMTP daemon that requires port 25 to be open in the firewall to allow users to send messages using this protocol. The imap daemon uses the IMAP4 protocol and needs port 143 open in the firewall to allow users to download messages to their e-mail client using this protocol. The pop3 daemon uses the POP3 protocol and needs port 110 open to allow users to download messages to their e-mail client using this protocol.

☒ **C** and **E** are incorrect. **C** is incorrect because port 123 is used by the NTP protocol to synchronize time among hosts on the network. **E** is incorrect because port 119 is used by the NNTP protocol to download messages from a newsgroup server.

5

TCP/IP Utilities

QUESTIONS

In the previous chapters, you were tested on how IP networks function from a conceptual point of view. In this chapter, you'll implement what you've learned to troubleshoot basic network issues using IP-based utilities. Most server and workstation operating systems provide a suite of IP-based configuration and troubleshooting utilities that you can use, including the following:

- ping
- tracert
- traceroute
- dig
- ipconfig
- ifconfig
- nslookup
- arp
- nbtstat
- netstat
- route
- ftp

Many of these commands are common to most operating systems, including Windows and Linux. However, the syntax used by these commands can vary between operating systems. Make sure you are familiar with the differences. You should also be familiar with commands that are unique to a particular operating system. For example, the **ifconfig** command is used only on Linux/UNIX/Mac operating systems, while the **ipconfig** command is used only on Windows operating systems (Windows 2000 and later).

For the Network+ exam, you'll need to be familiar with the various options that can be used with each of these commands. You'll also need to be familiar with the output generated by these commands. On your exam, you will likely be presented with output from one or more of these commands and be asked to identify the command that was used to generate it.

1. Your workstation needs to copy a file to a server on the same network segment with an IP address of 10.0.01. Part of this process involves resolving the server's IP address into its MAC address using the ARP protocol. ARP has already looked in the ARP cache on your workstation, but it couldn't find an entry for the server's IP address. What happens next?

   A. An ARP request packet is broadcast to all the machines on the network segment to determine the MAC address of the host with an IP address of 10.0.0.1.

   B. ARP sends a unicast ARP request packet to the host with an IP address of 10.0.0.1 requesting its MAC address.

C. An ARP request packet is broadcast to all the machines on the network segment to determine the MAC address of the default gateway router.

D. The file transfer fails and an error message is displayed to the end user.

2. You need to view the entries of the ARP cache on your Windows 7 workstation. Which options can you use with the **arp** command to do this? (Choose two.)

A. -n

B. -a

C. -s

D. -g

E. -d

3. You need to add an entry manually to your Windows workstation's ARP cache that maps the 192.168.1.1 IP address to the 00-17-08-3B-06-3B MAC address. Which command can you use at the command prompt to do this?

A. `arp -g 192.168.1.1 00-17-08-3B-06-3B`

B. `arp -a 192.168.1.1 00-17-08-3B-06-3B`

C. `arp -s 192.168.1.1 00-17-08-3B-06-3B`

D. `arp -a 192.168.1.1`

4. You need to connect to the Telnet service on a Linux server from your Windows 7 workstation to manage the system remotely. Assuming the Telnet daemon has been enabled, which port in the server's host firewall must be opened to allow Telnet access?

A. 20

B. 21

C. 22

D. 23

5. A night-shift employee has paged you at home indicating he forgot his password and can't log into your organization's Linux server. You need to access the server remotely from home over the Internet and reset the user's password. Which protocol would be the best choice in this scenario?

A. Telnet

B. SSH

C. FTP

D. VNC

6. You are having problems sending e-mail messages using the SMTP protocol between two Microsoft Exchange servers. The first server's hostname is mail1.mycorp.com, and the second server's hostname is mail2.mycorp.com. You want to test SMTP connectivity from the mail1

server to the mail2 server using the Telnet protocol. Which command can you use on the mail1 server to do this?

- **A.** `telnet mail2.mycorp.com`
- **B.** `telnet mail1.mycorp.com 25`
- **C.** `telnet mail2.mycorp.com 25`
- **D.** `telnet mail2.mycorp.com 22`

7. Consider the following output from a command entered at the command prompt of a Windows 7 workstation:

```
Interface: 192.168.1.105 --- 0x5
Internet Address       Physical Address      Type
192.168.1.1            00-19-5b-06-de-a4     dynamic
192.168.1.240          44-87-fc-e2-e5-d3     dynamic
```

Which command was used to generate this output?

- **A.** `arp -a`
- **B.** `nbtstat -c`
- **C.** `telnet localhost 20`
- **D.** `netstat -e`

8. The **nbtstat** command has returned the following output: `NTI-LINUX-W     <20> UNIQUE`. What type of system is NTI-LINUX-W?

- **A.** Workstation
- **B.** File server
- **C.** Mail server
- **D.** Domain controller

9. Which command was used at the command prompt of a Windows system to generate the following output?

```
Wireless Network Connection:
Node IpAddress: [192.168.1.105] Scope Id: []
                NetBIOS Local Name Table
       Name            Type          Status
    ---------------------------------------------
    WS1LAPTOP      <00>  UNIQUE      Registered
    MYWORKGROUP    <00>  GROUP       Registered
    WS1LAPTOP      <20>  UNIQUE      Registered
```

- **A.** `netstat -s`
- **B.** `nbtstat -c`
- **C.** `netstat -r`
- **D.** `nbtstat -n`

10. Which command was used to generate the following output from the shell prompt on a Linux server system?

```
Kernel IP routing table
Destination     Gateway         Genmask         Flags   MSS Window  irtt
Iface
192.168.1.0     *               255.255.255.0   U       0 0         0 eth0
link-local      *               255.255.0.0     U       0 0         0 eth0
loopback        *               255.0.0.0       U       0 0         0 lo
default         192.168.1.1     0.0.0.0         UG      0 0         0 eth0
```

A. netstat -r

B. netstat -s

C. arp -g

D. netstat -p TCP

11. While troubleshooting NetBIOS issues with Windows hosts on your network, you need to determine whether NetBIOS names are being resolved by your WINS server or with broadcasts. Which command can you use to do this?

A. nbtstat -r

B. nbtstat -c

C. nbtstat -A

D. nbtstat -n

12. Which protocol is used by the tracert utility on Windows to test network communications?

A. TCP

B. UDP

C. ICMP

D. IGMP

13. Based upon the output of the **tracert** command shown next, how many hops away from the sending host is the 63.146.27.230 router?

```
Tracing route to ns.novell.com [137.65.1.1]
over a maximum of 30 hops:

  1     1 ms    <1 ms    <1 ms  192.168.1.1
  2     2 ms     1 ms     1 ms  192.168.0.1
  3    41 ms    40 ms    40 ms  slkc-dsl-gw10-202.slkc.qwest.net
                                [67.41.239.202]
  4    42 ms    41 ms    41 ms  slkc-agw1.inet.qwest.net [67.41.238.73]
  5    59 ms    61 ms    68 ms  sjp-brdr-03.inet.qwest.net [67.14.34.10]
  6    59 ms    59 ms    61 ms  63.146.27.230
  7    79 ms    59 ms    58 ms  0.ae1.XL4.SJC7.ALTER.NET [152.63.51.41]
  8   122 ms    92 ms    91 ms  0.so-7-0-0.XT2.DEN4.ALTER.NET
                                [152.63.1.118]
```

```
 9    92 ms    92 ms    91 ms  POS7-0.GW3.DEN4.ALTER.NET [152.63.72.73]
10   101 ms   101 ms   101 ms  unknown.customer.alter.net [65.206.183.22]
11   164 ms   163 ms   182 ms  192.94.118.247
12   450 ms   105 ms   105 ms  137.65.2.66
13   104 ms   105 ms   105 ms  ns.novell.com [137.65.1.1]

Trace complete.
```

    A. 2

    B. 61

    C. 59

    D. 5

14. You are troubleshooting serious issues in your organization's network. You need to use the **tracert** command from a Windows 7 workstation to verify the route that packets are taking through your network from users' workstations to your domain controller. However, your organization's DNS server is down and name resolution is unavailable. Which option can you use with the **tracert** command to cause it not to resolve hostnames of each router as it processes the route?

    A. -w

    B. -d

    C. -h

    D. -j

15. Using the output from the **netstat -a** command shown here, which entry indicates the client received a TCP SYN message, indicating the connection is complete?

```
TCP    ws11laptop:49100       ws11laptop:0              LISTENING
TCP    ws11laptop:netbios-ssn ws11laptop:0              LISTENING
TCP    ws11laptop:1348        67-149-47-80.qwest.net:1935  ESTABLISHED
TCP    ws11laptop:1788        r-199-59-150-87.twttr.com:http  TIME_WAIT
TCP    ws11laptop:1790        addons-versioncheck.zlb.phx.mozilla.net:https
                              TIME_WAIT
TCP    ws11laptop:2869        192.168.1.1:1077          CLOSE_WAIT
UDP    ws11laptop:microsoft-ds  *:*
```

    A. TCP ws11laptop:1348   67-149-47-80. qwest.net:1935 ESTABLISHED

    B. TCP ws11laptop:1788   r-199-59-150-87.twttr.com:http TIME_WAIT

    C. TCP ws11laptop:2869   192.168.1.1:1077   CLOSE_WAIT

    D. TCP ws11laptop:netbios-ssn ws11laptop:0   LISTENING

16. You've just completed a migration of several network services to a different server in your network. Accordingly, you've changed the DNS records associated with these services to point to the new server's IP address. However, when you try to test the new services from a user's Windows 7 workstation, you notice that the host is still resolving the DNS records to the old

server's IP address. Which command can you use at the command prompt of the Windows system to clear its DNS resolver cache?

A. `ipconfig /displaydns`

B. `ipconfig /all`

C. `ipconfig /release`

D. `ipconfig /flushdns`

17. While monitoring a Windows Server 2008 server system using the **netstat** command, you notice that a new port has been opened on the system. You are concerned about this and need to find out which process opened the port. Which option can you use with the **netstat** command to display the process ID of the process that opened the port?

A. -o

B. -a

C. -r

D. -s

18. You need to assign the eth0 interface in a Linux system an IP address of 192.168.1.8 with a subnet mask of 255.255.255.0 and a broadcast address of 192.168.1.255. Which command will do this?

A. `ifconfig eth0 192.168.1.8 mask 255.255.255.0 bcast 192.168.1.255`

B. `ifconfig 192.168.1.8 netmask 255.255.255.0 broadcast 192.168.1.255`

C. `ifconfig eth0 192.168.1.8 subnetmask 255.255.255.0 bcast 192.168.1.255`

D. `ifconfig eth0 192.168.1.8 netmask 255.255.255.0 broadcast 192.168.1.255`

19. From the command prompt on a Windows system, you've connected to the ftp.downloads.com FTP server using the **ftp** command. You need to download an executable file named installer.exe located in a directory named STABLE. You've already entered the **cd STABLE** command to change to this directory. What should you do next?

A. Enter **put installer.exe** at the ftp> prompt.

B. Enter **get installer.exe** at the ftp> prompt.

C. Enter **binary** at the ftp> prompt.

D. Enter **verbose** at the ftp> prompt.

20. From the command prompt on a Windows system, you've connected to the ftp.downloads.com FTP server using the **ftp** command. You need to display a list of files and directories in the current directory on the FTP server. Which commands can you use to do this? (Choose two.)

A. ls

B. get

C. put

D. list

E. dir

21.   Which of the following is true regarding the TFTP protocol?

    A.   It runs on TCP port 69.

    B.   It runs on UDP port 69.

    C.   It runs on TCP ports 20 and 21.

    D.   It runs on UDP ports 20 and 21.

22.   Which command was used at the command prompt of a Windows system to generate the output shown here?

```
Pinging NTI-Linux [192.168.1.3] with 32 bytes of data:

Reply from 192.168.1.3: bytes=32 time<1ms TTL=64
Reply from 192.168.1.3: bytes=32 time<1ms TTL=64
Reply from 192.168.1.3: bytes=32 time<1ms TTL=64
Reply from 192.168.1.3: bytes=32 time<1ms TTL=64

Ping statistics for 192.168.1.3:
    Packets: Sent = 4, Received = 4, Lost = 0 (0% loss),
Approximate round trip times in milli-seconds:
    Minimum = 0ms, Maximum = 0ms, Average = 0ms
```

    A.   `ping 192.168.1.3`

    B.   `ping -t 192.168.1.3`

    C.   `ping -a 192.168.1.3`

    D.   `ping -f 192.168.1.3`

23.   You've just entered the **ping 192.168.1.1** command at the command prompt of a Windows system. This caused the **ping** command to send out an ICMP echo request (ICMP Type 8) message to the host with an IP address of 192.168.1.1. Assuming this host received the echo request correctly, what type of message is sent back to the source system where the **ping** command was run? (Choose two.)

    A.   ICMP Type 11

    B.   ICMP time exceeded

    C.   ICMP echo reply

    D.   ICMP Type 0

    E.   ICMP timestamp reply

24.   You've entered **nslookup** at the shell prompt of a Linux system. Which command can you use at the > prompt to cause nslookup to display a list of authoritative DNS servers for a DNS domain?

    A.   `set q=CNAME`

    B.   `set q=NS`

    C.   `set q=PTR`

    D.   `set q=SOA`

25. You need to use the **dig** command to query your DNS server for a list of all mail servers in the nebo-tech.com domain. Which command will do this?

A. `dig nebo-tech.com MX`

B. `dig nebo-tech.com MAIL`

C. `dig nebo-tech.com +short`

D. `dig nebo-tech.com`

26. Which command was entered at the command prompt of a Windows workstation to generate the output shown here?

```
===========================================================================
Interface List
0x1 ......................... MS TCP Loopback interface
0x2 ...00 0c 29 93 ce 0d ...... AMD PCNET Family PCI Ethernet Adapter -
Packet Scheduler Miniport
===========================================================================
===========================================================================
Active Routes:
Network Destination        Netmask          Gateway       Interface  Metric
          0.0.0.0          0.0.0.0      192.168.1.1    192.168.1.101     10
        127.0.0.0        255.0.0.0        127.0.0.1        127.0.0.1      1
      192.168.1.0    255.255.255.0    192.168.1.101    192.168.1.101     10
    192.168.1.101  255.255.255.255        127.0.0.1        127.0.0.1     10
    192.168.1.255  255.255.255.255    192.168.1.101    192.168.1.101     10
        224.0.0.0        240.0.0.0    192.168.1.101    192.168.1.101     10
  255.255.255.255  255.255.255.255    192.168.1.101    192.168.1.101      1
Default Gateway:       192.168.1.1
===========================================================================
Persistent Routes:
  None
```

A. `route print`

B. `route add 192.168.1.0 mask 255.255.255.0 192.168.1.1 IF 2`

C. `route change  192.168.1.0 mask 255.255.255.0 192.168.1.254 IF 2`

D. `route delete 192.168.1.0`

27. On your Linux workstation, you needed to add a route to the 192.168.2.0/24 network through the router with an IP address of 192.168.1.254. Which command will do this?

A. `route add -net 192.168.2.0 netmask 255.255.255.0 192.168.1.254`

B. `route add netmask 255.255.255.0 gw 192.168.1.254`

C. `route add -net 192.168.2.0 subnetmask 255.255.255.0 gw 192.168.1.254`

D. `route add -net 192.168.2.0 netmask 255.255.255.0 gw 192.168.1.254`

QUICK ANSWER KEY

1.	A	10.	A	19.	C
2.	B, D	11.	A	20.	A, E
3.	C	12.	C	21.	B
4.	D	13.	D	22.	C
5.	B	14.	B	23.	C, D
6.	C	15.	A	24.	B
7.	A	16.	D	25.	A
8.	B	17.	A	26.	A
9.	D	18.	D	27.	D

IN-DEPTH ANSWERS

1. Your workstation needs to copy a file to a server on the same network segment with an IP address of 10.0.01. Part of this process involves resolving the server's IP address into its MAC address using the ARP protocol. ARP has already looked in the ARP cache on your workstation, but it couldn't find an entry for the server's IP address. What happens next?

   A. An ARP request packet is broadcast to all the machines on the network segment to determine the MAC address of the host with an IP address of 10.0.0.1.

   B. ARP sends a unicast ARP request packet to the host with an IP address of 10.0.0.1 requesting its MAC address.

   C. An ARP request packet is broadcast to all the machines on the network segment to determine the MAC address of the default gateway router.

   D. The file transfer fails and an error message is displayed to the end user.

   ☑ **A.** If an entry for the destination system's IP address doesn't exist in the ARP cache, an ARP request packet is broadcast to all the machines on the network segment to determine the MAC address of the host with an IP address of 10.0.0.1. This happens because the originating host and the destination host are on the same network segment.

   ☒ **B, C,** and **D** are incorrect. **B** is incorrect because ARP uses broadcasts to resolve layer 3 IP addresses into layer 2 MAC addresses. **C** is incorrect because the originating system and the destination system reside on the same network segment. This response would be correct if the server resided on a different LAN segment. **D** is incorrect because ARP uses broadcasts to build its cache of IP address to MAC address mappings.

2. You need to view the entries of the ARP cache on your Windows 7 workstation. Which options can you use with the **arp** command to do this? (Choose two.)

   A. -n

   B. -a

   C. -s

   D. -g

   E. -d

   ☑ **B** and **D.** The -a and -g options can be used with the **arp** command on Windows workstations to view the local ARP cache. This will display a list of all IP address to MAC address mappings that ARP is aware of on your system.

☒ **A, C,** and **E** are incorrect. **A** is incorrect because the **-n** option is used to display the ARP cache entries for a specific network interface. **C** is incorrect because the **-s** option is used to add an entry to the ARP cache. **E** is incorrect because the **-d** option is used to remove an entry from the ARP cache.

3. You need to add an entry manually to your Windows workstation's ARP cache that maps the 192.168.1.1 IP address to the 00-17-08-3B-06-3B MAC address. Which command can you use at the command prompt to do this?
   A. `arp -g 192.168.1.1 00-17-08-3B-06-3B`
   B. `arp -a 192.168.1.1 00-17-08-3B-06-3B`
   C. `arp -s 192.168.1.1 00-17-08-3B-06-3B`
   D. `arp -a 192.168.1.1`

☑ **C.** The **arp -s 192.168.1.1 00-17-08-3B-06-3B** command will add this mapping into the ARP cache of the Windows workstation. Once entered into the cache, the ARP protocol will use this mapping when the local system needs to contact the host with the 192.168.1.1 IP address. It will no longer need to send broadcasts to resolve the IP address into a MAC address.

☒ **A, B,** and **D** are incorrect. **A** is incorrect because the **-g** option causes the **arp** command to display the ARP cache, not add entries to it. **B** and **D** are also incorrect because the **-a** option also causes the **arp** command to display the ARP cache, not add entries to it.

4. You need to connect to the Telnet service on a Linux server from your Windows 7 workstation to manage the system remotely. Assuming the Telnet daemon has been enabled, which port in the server's host firewall must be opened to allow Telnet access?
   A. 20
   B. 21
   C. 22
   D. 23

☑ **D.** The Telnet protocol uses TCP port 23. Therefore, for Telnet communications to occur, port 23 must be opened in the firewall of the server.

> ☒ **A, B,** and **C** are incorrect. **A** and **B** are incorrect because ports 20 and 21 are used by the FTP protocol. Port 20 is used for transferring data while port 21 is used for the control connection. **C** is incorrect because TCP port 22 is used by the Secure Shell (SSH) protocol, which is also used to establish remote access connections.

5. A night-shift employee has paged you at home indicating he forgot his password and can't log into your organization's Linux server. You need to access the server remotely from home over the Internet and reset the user's password. Which protocol would be the best choice in this scenario?
    A. Telnet
    B. SSH
    C. FTP
    D. VNC

> ☑ **B.** Because a remote access session will be established with the server over an untrusted public network (the Internet), you should use a protocol that encrypts all data before it is transferred. This is especially true if you will be working with usernames and passwords. The Secure Shell protocol (SSH) provides the best encryption mechanism of the choices in this scenario.
>
> ☒ **A, C,** and **D** are incorrect. **A** is incorrect because the Telnet protocol is notoriously insecure. When you establish a Telnet session, all data (including your administrative user's username and password) are sent in clear-text over the network, making them very easy to capture with a sniffer. **C** is incorrect because the FTP protocol provides access only to the file system of the server. **D** is incorrect because the VNC protocol is much less secure than the SSH protocol, although it can be tunneled through an SSH connection to increase security.

6. You are having problems sending e-mail messages using the SMTP protocol between two Microsoft Exchange servers. The first server's hostname is mail1.mycorp.com, and the second server's hostname is mail2.mycorp.com. You want to test SMTP connectivity from the mail1 server to the mail2 server using the Telnet protocol. Which command can you use on the mail1 server to do this?
    A. `telnet mail2.mycorp.com`
    B. `telnet mail1.mycorp.com 25`
    C. `telnet mail2.mycorp.com 25`
    D. `telnet mail2.mycorp.com 22`

☑ **C. The telnet mail2.mycorp.com 25** command can be used from the mail1 server to test SMTP communications from the mail1 server to the mail2 server. If SMTP communications are working correctly, you should receive a response from the SMTP service on mail2 similar to the following: `220 mail2.mycorp.com Microsoft Exchange Internet Mail Connector.`

☒ **A, B,** and **D** are incorrect. **A** is incorrect because the **telnet mail2.mycorp.com** command establishes a standard Telnet connection on port 23 and doesn't test SMTP communications. **B** is incorrect because it specifies the mail1 server in the command instead of the mail2 server. **D** is incorrect because it specifies the SSH port (22) instead of the SMTP port (25).

7. Consider the following output from a command entered at the command prompt of a Windows 7 workstation:

```
Interface: 192.168.1.105 --- 0x5
Internet Address      Physical Address      Type
192.168.1.1           00-19-5b-06-de-a4     dynamic
192.168.1.240         44-87-fc-e2-e5-d3     dynamic
```

Which command was used to generate this output?

A. `arp -a`

B. `nbtstat -c`

C. `telnet localhost 20`

D. `netstat -e`

☑ **A. The arp -a** command was used to generate the output shown in this question. The **-a** option causes the **arp** command to display the contents of the ARP cache.

☒ **B, C,** and **D** are incorrect. **B** is incorrect because the **nbtstat -c** command displays the contents of the NetBIOS name cache. **C** is incorrect because the **telnet localhost 20** command establishes a Telnet connection to the FTP service running on the local host. **D** is incorrect because the **netstat -e** command displays Ethernet statistics.

8. The **nbtstat** command has returned the following output: `NTI-LINUX-W      <20> UNIQUE`. What type of system is NTI-LINUX-W?

A. Workstation

B. File server

C. Mail server

D. Domain controller

☑ **B.** The output of the **nbtstat** command has shown that the NTI-LINUX-W host has a NetBIOS name suffix of 20. This name suffix indicates the host is a file and print server on the network.

☒ **A, C,** and **D** are incorrect. **A** is incorrect because workstations have a name suffix of 00. **C** is incorrect because mail servers have a name suffix of 03. **D** is incorrect because domain controllers have a name suffix of 1C.

9. Which command was used at the command prompt of a Windows system to generate the following output?

```
Wireless Network Connection:
Node IpAddress: [192.168.1.105] Scope Id: []
                 NetBIOS Local Name Table
       Name                Type          Status
    ---------------------------------------------
    WS1LAPTOP      <00>  UNIQUE      Registered
    MYWORKGROUP    <00>  GROUP        Registered
    WS1LAPTOP      <20>  UNIQUE      Registered
```

A. `netstat -s`
B. `nbtstat -c`
C. `netstat -r`
D. `nbtstat -n`

☑ **D.** The **nbtstat -n** command was used to generate the output shown in this question. The **-n** option causes **nbtstat** to list NetBIOS names for the local machine.

☒ **A, B,** and **C** are incorrect. **A** is incorrect because the **netstat -s** command is used to display network statistics for each protocol in the TCP/IP suite. **B** is incorrect because the **nbtstat -c** command is used to display the local NetBIOS cache. **C** is incorrect because the **netstat -r** command displays the routing table for the local machine.

10. Which command was used to generate the following output from the shell prompt on a Linux server system?

```
Kernel IP routing table
Destination     Gateway          Genmask          Flags  MSS Window  irtt
Iface
192.168.1.0     *                255.255.255.0    U      0 0         0 eth0
link-local      *                255.255.0.0      U      0 0         0 eth0
loopback        *                255.0.0.0        U      0 0         0 lo
default         192.168.1.1      0.0.0.0          UG     0 0         0 eth0
```

A. `netstat -r`

B. `netstat -s`

C. `arp -g`

D. `netstat -p TCP`

☑ **A.** The **netstat -r** command was used to generate the output shown in this question. The **-r** option causes **netstat** to display the host's routing table.

☒ **B, C,** and **D** are incorrect. **B** is incorrect because the **netstat -s** command is used to display network statistics for each protocol in the TCP/IP suite on the local machine. **C** is incorrect because the **arp -g** command is used to display the contents of the ARP cache on the local machine. **D** is incorrect because the **netstat -p** TCP command is used to display a list of current TCP connections.

---

11. While troubleshooting NetBIOS issues with Windows hosts on your network, you need to determine whether NetBIOS names are being resolved by your WINS server or with broadcasts. Which command can you use to do this?

A. `nbtstat -r`

B. `nbtstat -c`

C. `nbtstat -A`

D. `nbtstat -n`

☑ **A.** The **nbtstat -r** command displays name resolution statistics. In this scenario, you could use this command to determine whether or not NetBIOS names are being resolved by the WINS server on your network or whether broadcasts are being used.

☒ **B, C,** and **D** are not correct. **B** is incorrect because the **nbtstat -c** command displays the contents of the name cache. **C** is incorrect because the **nbtstat -A** command lists a remote network host's name table using its IP address. **D** is incorrect because the **nbtstat -n** command displays NetBIOS names for the local host.

---

12. Which protocol is used by the tracert utility on Windows to test network communications?

A. TCP

B. UDP

C. ICMP

D. IGMP

☑ **C.** The tracert utility on Windows uses the ICMP protocol to test network communications. Each time a packet crosses a router between the sender and the target system, an ICMP time exceeded message is sent to the sender, allowing you to trace the route a packet takes through the network. The traceroute utility on Linux uses UDP instead of ICMP.

☒ **A, B,** and **D** are incorrect. **A** and **B** are incorrect because the TCP and UDP are transport protocols and are not capable of sending echo response packets. **D** is incorrect because IGMP is used to establish multicast group memberships. It is also incapable of sending echo response packets.

13. Based upon the output of the **tracert** command shown next, how many hops away from the sending host is the 63.146.27.230 router?

```
Tracing route to ns.novell.com [137.65.1.1]
over a maximum of 30 hops:

  1      1 ms     <1 ms     <1 ms   192.168.1.1
  2      2 ms      1 ms      1 ms   192.168.0.1
  3     41 ms     40 ms     40 ms   slkc-dsl-gw10-202.slkc.qwest.net
                                    [67.41.239.202]
  4     42 ms     41 ms     41 ms   slkc-agw1.inet.qwest.net [67.41.238.73]
  5     59 ms     61 ms     68 ms   sjp-brdr-03.inet.qwest.net [67.14.34.10]
  6     59 ms     59 ms     61 ms   63.146.27.230
  7     79 ms     59 ms     58 ms   0.ae1.XL4.SJC7.ALTER.NET [152.63.51.41]
  8    122 ms     92 ms     91 ms   0.so-7-0-0.XT2.DEN4.ALTER.NET
                                    [152.63.1.118]
  9     92 ms     92 ms     91 ms   POS7-0.GW3.DEN4.ALTER.NET [152.63.72.73]
 10    101 ms    101 ms    101 ms   unknown.customer.alter.net [65.206.183.22]
 11    164 ms    163 ms    182 ms   192.94.118.247
 12    450 ms    105 ms    105 ms   137.65.2.66
 13    104 ms    105 ms    105 ms   ns.novell.com [137.65.1.1]

Trace complete.
```

A. 2
B. 61
C. 59
D. 5

☑ **D.** The router with an IP address of 63.146.27.230 is identified as being 5 hops away from the system where the **tracert** command was run in this example. The **tracert** command sent three ICMP echo request packets to this router and the response times for these packets were 59, 61, and 68 milliseconds.

☒ **A, B,** and **C** are incorrect. **A** is incorrect because the **tracert** command identified the 63.146.27.230 router as being 5 hops away, not 2. **B** and **C** are incorrect because these statistics in the output of the **tracert** command are response times, not hop counts.

14. You are troubleshooting serious issues in your organization's network. You need to use the **tracert** command from a Windows 7 workstation to verify the route that packets are taking through your network from users' workstations to your domain controller. However, your organization's DNS server is down and name resolution is unavailable. Which option can you use with the **tracert** command to cause it not to resolve hostnames of each router as it processes the route?

A. -w
B. -d
C. -h
D. -j

☑ **B.** When you use the **-d** option with the **tracert** command, it will not try to resolve the IP address of each router it reaches into a hostname (which is the default behavior of the utility). By not resolving IP addresses into hostnames, the **tracert** command is not dependent upon the availability of a DNS server and also runs much faster.

☒ **A, C,** and **D** are incorrect. **A** is incorrect because the **-w** option is used to specify a timeout period (in milliseconds) to wait for a reply from each router. **C** is incorrect because the **-h** option is used to specify a maximum number of hops allowed between the source and target systems. **D** is incorrect because the **-j** option is used to force the **tracert** command to use loose source routing.

15. Using the output from the **netstat -a** command shown here, which entry indicates the client received a TCP SYN message, indicating the connection is complete?

```
TCP    ws1laptop:49100        ws1laptop:0              LISTENING
TCP    ws1laptop:netbios-ssn  ws1laptop:0              LISTENING
TCP    ws1laptop:1348         67-149-47-80.qwest.net:1935   ESTABLISHED
TCP    ws1laptop:1788         r-199-59-150-87.twttr.com:http  TIME_WAIT
```

```
TCP     ws1laptop:1790        addons-versioncheck.zlb.phx.mozilla.net:https
                              TIME_WAIT
TCP     ws1laptop:2869        192.168.1.1:1077        CLOSE_WAIT
UDP     ws1laptop:microsoft-ds  *:*
```

A. TCP   ws1laptop:1348   67-149-47-80. qwest.net:1935 ESTABLISHED

B. TCP   ws1laptop:1788   r-199-59-150-87.twttr.com:http TIME_WAIT

C. TCP   ws1laptop:2869   192.168.1.1:1077   CLOSE_WAIT

D. TCP   ws1laptop:netbios-ssn ws1laptop:0   LISTENING

☑ **A.** This entry is in an ESTABLISHED state. This indicates that the 3-way handshake used by the TCP protocol completed correctly, establishing the connection.

☒ **B, C,** and **D** are incorrect. **B** is incorrect because clients enter the TIME_WAIT state after an active close operation is complete. **C** is incorrect because the CLOSE_WAIT state indicates a passive close operation. **D** is incorrect because the LISTENING state indicates the host is waiting for a connection.

16. You've just completed a migration of several network services to a different server in your network. Accordingly, you've changed the DNS records associated with these services to point to the new server's IP address. However, when you try to test the new services from a user's Windows 7 workstation, you notice that the host is still resolving the DNS records to the old server's IP address. Which command can you use at the command prompt of the Windows system to clear its DNS resolver cache?

A. `ipconfig /displaydns`

B. `ipconfig /all`

C. `ipconfig /release`

D. `ipconfig /flushdns`

☑ **D.** The **ipconfig /flushdns** command clears out (flushes) the DNS resolver cache on the workstation. This causes the host to query your DNS server when it needs to resolve a hostname to an IP address instead of just looking in its local cache of resolved hostnames. In this scenario, this will allow the host to get the new DNS record information you configured in your DNS server and resolve the hostnames into the new server's IP address.

☒ **A, B,** and **C** are incorrect. **A** is incorrect because the **/displaydns** option displays the DNS resolve cache on the workstation, but it doesn't clear it. **B** is incorrect because the **/all** option causes the **ipconfig** command simply to display all IP addressing configuration information on the host. **C** is incorrect because the **/release** option causes the **ipconfig** command to release any dynamically-assigned IP addressing configuration information on the host.

17. While monitoring a Windows Server 2008 server system using the **netstat** command, you notice that a new port has been opened on the system. You are concerned about this and need to find out which process opened the port. Which option can you use with the **netstat** command to display the process ID of the process that opened the port?

    A. -o

    B. -a

    C. -r

    D. -s

☑ **A.** The **-o** option causes the **netstat** command to display the PID of the process that opened each port on the system. You can then use this information to determine which process is responsible and decide whether it is a legitimate process or some form of malware.

☒ **B, C,** and **D** are incorrect. **B** is incorrect because the **-a** option causes **netstat** to display all connections and ports, but it doesn't display the associated PIDs. **C** is incorrect because the **-r** option causes **netstat** to display the host's routing table. **D** is incorrect because the **-s** option causes **netstat** to display summary statistics for each protocol on the system (IP, ICMP, TCP, and UDP).

18. You need to assign the eth0 interface in a Linux system an IP address of 192.168.1.8 with a subnet mask of 255.255.255.0 and a broadcast address of 192.168.1.255. Which command will do this?

    A. `ifconfig eth0 192.168.1.8 mask 255.255.255.0 bcast 192.168.1.255`

    B. `ifconfig 192.168.1.8 netmask 255.255.255.0 broadcast 192.168.1.255`

    C. `ifconfig eth0 192.168.1.8 subnetmask 255.255.255.0 bcast 192.168.1.255`

    D. `ifconfig eth0 192.168.1.8 netmask 255.255.255.0 broadcast 192.168.1.255`

☑ **D.** This command assigns the eth0 interface an IP address of 192.168.18 with a subnet mask of 255.255.255.0, and a broadcast address of 192.168.1.255. Be aware that any IP address changes you make with the **ifconfig** command are not persistent. If you reboot the system, all changes you made with the command will be lost.

☒ **A, B,** and **C** are incorrect. **A** is incorrect because the command uses incorrect options with the **ifconfig** command (**mask** and **bcast**). **B** is incorrect because the command omits the network interface to be configured. **C** is incorrect because the command uses incorrect options with the **ifconfig** command (**subnetmask** and **broadcast**).

19. From the command prompt on a Windows system, you've connected to the ftp.downloads.com FTP server using the **ftp** command. You need to download an executable file named installer.exe located in a directory named STABLE. You've already entered the **cd STABLE** command to change to this directory. What should you do next?
    A. Enter **put installer.exe** at the ftp> prompt.
    B. Enter **get installer.exe** at the ftp> prompt.
    C. Enter **binary** at the ftp> prompt.
    D. Enter **verbose** at the ftp> prompt.

☑ **C.** Because the file to be downloaded is a binary executable, you should switch the ftp client to binary mode using the **binary** command at the ftp> prompt. This prevents the FTP client from trying to download the file as an ASCII text file.

☒ **A, B,** and **D** are incorrect. **A** is incorrect because the **put** command is used to upload a file. **B** is an incorrect answer, though partially correct. After switching the FTP client into binary mode, you would next use the **get** command to download the file. **D** is incorrect because the **verbose** command turns verbose mode in the FTP client on or off. It is optional and not required to download the file.

20. From the command prompt on a Windows system, you've connected to the ftp.downloads.com FTP server using the **ftp** command. You need to display a list of files and directories in the current directory on the FTP server. Which commands can you use to do this? (Choose two.)
    A. ls
    B. get
    C. put
    D. list
    E. dir

☑ **A and E.** You can use either the **ls** or the **dir** command to display a list of files in the current directory on the FTP server. On most FTP servers, the **ls** command displays just a list of files and subdirectories in the current directory. The **dir** command displays extended information about files and subdirectories in the current directory, such as permissions, file sizes, and last modification date.

☒ **B, C, and D are incorrect. B** is incorrect because the **get** command is used to download files from the FTP server. **C** is incorrect because the **put** command is used to upload files to the FTP server. **D** is incorrect because the **list** command is not a valid FTP server command.

21. Which of the following is true regarding the TFTP protocol?

A. It runs on TCP port 69.

B. It runs on UDP port 69.

C. It runs on TCP ports 20 and 21.

D. It runs on UDP ports 20 and 21.

☑ **B.** The TFTP protocol runs on UDP port 69. Unlike FTP, TFTP does not use a control connection on a separate IP port, nor does it support user authentication. This is done to simplify the way the protocol works and to increase the speed of data transfers.

☒ **A, C, and D are incorrect. A** is incorrect because the TFTP protocol uses the UDP protocol, not TCP. **C** is incorrect because TFTP uses the UDP protocol and runs on port 69 instead of the FTP ports of 20 and 21. **D** is incorrect for the same reason.

22. Which command was used at the command prompt of a Windows system to generate the output shown here?

```
Pinging NTI-Linux [192.168.1.3] with 32 bytes of data:

Reply from 192.168.1.3: bytes=32 time<1ms TTL=64
Reply from 192.168.1.3: bytes=32 time<1ms TTL=64
Reply from 192.168.1.3: bytes=32 time<1ms TTL=64
Reply from 192.168.1.3: bytes=32 time<1ms TTL=64

Ping statistics for 192.168.1.3:
    Packets: Sent = 4, Received = 4, Lost = 0 (0% loss),
Approximate round trip times in milli-seconds:
    Minimum = 0ms, Maximum = 0ms, Average = 0ms
```

A. `ping 192.168.1.3`
B. `ping -t 192.168.1.3`
C. `ping -a 192.168.1.3`
D. `ping -f 192.168.1.3`

☑ **C.** The **ping -a 192.168.1.3** command was entered at the command prompt of the Windows system to generate the output shown in this question. The **-a** option causes the **ping** command to resolve addresses into computer names. In this example, the IP address 192.168.1.3 was resolved into a computer name of NTI-Linux.

☒ **A, B,** and **D** are incorrect. **A** is incorrect because the command in this response omits the **-a** option with the **ping** command. **B** is incorrect because the **-t** option causes the **ping** command to continue pinging until interrupted by a CTRL-C key keypress. **D** is incorrect because the **-f** option causes the **ping** command not to fragment packets.

23. You've just entered the **ping 192.168.1.1** command at the command prompt of a Windows system. This caused the **ping** command to send out an ICMP echo request (ICMP Type 8) message to the host with an IP address of 192.168.1.1. Assuming this host received the echo request correctly, what type of message is sent back to the source system where the **ping** command was run? (Choose two.)

A. ICMP Type 11
B. ICMP time exceeded
C. ICMP echo reply
D. ICMP Type 0
E. ICMP timestamp reply

☑ **C** and **D.** When an IP host receives an ICMP echo request (Type 8) message from a host running the **ping** command, it responds with an ICMP echo reply (Type 0) message. This is a very useful tool for testing basic network communications. Using the **ping** command, you can test whether a remote host is up and responding to network requests.

☒ **A, B,** and **E** are incorrect. **A** and **B** are incorrect because ICMP Type 11 (time exceeded) messages are sent when the ICMP packet's TTL expired during transit. **E** is incorrect because ICMP timestamp reply messages are sent in response to an ICMP timestamp message.

24. You've entered **nslookup** at the shell prompt of a Linux system. Which command can you use at the > prompt to cause nslookup to display a list of authoritative DNS servers for a DNS domain?

    A. `set q=CNAME`

    B. `set q=NS`

    C. `set q=PTR`

    D. `set q=SOA`

    ☑ **B.** While running nslookup in interactive mode, you can use the **set q=NS** command at the nslookup prompt to configure nslookup to display a list of authoritative DNS servers for a DNS zone. For example, if you were to enter **nebo-tech.com** after entering **set q=NS** at the nslookup prompt, you would see list of authoritative DNS servers for the nebo-tech.com domain.

    ☒ **A, C,** and **D** are incorrect. **A** is incorrect because the **set q=CNAME** command causes nslookup to display the canonical name for an alias. **C** is incorrect because the **set q=PTR** command causes nslookup to resolve IP addresses into DNS hostnames (a reverse DNS lookup). **D** is incorrect because the **set q=SOA** command causes nslookup to display the start of authority (SOA) record for a DNS domain.

25. You need to use the **dig** command to query your DNS server for a list of all mail servers in the nebo-tech.com domain. Which command will do this?

    A. `dig nebo-tech.com MX`

    B. `dig nebo-tech.com MAIL`

    C. `dig nebo-tech.com +short`

    D. `dig nebo-tech.com`

    ☑ **A.** The **dig nebo-tech.com MX** command will query your DNS server for a list of all MX records in the nebo-tech.com domain. MX records are a special type of DNS record that is used only for mail servers. Therefore, by listing all MX records for a domain, you are able to view a list of all mail servers for that domain.

    ☒ **B, C,** and **D** are incorrect. **B** is incorrect because the MAIL DNS record type doesn't exist. **C** and **D** are incorrect because both commands in these responses perform an A record lookup of the nebo-tech.com domain instead of an MX record lookup.

26. Which command was entered at the command prompt of a Windows workstation to generate the output shown here?

```
=============================================================================
Interface List
0x1 .......................... MS TCP Loopback interface
0x2 ...00 0c 29 93 ce 0d ...... AMD PCNET Family PCI Ethernet Adapter -
                                Packet Scheduler Miniport
=============================================================================
=============================================================================
Active Routes:
Network Destination        Netmask          Gateway       Interface  Metric
          0.0.0.0          0.0.0.0      192.168.1.1   192.168.1.101     10
        127.0.0.0        255.0.0.0        127.0.0.1       127.0.0.1      1
      192.168.1.0    255.255.255.0    192.168.1.101   192.168.1.101     10
    192.168.1.101  255.255.255.255        127.0.0.1       127.0.0.1     10
    192.168.1.255  255.255.255.255    192.168.1.101   192.168.1.101     10
        224.0.0.0        240.0.0.0    192.168.1.101   192.168.1.101     10
  255.255.255.255  255.255.255.255    192.168.1.101   192.168.1.101      1
Default Gateway:        192.168.1.1
=============================================================================
Persistent Routes:
  None
```

A. route print

B. route add 192.168.1.0 mask 255.255.255.0 192.168.1.1 IF 2

C. route change 192.168.1.0 mask 255.255.255.0 192.168.1.254 IF 2

D. route delete 192.168.1.0

☑ **A.** The **route print** command was used to generate the output shown in this question. This command displays the routing table for the local computer system. In this example, you can see that the default gateway router for this network segment is 192.168.1.1.

☒ **B, C,** and **D** are incorrect. **B** is incorrect because this command adds a route for the 192.168.1.0 network to the local routing table for the first physical interface (IF 2) in the system. (The IF 1 interface is the loopback adapter on Windows systems.) **C** is incorrect because this command modifies the 192.168.1.0 route to use the 192.168.1.254 router. **D** is incorrect because it removes the route to the 192.168.1.0 network from the routing table.

27. On your Linux workstation, you needed to add a route to the 192.168.2.0/24 network through the router with an IP address of 192.168.1.254. Which command will do this?

    A. `route add -net 192.168.2.0 netmask 255.255.255.0 192.168.1.254`

    B. `route add netmask 255.255.255.0 gw 192.168.1.254`

    C. `route add -net 192.168.2.0 subnetmask 255.255.255.0 gw 192.168.1.254`

    D. `route add -net 192.168.2.0 netmask 255.255.255.0 gw 192.168.1.254`

    ☑ **D.** The **route add -net 192.168.2.0 netmask 255.255.255.0 gw 192.168.1.254** command will add a route to the 192.168.2.0/24 network through the router with an IP address of 192.168.1.254.

    ☒ **A, B,** and **C** are incorrect. **A** is incorrect because it omits the **gw** option. **B** is incorrect because it omits the **-net** option. **C** is incorrect because it uses an invalid option (**subnetmask**) with the **route** command.

6

Configuring Routers and Switches

CERTIFICATION OBJECTIVES

❏ **1.4** Explain the purpose and properties of routing and switching.

❏ **2.1** Given a scenario, install and configure routers and switches.

❏ **2.5** Given a scenario, troubleshoot common router and switch problems.

QUESTIONS

As a network administrator, you need to ensure that the basic infrastructure used by your network is functioning properly. Infrastructure failures in the network prevent connectivity and will result in many help desk calls.

The problems you might experience with your network infrastructure can range from incorrect implementations, to malfunctioning equipment, to deliberate security exploits. To deal with these widely varying causes, you need to develop excellent network troubleshooting skills. In this chapter, you are presented with questions that test your ability to diagnose correctly, problems with network devices, wiring, and configurations.

1. You need to make configuration changes to your Cisco router. What should you do? (Choose two.)
   A. Enter **enable** at the command prompt.
   B. Enter **disable** at the command prompt.
   C. Enter **config term** at the command prompt.
   D. Enter **exit** at the command prompt.
   E. Enter **configure** at the command prompt.

2. You are configuring the ports on your switch. Your network is composed of a variety of devices and you are unsure as to which duplex settings they have been configured to use. What should you do? (Choose two.)
   A. Configure the duplex settings on all network devices to half duplex.
   B. Configure the duplex settings on your switch ports to full duplex.
   C. Configure the duplex settings on your switch ports to half duplex.
   D. Configure the duplex settings on your switch ports to auto.
   E. Configure the duplex settings on all network devices to auto.

3. You need to configure an Ethernet interface in a Cisco router to support Fast Ethernet speeds. Which command should you use to do this?
   A. port speed 1000
   B. speed 10
   C. speed 100
   D. port speed Fast Ethernet

4. You need to configure an Ethernet interface in a Cisco router with an IP address of 192.168.1.254 using the default Class C subnet mask. What should you do?
   A. Enter **ip address 192.168.1.254 255.255.0.0** at the router's command prompt.
   B. Enter **ip address 192.168.1.254 255.255.255.0** at the router's command prompt.
   C. Enter **ipaddr 192.168.1.254 255.255.255.0** at the router's command prompt.
   D. Enter **ifconfig eth0 192.168.1.254 netmask 255.255.255.0** at the router's command prompt.

5. Which VLAN feature allows you to connect multiple switches together and assign one port to carry VLAN traffic to the other switch?

   A. Trunking

   B. Spanning Tree Protocol

   C. Port mirroring

   D. QoS

6. Which switch feature allows you to restrict hosts that are allowed to connect to a particular port by their MAC address?

   A. Port authentication

   B. Packet filtering

   C. Smartjack

   D. Load balancing

7. You are designing a network implementation for a startup business. Your Ethernet network design calls for the implementation of VLANs to separate design and development network traffic from administration and human resources traffic. In addition, you need to be able to customize each network port on your network switches to support the manufacturing devices used by the design and development teams. What should you do?

   A. Implement managed Ethernet switches.

   B. Implement unmanaged Ethernet switches.

   C. Purchase your network Ethernet switches and network interface cards from the same vendor.

   D. Implement Ethernet hubs.

8. A client has hired you to implement a number of IP security cameras and IP security phones. Ethernet wire and RJ-45 jacks have already been run to the locations where the cameras and phones are to be installed. However, upon investigation, you notice that most of the locations are far away from the nearest power outlet. What should you do?

   A. Implement PLT switches, cameras, and phones.

   B. Implement PDSL switches, cameras, and phones.

   C. Implement BPL switches, cameras, and phones.

   D. Implement PoE switches, cameras, and phones.

9. What can be used by an Ethernet switch to filter network traffic?

   A. Source IP address

   B. Destination IP address

   C. MAC address

   D. TCP connection state

10. Which Cisco technology can be used to extend a VLAN to multiple network switches?
    A. Spanning Tree Protocol
    B. VTP
    C. OSPF
    D. RIP

11. Which standard allows VLAN tags to be assigned to Ethernet frames, allowing VLAN information to be distributed among multiple network switches?
    A. 802.5
    B. 802.3
    C. 802.1q
    D. 802.14

12. A new employee has been hired by your organization and you are setting up her desktop workstation. You've connected the network interface card in her system to the wall jack, but the link light for the port to which it's connected on your switch does not come on. You recently tested the wiring for this wall jack and know that it is wired correctly. You check the driver status in Device Manager in Windows and it reports that the device is working correctly. What could be wrong? (Choose two possibilities.)
    A. The workstation has the wrong default gateway address assigned.
    B. The workstation has the wrong subnet mask assigned.
    C. The drop cable between the workstation and the wall jack may be a crossover cable.
    D. The drivers for the network interface need to be updated.
    E. The port may be disabled on the switch.

13. You've organized the hosts connected to your network switch into two VLANs: one for your design and development group and one for administration and human resources. A new software developer has been hired who needs access to design and development network resources. You've set up her workstation and connected it to your network switch. The link light for the port is lit; however, the developer is unable to see the server shares used by the design and development group on the network. What should you do?
    A. Verify that a crossover drop cable was not used to connect the workstation to the wall jack.
    B. Verify that the port is enabled on the switch to which the workstation is connected.
    C. Check the routing table on the network segment's default gateway router for wrong or missing routes.
    D. Check to see if the workstation has been made a member of the VLAN used by the design and development group.

14. Upon arrival at work, you are met with chaos as no one in the organization is able to access any network resources on your mixed fiber-optic and copper UTP Gigabit Ethernet network. Users are not able to authenticate to their configured Active Directory domain controllers, and they cannot see any network resources on the network. You've checked and all of your servers are up and running, but none of them can be pinged from workstations. You check the IP configuration on several workstations and see that they are all using IP addresses in the 169.254.1.*x* range with a subnet mask of 255.255.0.0. However, none of the workstations can ping any of the others. What should you do? (Choose the best two.)

   A. Manually assign static IP addresses to all workstations until you can get your DHCP server working correctly.

   B. Verify the network switch has power and is turned on.

   C. Verify your DNS server is up and responding to requests.

   D. Check for bad SFP or GBIC modules.

   E. Check the routing table on the network segment's default gateway router for wrong or missing routes.

15. You are experiencing errors caused by an MTU black hole. TCP connections between hosts on different network segments frequently hang after successfully completing the three-way handshake. What should you do to fix this?

   A. Configure network security devices to allow ICMP messages.

   B. Implement a stateful firewall to monitor the state of TCP connections.

   C. Move all network hosts onto the same network segment.

   D. Implement VLANs to subdivide each network segment.

16. The workstations on your network are unable to reach a Linux-based file and print server on the same network segment. You've checked and the server has been assigned a static IP address of 172.17.0.1. Your workstations are assigned IP addresses via DHCP in the 172.17.8.100– 172.17.8.253 range with a subnet mask of 255.255.0.0. You are unable to ping the server from any workstation, yet the workstations are able to ping each other. What should you do?

   A. Assign the Linux server an IP address of 172.17.8.1.

   B. Verify that the workstations have the correct default gateway router address assigned.

   C. Verify that the network switch has power and is turned on.

   D. Check the subnet mask assigned to the Linux server.

17. A user has called the help desk indicating that his Windows workstation is displaying a "Duplicate IP address…" error message. You check the workstation and find that it is using DHCP to get its IP addressing information. What should you do to fix this issue?

   A. Reboot the workstation.

   B. Check the network for another host that has been statically assigned the duplicated IP address.

   C. Clear all lease information on your DHCP server.

   D. Restart the DHCP service on your DHCP server.

18. Users are complaining that they can't access the company intranet site. You check and find that you can ping the intranet web server by IP address, but not by its DNS name. What should you do?

A. Verify that users' workstations have the correct default gateway router address configured.

B. Verify that users' workstations have the correct DNS resolver address configured.

C. Check your network switches for a switching loop.

D. Verify that the intranet web server doesn't have an incorrect subnet mask assigned.

QUICK ANSWER KEY

1.	A, C	**7.**	A	**13.**	D
2.	D, E	**8.**	D	**14.**	B, D
3.	C	**9.**	C	**15.**	A
4.	B	**10.**	B	**16.**	D
5.	A	**11.**	C	**17.**	B
6.	A	**12.**	C, E	**18.**	B

IN-DEPTH ANSWERS

1. You need to make configuration changes to your Cisco router. What should you do? (Choose two.)
   A. Enter **enable** at the command prompt.
   B. Enter **disable** at the command prompt.
   C. Enter **config term** at the command prompt.
   D. Enter **exit** at the command prompt.
   E. Enter **configure** at the command prompt.

   ☑ **A and C.** The **enable** command is used on a Cisco router to switch from user exec mode (which is a read-only mode) to privilege exec mode. You then need to change to global configuration mode by entering config term, which allows you to make actual configuration changes to the router.

   ☒ **B, D, and E** are incorrect. **B** is incorrect because the **disable** command is used to switch from privilege exec mode to user exec mode. **D** is incorrect because the **exit** command is used to switch from global configuration mode to privilege exec mode. **E** is incorrect because **configure** is not a valid command on a Cisco router.

2. You are configuring the ports on your switch. Your network is composed of a variety of devices and you are unsure as to which duplex settings they have been configured to use. What should you do? (Choose two.)
   A. Configure the duplex settings on all network devices to half duplex.
   B. Configure the duplex settings on your switch ports to full duplex.
   C. Configure the duplex settings on your switch ports to half duplex.
   D. Configure the duplex settings on your switch ports to auto.
   E. Configure the duplex settings on all network devices to auto.

   ☑ **D and E.** Setting your switch ports and your network devices to a duplex setting of auto will allow the ports and the network interfaces to which they are connected to configure their duplex settings automatically to match each other. Another option would be to configure your switch ports and network devices to use full duplex communications.

   ☒ **A, B, and C** are incorrect. **A** and **C** are incorrect because setting the switch ports and network devices to use half duplex would dramatically reduce the overall throughput of the network. **B** is incorrect because setting your switch ports to full duplex without configuring your network devices to match could result in duplex mismatch, which will reduce the network throughput for the mismatched devices.

3. You need to configure an Ethernet interface in a Cisco router to support Fast Ethernet speeds. Which command should you use to do this?

   A. port speed 1000

   B. speed 10

   C. speed 100

   D. port speed Fast Ethernet

   ☑ **C.** First, you must enter **interface f0/0** at the command prompt of the Cisco router to tell the operating system that you want to configure the first Ethernet interface installed in it. Then you can enter the **speed 100** command to set the port speed to 100 Mbps (Fast Ethernet).

   ☒ **A, B,** and **D** are incorrect. **A** and **D** are incorrect because **port speed** is an invalid command on a Cisco router. **B** is incorrect because this command sets the port speed to 10 Mbps, and Fast Ethernet requires 100 Mbps.

4. You need to configure an Ethernet interface in a Cisco router with an IP address of 192.168.1.254 using the default Class C subnet mask. What should you do?

   A. Enter **ip address 192.168.1.254 255.255.0.0** at the router's command prompt.

   B. Enter **ip address 192.168.1.254 255.255.255.0** at the router's command prompt.

   C. Enter **ipaddr 192.168.1.254 255.255.255.0** at the router's command prompt.

   D. Enter **ifconfig eth0 192.168.1.254 netmask 255.255.255.0** at the router's command prompt.

   ☑ **B.** To set the IP address used by an interface in a Cisco router, you first enter **interface f0/0** at the command prompt of the Cisco router to tell the operating system that you want to configure the first Ethernet interface installed in it. Then you enter **ip address 192.168.1.254 255.255.255.0** at the router's command prompt.

   ☒ **A, C,** and **D** are incorrect. **A** is incorrect because the command specifies the wrong subnet mask (Class B). **C** is incorrect because it uses an invalid command for a Cisco router (**ipaddr**). **D** is incorrect because it uses the **ifconfig** command, which is used to set the IP address on a Linux system, not a Cisco router.

5. Which VLAN feature allows you to connect multiple switches together and assign one port to carry VLAN traffic to the other switch?

   A. Trunking

   B. Spanning Tree Protocol

C. Port mirroring

D. QoS

☑ **A.** Trunking allows you to connect two switches together and assign one port as a trunk port. The trunk port is used to carry VLAN traffic to the other switch.

☒ **B, C,** and **D** are incorrect. **B** is incorrect because the Spanning Tree Protocol is used by switches to prevent switching loops that could occur if multiple switches were wired together incorrectly. **C** is incorrect because port mirroring allows the switch to send a copy of data that reaches certain ports to a monitored port, which allows you as the administrator to monitor network traffic. **D** is incorrect because QoS settings allow you to prioritize certain types of network traffic over other types.

---

6. Which switch feature allows you to restrict hosts that are allowed to connect to a particular port by their MAC address?

A. Port authentication

B. Packet filtering

C. Smartjack

D. Load balancing

☑ **A.** Port authentication lets you restrict hosts that are allowed to connect to a specific port on a network switch based on the MAC address assigned to their network interface. This security measure can prevent unauthorized users from connecting their network devices, such as a laptop, to your wired network.

☒ **B, C,** and **D** are incorrect. **B** is incorrect because packet filtering is a function provided by a network router. **C** is incorrect because a Smartjack is a type of network interface device that is used with T1 lines. **D** is incorrect because load balancing is a technology used to distribute network tasks among multiple systems, devices, or interfaces.

---

7. You are designing a network implementation for a startup business. Your Ethernet network design calls for the implementation of VLANs to separate design and development network traffic from administration and human resources traffic. In addition, you need to be able to customize each network port on your network switches to support the manufacturing devices used by the design and development teams. What should you do?

A. Implement managed Ethernet switches.

B. Implement unmanaged Ethernet switches.

C. Purchase your network Ethernet switches and network interface cards from the same vendor.

D. Implement Ethernet hubs.

☑ **A.** You should use managed Ethernet switches in this scenario. Managed switches provide VLAN functionality and allow you to configure a variety of settings for each port, such as speed, duplexing, and so on.

☒ **B, C,** and **D** are incorrect. **B** is incorrect because unmanaged switches, while less expensive, usually don't provide VLAN functionality; nor do they allow you to customize port settings. **C** is incorrect because purchasing your switches and interfaces from the same vendor doesn't guarantee that the switch can be managed. **D** is incorrect because hubs don't provide VLANs.

8. A client has hired you to implement a number of IP security cameras and IP security phones. Ethernet wire and RJ-45 jacks have already been run to the locations where the cameras and phones are to be installed. However, upon investigation, you notice that most of the locations are far away from the nearest power outlet. What should you do?

A. Implement PLT switches, cameras, and phones.

B. Implement PDSL switches, cameras, and phones.

C. Implement BPL switches, cameras, and phones.

D. Implement PoE switches, cameras, and phones.

☑ **D.** You can implement Power over Ethernet (PoE) switches, cameras, and phones. PoE transmits 12v DC current over CAT 5 twisted pair cabling to power remote devices. In this scenario, you could use a PoE switch to power each PoE-enabled camera and phone over the Ethernet network.

☒ **A, B,** and **C** are incorrect because Power Line Telecom (PLT), Power Line Digital Subscriber Line (PDSL), and Broadband Over Power Lines (BPL) technologies all transmit network data over standard electrical wiring. Because of the lack of electrical wiring in this scenario, none of these technologies is feasible.

9. What can be used by an Ethernet switch to filter network traffic?
   A. Source IP address
   B. Destination IP address
   C. MAC address
   D. TCP connection state

   ☑ **C.** Because switches are data link layer devices, they can filter only network traffic based on MAC address.

   ☒ **A, B,** and **D** are incorrect. **A** and **B** are functions of the network layer and can be used by packet filtering network firewalls to manage traffic. **D** is incorrect because TCP connection state is a function of the transport layer and can be used by stateful firewalls to manage traffic.

10. Which Cisco technology can be used to extend a VLAN to multiple network switches?
    A. Spanning Tree Protocol
    B. VTP
    C. OSPF
    D. RIP

    ☑ **B.** The VLAN Trunking Protocol (VTP) is a proprietary Cisco protocol that allows you to extend a VLAN to multiple network switches.

    ☒ **A, C,** and **D** are incorrect. **A** is incorrect because the Spanning Tree Protocol is used to prevent switching loops. **C** and **D** are incorrect because OSPF and RIP are routing protocols that operate at the network layer of the OSI model.

11. Which standard allows VLAN tags to be assigned to Ethernet frames, allowing VLAN information to be distributed among multiple network switches?
    A. 802.5
    B. 802.3
    C. 802.1q
    D. 802.14

    ☑ **C.** The IEEE 802.1q standard defines a method for adding VLAN tags to Ethernet frames. By doing this, you can extend a VLAN beyond a single network switch.

☒ **A, B,** and **D** are incorrect. **A** is incorrect because the IEEE 802.5 standard defines the token passing method used by Token Ring networks. **B** is incorrect because the IEEE 802.3 standard defines Ethernet networking. **D** is incorrect because the IEEE 802.14 standard defines how cable modems function.

12. A new employee has been hired by your organization and you are setting up her desktop workstation. You've connected the network interface card in her system to the wall jack, but the link light for the port to which it's connected on your switch does not come on. You recently tested the wiring for this wall jack and know that it is wired correctly. You check the driver status in Device Manager in Windows and it reports that the device is working correctly. What could be wrong? (Choose two possibilities.)

    A. The workstation has the wrong default gateway address assigned.
    B. The workstation has the wrong subnet mask assigned.
    C. The drop cable between the workstation and the wall jack may be a crossover cable.
    D. The drivers for the network interface need to be updated.
    E. The port may be disabled on the switch.

☑ **C** and **E.** Because you know the cabling behind the wall is good and that the network interface is working correctly, the most likely cause of the symptoms in this scenario could be either a bad drop cable or a disabled switch port.

☒ **A, B,** and **D** are incorrect. **A** and **B** are incorrect because incorrect IP addressing parameters would not prevent the link light from coming on. **D** is incorrect because it's unlikely that outdated drivers would prevent the link light from coming on.

13. You've organized the hosts connected to your network switch into two VLANs: one for your design and development group and one for administration and human resources. A new software developer has been hired who needs access to design and development network resources. You've set up her workstation and connected it to your network switch. The link light for the port is lit; however, the developer is unable to see the server shares used by the design and development group on the network. What should you do?

    A. Verify that a crossover drop cable was not used to connect the workstation to the wall jack.
    B. Verify that the port is enabled on the switch to which the workstation is connected.
    C. Check the routing table on the network segment's default gateway router for wrong or missing routes.
    D. Check to see if the workstation has been made a member of the VLAN used by the design and development group.

☑ **D.** The most likely cause of the issue in this scenario is an incorrect VLAN assignment for the workstation and network switch port. The port or workstation needs to be added to the VLAN used by the design and development group.

☒ **A, B,** and **C** are incorrect. **A** is incorrect because a lit link light usually indicates the correct type of drop cable has been used. **B** is incorrect because a lit link light indicates the port is enabled on the switch. **C** could potentially be a cause of the problem in this scenario. However, the symptoms would affect all workstations on the segment, not just one.

14. Upon arrival at work, you are met with chaos as no one in the organization is able to access any network resources on your mixed fiber-optic and copper UTP Gigabit Ethernet network. Users are not able to authenticate to their configured Active Directory domain controllers, and they cannot see any network resources on the network. You've checked and all of your servers are up and running, but none of them can be pinged from workstations. You check the IP configuration on several workstations and see that they are all using IP addresses in the 169.254.1.*x* range with a subnet mask of 255.255.0.0. However, none of the workstations can ping any of the others. What should you do? (Choose the best two.)

    A. Manually assign static IP addresses to all workstations until you can get your DHCP server working correctly.
    B. Verify the network switch has power and is turned on.
    C. Verify your DNS server is up and responding to requests.
    D. Check for bad SFP or GBIC modules.
    E. Check the routing table on the network segment's default gateway router for wrong or missing routes.

☑ **B** and **D.** The two best responses for this scenario are to verify that the network switch has power and is turned on and then to check for bad SFP or GBIC modules. Based on the fact that hosts are auto-assigning themselves addresses and that none of the hosts can ping any others, you know that the switch is malfunctioning in some way. This could be caused by a switch with a bad power supply or bad SFP/GBIC modules used to connect fiber and copper devices together (depending on how the network is wired).

☒ **A, C,** and **E** are incorrect. **A** is incorrect because manually assigning static IP addresses will not resolve a situation in which the network switch has failed. **C** and **E** are incorrect because verifying DNS or routing functionality will not resolve a situation in which the network switch has failed.

15. You are experiencing errors caused by an MTU black hole. TCP connections between hosts on different network segments frequently hang after successfully completing the three-way handshake. What should you do to fix this?
    A. Configure network security devices to allow ICMP messages.
    B. Implement a stateful firewall to monitor the state of TCP connections.
    C. Move all network hosts onto the same network segment.
    D. Implement VLANs to subdivide each network segment.

    ☑ **A.** Many network security devices are configured by default to block ICMP traffic. MTU black holes are caused when routers with a small MTU size configured are unable to send ICMP Fragmentation Needed messages to transmitting hosts telling them to reduce their MTU size. As a result, TCP connections are set up correctly, but then oversized packets are lost when the ICMP notification messages are blocked. Allowing ICMP messages will fix the issue.

    ☒ **B, C, and D** are incorrect. **B** is incorrect because the size of the MTU is causing the issue in this scenario, not the state of the TCP connection. **C** is incorrect because moving all hosts to the same network segment is usually infeasible in all but the smallest of networks. **D** is incorrect because implementing VLANs will not address the issue of oversized MTUs.

16. The workstations on your network are unable to reach a Linux-based file and print server on the same network segment. You've checked and the server has been assigned a static IP address of 172.17.0.1. Your workstations are assigned IP addresses via DHCP in the 172.17.8.100–172.17.8.253 range with a subnet mask of 255.255.0.0. You are unable to ping the server from any workstation, yet the workstations are able to ping each other. What should you do?
    A. Assign the Linux server an IP address of 172.17.8.1.
    B. Verify that the workstations have the correct default gateway router address assigned.
    C. Verify that the network switch has power and is turned on.
    D. Check the subnet mask assigned to the Linux server.

    ☑ **D.** The most likely cause of the issue in the scenario is a misconfigured subnet mask on the server. The fact that the workstations can ping each other indicates that the basic network infrastructure is functioning. A misconfigured subnet mask effectively places the server on a different logical network, requiring a router for the workstations to reach it.

> ☒ **A, B**, and **C** are incorrect. **A** is incorrect because changing the IP address of the server to 172.17.8.1 won't fix the issue. 172.17.0.1 and 172.17.8.*x* are on the same logical network if they use the correct subnet mask of 255.255.0.0. **B** is incorrect because routing isn't an issue if the server and workstations are on the same network segment. **C** is incorrect because workstations on the segment can ping each other, indicating the network switch is functioning correctly.

17. A user has called the help desk indicating that his Windows workstation is displaying a "Duplicate IP address…" error message. You check the workstation and find that it is using DHCP to get its IP addressing information. What should you do to fix this issue?

    A. Reboot the workstation.

    B. Check the network for another host that has been statically assigned the duplicated IP address.

    C. Clear all lease information on your DHCP server.

    D. Restart the DHCP service on your DHCP server.

> ☑ **B.** The most likely cause of the issue in this scenario is a workstation or server that has been statically assigned an IP address that is included in the range of addresses being handed out by your DHCP server. You should track down the offending host and configure it to use DHCP if it is a workstation. If it is a server, reassign it an appropriate static IP address or create an exclusion for the address on your DHCP server. Note that some DHCP services will ping ahead to see if the address they are about to hand out is in use or not, but many services do not do this.
>
> ☒ **A, C**, and **D** are incorrect. **A** is incorrect because the duplicate IP address error will reoccur the next time the DHCP server hands out the duplicated IP address to that (or another) network host. **C** is incorrect because clearing lease information from the DHCP server will not fix the issue. The duplicate IP address error will reoccur the next time the DHCP server hands out the duplicated IP address. **D** is incorrect because restarting the DHCP service will not prevent it from handing out the duplicated IP address.

18. Users are complaining that they can't access the company intranet site. You check and find that you can ping the intranet web server by IP address, but not by its DNS name. What should you do?

    A. Verify that users' workstations have the correct default gateway router address configured.

    B. Verify that users' workstations have the correct DNS resolver address configured.

C. Check your network switches for a switching loop.

D. Verify that the intranet web server doesn't have an incorrect subnet mask assigned.

☑ **B.** The most likely cause of the issue in this scenario is a misconfigured DNS server address on the workstations. This may happen when workstations use a DNS server provided by a service provider that doesn't have records for your internal hosts, instead of your internal DNS server.

☒ **A, C,** and **D** are incorrect because an incorrectly configured gateway address, switching loop, or incorrect subnet mask would prevent the web server from responding to pings by IP address.

7

Subnetting and Routing

QUESTIONS

As a network administrator, you'll likely be responsible for configuring multiple networks to communicate with one another. For example, suppose your organization has multiple buildings in different geographical locations, each with its own network. To support these networks, you may need to divide the IP address range assigned to your organization into multiple subnets.

You will also need to connect these systems using routers, so users on one network can communicate with users and resources on your organization's other networks. A key step in doing this is implementing routing protocols, which enables your routers to make decisions about the best way to get data from one network to another.

1. Your organization's network is composed of four separate physical network segments connected by routers. Your organization uses the 10.0.0.0 private IP addressing scheme. You want to divide the 10.0.0.0 network into four separate networks. What should you do to accomplish this?

   A. Configure the subnet mask to include the first 2 bits of the second octet in the network address to create four subnets.

   B. Configure the subnet mask to include the last 2 bits of the second octet in the network address to create four subnets.

   C. Configure the subnet mask to include the first 3 bits of the second octet in the network address to create four subnets.

   D. Configure the subnet mask to include the last 2 bits of the third octet in the network address to create four subnets.

2. You've decided to use a subnet mask of 255.255.192.0 with your 172.17.0.0 network to create four separate subnets. Which network IDs can be used for these subnets in this configuration? (Choose two.)

   A. 172.17.8.0

   B. 172.17.128.0

   C. 172.17.0.0

   D. 172.17.32.0

   E. 172.17.2.0

3. You've decided to use a subnet mask of 255.255.192.0 with your 172.17.0.0 network to create four separate subnets. Which broadcast addresses can you use for these subnets in this configuration? (Choose two.)

   A. 172.17.191.255

   B. 172.17.8.255

   C. 172.17.32.255

   D. 172.17.63.255

   E. 172.17.2.255

4. Consider the following IP address that uses CIDR notation: 10.0.0.5/12. Which of the following subnet masks corresponds to the CIDR prefix used in this address?

    A. 255.0.0.0

    B. 255.240.0.0

    C. 255.224.0.0

    D. 255.252.0.0

5. You've decided to use a subnet mask of 255.255.192.0 with your 172.17.0.0 network to create four separate subnets. The network ID for one of the subnets is 172.17.0.0. You are installing the first host (a server) on this subnet and want to assign the lowest numbered IP address possible to this system. What should you do?

    A. Assign the system an IP address of 172.17.0.1.

    B. Assign the system an IP address of 172.17.64.1.

    C. Assign the system an IP address of 172.17.128.1.

    D. Assign the system an IP address of 172.17.192.1.

6. You've decided to use a subnet mask of 255.255.192.0 with your 172.17.0.0 network to create four separate subnets. The network ID for one of the subnets is 172.17.128.0. You are installing a DNS/DHCP server on this subnet and want to assign the highest numbered IP address possible to this system. What should you do?

    A. Assign the system an IP address of 172.17.63.254.

    B. Assign the system an IP address of 172.17.255.254.

    C. Assign the system an IP address of 172.17.127.254.

    D. Assign the system an IP address of 172.17.191.254.

7. A workstation on your network has just sent several packets to a host that does not reside on the current network segment. The packets are sent to the default gateway router for the network segment. What happens next?

    A. The packets are dropped.

    B. The packets are translated from private IP addresses used on the internal network to the public IP address configured on the router.

    C. The default gateway router checks its routing table to determine where to send the packets next.

    D. The default gateway router performs a DNS lookup to determine the IP address of the target host.

8. You've just enabled routing on a Cisco router. You need to verify that the appropriate routes exist in the routing table. What should you do?

    A. Restart the router.

    B. Enter **ip routing** at the command prompt of the router.

    C. Enter **ip route add local** at the command prompt of the router.

    D. Enter **show ip route** at the command prompt of the router.

9. Your Windows Server 2008 system functions as a router for a network segment. You need to add a static route in the routing table to the 137.65.0.0 network. This network uses the default subnet mask for its address class. The next hop to reach this network is 137.64.1.254. What should you do?

   A. Enter **route add 137.65.0.0 MASK 255.255.0.0 137.64.1.254** at the command prompt.

   B. Enter **route add 137.65.0.0 MASK 255.0.0.0 137.64.1.254** at the command prompt.

   C. Enter **ip route 137.65.0.0 255.255.0.0 137.64.1.254** at the command prompt.

   D. Enter **route add 137.64.1.254 MASK 255.0.0.0 137.65.0.0** at the command prompt.

10. You need to view the routing table on your Windows Server 2008 system that has been configured as a router. What should you do?

   A. Enter **route add** at the command prompt.

   B. Enter **route print** at the command prompt.

   C. Enter **route table print** at the command prompt.

   D. Enter **route view** at the command prompt.

11. Which dynamic routing protocols are Interior Gateway Protocols (IGPs)? (Choose two.)

   A. Exterior Gateway Protocol 3 (EGP3)

   B. Spanning Tree Protocol (STP)

   C. Border Gateway Protocol (BGP)

   D. Routing Information Protocol (RIP)

   E. Open Shortest Path First (OSPF)

12. In your network, none of your routers has a complete picture of your network topology. Instead, each router advertises its distance value to the other routers in the network to populate each router's routing table automatically. What type of dynamic routing protocol is in use in this network?

   A. Hybrid routing protocol

   B. Link state routing protocol

   C. Distance vector routing protocol

   D. Exterior Gateway Protocol

13. Which Interior Gateway Protocol does not use advertisements to populate each router's routing table?

   A. Routing Information Protocol (RIP)

   B. Open Shortest Path First (OSPF)

   C. Interior Gateway Routing Protocol (IGRP)

   D. Enhanced Interior Gateway Routing Protocol (EIGRP)

14. The Cisco routers in your network use the Routing Information Protocol (RIP) to advertise routing information with one another. You've just finished making several changes to your network topology. From a routing perspective, what should you do next?

    A. Wait while the routers advertise the changes to one another and they all converge.

    B. Manually update all of your routers with the changes using the **ip route** command.

    C. Manually update all of your routers with the changes using the **route add** command.

    D. Reset each router to allow it to detect the new topology on restart.

15. Some routing protocols determine the best route to take based on the bandwidth of network links. Which metric is used by these protocols to determine the bandwidth of a link?

    A. Hop count

    B. MTU

    C. Distance vector

    D. Link state

16. Which routing metric measures how long it takes a packet to travel from one network to another?

    A. Hop count

    B. MTU

    C. Latency

    D. Cost

17. Which routing protocols are examples of Exterior Gateway Protocols that can be used on global public networks such as the Internet? (Choose two.)

    A. Intermediate System–to–Intermediate System (IS-IS)

    B. Exterior Gateway Protocol (EGP)

    C. Interior Gateway Routing Protocol (IGRP)

    D. Border Gateway Protocol (BGP)

    E. Open Shortest Path First (OSPF)

18. Which interior gateway protocol was designed by Cisco to replace IGRP and uses both distance vector as well as link state routing techniques?

    A. Intermediate System–to–Intermediate System (IS-IS)

    B. Open Shortest Path First (OSPF)

    C. Routing Information Protocol (RIP)

    D. Enhanced Interior Gateway Routing Protocol (EIGRP)

19. Which link state interior gateway protocols were designed to support VLSM IP addressing? (Choose two.)

A. Enhanced Interior Gateway Routing Protocol (EIGRP)

B. Routing Information Protocol (RIP)

C. Open Shortest Path First (OSPF)

D. Interior Gateway Routing Protocol (IGRP)

E. Intermediate System–to–Intermediate System (IS-IS)

20. You are configuring a Cisco router and need to enable the RIP routing protocol on the router. What should you do?

A. Enter **/etc/init.d/routed start** at the command prompt of the router.

B. Enter **enable rip** at the command prompt of the router.

C. Enter **router rip** at the command prompt of the router.

D. Enter **router rip enable** at the command prompt of the router.

QUICK ANSWER KEY

1.	A	8.	D	15.	B
2.	B, C	9.	A	16.	C
3.	A, D	10.	B	17.	B, D
4.	B	11.	D, E	18.	D
5.	A	12.	C	19.	C, E
6.	D	13.	B	20.	C
7.	C	14.	A		

IN-DEPTH ANSWERS

1. Your organization's network is composed of four separate physical network segments connected by routers. Your organization uses the 10.0.0.0 private IP addressing scheme. You want to divide the 10.0.0.0 network into four separate networks. What should you do to accomplish this?
    A. Configure the subnet mask to include the first 2 bits of the second octet in the network address to create four subnets.
    B. Configure the subnet mask to include the last 2 bits of the second octet in the network address to create four subnets.
    C. Configure the subnet mask to include the first 3 bits of the second octet in the network address to create four subnets.
    D. Configure the subnet mask to include the last 2 bits of the third octet in the network address to create four subnets.

    ☑ **A.** This network uses a Class A address (10.0.0.0). This means the first octet is used for the network address and the last three octets are used for node addresses. To create four additional networks, you can configure the subnet mask to include the first 2 bits of the second octet in the network address to create additional networks. Instead of using the default Class A subnet mask of 11111111.00000000.00000000.00000000 (255.0.0.0), you would use a subnet mask of 11111111.11000000.00000000.00000000 (255.192.0.0).

    ☒ **B, C,** and **D** are incorrect. **B** is incorrect because using the last 2 bits of the second octet would produce an invalid subnet mask of 11111111.00000011.00000000.00000000. **C** would actually work, because using the first 3 bits of the second octet would produce a subnet mask of 11111111.11100000.00000000.00000000. However, this mask creates eight possible subnets instead of the required four. **D** is incorrect because using the last 2 bits of the third octet would produce an invalid subnet mask of 11111111.00000000.00000011.00000000.

2. You've decided to use a subnet mask of 255.255.192.0 with your 172.17.0.0 network to create four separate subnets. Which network IDs can be used for these subnets in this configuration? (Choose two.)
    A. 172.17.8.0
    B. 172.17.128.0
    C. 172.17.0.0
    D. 172.17.32.0
    E. 172.17.2.0

☑ **B and C.** The subnet mask used for this network is 11111111.11111111.11000000.000000. Because the first 2 bits of the third octet are reallocated to the network portion of the address, four subnets are possible: 172.17.0.0 (00), 172.17.64.0 (01), 172.17.128.0 (10), and 172.17.192.0 (11).

☒ **A, D, and E are incorrect.** A is incorrect because a subnet network ID of 172.17.8.0 would require the first 5 bits of the third octet to be used for the network address. This would require a subnet mask of 255.255.248.0. **D** is incorrect because a subnet network ID of 172.17.32.0 would require the first 3 bits of the third octet to be used for the network address. This would require a subnet mask of 255.255.224.0. **E** is incorrect because a subnet network ID of 172.17.2.0 would require the first 7 bits of the third octet to be used for the network address. This would require a subnet mask of 255.255.254.0.

3. You've decided to use a subnet mask of 255.255.192.0 with your 172.17.0.0 network to create four separate subnets. Which broadcast addresses can you use for these subnets in this configuration? (Choose two.)
   A. 172.17.191.255
   B. 172.17.8.255
   C. 172.17.32.255
   D. 172.17.63.255
   E. 172.17.2.255

☑ **A and D.** The subnet mask used for this network is 11111111.11111111.11000000 .000000. Because the first 2 bits of the third octet are reallocated to the network portion of the address, four subnets are possible: 172.17.0.0 (00), 172.17.64.0 (01), 172.17.128.0 (10), and 172.17.192.0 (11). To calculate the corresponding broadcast addresses for these subnets, you must set the value of each bit in the host portion of the address to a value of 1. The resulting broadcast addresses are 172.17.63.255, 172.17.127.255, 172.17.191.255, and 172.17.255.255.

☒ **B, C, and E are incorrect.** B is incorrect because the address 172.17.8.255 has only 1 bit set to a value of 1 in the third octet (00001000). **C** is incorrect because the address 172.17.32.255 also has only 1 bit set to a value of 1 in the third octet (00010000). **E** is also incorrect because the address 172.17.2.255 has only 1 bit set to a value of 1 in the third octet (00000010).

4. Consider the following IP address that uses CIDR notation: 10.0.0.5/12. Which of the following subnet masks corresponds to the CIDR prefix used in this address?

   A. 255.0.0.0
   B. 255.240.0.0
   C. 255.224.0.0
   D. 255.252.0.0

   ☑ **B.** A CIDR IP address of 10.0.0.5/12 specifies a 12-bit prefix length. The subnet mask for this address is therefore 12-bits long (11111111.11110000.00000000.00000000). In decimal notation, this would be a subnet mask of 255.240.0.0.

   ☒ **A, C,** and **D** are incorrect. **A** is incorrect because it specifies an 8-bit subnet mask. **C** is incorrect because it specifies an 11-bit subnet mask. **D** is incorrect because it specifies a 14-bit subnet mask.

5. You've decided to use a subnet mask of 255.255.192.0 with your 172.17.0.0 network to create four separate subnets. The network ID for one of the subnets is 172.17.0.0. You are installing the first host (a server) on this subnet and want to assign the lowest numbered IP address possible to this system. What should you do?

   A. Assign the system an IP address of 172.17.0.1.
   B. Assign the system an IP address of 172.17.64.1.
   C. Assign the system an IP address of 172.17.128.1.
   D. Assign the system an IP address of 172.17.192.1.

   ☑ **A.** Using a subnet mask of 255.255.192.0 on the 172.17.0.0 network creates four subnets: 172.17.0.0, 172.17.64.0, 172.17.128.0, and 172.17.192.0. The first available IP address on the 172.17.0.0 subnet is 172.17.0.1.

   ☒ **B, C,** and **D** are incorrect. **B** is incorrect because 172.17.64.1 is the first available IP address on the 172.17.64.0 subnet. **C** is incorrect because 172.17.128.1 is the first available IP address on the 172.17.128.0 subnet. **D** is incorrect because 172.17.192.1 is the first available IP address on the 172.17.192.0 subnet.

6. You've decided to use a subnet mask of 255.255.192.0 with your 172.17.0.0 network to create four separate subnets. The network ID for one of the subnets is 172.17.128.0. You are installing a DNS/DHCP server on this subnet and want to assign the highest numbered IP address possible to this system. What should you do?

   A. Assign the system an IP address of 172.17.63.254.
   B. Assign the system an IP address of 172.17.255.254.

C. Assign the system an IP address of 172.17.127.254.

D. Assign the system an IP address of 172.17.191.254.

> ☑ **D.** Using a subnet mask of 255.255.192.0 on the 172.17.0.0 network creates four subnets: 172.17.0.0, 172.17.64.0, 172.17.128.0, and 172.17.192.0. The last available IP address on the 172.17.128.0 subnet is 172.17.191.254.
>
> ☒ **A, B,** and **C** are incorrect. **A** is incorrect because 172.17.63.254 is the last valid IP address on the 172.17.0.0 subnet. **B** is incorrect because 172.17.255.254 is the last valid IP address on the 172.17.192.0 subnet. **C** is incorrect because 172.17.127.254 is the last valid IP address on the 172.17.64.0 subnet.

7. A workstation on your network has just sent several packets to a host that does not reside on the current network segment. The packets are sent to the default gateway router for the network segment. What happens next?

A. The packets are dropped.

B. The packets are translated from private IP addresses used on the internal network to the public IP address configured on the router.

C. The default gateway router checks its routing table to determine where to send the packets next.

D. The default gateway router performs a DNS lookup to determine the IP address of the target host.

> ☑ **C.** Because the packets are being sent to a host that does not reside on the current network segment, they are automatically forwarded to the default gateway router configured on the segment. The default gateway router checks its routing table to determine where to send the packets next.
>
> ☒ **A, B,** and **D** are incorrect. **A** is correct only if the destination is not in the routing table on the default gateway router and the default gateway router itself does not have a default route. **B** is incorrect because this process occurs only if the router is also configured as a Network Address Translation (NAT) router. **D** is incorrect because the source system sending the packets performs a DNS lookup to determine the IP address of the target host.

8. You've just enabled routing on a Cisco router. You need to verify that the appropriate routes exist in the routing table. What should you do?

A. Restart the router.

B. Enter **ip routing** at the command prompt of the router.

C. Enter **ip route add local** at the command prompt of the router.

D. Enter **show ip route** at the command prompt of the router.

☑ **D.** Entering **show ip route** at the command prompt of the router will cause the router to display its routing table. A route should have been automatically added for each of the networks to which it is connected.

☒ **A, B,** and **C** are incorrect. **A** is incorrect because restarting the router will not display the routing table. **B** is incorrect because the **ip routing** command is used to enable routing; it doesn't display the routing table. **C** is incorrect because the **ip route add local** command is not a valid command on a Cisco router.

9. Your Windows Server 2008 system functions as a router for a network segment. You need to add a static route in the routing table to the 137.65.0.0 network. This network uses the default subnet mask for its address class. The next hop to reach this network is 137.64.1.254. What should you do?

A. Enter **route add 137.65.0.0 MASK 255.255.0.0 137.64.1.254** at the command prompt.

B. Enter **route add 137.65.0.0 MASK 255.0.0.0 137.64.1.254** at the command prompt.

C. Enter **ip route 137.65.0.0 255.255.0.0 137.64.1.254** at the command prompt.

D. Enter **route add 137.64.1.254 MASK 255.0.0.0 137.65.0.0** at the command prompt.

☑ **A.** Entering **route add 137.65.0.0 MASK 255.255.0.0 137.64.1.254** at the command prompt of the Windows server functioning as a router will add a route to the 137.65.0.0 network through the router with an IP address of 137.64.1.254. This router will then know where to send packets destined for a host on the 137.65.0.0 network.

☒ **B, C,** and **D** are incorrect. **B** is incorrect because the command uses an incorrect subnet mask for the 137.65.0.0 network. **C** is the correct command for adding the route to a Cisco router, but not to a Windows-based router. **D** is incorrect because it reverses the destination network and the next hop router.

10. You need to view the routing table on your Windows Server 2008 system that has been configured as a router. What should you do?

A. Enter **route add** at the command prompt.

B. Enter **route print** at the command prompt.

C. Enter **route table print** at the command prompt.

D. Enter **route view** at the command prompt.

☑ **B.** Entering **route print** at the command prompt of a Windows server will display the system's routing table.

☒ **A, C,** and **D** are incorrect. **A** is incorrect because entering the **route add** command is used to add a route to a destination network. **C** is incorrect because the **route table print** command is invalid. **D** is incorrect because the **route view** command is invalid.

11. Which dynamic routing protocols are Interior Gateway Protocols (IGPs)? (Choose two.)
A. Exterior Gateway Protocol 3 (EGP3)
B. Spanning Tree Protocol (STP)
C. Border Gateway Protocol (BGP)
D. Routing Information Protocol (RIP)
E. Open Shortest Path First (OSPF)

☑ **D and E.** The Routing Information Protocol (RIP) and the Open Shortest Path First (OSPF) protocols are examples of Interior Gateway Protocols. IGPs are used to exchange routing information within an autonomous system.

☒ **A, B,** and **C** are incorrect. **A** and **C** are incorrect because the EGP3 and BGP protocols are examples of Exterior Gateway Protocols (EGP). **B** is incorrect because the Spanning Tree Protocol is a switching protocol used to prevent switching loops.

12. In your network, none of your routers has a complete picture of your network topology. Instead, each router advertises its distance value to the other routers in the network to populate each router's routing table automatically. What type of dynamic routing protocol is in use in this network?
A. Hybrid routing protocol
B. Link state routing protocol
C. Distance vector routing protocol
D. Exterior Gateway Protocol

☑ **C.** Because none of the routers has a complete picture of the network topology, and each router advertises its distance value to the other routers in the network to populate each router's routing table, this network uses a distance vector routing protocol. The Routing Information Protocol (RIP) is an example of a distance vector routing protocol.

☒ **A, B,** and **D** are incorrect. **A** is incorrect because hybrid routing protocols include features of both distance vector and link state protocols. **B** is incorrect because link state routing protocols do not use advertisements to populate routing tables. **D** is incorrect because distance vector routing protocols are types of Interior Gateway Protocols, not Exterior Gateway Protocols.

13. Which Interior Gateway Protocol does not use advertisements to populate each router's routing table?
    A. Routing Information Protocol (RIP)
    B. Open Shortest Path First (OSPF)
    C. Interior Gateway Routing Protocol (IGRP)
    D. Enhanced Interior Gateway Routing Protocol (EIGRP)

    ☑ **B.** The Open Shortest Path First (OSPF) protocol is a link state routing protocol. This category of Interior Gateway Protocol requires each router in the network to have a complete picture of the entire network topology. Instead of using advertisements to share routing information, OSPF allows routers to use their information about the network topology to calculate independently the best route to every destination network.

    ☒ **A, C,** and **D** are incorrect. **A** and **C** are incorrect because RIP and IGRP are distance vector routing protocols, which use advertisements to share routing information. **D** is incorrect because EIGRP is a hybrid routing protocol, which uses features of both distance vector and link state routing protocols.

14. The Cisco routers in your network use the Routing Information Protocol (RIP) to advertise routing information with one another. You've just finished making several changes to your network topology. From a routing perspective, what should you do next?
    A. Wait while the routers advertise the changes to one another and they all converge.
    B. Manually update all of your routers with the changes using the **ip route** command.
    C. Manually update all of your routers with the changes using the **route add** command.
    D. Reset each router to allow it to detect the new topology on restart.

    ☑ **A.** RIP is a distance vector protocol. As such, each router uses advertisements to share its routing table with its neighboring routers. This process continues until all of the routers have a complete picture of the network topology, which is called convergence.

    ☒ **B, C,** and **D** are incorrect. **B** and **C** are incorrect because RIP uses network advertisements to share routing information. **D** is incorrect because it is not necessary to reboot the routers to allow RIP to update routing information among the network routers.

15. Some routing protocols determine the best route to take based on the bandwidth of network links. Which metric is used by these protocols to determine the bandwidth of a link?
    A. Hop count
    B. MTU

C. Distance vector

D. Link state

☑ **B.** The maximum transmission unit (MTU) metric measures the bandwidth of the link. Using this metric, the routing protocol will give preference to high-bandwidth routes over low-bandwidth routes.

☒ **A, C,** and **D** are incorrect. **A** is incorrect because the hop count metric measures how many routers a packet must traverse to reach its destination. Some routing protocols use this metric instead of the MTU to determine the best route to take. **C** and **D** are incorrect because the terms "distance vector" and "link state" are used to categorize different types of routing protocols. They are not routing metrics.

16. Which routing metric measures how long it takes a packet to travel from one network to another?

A. Hop count

B. MTU

C. Latency

D. Cost

☑ **C.** Latency is used to measure how long it takes for a packet to travel from one network to another. Using this metric, some routing protocols choose routes with the least latency.

☒ **A, B,** and **D** are incorrect. **A** is incorrect because the hop count metric measures how many routers a packet must traverse to reach its destination. **B** is incorrect because the maximum transmission unit (MTU) metric measures the bandwidth of the link. **D** is incorrect because the cost metric measures the cost associated with each route.

17. Which routing protocols are examples of Exterior Gateway Protocols that can be used on global public networks such as the Internet? (Choose two.)

A. Intermediate System–to–Intermediate System (IS-IS)

B. Exterior Gateway Protocol (EGP)

C. Interior Gateway Routing Protocol (IGRP)

D. Border Gateway Protocol (BGP)

E. Open Shortest Path First (OSPF)

☑ **B** and **D.** The Exterior Gateway Protocol (EGP) and the Border Gateway Protocol (BGP) are examples of Exterior Gateway Protocols. EGP is a routing protocol that was used in the early days of the Internet, but has been largely replaced by BGP since the early 1990s. BGP does not use traditional IGP metrics (such as hop count, MTU, or latency). Instead, it uses network path information along with network rules to determine the best route to use.

☒ **A, C,** and **E** are incorrect. **A** is incorrect because the Intermediate System–to–Intermediate System (IS-IS) protocol is an example of a link state interior gateway protocol. **C** is incorrect because the Interior Gateway Routing Protocol (IGRP) is an example of a distance vector interior gateway protocol. **E** is incorrect because the Open Shortest Path First (OSPF) protocol is an example of a link state interior gateway protocol.

18. Which interior gateway protocol was designed by Cisco to replace IGRP and uses both distance vector as well as link state routing techniques?
   A. Intermediate System–to–Intermediate System (IS-IS)
   B. Open Shortest Path First (OSPF)
   C. Routing Information Protocol (RIP)
   D. Enhanced Interior Gateway Routing Protocol (EIGRP)

☑ **D.** The Enhanced Interior Gateway Routing Protocol (EIGRP) is an interior gateway protocol designed by Cisco to replace IGRP. EIGRP uses primarily distance-vector techniques to make routing decisions, including metrics such as latency and hop count. However, EIGRP is sometimes referred to as a *hybrid* routing protocol because it also includes some link state routing techniques, such as the use of HELLO packets to discover routers.

☒ **A, B,** and **C** are incorrect. **A** and **B** are incorrect because IS-IS and OSPF are link state routing protocols that are not descended from IGRP. **C** is incorrect because RIP is a distance vector routing protocol that is also not descended from IGRP.

19. Which link state interior gateway protocols were designed to support VLSM IP addressing? (Choose two.)
   A. Enhanced Interior Gateway Routing Protocol (EIGRP)
   B. Routing Information Protocol (RIP)
   C. Open Shortest Path First (OSPF)
   D. Interior Gateway Routing Protocol (IGRP)
   E. Intermediate System–to–Intermediate System (IS-IS)

☑ **C** and **E.** Both OSPF and IS-IS are link state interior gateway protocols that support VLSM IP addressing. The conceptual functioning of both protocols is very similar. However, of the two, OSPF is probably the most widely used link state interior gateway routing protocol.

☒ **A, B,** and **D** are incorrect. **A** is partially correct from the standpoint that EIGRP supports VLSM IP addressing and does use some link state routing functionality. However, EIGRP is a hybrid routing protocol that primarily relies on distance vector techniques to make routing decisions. **B** and **D** are incorrect because RIP and IGRP are both distance vector routing protocols. RIPv2 does support VLSM IP addressing, but IGRP does not.

20. You are configuring a Cisco router and need to enable the RIP routing protocol on the router. What should you do?

A. Enter **/etc/init.d/routed start** at the command prompt of the router.

B. Enter **enable rip** at the command prompt of the router.

C. Enter **router rip** at the command prompt of the router.

D. Enter **router rip enable** at the command prompt of the router.

☑ **C.** You can use the **router rip** command to enable the RIP routing protocol on a Cisco router. Once done, it will begin sharing its routing table with other routers on the network using the RIP protocol. The other routers, in turn, will share their routing tables with the router until all the routers have the same routing information and a steady state called *convergence* is reached.

☒ **A, B,** and **D** are incorrect. **A** is used to enable RIP routing on some Linux distributions. **B** and **D** are invalid commands for a Cisco router.

8

Configuring
Network Services

QUESTIONS

As a network administrator, one of your key job roles is to configure and maintain the infrastructure that makes the network function. You must be familiar with three key infrastructure components:

- **Domain Name System (DNS)**   DNS maps easy-to-remember domain names (such as www .mycorp.com) to numeric IP addresses.
- **Dynamic Host Configuration Protocol (DHCP)**   DHCP allows you to assign IP addressing information dynamically to network hosts.
- **Network Address Translation (NAT)**   NAT allows a large number of network hosts to use a limited number of registered public IP addresses.

In this chapter, you test your knowledge of DNS, DHCP, and NAT by answering questions about each of these technologies.

1. A print server in your network has gone down and you've migrated the service to a different server. Your want to allow clients to continue sending Internet Printing Protocol (IPP) print jobs without reconfiguration. To do this, you need to modify the IP address assigned to the A record for printers.mycorp.com and point it to the new server. Because your DNS servers are Linux systems running BIND, you've decided to open the zone configuration file in a text editor on the secondary DNS server and make the change. Will this strategy work?
   A. Yes, the DNS record change will take effect and users will be able to send print jobs to the new print server.
   B. No, the change should be made on the primary DNS server for the zone.
   C. No, you must create an alias (CNAME) record that points to the existing record for the new print server.
   D. No, you must leave the DNS servers as they are and manually reconfigure each client system to point to the new print server.

2. Which type of DNS record is used to resolve IP addresses for a mail server?
   A. A record
   B. CNAME record
   C. NS record
   D. MX record

3. Which type of DNS record resolves an IP address into a hostname instead of a hostname into an IP address?
   A. PTR record
   B. SOA record
   C. MX record
   D. AAAA record

4. Which type of DNS zone contains PTR records?

   A. Forward-lookup zone

   B. Reverse-lookup zone

   C. Stub zone

   D. Primary zone

5. You are using your web browser to access the http://www.mycorp.com URL. Because your workstation has never accessed this URL before, it sends a request to resolve www.mycorp.com to your organization's DNS server (ns.yourcorp.com). What happens next?

   A. Your name server looks up the www.mycorp.com domain name in the yourcorp.com zone and returns the IP address to your workstation.

   B. Your name server forwards the request to the server that is authoritative for the mycorp.com zone and asks it to resolve www.mycorp.com into an IP address.

   C. Your name server forwards the request to a root-level DNS server.

   D. Your name server forwards the request to a server that is authoritative for the .com zone.

6. You've installed a web application in your network that sales and customer service employees will use to view current trends in commodity pricing. To prevent spoofing, the application performs a reverse lookup of workstation hostnames on your DNS server when your users access it. Given that the workstations in your network are configured to use DHCP to get IP addressing information, what should you do? (Choose two.)

   A. Configure your DNS server to allow dynamic updates.

   B. Configure your DHCP server to deliver DNS server information as a DHCP option to workstations in your network.

   C. Configure your workstations to use static IP addresses.

   D. Manually add an A record to your DNS server for each workstation on your network.

   E. Configure your DHCP server to update your DNS server with hostname and IP address information each time it establishes or releases a DHCP lease.

7. Zone information for the yourcorp.com domain is stored in a primary zone on the fs1.yourcorp .com server, which is located in your organization's Phoenix office. Your organization uses a T1 line to link the Phoenix with the Albuquerque office, but it is heavily utilized by VPN traffic between the two sites. As a result, name resolution requests for the Albuquerque office can be very slow during high-traffic times. What should you do?

   A. Install a secondary DNS server for the yourcorp.com zone in the Albuquerque office.

   B. Install a primary DNS server for the yourcorp.com zone in the Albuquerque office.

   C. Install a DNS server in the Albuquerque office and configure it with an in-addr.arpa zone for the yourcorp.com zone.

   D. Install a primary DNS server in the Albuquerque office and create a new zone called albuquerque.yourcorp.com on it containing host records in the Albuquerque office.

8. Consider the following record from a zone file on a DNS server:

```
yourcorp.com.      IN      NS      ns1.yourcorp.com.
```

What does this record do?

A. It contains the start of authority information for the zone.

B. It contains the mail exchanger record for the yourcorp.com zone.

C. It points to the name server used by the yourcorp.com zone.

D. It contains an alias for the ns1.yourcorp.com host.

9. What information is contained within an SOA record in a primary DNS server zone? (Choose two.)

A. IP addresses of secondary DNS servers

B. Serial number

C. Refresh time

D. Reverse-lookup domain names

E. Associated Active Directory domain controller IP addresses

10. Consider the following records from a DNS zone file:

```
printers.yourcorp.com.      CNAME      fs2.yourzone.com.
fs2.yourzone.com.           A             10.0.0.3
```

What do these records do? (Choose two.)

A. Create a host record that resolves fs2.yourzone.com to an IP address of 10.0.0.3.

B. Create an alias that points printers.yourcorp.com to the fs2.yourzone.com host record.

C. Create an in-addr.arpa record that resolves the IP address of 10.0.0.3 to a hostname of fs2.yourzone.com.

D. Create an alias that points fs2.yourzone.com to the printers.yourcorp.com host record.

E. Create a host record that resolves printers.yourcorp.com to an IP address of 10.0.0.3.

11. Your workstation is configured to use DHCP to get its IP addressing information. When you boot the system and the operating system loads, it sends out a DHCPDISCOVER broadcast on the network. What happens next?

A. The DHCP server receives the message and responds with an IP address assignment.

B. The DHCP server receives the message and responds with a DHCPOFFER to the workstation.

C. The workstation sends a DHCPREQUEST message on the network.

D. The DHCP server sends a DHCPACK message with IP address configuration information.

12. Which mechanism can be used by DHCP servers to deliver configuration information, such as the default gateway router address and DNS server addresses, to DHCP client systems?

A. DHCP scope

B. DHCP subnet address range

    C. DHCP option

    D. DHCP address exclusion

13. What is always contained in a DHCPOFFER message? (Choose two.)

    A. The DHCP client's MAC address

    B. The DHCP server's MAC address

    C. DHCP lease information

    D. An option for the default gateway address

    E. An option for the DNS server address

14. Your organization's network is composed of four segments (A, B, C, and D) connected by routers. Your DHCP server is on segment A, while your DNS server is on segment B. Workstations are connected to all segments; however, you've discovered that only the workstations on segment A are able to get IP addresses from the DHCP server. What should you do?

    A. Configure DHCP relay agents on segments B, C, and D.

    B. Configure your routers to forward broadcasts.

    C. Configure your DHCP server with an option that distributes the appropriate gateway router address.

    D. Configure the workstations on segments B, C, and D with static IP addresses.

15. Many users have called to complain that they can't log into the network server, nor can they access the Internet. However, the symptoms seem to be affecting only some workstations on the network. Upon inspection, you find that the affected hosts are being assigned IP addresses in the 10.0.0.*x* range, but they should be using the 172.17.*x*.*x* address range. Given that your network uses DHCP for IP address assignments, what should you do?

    A. Configure a DHCP relay agent to forward DHCPDISCOVER messages to your DHCP server.

    B. Reboot your DHCP server, and then reboot all affected workstations.

    C. Check network connectivity, because the affected workstations are using Automatic Private IP Addressing (APIPA).

    D. Check the network for a rogue DHCP server.

16. You are implementing a home network using a DSL connection for Internet access. Your service provider gave you only a single registered IP address for the connection. However, you want to connect several home computers, your DVD player, and your IP phone to the Internet through this connection. What should you do?

    A. Restrict Internet access to a single host on your network.

    B. Switch to a cable TV provider for Internet access.

    C. Implement internal private IP addressing with a Network Address Translation (NAT) router facing the Internet.

    D. Purchase additional registered addresses from the service provider for each device.

17. A network segment has two web servers connected to it, but no workstations. The segment is connected to the network backbone by a NAT router. The web servers use private IP addresses, while the network backbone uses routable public IP addresses. You want users to be able to come in from the backbone side of the NAT router and access content on the web servers on the private network. What should you do?

A. Configure static NAT on the NAT router.

B. Configure NAT overload on the NAT router.

C. Configure dynamic NAT on the NAT router.

D. Configure many-to-one NAT on the NAT router.

18. A private network uses a dynamic NAT router to connect to the Internet. A workstation on the private network behind the NAT router sends a packet to the Internet, and the NAT router replaces the private IP address of the sender in the source field of the packet header with the NAT router's public IP address. What happens next?

A. The NAT router adds an entry to its translation table listing the packet's private IP address, source port, and translated port.

B. The destination host receives the translated packet and establishes a connection to the port and IP address contained in the translated packet's header.

C. The destination host sends a message to the NAT router requesting the private IP address and source port of the sender.

D. PAT assigns the connection a port number from a pool of available ports, inserting this port number in the source port field.

QUICK ANSWER KEY

1.	B	7.	A	13.	A, C
2.	D	8.	C	14.	A
3.	A	9.	B, C	15.	D
4.	B	10.	A, B	16.	C
5.	C	11.	B	17.	A
6.	A, E	12.	C	18.	D

IN-DEPTH ANSWERS

I. A print server in your network has gone down and you've migrated the service to a different server. Your want to allow clients to continue sending Internet Printing Protocol (IPP) print jobs without reconfiguration. To do this, you need to modify the IP address assigned to the A record for printers.mycorp.com and point it to the new server. Because your DNS servers are Linux systems running BIND, you've decided to open the zone configuration file in a text editor on the secondary DNS server and make the change. Will this strategy work?

    A. Yes, the DNS record change will take effect and users will be able to send print jobs to the new print server.

    B. No, the change should be made on the primary DNS server for the zone.

    C. No, you must create an alias (CNAME) record that points to the existing record for the new print server.

    D. No, you must leave the DNS servers as they are and manually reconfigure each client system to point to the new print server.

    ☑ **B.** The change should be made on the primary server for the DNS zone, not the secondary. After making the change to the primary server, it will be automatically synchronized to all secondary DNS servers. If you make the change to the secondary DNS server, the change will be overwritten with old information from the primary DNS server the next time it syncs with the secondary.

    ☒ **A, C,** and **D** are incorrect. **A** is incorrect because the change should be made on the primary server for the DNS zone, not on the secondary. **C** is incorrect because using a CNAME record will require you to reconfigure every client system manually with the new hostname where print jobs should be sent. **D** will work but could represent a significant amount of work, especially if the network is large. Simply editing the existing A record will allow all clients to send print jobs to the new print server without making any client configuration changes.

2. Which type of DNS record is used to resolve IP addresses for a mail server?

    A. A record

    B. CNAME record

    C. NS record

    D. MX record

☑ **D.** Mail exchanger (MX) records are used to resolve IP addresses for an e-mail server.

☒ **A, B,** and **C** are incorrect. **A** is incorrect because A records are used to resolve standard hostnames into IPv4 addresses. **B** is incorrect because CNAME records create aliases that point to existing records in the DNS zone. **C** is incorrect because NS records point to the host records for the hosts that are DNS servers for the zone.

3. Which type of DNS record resolves an IP address into a hostname instead of a hostname into an IP address?

   A. PTR record

   B. SOA record

   C. MX record

   D. AAAA record

☑ **A.** PTR records are used in the opposite fashion of A records. Instead of resolving a hostname into an IP address, a PTR record resolves an IP address into its corresponding hostname.

☒ **B, C,** and **D** are incorrect. **B** is incorrect because SOA records contain configuration information for the DNS zone itself. **C** is incorrect because MX records are used to resolve e-mail domain names into hostnames. **D** is incorrect because AAAA records are used to resolve hostnames into IPv6 addresses.

4. Which type of DNS zone contains PTR records?

   A. Forward-lookup zone

   B. Reverse-lookup zone

   C. Stub zone

   D. Primary zone

☑ **B.** Reverse-lookup zones contain PTR records, which are used to resolve IP addresses into hostnames in the zone. A reverse-lookup zone is tied to a standard forward lookup zone. They are named using the reverse network IP address used by the zone. For example, if the network address of the zone is 192.168.1.0, the name of the reverse-lookup zone would be 1.168.192.in-addr.arpa.

☒   **A, C,** and **D** are incorrect. **A** is incorrect because forward-lookup zones do not contain PTR records. **C** is incorrect because stub zones are a special type of DNS zone used by Windows servers that contain only records for other DNS servers. **D** is incorrect because a primary zone can be a forward- or reverse-lookup zone.

5.   You are using your web browser to access the http://www.mycorp.com URL. Because your workstation has never accessed this URL before, it sends a request to resolve www.mycorp.com to your organization's DNS server (ns.yourcorp.com). What happens next?

A.   Your name server looks up the www.mycorp.com domain name in the yourcorp.com zone and returns the IP address to your workstation.

B.   Your name server forwards the request to the server that is authoritative for the mycorp.com zone and asks it to resolve www.mycorp.com into an IP address.

C.   Your name server forwards the request to a root-level DNS server.

D.   Your name server forwards the request to a server that is authoritative for the .com zone.

☑   **C.** Because your name server is not authoritative for the mycorp.com zone, it doesn't have a record for www.mycorp.com. It also doesn't know which DNS server is authoritative for this zone, so it forwards the request to a root-level name server on the Internet.

☒   **A, B,** and **D** are incorrect. **A** is incorrect because the ns.yourcorp.com name server is not authoritative for the mycorp.com zone where the www record requested resides. **B** is incorrect because your name server doesn't know what server is authoritative for the mycorp.com zone yet. It relies on the root-level name server to lead it to the appropriate name server for mycorp.com. **D** is incorrect because a root-level name server hasn't told your name server which server is authoritative for .com yet.

6.   You've installed a web application in your network that sales and customer service employees will use to view current trends in commodity pricing. To prevent spoofing, the application performs a reverse lookup of workstation hostnames on your DNS server when your users access it. Given that the workstations in your network are configured to use DHCP to get IP addressing information, what should you do? (Choose two.)

A.   Configure your DNS server to allow dynamic updates.

B.   Configure your DHCP server to deliver DNS server information as a DHCP option to workstations in your network.

C.   Configure your workstations to use static IP addresses.

D.   Manually add an A record to your DNS server for each workstation on your network.

E.   Configure your DHCP server to update your DNS server with hostname and IP address information each time it establishes or releases a DHCP lease.

☑ **A** and **E**. You can use Dynamic DNS (DDNS) to address this issue. To do this, you must first configure your DNS server to accept dynamic updates. Then you must configure your DHCP server to update the DNS server with hostname and IP address information each time it establishes or releases a DHCP lease. By doing this, your DNS server will be automatically populated with host records for each of your users' workstations.

☒ **B, C**, and **D** are incorrect. **B** is incorrect because delivering name resolver information will not rectify the issue in this scenario. In fact, it's likely that your DHCP server is already configured to deliver your organization's DNS server addresses as DHCP options whenever a DHCP lease is established. **C** and **D** will address the issue in this scenario, but the amount of administrative overhead these solutions would add to your network makes them unfeasible on all but the smallest of networks.

7. Zone information for the yourcorp.com domain is stored in a primary zone on the fs1.yourcorp .com server, which is located in your organization's Phoenix office. Your organization uses a T1 line to link the Phoenix with the Albuquerque office, but it is heavily utilized by VPN traffic between the two sites. As a result, name resolution requests for the Albuquerque office can be very slow during high-traffic times. What should you do?
   A. Install a secondary DNS server for the yourcorp.com zone in the Albuquerque office.
   B. Install a primary DNS server for the yourcorp.com zone in the Albuquerque office.
   C. Install a DNS server in the Albuquerque office and configure it with an in-addr.arpa zone for the yourcorp.com zone.
   D. Install a primary DNS server in the Albuquerque office and create a new zone called albuquerque.yourcorp.com on it containing host records in the Albuquerque office.

☑ **A**. An efficient way to address the issue in this scenario is to install a secondary DNS server for the yourcorp.com zone in the Albuquerque office. All changes made to the primary zone in Phoenix will be automatically replicated to the secondary server in Albuquerque. However, after configuring clients in the Albuquerque office to use the local DNS server, name resolution requests will no longer need to cross the busy WAN connection.

☒ **B, C**, and **D** are incorrect. **B** is incorrect because configuring a second primary DNS server in the Albuquerque office would require you to update it manually each time a change is made to the DNS server in the Phoenix office. **C** is incorrect because an in-addr.arpa zone is a reverse-lookup zone, which won't address the issue in this scenario. **D** is incorrect because, judging by the traffic on the WAN link, users in both offices frequently need access to resources at both sites.

8. Consider the following record from a zone file on a DNS server:

```
yourcorp.com.        IN      NS      ns1.yourcorp.com.
```

What does this record do?

A. It contains the start of authority information for the zone.

B. It contains the mail exchanger record for the yourcorp.com zone.

C. It points to the name server used by the yourcorp.com zone.

D. It contains an alias for the ns1.yourcorp.com host.

☑ **C.** The record shown in this example is an NS record. It is used to specify the name server for the yourcorp.com zone.

☒ **A, B,** and **D** are incorrect. **A** is incorrect because an SOA record contains zone configuration information. **B** is incorrect because MX records are used to point to e-mail servers. **D** is incorrect because an alias is configured by a CNAME record.

9. What information is contained within an SOA record in a primary DNS server zone? (Choose two.)

A. IP addresses of secondary DNS servers

B. Serial number

C. Refresh time

D. Reverse-lookup domain names

E. Associated Active Directory domain controller IP addresses

☑ **B** and **C.** An SOA record contains, among other things, the zone's serial number and refresh time parameter. The serial number is really a revision number for the zone file. The serial number is incremented each time the zone file is modified. Whenever the serial number for a primary zone is incremented, it tells any secondary servers for the zone that they need to update themselves with the new zone information. The refresh time specifies how many seconds a secondary DNS server waits before querying the primary DNS server's SOA record to check for changes.

☒ **A, D,** and **E** are incorrect because none of this information is contained within a zone's SOA record.

10. Consider the following records from a DNS zone file:

```
printers.yourcorp.com.      CNAME       fs2.yourzone.com.
fs2.yourzone.com.           A           10.0.0.3
```

What do these records do? (Choose two.)

A. Create a host record that resolves fs2.yourzone.com to an IP address of 10.0.0.3.

B. Create an alias that points printers.yourcorp.com to the fs2.yourzone.com host record.

C. Create an in-addr.arpa record that resolves the IP address of 10.0.0.3 to a hostname of fs2.yourzone.com.

D. Create an alias that points fs2.yourzone.com to the printers.yourcorp.com host record.

E. Create a host record that resolves printers.yourcorp.com to an IP address of 10.0.0.3.

☑ **A** and **B.** The first record creates an alias (CNAME record) that points printers.yourcorp .com to the fs2.yourzone.com host record. The second record is a host record (A record) that resolves fs2.yourzone.com to an IP address of 10.0.0.3.

☒ **C, D,** and **E** are incorrect. **C** is incorrect because neither record is a reverse-lookup record. **D** is incorrect because the CNAME record in this example points printers .yourcorp.com to the fs2.yourzone.com host record, not the other way around. **E** is partially correct because using these two records, printers.yourcorp.com eventually will resolve to 10.0.0.3. However, no host record exists in this example that does this directly.

11. Your workstation is configured to use DHCP to get its IP addressing information. When you boot the system and the operating system loads, it sends out a DHCPDISCOVER broadcast on the network. What happens next?

A. The DHCP server receives the message and responds with an IP address assignment.

B. The DHCP server receives the message and responds with a DHCPOFFER to the workstation.

C. The workstation sends a DHCPREQUEST message on the network.

D. The DHCP server sends a DHCPACK message with IP address configuration information.

☑ **B.** Any DHCP server on the network that receives the DHCPDISCOVER message from the workstation will respond with a DHCPOFFER message containing a proposed DHCP configuration.

☒ **A, C,** and **D** are incorrect. **A** is incorrect because the DHCP server does not immediately respond to the DHCPDISCOVER message with an address assignment. Instead, it sends a proposed configuration and waits for the client to accept it. **C** is incorrect because a DHCPREQUEST message is sent from the client after it has decided which offer to accept. **D** is incorrect because a DHCPACK message is not sent until after the client has decided which offer to accept.

12. Which mechanism can be used by DHCP servers to deliver configuration information, such as the default gateway router address and DNS server addresses, to DHCP client systems?

A. DHCP scope

B. DHCP subnet address range

C. DHCP option

D. DHCP address exclusion

☑ **C.** You can use DHCP options with your DHCP server to deliver a wide variety of configuration parameters to DHCP clients. For example, you can deliver the IP address of the default gateway router, the IP address of your DNS server, the IP address of your WINS server, and so on.

☒ **A, B**, and **D** are incorrect. **A** is incorrect because a DHCP scope is a logical grouping of IP addresses. **B** is incorrect because a subnet address range is used to define a range of IP addresses that the DHCP server will hand out to clients. **D** is incorrect because address exclusions are used to reserve IP addresses in a range so that they will not be distributed by the DHCP server.

13. What is always contained in a DHCPOFFER message? (Choose two.)

A. The DHCP client's MAC address

B. The DHCP server's MAC address

C. DHCP lease information

D. An option for the default gateway address

E. An option for the DNS server address

☑ **A** and **C.** A DHCPOFFER message always contains the DHCP client's MAC address as well as DHCP lease information. It also contains the IP address and subnet mask being offered as well as the IP address of the DHCP server itself.

☒ **B, D**, and **E** are incorrect. **B** is incorrect because the DHCPOFFER doesn't contain the DHCP server's MAC address. **D** and **E** are incorrect because options are just that, optional. A DHCPOFFER may or may not include options to deliver the default gateway address or DNS server addresses, depending on how the DHCP server is configured.

14. Your organization's network is composed of four segments (A, B, C, and D) connected by routers. Your DHCP server is on segment A, while your DNS server is on segment B. Workstations are connected to all segments; however, you've discovered that only the workstations on segment A are able to get IP addresses from the DHCP server. What should you do?

   A. Configure DHCP relay agents on segments B, C, and D.

   B. Configure your routers to forward broadcasts.

   C. Configure your DHCP server with an option that distributes the appropriate gateway router address.

   D. Configure the workstations on segments B, C, and D with static IP addresses.

   ☑ **A.** Most routers are configured by default not to forward broadcast messages. This is done to reduce network traffic and prevent DoS attacks. Therefore, the DHCPDISCOVER broadcasts sent from clients on segments B, C, and D can't reach the DHCP server. To fix this, you can configure DHCP relay agents on segments B, C, and D that manage DHCP messages between the clients on these segments and the DHCP server on segment A.

   ☒ **B, C,** and **D** are incorrect. **B** is incorrect because configuring routers to forward broadcasts would increase network traffic and could expose your network to certain DoS exploits. **C** is incorrect because the client systems on segments B, C, and D can't reach the DHCP server in the first place and, therefore, do not have routable IP addresses. **D** would work, but it isn't necessary and would increase your administrative workload significantly.

15. Many users have called to complain that they can't log into the network server, nor can they access the Internet. However, the symptoms seem to be affecting only some workstations on the network. Upon inspection, you find that the affected hosts are being assigned IP addresses in the 10.0.0.*x* range, but they should be using the 172.17.*x.x* address range. Given that your network uses DHCP for IP address assignments, what should you do?

   A. Configure a DHCP relay agent to forward DHCPDISCOVER messages to your DHCP server.

   B. Reboot your DHCP server, and then reboot all affected workstations.

   C. Check network connectivity, because the affected workstations are using Automatic Private IP Addressing (APIPA).

   D. Check the network for a rogue DHCP server.

☑ **D.** The most likely cause of this issue is a rogue DHCP server on the network. DHCP clients usually accept the first DHCPOFFER they receive from a DHCP server. In this scenario, workstations closest to the rogue server receive DHCPOFFER messages from it first and accept them. Workstations closer to your authorized DHCP server receive their IP addressing information from it.

☒ **A, B,** and **C** are incorrect. **A** is incorrect because broadcast filtering is not an issue in this scenario and, hence, a DHCP relay agent won't solve the problem. **B** is incorrect because rebooting the DHCP server will not fix issues associated with rogue DHCP servers. **C** is incorrect because APIPA comes into effect when no DHCP servers can be reached.

16. You are implementing a home network using a DSL connection for Internet access. Your service provider gave you only a single registered IP address for the connection. However, you want to connect several home computers, your DVD player, and your IP phone to the Internet through this connection. What should you do?

   A. Restrict Internet access to a single host on your network.

   B. Switch to a cable TV provider for Internet access.

   C. Implement internal private IP addressing with a Network Address Translation (NAT) router facing the Internet.

   D. Purchase additional registered addresses from the service provider for each device.

☑ **C.** You should implement a private IP addressing scheme, such as 192.168.1.x, on your internal network and use a NAT router to connect to the DSL interface. (In fact, many DSL modems include this functionality in their firmware.) The NAT router will translate the private IP addresses into the single registered IP address whenever an internal host accesses an Internet resource.

☒ **A, B,** and **D** are incorrect. **A** is incorrect because it would be frustrating and unnecessary to restrict Internet access to a single host. **B** is incorrect because cable Internet providers usually provide only a single registered IP address, just as was provided with the DSL line in this scenario. **D** would work, but it is more expensive and isn't necessary.

17. A network segment has two web servers connected to it, but no workstations. The segment is connected to the network backbone by a NAT router. The web servers use private IP addresses, while the network backbone uses routable public IP addresses. You want users to be able to come in from the backbone side of the NAT router and access content on the web servers on the private network. What should you do?
   A. Configure static NAT on the NAT router.
   B. Configure NAT overload on the NAT router.
   C. Configure dynamic NAT on the NAT router.
   D. Configure many-to-one NAT on the NAT router.

   ☑ **A.** You should configure static NAT on the NAT router. Static NAT is also called one-to-one NAT. Static NAT, in this scenario, allows you to translate two specific public address on the backbone to two specific private address on the private network segment. This can be done by installing multiple network interfaces in the NAT router or by simply configuring multiple addresses on a single interface.

   ☒ **B, C,** and **D** are incorrect because NAT overload, dynamic NAT, and many-to-one NAT use the same mechanism of translating a single routable public IP address to multiple private IP addresses on the private network. This mechanism essentially hides the private network from the public network and would not allow external users to access web servers on the network behind the NAT router.

18. A private network uses a dynamic NAT router to connect to the Internet. A workstation on the private network behind the NAT router sends a packet to the Internet, and the NAT router replaces the private IP address of the sender in the source field of the packet header with the NAT router's public IP address. What happens next?
   A. The NAT router adds an entry to its translation table listing the packet's private IP address, source port, and translated port.
   B. The destination host receives the translated packet and establishes a connection to the port and IP address contained in the translated packet's header.
   C. The destination host sends a message to the NAT router requesting the private IP address and source port of the sender.
   D. PAT assigns the connection a port number from a pool of available ports, inserting this port number in the source port field.

☑ **D.** After translating the private IP address to the public IP address, the NAT router uses Port Address Translation (PAT) to assign the connection a port number from a pool of available ports, inserting this port number in the source port field. This allows the NAT router to keep track of which external requests originated from which internal hosts and ensures the information sent in response makes it back to the appropriate system on the private network.

☒ **A, B,** and **C** are incorrect. **A** is incorrect because PAT must occur before the connection is added to the NAT router's translation table. **B** is incorrect because PAT must occur and an entry added to the NAT router's translation table before the packet can be transmitted to the destination host and a connection established. **C** is incorrect because the destination host doesn't know that the packet came from a NAT router.

9

Wireless Networking

QUESTIONS

Wireless networks provide a degree of mobility and flexibility that modern network users demand. However, a wireless network must be implemented correctly to provide adequate performance while preventing network security issues. For example, you must manage the placement and power level of wireless networking components to provide adequate service to your users. At the same time, you must prevent the signal from leaking outside your organization. In addition, you must implement encryption and authentication mechanisms to ensure that only authorized users are able to access the wireless network.

1. You are implementing a wireless network in an office suite. Due to the rectangular shape of the building, you need to implement a single wireless access point in the center of the office suite along with four additional wireless access points in each corner. What should you do? (Choose two.)
   A. Implement a WAP with an omni-directional antenna in the center of the office complex.
   B. Implement a WAP with a semi-directional antenna in each corner of the office complex.
   C. Implement a WAP with a highly-directional antenna in the center of the office complex.
   D. Implement a WAP with a semi-directional antenna in the center of the office complex.
   E. Implement a WAP with an omni-directional antenna in each corner of the office complex.

2. You've discovered that the signal from your wireless network is emanating some distance out into the parking lot of your facility. What can you do to stop this? (Choose three.)
   A. Implement wireless repeaters at strategic locations within your building.
   B. Relocate the wireless access point to a central location in your building.
   C. Increase the gain on the wireless access point antenna.
   D. Reduce the power level of the wireless access point.
   E. Implement a Faraday cage on the exterior of your building.
   F. Implement omni-directional wireless access points.

3. Which type of wireless network does not use a wireless access point?
   A. Infrastructure
   B. Bus
   C. Star
   D. Ad hoc

4. Which wireless networking standard runs at a frequency of 5 GHz? (Choose two.)
   A. 802.11a
   B. 802.11b
   C. 802.11g
   D. 802.11n
   E. 802.11z

5. You've discovered an older laptop in your equipment closet that has in integrated 802.11b wireless network adapter. Your organization uses 802.11n wireless access points to provide wireless connectivity to your network. What must you do to connect this device to the network?

   A. Disable the integrated 802.11b adapter and install an 802.11n USB wireless network adapter.

   B. Disable the integrated 802.11b adapter and install an 802.11g USB wireless network adapter.

   C. Install a wireless bridge and connect the integrated 802.11b adapter to the 802.11b side of the bridge.

   D. Connect the integrated 802.11b adapter directly to the 802.11n wireless network.

6. Which technologies allows the 802.11n standard to provide dramatically more wireless bandwidth than that available with 802.11b and 802.11g? (Choose two.)

   A. Lempel-Ziv (LZ) compression

   B. Time-division multiplexing

   C. 3DES data encryption

   D. MIMO

   E. Channel bonding

7. You are implementing an 802.11n wireless network for a small business in a rented office suite within a large, multitenant office complex. You are experiencing significant interference in the wireless network, causing dropped connections. You've discovered that the 2.4 GHz cordless phone system used in the office is set to use channel 3. You also discovered that neighboring tenants are using channels 1 and 5 for their 802.11x wireless networks. What should you do?

   A. Set your wireless access point to use channel 2.

   B. Set your wireless access point to use channel 4.

   C. Set your wireless access point to use channel 7.

   D. Set your wireless access point to use channel 3.

8. A small business has hired you to manage its 802.11g wireless network. Upon investigation, you find that 128-bit WEP is being used to secure transmissions on the wireless network. Which components comprise the encryption keys used on this network? (Choose two.)

   A. 24-bit initialization vector

   B. 40-bit encryption key

   C. 48-bit initialization vector

   D. 104-bit encryption key

   E. 80-bit encryption key

9. Which security standard uses the AES-CCMP algorithm to secure data on a wireless network?
   A. WEP
   B. WPA2
   C. WPA
   D. WAPI

10. You are implementing a new wireless network for a financial services firm. You need to ensure that the network is as secure as possible. What should you do? (Choose two.)
    A. Implement WEP encryption on wireless access points and all client systems that will connect to them.
    B. Hide the SSID.
    C. Implement MAC address filtering.
    D. Implement WPA encryption on wireless access points and all client systems that will connect to them.
    E. Use omni-directional antennae on the wireless access points and locate them along the exterior walls of the firm's physical structure.

11. A nefarious individual has used Kismet on his laptop to determine the SSID of a public access WAP at an airport. Using this information, he has set up a rogue access point and web server on a laptop within the airport using the same SSID. On the web server, he has created bogus web pages that look like the pages used by several large banks and credit card companies. These pages are used to capture bank and credit card account information and account credentials. What kind of wireless exploit is in use in this scenario?
    A. Evil twin
    B. WPA cracking
    C. War chalking
    D. War driving

12. Which security weakness is found within the WEP encryption scheme and makes it relatively easy to crack?
    A. The DES encryption used by WEP is relatively easy to crack.
    B. The RSA encryption used by WEP is relatively easy to crack.
    C. Short passphrases using words found in the dictionary can be cracked using a dictionary attack.
    D. The 24-bit IVs are reused and transmitted in clear-text.

13. Which mechanism can be used with WPA security to encapsulate Extensible Authentication Protocol (EAP) information within an encrypted SSL/TLS tunnel?
    A. Lightweight Extensible Authentication Protocol (LEAP)
    B. Protected Extensible Authentication Protocol (PEAP)
    C. Temporal Key Integrity Protocol (TKIP)
    D. Extensible Authentication Protocol-MD5 (EAP-MD5)

14. The wireless users located in a portable office building situated next to your organization's main physical structure are complaining of slow data transfers over the network. Given that your organization uses an 802.11n wireless network with WAPs implemented within the main physical structure, what should you do? (Choose two.)

    A. Implement MAC address filtering.

    B. Move the users closer to the WAP to see if the signal strength improves.

    C. Upgrade the users' computers to 802.11a network interfaces.

    D. Implement an additional WAP in the location where the users work.

    E. Change the channel used by the WAP nearest the users to a higher numbered channel.

15. Your 802.11n wireless network is experiencing a significant amount of latency. You've used the IPERF utility to determine that your wireless network is experiencing a significant number of packets arriving out of order, arriving late, and being completely lost. What should you do? (Choose two.)

    A. Check for sources of interference, such as microwave ovens or 2.4 GHz cordless phones.

    B. Verify that all devices on the wireless network are using the correct encryption mechanism.

    C. Try using a different channel on the WAP to reduce interference from other 2.4 GHz devices.

    D. Verify that wireless devices are not using mismatched SSIDs.

    E. Move the WAP's antenna to a lower physical location.

16. A user has reported that he can't connect to your organization's 802.11n wireless network from his newly issued laptop computer. The user works in a location at which you know a good wireless signal is available. In addition, none of his co-workers are having trouble connecting to the wireless network. The user checked the documentation that came with his laptop and verified that it has an integrated wireless adapter and that it is enabled. What should you do? (Choose three.)

    A. Verify that the user is using the correct SSID when connecting.

    B. Install an 802.11n wireless USB adapter in the laptop.

    C. Check to see if MAC filtering is in use on the WAP.

    D. Change the channel used by the WAP to eliminate interference from other 2.4 GHz devices.

    E. Check for surfaces or objects that might be causing the wireless network signal to bounce.

    F. Verify that the user has configured the wireless adapter to use the correct wireless encryption mechanism.

17. Given optimal wireless conditions, which wireless networking standard provides the longest range?

    A. 802.11a

    B. 802.11b

    C. 802.11g

    D. 802.11n

18. Which wireless networking standard is limited to a maximum bitrate of 11 Mbps?

    A. 802.11a

    B. 802.11b

    C. 802.11g

    D. 802.11n

19. Which wireless security mechanism uses a preshared key (PSK)?

    A. WEP

    B. WPA2 Enterprise

    C. WPA Personal

    D. WAPI

20. The Marketing workgroup in your organization decided that they need a stronger wireless signal in their workspace to support the tablet devices they are using to develop a new marketing app. To do this, they purchased a WAP and plugged it into an open network jack within an empty cubicle. Which term best describes the security risk in this scenario?

    A. Rogue access point

    B. Evil twin

    C. War driving

    D. Data emanation

QUICK ANSWER KEY

1.	A, B	**8.**	A, D	**15.**	A, C
2.	B, D, E	**9.**	B	**16.**	A, C, F
3.	D	**10.**	B, C	**17.**	D
4.	A, D	**11.**	A	**18.**	B
5.	D	**12.**	D	**19.**	C
6.	D, E	**13.**	B	**20.**	A
7.	C	**14.**	B, D		

IN-DEPTH ANSWERS

1. You are implementing a wireless network in an office suite. Due to the rectangular shape of the building, you need to implement a single wireless access point in the center of the office suite along with four additional wireless access points in each corner. What should you do? (Choose two.)
   A. Implement a WAP with an omni-directional antenna in the center of the office complex.
   B. Implement a WAP with a semi-directional antenna in each corner of the office complex.
   C. Implement a WAP with a highly-directional antenna in the center of the office complex.
   D. Implement a WAP with a semi-directional antenna in the center of the office complex.
   E. Implement a WAP with an omni-directional antenna in each corner of the office complex.

   ☑ **A and B.** The goal of wireless antenna placement is to achieve the best coverage without excessive signal emanation outside the facility. Therefore, an omni-directional antenna in the center of the rectangular suite would provide the best coverage. Using semi-directional antennae in each corner would fill in the dead spots left by the omni-directional antenna but reduce signal emanation outside.

   ☒ **C, D,** and **E** are incorrect. **C** and **D** are incorrect because using a semi- or highly-directional antenna in the center of the complex would provide poor coverage in a rectangular office suite. **E** is incorrect because using omni-directional antennae in each corner of the office would excessively emanate the wireless signal outside the facility.

2. You've discovered that the signal from your wireless network is emanating some distance out into the parking lot of your facility. What can you do to stop this? (Choose three.)
   A. Implement wireless repeaters at strategic locations within your building.
   B. Relocate the wireless access point to a central location in your building.
   C. Increase the gain on the wireless access point antenna.
   D. Reduce the power level of the wireless access point.
   E. Implement a Faraday cage on the exterior of your building.
   F. Implement omni-directional wireless access points.

   ☑ **B, D,** and **E.** You could employ several strategies to reduce signal emanation. One is to relocate the WAP to the center of your facility. Another is to reduce the power level of your WAP. However, depending upon the layout of your building, you may need to implement additional directional WAPs to cover dead spots created by the reduced signal strength. Many organizations with very high security requirements implement a metal mesh around the exterior of their buildings to form a Faraday cage that stops signal emanation completely. However, it will also block cell phone signals.

☒ **A, C,** and **F** are incorrect. **A** is incorrect because wireless repeaters would likely increase signal emanation unless they used directional antennae. **C** and **F** are incorrect because they would both likely increase signal emanation rather than reduce it.

3. Which type of wireless network does not use a wireless access point?

   A. Infrastructure
   B. Bus
   C. Star
   D. Ad hoc

☑ **D.** An ad hoc wireless network allows wireless hosts to connect directly to one another without the use of a WAP. This essentially forms a wireless mesh network topology.

☒ **A, B,** and **C** are incorrect. **A** is incorrect because infrastructure wireless networks use a WAP. **B** is incorrect because wireless Ethernet networks still function as a logical bus, regardless of whether they run in infrastructure or ad hoc mode. **C** is incorrect because a wireless network that uses a star topology would require a WAP as a central connecting point.

4. Which wireless networking standard runs at a frequency of 5 GHz? (Choose two.)

   A. 802.11a
   B. 802.11b
   C. 802.11g
   D. 802.11n
   E. 802.11z

☑ **A** and **D.** 802.11a is an older wireless networking standard that operates in the 5 GHz frequency range and transmits data at 54 Mbps. 802.11a devices are incompatible with 802.11b and 802.11g devices as these standards all operate in the 2.4 GHz frequency range. However 802.11a devices are usually compatible with 802.11n devices, because the 802.11n standard operates at either 2.4 or 5 GHz.

☒ **B, C,** and **E** are incorrect. **B** and **C** are incorrect because the 802.11b and 802.11g standards all operate in the 2.4 GHz frequency range. **E** is incorrect because the 802.11z standard specifies extensions to Direct Link Setup.

5. You've discovered an older laptop in your equipment closet that has in integrated 802.11b wireless network adapter. Your organization uses 802.11n wireless access points to provide wireless connectivity to your network. What must you do to connect this device to the network?
    A. Disable the integrated 802.11b adapter and install an 802.11n USB wireless network adapter.
    B. Disable the integrated 802.11b adapter and install an 802.11g USB wireless network adapter.
    C. Install a wireless bridge and connect the integrated 802.11b adapter to the 802.11b side of the bridge.
    D. Connect the integrated 802.11b adapter directly to the 802.11n wireless network.

    ☑ **D.** All 802.11b/g/n devices are compatible with each other. Therefore, you can connect the integrated 802.11b wireless network interface in the laptop directly to the 802.11n wireless network. However, the adapter will run at a rather sedate 11 Mbps.

    ☒ **A, B,** and **C** are incorrect. **A** will work; it's incorrect, however, because the integrated 802.11b wireless network interface in the laptop can connect directly to the 802.11n wireless network. **B** will also work, but it's incorrect because the integrated 802.11b wireless network interface in the laptop can connect directly to the 802.11n wireless network. **C** is incorrect because a bridge isn't necessary to connect an 802.11b wireless network to an 802.11n network.

6. Which technologies allows the 802.11n standard to provide dramatically more wireless bandwidth than that available with 802.11b and 802.11g? (Choose two.)
    A. Lempel-Ziv (LZ) compression
    B. Time-division multiplexing
    C. 3DES data encryption
    D. MIMO
    E. Channel bonding

    ☑ **D** and **E.** The 802.11n wireless networking standard employs multiple input multiple output (MIMO) and channel bonding to increase bandwidth. MIMO involves the use of multiple antennae, while channel bonding allows data to be transferred over two channels simultaneously.

    ☒ **A, B,** and **C** are incorrect. **A** is incorrect because 802.11n does not compress data to increase throughput. **B** is incorrect because 802.11n does not use time-division multiplexing. It does, however, use space-division multiplexing to implement MIMO. **C** is incorrect because 802.11n does not specify the use of 3DES encryption (nor would the use of encryption increase bandwidth).

7. You are implementing an 802.11n wireless network for a small business in a rented office suite within a large, multitenant office complex. You are experiencing significant interference in the wireless network, causing dropped connections. You've discovered that the 2.4 GHz cordless phone system used in the office is set to use channel 3. You also discovered that neighboring tenants are using channels 1 and 5 for their 802.11x wireless networks. What should you do?

A. Set your wireless access point to use channel 2.

B. Set your wireless access point to use channel 4.

C. Set your wireless access point to use channel 7.

D. Set your wireless access point to use channel 3.

☑ **C.** Because there is frequency overlap between channels within the 2.4 GHz range, you need to select a channel far away from those already in use. In this example, channels 1, 3, and 5 are used by nearby equipment. Therefore setting your WAP to use channel 7 should eliminate interference from these devices.

☒ **A, B,** and **D** are incorrect. **A** is incorrect because there is overlap between the frequencies used by channels 1 (2.3995–2.4245 GHz) and 2 (2.4045–2.4295 GHz) in the 2.4 GHz range. **B** is incorrect because there is overlap between the frequencies used by channels 3 (2.4095–2.4345 GHz) and 4 (2.4145–2.4395 GHz) in the 2.4 GHz range. **D** is incorrect because channel 3 is already in use by the cordless phone system. If set to the same channel, the wireless network will work only until someone in the office uses the telephone.

8. A small business has hired you to manage its 802.11g wireless network. Upon investigation, you find that 128-bit WEP is being used to secure transmissions on the wireless network. Which components comprise the encryption keys used on this network? (Choose two.)

A. 24-bit initialization vector

B. 40-bit encryption key

C. 48-bit initialization vector

D. 104-bit encryption key

E. 80-bit encryption key

☑ **A and D.** 128-bit WEP security uses a 24-bit initialization vector and then a 104-bit encryption key. 64-bit WEP security uses the same 24-bit initialization vector, but uses a 40-bit key for encryption only.

☒ **B, C,** and **E** are incorrect. **B** is incorrect because a 40-bit encryption key is used by 64-bit WEP security. **C** is incorrect because the initialization vector used by WEP is 24-bits, not 48 bits, long. **E** is incorrect because WEP uses either 40- or 104-bit encryption keys.

9. Which security standard uses the AES-CCMP algorithm to secure data on a wireless network?
   A. WEP
   B. WPA2
   C. WPA
   D. WAPI

   ☑ **B.** The key difference between WPA and WPA2 is the inclusion of AES-CCMP to secure data on the wireless network. WPA2 is considered more secure than WPA and much more secure than WEP.

   ☒ **A, C,** and **D** are incorrect. **A** and **C** are incorrect because neither WEP nor WPA use AES-CCMP to secure data. **D** is incorrect because WAPI is a wireless security standard defined by the government of China that uses SMS4 symmetric encryption instead of AES-CCMP.

10. You are implementing a new wireless network for a financial services firm. You need to ensure that the network is as secure as possible. What should you do? (Choose two.)
    A. Implement WEP encryption on wireless access points and all client systems that will connect to them.
    B. Hide the SSID.
    C. Implement MAC address filtering.
    D. Implement WPA encryption on wireless access points and all client systems that will connect to them.
    E. Use omni-directional antennae on the wireless access points and locate them along the exterior walls of the firm's physical structure.

    ☑ **B and C.** You can configure each WAP not to broadcast the SSID of the network to make it more difficult to locate. Implementing MAC address filtering to control which hosts are allowed to connect will help increase the security of the wireless network. Be aware that these measures provide only a basic level of security. Encryption and authentication should be enabled on the wireless network. Because of the sensitive nature of the information on this network, you should also consider implementing a VPN to restrict access to the wired network from the wireless network.

    ☒ **A, D,** and **E** are incorrect. **A** is incorrect because WEP encryption is notoriously weak and can be compromised with relative ease. **D** is incorrect because the sensitive nature of the data on this network would dictate the use of WPA2 or (better yet) WPA-Enterprise encryption. **E** is incorrect because omni-directional antennae installed on the exterior walls of the physical structure would emanate a strong wireless signal outside the firm.

11. A nefarious individual has used Kismet on his laptop to determine the SSID of a public access WAP at an airport. Using this information, he has set up a rogue access point and web server on a laptop within the airport using the same SSID. On the web server, he has created bogus web pages that look like the pages used by several large banks and credit card companies. These pages are used to capture bank and credit card account information and account credentials. What kind of wireless exploit is in use in this scenario?

A. Evil twin

B. WPA cracking

C. War chalking

D. War driving

☑ **A.** This is an example of an evil twin wireless exploit. The victims connect to the rogue WAP thinking it is the airport's public access WAP. Then they send their confidential information to the criminal's web server, thinking they are logging into their legitimate bank or credit card accounts.

☒ **B, C,** and **D** are incorrect. **B** is incorrect because WPA cracking involves using software to capture packets transmitted on the wireless network and crack the WPA encryption used to secure them. **C** and **D** are incorrect because war chalking and war driving involve searching out wireless network signals and marking their location either on a map or on the sidewalk with chalk using special symbols to identify the characteristics of the network.

12. Which security weakness is found within the WEP encryption scheme and makes it relatively easy to crack?

A. The DES encryption used by WEP is relatively easy to crack.

B. The RSA encryption used by WEP is relatively easy to crack.

C. Short passphrases using words found in the dictionary can be cracked using a dictionary attack.

D. The 24-bit IVs are reused and transmitted in clear-text.

☑ **D.** WEP wireless security uses an RC4 wireless stream cipher, which has a key weakness of reusing 24-bit IVs and transmitting them as clear-text in the header of packets containing a WEP-encrypted payload. If enough packets are captured (around 10,000 or so), software can be used to crack the complete encryption key, thus exposing the encrypted network transmissions.

☒ **A, B,** and **C** are not correct. **A** and **B** are incorrect because WEP does not use DES or RSA encryption, although RC4 was initially developed by the RSA organization. **C** is incorrect because the use of short passphrases containing dictionary terms is a weakness associated with the WPA encryption mechanism.

13. Which mechanism can be used with WPA security to encapsulate Extensible Authentication Protocol (EAP) information within an encrypted SSL/TLS tunnel?
    A. Lightweight Extensible Authentication Protocol (LEAP)
    B. Protected Extensible Authentication Protocol (PEAP)
    C. Temporal Key Integrity Protocol (TKIP)
    D. Extensible Authentication Protocol-MD5 (EAP-MD5)

    ☑ **B.** The PEAP authentication mechanism was created in cooperation by Cisco, Microsoft, and RSA Security. PEAP encapsulates EAP authentication information within an encrypted SSL/TLS tunnel. PEAP provides better security and is preferred over other mechanisms such as LEAP and EAP-MD5.

    ☒ **A, C,** and **D** are incorrect. **A** is incorrect because LEAP uses passwords only. No digital certificates or any other type of PKI mechanism is used, so some information is sent as clear-text. **C** is incorrect because TKIP is a protocol designed to improve upon WEP's key-based flaws. It provides dynamic key generation and rotation, ensuring that each packet gets a unique encryption key. **D** is incorrect because EAP-MD5 is an early authentication mechanism that offers very little security. It uses an MD5 hash to secure data, which is vulnerable to a variety of attacks.

14. The wireless users located in a portable office building situated next to your organization's main physical structure are complaining of slow data transfers over the network. Given that your organization uses an 802.11n wireless network with WAPs implemented within the main physical structure, what should you do? (Choose two.)
    A. Implement MAC address filtering.
    B. Move the users closer to the WAP to see if the signal strength improves.
    C. Upgrade the users' computers to 802.11a network interfaces.
    D. Implement an additional WAP in the location where the users work.
    E. Change the channel used by the WAP nearest the users to a higher numbered channel.

    ☑ **B** and **D.** The bandwidth available to wireless network client decreases as the distance from the WAP increases. In this scenario, the users are probably too far away to get a good signal. Moving the users closer to the WAP or implementing an additional WAP within the portable structure will probably fix the issue.

☒ **A, C,** and **E** are incorrect. **A** is incorrect because MAC address filtering controls who can and who can't connect to the wireless network. It does not improve signal strength. **C** is incorrect because the 802.11a is an older, seldom implemented network standard that would not fix the issue in this scenario. **E** is incorrect because interference caused by a misconfigured channel setting on the WAP would affect all wireless users, not just those working in the auxiliary building.

15. Your 802.11n wireless network is experiencing a significant amount of latency. You've used the IPERF utility to determine that your wireless network is experiencing a significant number of packets arriving out of order, arriving late, and being completely lost. What should you do? (Choose two.)

    A. Check for sources of interference, such as microwave ovens or 2.4 GHz cordless phones.
    B. Verify that all devices on the wireless network are using the correct encryption mechanism.
    C. Try using a different channel on the WAP to reduce interference from other 2.4 GHz devices.
    D. Verify that wireless devices are not using mismatched SSIDs.
    E. Move the WAP's antenna to a lower physical location.

    ☑ **A** and **C.** Latency can be caused by a variety of factors. In this scenario, interference is the most likely culprit. Checking for interference emitters (such as a microwave oven) is a good place start. You should also check to see if the WAP is set to use the same channel as another WAP (perhaps in a neighboring office or apartment) or a 2.4 GHz cordless phone system.

    ☒ **B, D,** and **E** are incorrect. **B** and **D** are incorrect because incorrect encryption settings and mismatched SSIDs would not result in latency, but would instead result in the client system not being able to connect at all. **E** is incorrect because moving the WAP to a lower physical location would most likely decrease signal quality and increase latency.

16. A user has reported that he can't connect to your organization's 802.11n wireless network from his newly issued laptop computer. The user works in a location at which you know a good wireless signal is available. In addition, none of his co-workers are having trouble connecting to the wireless network. The user checked the documentation that came with his laptop and verified that it has an integrated wireless adapter and that it is enabled. What should you do? (Choose three.)

    A. Verify that the user is using the correct SSID when connecting.
    B. Install an 802.11n wireless USB adapter in the laptop.
    C. Check to see if MAC filtering is in use on the WAP.

D. Change the channel used by the WAP to eliminate interference from other 2.4 GHz devices.

E. Check for surfaces or objects that might be causing the wireless network signal to bounce.

F. Verify that the user has configured the wireless adapter to use the correct wireless encryption mechanism.

☑ **A, C,** and **F.** You should first verify that the user is using the correct SSID when trying to connect to the wireless network. Because this is a newly issued laptop, you should also check to see if MAC address filtering is preventing it from connecting. You should also verify that the user has configured his wireless network interface to use the correct type of encryption for your network.

☒ **B, D,** and **E** are incorrect. **B** is incorrect because 802.11n WAPs are backward-compatible with 802.11b and 802.11g network interfaces. Installing a new wireless network interface probably isn't necessary. **D** and **E** are incorrect because interference or signal bounce issues would affect all wireless users in the location, not just one user.

17. Given optimal wireless conditions, which wireless networking standard provides the longest range?

A. 802.11a

B. 802.11b

C. 802.11g

D. 802.11n

☑ **D.** All things being equal, the 802.11n standard offers the longest wireless range. Under ideal outdoor conditions, it can extend the wireless signal out to around 800 feet. Under indoor conditions, it has a maximum range of about 200 feet.

☒ **A, B,** and **C** are incorrect. **A** is incorrect because 802.11a has a maximum outdoor range of about 400 feet with a maximum indoor range of about 120 feet. **B** and **C** are incorrect because the 802.11b and 802.11g standards are limited to a maximum outdoor range of about 450 feet and a maximum indoor range of about 125 feet.

18. Which wireless networking standard is limited to a maximum bitrate of 11 Mbps?

A. 802.11a

B. 802.11b

C. 802.11g

D. 802.11n

☑ **B.** The 802.11b standard is limited to a maximum bitrate of 11 Mbps. Of course, the bitrate drops from the maximum as the distance between the WAP and the network interface increases.

☒ **A, C,** and **D** are incorrect. **A** and **C** are incorrect because the maximum bitrate supported by the 802.11a and 802.11g standards is 54 Mbps. **D** is incorrect because 802.11n supports a maximum practical bitrate of 150 Mbps.

19. Which wireless security mechanism uses a preshared key (PSK)?
    A. WEP
    B. WPA2 Enterprise
    C. WPA Personal
    D. WAPI

☑ **C.** WPA Personal uses a preshared key created from either an 8- to 63-character passphrase or a 64-character hexadecimal passphrase. WPA Personal is commonly used with home networks, but is generally considered inadequate for enterprise networks.

☒ **A, B,** and **D** are incorrect. **A** is incorrect because, although WEP devices use a common security key, they do not use the type of preshared key used by WPA security. **B** is incorrect because WPA2 Enterprise uses a RADIUS server for authentication instead of preshared keys. **D** is incorrect because WAPI uses a central Authentication Service Unit (ASU) instead of preshared keys to authenticate devices to the wireless network.

20. The Marketing workgroup in your organization decided that they need a stronger wireless signal in their workspace to support the tablet devices they are using to develop a new marking app. To do this, they purchased a WAP and plugged it into an open network jack within an empty cubicle. Which term best describes the security risk in this scenario?
    A. Rogue access point
    B. Evil twin
    C. War driving
    D. Data emanation

☑ **A.** The WAP in this scenario is considered a rogue access point because it wasn't authorized and isn't managed by your organization's IT department. Depending upon how the Marketing employees configured the WAP, it could potentially represent a significant security hole into your network.

☒ **B, C,** and **D** are incorrect. **B** describes a situation in which a rogue WAP is configured with the same SSID as a legitimate WAP to steal information from unsuspecting wireless clients. **C** refers to the practice of driving around looking for open wireless networks. **D** could potentially be a legitimate issue in this scenario, depending upon where the Marketing employees physically located the WAP.

10

Remote Access and VPN Connectivity

QUESTIONS

In the last decade, the workforce of the average organization has become increasingly mobile. In prior decades, network users typically worked at a desk within the organization's physical structure. However, with the proliferation of broadband Internet access, network users can now access internal network resources from remote locations at speeds fast enough to make productive work feasible.

Today, your average network user may be a user sitting at a desk within the organization, a traveling salesperson accessing your network through a 4G broadband wireless connection, or a contractor working from a home office using a Digital Subscriber Line (DSL) Internet connection. Your organization might even partner with another company and require that you provide its users with access to resources in your organization's network.

If this is the case, you'll need to configure your network to provide remote access for external users. In this chapter, you'll answer questions about commonly used remote access solutions such as Remote Access Server (RAS) and virtual private networks (VPN).

I. Your company's traveling sales force use modems in their laptop systems to dial remotely into your network each night to update the company's order processing database. Given that they are using a dial-up connection over the public switched telephone network (PSTN), what's the fastest data rate these users can achieve?

    A. 56 Kbps

    B. 256 Kbps

    C. 512 Kbps

    D. 1.5 Mbps

2. What components make up a North American Primary Rate Interface (PRI) ISDN connection? (Choose two.)

    A. 30, 64 Kbps B channels

    B. One, 64 Kbps D channel

    C. 23, 64 Kbps B channels

    D. Two, 64 Kbps B channels

    E. One, 16 Kbps D channel

3. Which type of ISDN devices manage data link and network layer functions, such as routing, in ISDN networks with multiple devices?

    A. Terminal adapter (TA)

    B. Terminal equipment 1 (TE1)

    C. Network terminator 2 (NT2)

    D. Network terminator 1 (NT1)

4. Which of the following is true regarding the SLIP remote access protocol? (Choose two.)

    A. It supports the NetBEUI protocol.

    B. It does not support TCP/IP.

    C. It does not support password encryption.

    D. It supports data encryption during transmission.

    E. It does not support the use of dynamic IP address assignment via DHCP.

5. You are implementing an RAS and routing solution. The network to which remote clients will connect contains a Windows server and a Linux server that communicate using TCP/IP. It also contains a legacy NetWare 4.2 server running a custom mission-critical application for your organization that uses the IPX/SPX protocol. Given that the clients' systems that will connect to the network through the RAS server, as well as the RAS server itself, already have TCP/IP configured, what should you do? (Choose two.)

    A. Configure the IPX/SPX protocol on the client workstations.

    B. Implement TCP/IP on the NetWare server.

    C. Migrate the NetWare server data to a Windows Server 2008 system.

    D. Configure the IPX/SPX protocol on the RAS server.

    E. Configure the RAS server to support SLIP connections to enable TCP/IP and IPX/SPX to be used simultaneously by remote connections.

6. Which PPP component is responsible for encapsulating data for transmission over a PPP connection?

    A. Network Control Protocols (NCPs)

    B. Link Control Protocol (LCP)

    C. High-Level Data Link Control (HDLC)

    D. Internet Protocol Control Protocol (IPCP)

7. A PPP connection is being established between your Windows 7 workstation and a Windows Server 2008 RAS server. The connection is started when your workstation sends LCP frames to establish, configure, and then test the link. What happens next?

    A. The authentication protocols to be used in the connection are negotiated.

    B. Your workstation sends NCP frames to setup the network layer protocols to be used in the connection.

    C. HDLC is used to encapsulate the data stream and transmits it through the PPP connection.

    D. The configured network protocols pass data through the PPP connection.

8. You are configuring a RAS implementation using a Windows Server 2008 system. You want to enhance security by using a RADIUS server for authentication. What should you do?

    A. Configure the RAS server to use PAP for authentication.

    B. Configure the RAS server to use EAP for authentication.

    C. Configure the RAS server to use CHAP for authentication.

    D. Configure the RAS server to use MS-CHAPv2 for authentication.

9. You need to establish a remote connection to a Linux server from a Linux workstation using the Secure Shell (SSH) protocol. You are currently logged into your workstation as the rbutler user. You need to access the Linux server as the dbadmin user to update the data in the MySQL database service. Given that the hostname of the Linux server is db1, what should you do?

   A. Enter **ssh db1** at the shell prompt of your Linux workstation, and then log in as dbadmin.
   B. Enter **ssh -l dbadmin db1** at the shell prompt of your Linux workstation.
   C. Enter **ssh -u mysqladmin db1** at the shell prompt of your Linux workstation.
   D. Enter **telnet db1** at the shell prompt of your Linux workstation, and then authenticate as the dbadmin user.

10. Which of the following are functions of the Point-to-Point Protocol over Ethernet (PPPoE) protocol? (Choose two.)

    A. It encapsulates PPP frames within traditional Ethernet frames.
    B. It establishes a PPP connection through a traditional Ethernet network.
    C. It enables data transfers from a remote client to a server by creating a VPN.
    D. It encrypts VPN traffic using the IPSec protocol.
    E. It encrypts VPN traffic using the SSL protocol.

11. You need to access an application running in a Citrix server farm from your Windows workstation. You need to configure your workstation's firewall to allow this type of traffic. What should you do? (Choose two.)

    A. Open port 80 in the firewall.
    B. Open port 636 in the firewall.
    C. Open port 1494 in the firewall.
    D. Open port 1293 in the firewall.
    E. Open port 389 in the firewall.

12. You want to be able to access the desktop of a Windows Server 2003 system in your data center remotely from a Windows workstation at your desk. What do you need to do? (Choose two.)

    A. Enable the Remote Desktop option on the Remote tab in the properties of My Computer on the workstation.
    B. Open TCP port 5800 in the firewall of the server and the desktop system.
    C. Add your user account to the list of allowed remote users on the Remote tab in the properties of My Computer on the workstation.
    D. Enable the Remote Desktop option on the Remote tab in the properties of My Computer on the server.
    E. Open TCP port 3389 in the firewall of the server and the desktop system.

13. Which authentication protocol authenticates both the client and the server when setting up a PPP connection?

    A. PAP

    B. CHAP

    C. MS-CHAP

    D. MS-CHAPv2

14. You are establishing a VPN connection over the Internet to your organization's home network from your hotel room. Which protocols could be used to create a VPN tunnel through the Internet, depending upon how your VPN server and client software are configured? (Choose two.)

    A. PPP

    B. SLIP

    C. PPTP

    D. L2TP

    E. ICA

15. You want to establish a VPN connection from your laptop at home to your company's internal network through the Internet. Your company's VPN server uses L2TP to create the tunnel. You need to configure your workstation's firewall to allow the VPN traffic through. What must you do? (Choose two.)

    A. Open TCP port 1723 in the firewall.

    B. Open UDP port 1701 in the firewall.

    C. Open TCP port 80 in the firewall.

    D. Open TCP port 1677 in the firewall

    E. Open UDP port 5500 in the firewall.

16. You are establishing a VPN connection from your home computer to your office network through the Internet. Your VPN server and client are configured to use L2TP/IPSec to create and secure the tunnel. What is the first process that occurs during the establishment of the connection?

    A. A security association (SA) is negotiated between the client and the server using Internet key exchange (IKE).

    B. Encapsulating Security Payload (ESP) communication is established between the client and the server.

    C. An L2TP tunnel is established between the client and the server.

    D. L2TP packets are encapsulated by IPSec and transmitted between the client and the server.

17. What security protocol is used by IKE to establish a security association between endpoints during the setup of an L2TP/IPSec VPN connection?

   A. Internet Protocol Security (IPSec)

   B. Transport Layer Security (TLS)

   C. Internet Security Association and Key Management Protocol (ISAKMP)

   D. Secure Shell (SSH)

18. Which of the following are advantages of using an SSL VPN instead of a traditional VPN? (Choose two.)

   A. An SSL VPN requires fewer open ports in the firewall.

   B. An SSL VPN uses IKE to establish a security association between endpoints in the tunnel.

   C. An SSL VPN doesn't require special client software.

   D. An SSL VPN doesn't require digital certificates to authenticate users.

   E. An SSL VPN can handle any protocol in the VPN tunnel that can be handled by other types of VPN tunnels, such as an L2TP/IPSec tunnel.

19. Your VPN is configured to use PPTP to establish VNP tunnels between the VPN server and clients. Which security protocol is used to encrypt the traffic transmitted through the tunnel?

   A. IPSec

   B. MPPE

   C. TLS

   D. MS-CHAP

20. Your organization is composed of a main office and three remote branch offices. An L2TP/IPSec VPN tunnel is used to connect the network at each branch office to the network at the main office through the Internet. When a branch office user accesses a resource, such as a shared folder on a server, on the main office network, her network request goes to the local branch office network first, then through the appropriate VPN tunnel to the main office network, and finally reaches the desired resource on the main office network. What type of VPN is in use in this scenario?

   A. Client-to-site

   B. Point-to-point

   C. Client-server

   D. Site-to-site

QUICK ANSWER KEY

1.	A	**8.**	B	**15.**	B, E
2.	B, C	**9.**	B	**16.**	A
3.	C	**10.**	A, B	**17.**	C
4.	C, E	**11.**	A, C	**18.**	A, C
5.	A, D	**12.**	D, E	**19.**	B
6.	C	**13.**	D	**20.**	D
7.	A	**14.**	C, D		

IN-DEPTH ANSWERS

1. Your company's traveling sales force use modems in their laptop systems to dial remotely into your network each night to update the company's order processing database. Given that they are using a dial-up connection over the public switched telephone network (PSTN), what's the fastest data rate these users can achieve?
    A. 56 Kbps
    B. 256 Kbps
    C. 512 Kbps
    D. 1.5 Mbps

    ☑ **A.** The fastest data rate the remote users will be able to achieve is 56 Kbps. This is because the modems used to establish dial-up connections transmit analog signals over the PSTN.

    ☒ **B, C,** and **D** are incorrect. **B, C,** and **D** are incorrect because speeds greater than 56 Kbps can be achieved only by a technology other than dial-up, such as DSL, cable, or satellite.

2. What components make up a North American Primary Rate Interface (PRI) ISDN connection? (Choose two.)
    A. 30, 64 Kbps B channels
    B. One, 64 Kbps D channel
    C. 23, 64 Kbps B channels
    D. Two, 64 Kbps B channels
    E. One, 16 Kbps D channel

    ☑ **B** and **C.** A North American PRI ISDN connection uses one, 64 Kbps D channel and 23, 64 Kbps B channels for a total of 1536 Kbps of bandwidth. The bearer B channels are used to transfer data while the data D channel handles signaling for the connection.

    ☒ **A, D,** and **E** are incorrect. **A** is incorrect because European PRI ISDN connections use 30, 64 Kbps B channels. **D** is incorrect because BRI ISDN connections use two, 64 Kbps B channels. **E** is incorrect because BRI ISDN connections use one, 16 Kbps D channel.

3. Which type of ISDN devices manage data link and network layer functions, such as routing, in ISDN networks with multiple devices?

A. Terminal adapter (TA)

B. Terminal equipment 1 (TE1)

C. Network terminator 2 (NT2)

D. Network terminator 1 (NT1)

☑ **C.** Network terminator 2 (NT2) devices manage data link and network layer functions in networks with multiple devices. An ISDN router is an example of an NT2 device.

☒ **A, B**, and **D** are incorrect. **A** is incorrect because a terminal adapter (TA) connects TE2 devices to an ISDN network. For example, the ISDN interface in a computer is an example of a TA. **B** is incorrect because terminal equipment 1 (TE1) devices can be directly connected to the NT1 or NT2 devices. An example is an ISDN telephone. **D** is incorrect because network terminator 1 devices communicate directly with the ISDN service provider's central office switch.

4. Which of the following is true regarding the SLIP remote access protocol? (Choose two.)

A. It supports the NetBEUI protocol.

B. It does not support TCP/IP.

C. It does not support password encryption.

D. It supports data encryption during transmission.

E. It does not support the use of dynamic IP address assignment via DHCP.

☑ **C and E.** SLIP was an early remote access protocol used primarily to connect to UNIX servers. As such, it doesn't include many key features, such as the ability to encrypt user passwords. In addition, it doesn't support the use of DHCP to assign IP addresses dynamically to systems on the client end of the connection. In fact, because of these limitations, RAS in Windows Server 2008 does not support SLIP connections.

☒ **A, B**, and **D** are incorrect. **A** is incorrect because SLIP does not support the NetBEUI protocol. **B** is incorrect because TCP/IP is the only protocol supported by SLIP. **D** is incorrect because SLIP does not support data encryption.

5. You are implementing a RAS and routing solution. The network to which remote clients will connect contains a Windows server and a Linux server that communicate using TCP/IP. It also contains a legacy NetWare 4.2 server running a custom mission-critical application for your organization that uses the IPX/SPX protocol. Given that the clients' systems that will connect to the network through the RAS server, as well as the RAS server itself, already have TCP/IP configured, what should you do? (Choose two.)

    A. Configure the IPX/SPX protocol on the client workstations.
    B. Implement TCP/IP on the NetWare server.
    C. Migrate the NetWare server data to a Windows Server 2008 system.
    D. Configure the IPX/SPX protocol on the RAS server.
    E. Configure the RAS server to support SLIP connections to enable TCP/IP and IPX/SPX to be used simultaneously by remote connections.

    ☑ **A** and **D.** When implementing an RAS solution, the client systems and the RAS server must use the same protocols to make a connection. In addition, if clients need to access resources on the internal network, the clients must use the same protocols as those used by those resources. In this example, the NetWare server on internal network is running IPX/SPX; therefore, the clients and the RAS server must also be configured to use IPX/SPX.

    ☒ **B**, **C**, and **E** are incorrect. **B** could be correct if a later version of NetWare were being used. However, the NetWare 4.2 server can use only IPX/SPX. **C** is incorrect because migrating the server data and applications isn't necessary in this scenario and could prove to be expensive and time-consuming to complete. **E** is incorrect because SLIP doesn't support the IPX/SPX protocol.

6. Which PPP component is responsible for encapsulating data for transmission over a PPP connection?

    A. Network Control Protocols (NCPs)
    B. Link Control Protocol (LCP)
    C. High-Level Data Link Control (HDLC)
    D. Internet Protocol Control Protocol (IPCP)

    ☑ **C.** The High-Level Data Link Control (HDLC) is responsible for encapsulating data for transmission over a PPP connection.

☒ **A, B,** and **D** are incorrect. **A** is incorrect because NCPs are used to set up the protocols, such as IP or IPX, that will be used on the PPP connection. **B** is incorrect because the LCP is used to establish the PPP connection, configure it, and verify that it is working correctly. **D** is incorrect because IPCP is an example of an NCP. It is used to configure IP on each end of the PPP connection.

7. A PPP connection is being established between your Windows 7 workstation and a Windows Server 2008 RAS server. The connection is started when your workstation sends LCP frames to establish, configure, and then test the link. What happens next?
   A. The authentication protocols to be used in the connection are negotiated.
   B. Your workstation sends NCP frames to setup the network layer protocols to be used in the connection.
   C. HDLC is used to encapsulate the data stream and transmits it through the PPP connection.
   D. The configured network protocols pass data through the PPP connection.

☑ **A.** After the connection is started by sending LCP frames to establish the link, the authentication protocols to be used in the connection are negotiated. For example, the connection could use the Challenge Handshaking Authentication Protocol (CHAP) or the Password Authentication Protocol (PAP).

☒ **B, C,** and **D** are incorrect. **B** is incorrect because NCP frames are not sent until after the authentication protocols to be used have been negotiated. **C** is incorrect because HDLC is not used to encapsulate data until after the connection is completely set up. **D** is incorrect for the same reason as **C**.

8. You are configuring a RAS implementation using a Windows Server 2008 system. You want to enhance security by using a RADIUS server for authentication. What should you do?
   A. Configure the RAS server to use PAP for authentication.
   B. Configure the RAS server to use EAP for authentication.
   C. Configure the RAS server to use CHAP for authentication.
   D. Configure the RAS server to use MS-CHAPv2 for authentication.

☑ **B.** The EAP-RADIUS authentication method can be used with PPP to enable the use of a RADIUS server for authentication. You must configure Windows RAS to point to the RADIUS server you want to use for authentication. You must also install and configure EAP on the RADIUS server itself.

☒ **A, C,** and **D** are incorrect. **A, C,** and **D** are incorrect because the PAP, CHAP, and MS-CHAPv2 protocols can't be used with a RADIUS server.

9. You need to establish a remote connection to a Linux server from a Linux workstation using the Secure Shell (SSH) protocol. You are currently logged into your workstation as the rbutler user. You need to access the Linux server as the dbadmin user to update the data in the MySQL database service. Given that the hostname of the Linux server is db1, what should you do?

   A. Enter **ssh db1** at the shell prompt of your Linux workstation, and then log in as dbadmin.
   B. Enter **ssh -l dbadmin db1** at the shell prompt of your Linux workstation.
   C. Enter **ssh -u mysqladmin db1** at the shell prompt of your Linux workstation.
   D. Enter **telnet db1** at the shell prompt of your Linux workstation, and then authenticate as the dbadmin user.

☑ **B.** You should enter **ssh -l dbadmin db1** at the shell prompt of your Linux workstation. This command will establish an SSH connection between your workstation and the SSH server. You will be prompted to enter the password of the dbadmin user on the server.

☒ **A, C,** and **D** are incorrect. **A** is incorrect because the **ssh** command on Linux attempts to authenticate you to the remote system using the same username with which you are currently logged into the local system, unless you explicitly specify a remote username with the **-l** option. **C** is incorrect because it uses an incorrect option to specify the username (**-u**) and it specifies the wrong user account. **D** will establish a remote connection with the server. However, it does so with the Telnet protocol, which transmits usernames and passwords as clear-text. In this example, the username and password for the dbadmin user on the server would be sent over the network as clear-text, significantly compromising security.

10. Which of the following are functions of the Point-to-Point Protocol over Ethernet (PPPoE) protocol? (Choose two.)

   A. It encapsulates PPP frames within traditional Ethernet frames.
   B. It establishes a PPP connection through a traditional Ethernet network.
   C. It enables data transfers from a remote client to a server by creating a VPN.
   D. It encrypts VPN traffic using the IPSec protocol.
   E. It encrypts VPN traffic using the SSL protocol.

☑ **A and B.** The PPPoE protocol encapsulates PPP frames within Ethernet frames, allowing you to establish a PPP connection through a traditional Ethernet network.

☒ **C, D, and E** are incorrect. **C** is incorrect because it describes the function of the PPTP protocol. **D** is incorrect because it describes the function of the L2TP protocol. **E** is incorrect because it describes the function of SSL VPNs.

11. You need to access an application running in a Citrix server farm from your Windows workstation. You need to configure your workstation's firewall to allow this type of traffic. What should you do? (Choose two.)
    A. Open port 80 in the firewall.
    B. Open port 636 in the firewall.
    C. Open port 1494 in the firewall.
    D. Open port 1293 in the firewall.
    E. Open port 389 in the firewall.

☑ **A and C.** Citrix systems use the Independent Computing Architecture (ICA) thin client protocol to provide remote access to applications running on the server. This protocol allows you to view and interact with the application locally, but it actually executes on the remote Citrix server. Only keystrokes, mouse actions, and screen updates are transmitted on the network. ICA runs on IP port 1494, so this port must be open in your workstation's firewall. Port 80 must also be open to allow browsing of available applications in the server farm. (Port 80 is sometimes called the ICA browsing port.)

☒ **B, D, and E** are incorrect. **B** is incorrect because port 636 is used for secure LDAP communications and isn't needed to access the server. **D** is incorrect because port 1293 is used for IPSec. **E** is incorrect because port 389 is used for clear-text LDAP communications.

12. You want to be able to access the desktop of a Windows Server 2003 system in your data center remotely from a Windows workstation at your desk. What do you need to do? (Choose two.)
    A. Enable the Remote Desktop option on the Remote tab in the properties of My Computer on the workstation.
    B. Open TCP port 5800 in the firewall of the server and the desktop system.
    C. Add your user account to the list of allowed remote users on the Remote tab in the properties of My Computer on the workstation.
    D. Enable the Remote Desktop option on the Remote tab in the properties of My Computer on the server.
    E. Open TCP port 3389 in the firewall of the server and the desktop system.

☑ **D** and **E.** To enable remote access to the desktop of the server, you need to enable the Remote Desktop option on the Remote tab in the properties of My Computer on the *server* and add your user account to the list of allowed remote users. You must also open TCP port 3389 in the firewall of the server and the desktop system to allow RDP traffic through.

☒ **A, B,** and **C** are incorrect. **A** is incorrect because it is not necessary to enable the Remote Desktop option on the workstation. **B** is incorrect because port 5800 is used by the VNC remote desktop protocol, not RDP. **C** is incorrect because you must add your user account to the list of allowed remote users on the Remote tab in the properties of My Computer on the server, not the workstation.

13. Which authentication protocol authenticates both the client and the server when setting up a PPP connection?
    A. PAP
    B. CHAP
    C. MS-CHAP
    D. MS-CHAPv2

☑ **D.** MS-CHAPv2 authenticates both the client and the server when setting up a PPP connection. Like MS-CHAP, MS-CHAP2 uses the MD4 hashing algorithm instead of MD5 used by CHAP.

☒ **A, B,** and **C** are incorrect. **A** is incorrect because PAP authenticates only the client end of the remote session. It is considered insecure because the client credentials are sent in clear-text. **B** and **C** are incorrect because both CHAP and MS-CHAP use a challenge-response mechanism for authentication, but they authenticate only the client end of the connection.

14. You are establishing a VPN connection over the Internet to your organization's home network from your hotel room. Which protocols could be used to create a secure VPN tunnel through the Internet, depending upon how your VPN server and client software are configured? (Choose two.)
    A. PPP
    B. SLIP
    C. PPTP
    D. L2TP
    E. ICA

☑ **C and D.** The PPTP and L2TP protocols could be used in this scenario to create a secure VPN tunnel through the Internet between your hotel room and your organization's home network. Which one is actually used depends upon how your VPN server and client software are configured.

☒ **A, B, and E** are incorrect. **A** and **B** are incorrect because the PPP and SLIP protocols are usually used to establish point-to-point connections using a modem through the PSTN. However, PPTP does use PPP to establish connections within the VPN tunnel. **E** is incorrect because the ICA protocol is used to provide remote access to applications running in Citrix server farms.

15. You want to establish a VPN connection from your laptop at home to your company's internal network through the Internet. Your company's VPN server uses L2TP to create the encrypted tunnel. You need to configure your workstation's firewall to allow the VPN traffic through. What must you do? (Choose two.)

   A. Open TCP port 1723 in the firewall.

   B. Open UDP port 1701 in the firewall.

   C. Open TCP port 80 in the firewall.

   D. Open TCP port 1677 in the firewall

   E. Open UDP port 5500 in the firewall.

☑ **B and E.** To allow traffic from a VPN tunnel created with L2TP, you need to open UDP port 1701 in your workstation's firewall. You must also open UDP port 5500 (for IPSec) and UDP port 500 (for key exchange via ISAKMP).

☒ **A, C, and D** are incorrect. **A** is incorrect because TCP port 1723 is used by VPN tunnels created using PPTP. **C** is incorrect because TCP port 80 is typically used for web servers using HTTP. **D** is incorrect because TCP port 1677 is used by Novell GroupWise servers and clients to manage messaging.

16. You are establishing a VPN connection from your home computer to your office network through the Internet. Your VPN server and client are configured to use L2TP/IPSec to create and secure the tunnel. What is the first process that occurs during the establishment of the connection?

   A. A security association (SA) is negotiated between the client and the server using Internet key exchange (IKE).

   B. Encapsulating Security Payload (ESP) communication is established between the client and the server.

    C. An L2TP tunnel is established between the client and the server.

    D. L2TP packets are encapsulated by IPSec and transmitted between the client and the server.

> ☑ **A.** The first step in establishing an L2TP/IPSec VPN tunnel occurs when an IPSec security association (SA) is negotiated between the client and the server using Internet key exchange (IKE). This process occurs over UDP port 500 using digital certificates.
>
> ☒ **B, C,** and **D** are incorrect. **B** occurs only after the security association is established. **C** occurs only after ESP communications have been established. **D** occurs only after all of the steps required to establish the L2TP/IPSec VPN tunnel have completed.

17. What security protocol is used by IKE to establish a security association between endpoints during the setup of an L2TP/IPSec VPN connection?

    A. Internet Protocol Security (IPSec)

    B. Transport Layer Security (TLS)

    C. Internet Security Association and Key Management Protocol (ISAKMP)

    D. Secure Shell (SSH)

> ☑ **C.** The ISAKMP security protocol is used by IKE to establish a security association between endpoints during the setup of an L2TP/IPSec VPN connection. This is the first process required to establish the VPN tunnel.
>
> ☒ **A, B,** and **D** are incorrect. **A** is incorrect because IPSec relies on ISAKMP and IKE to create a security association between the two endpoints of the VPN tunnel. **B** is incorrect because TLS is an alternative security mechanism to IPSec. **D** is incorrect because SSH is used to establish encrypted remote connections between systems running the SSH server and SSH client. SSH can be used, however, to create an encrypted tunnel through which network traffic can pass, essentially creating a very basic VPN.

18. Which of the following are advantages of using an SSL VPN instead of a traditional VPN? (Choose two.)

    A. An SSL VPN requires fewer open ports in the firewall.

    B. An SSL VPN uses IKE to establish a security association between endpoints in the tunnel.

    C. An SSL VPN doesn't require special client software.

    D. An SSL VPN doesn't require digital certificates to authenticate users.

    E. An SSL VPN can handle any protocol in the VPN tunnel that can be handled by other types of VPN tunnels, such as an L2TP/IPSec tunnel.

☑ **A and C.** An SSL VPN requires fewer ports to be opened in the firewalls at both ends of the VPN tunnel. Because SSL (or TLS) is used for security, the standard HTTPS port (443) is used for the VPN tunnel. It's very likely that this port is already opened in most organization's firewalls. An SSL VPN also doesn't require any special VPN client software to be installed. The client system's web browser is used as the client, which will probably already be installed and available.

☒ **B, D,** and **E** are incorrect. **B** is incorrect because IPSec relies on ISAKMP and IKE to create a security association between the two endpoints of the VPN tunnel. This process is not used in an SSL VPN. **D** is incorrect because SSL (and TLS) use PKI digital certificates to authenticate users. **E** is incorrect because SSL VPNs have the disadvantage of not supporting as many protocols as are supported by other types of VPN solutions.

19. Your VPN is configured to use PPTP to establish VNP tunnels between the VPN server and clients. Which security protocol is used to encrypt the traffic transmitted through the tunnel?
    A. IPSec
    B. MPPE
    C. TLS
    D. MS-CHAP

☑ **B.** The PPTP protocol is responsible for establishing the VPN tunnel, but it doesn't encrypt the contents of the tunnel. Instead, it relies on the Microsoft Point-to-Point Encryption (MPPE) protocol to secure the VPN tunnel.

☒ **A, C,** and **D** are incorrect. **A** is incorrect because the IPSec protocol is used to secure L2TP/IPSec VPNs. **C** is incorrect because TLS, or SSL can be used to secure SSL VPNs. These protocols are not used in a PPTP VPN. **D** is incorrect because MS-CHAP is an authentication protocol. It can be used to authenticate users in a PPTP VPN tunnel, but it isn't capable of encrypting data transmissions.

20. Your organization is composed of a main office and three remote branch offices. An L2TP/IPSec VPN tunnel is used to connect the network at each branch office to the network at the main office through the Internet. When a branch office user accesses a resource, such as a shared folder on a server, on the main office network, her network request goes to the local branch office network first, then through the appropriate VPN tunnel to the main office network, and finally reaches the desired resource on the main office network. What type of VPN is in use in this scenario?
    A. Client-to-site
    B. Point-to-point

C. Client-server

D. Site-to-site

☑ **D.** In this scenario, site-to-site VPNs are in use because there is a VPN tunnel between each location. Network traffic from branch office users traverses through their local LAN and then through these tunnels instead of going directly to the main office network.

☒ **A, B,** and **C** are incorrect. **A** is incorrect because a client-to-site VPN would require branch office users in this scenario to establish individual VPN tunnels to the main office network from their various workstations. **B** is partially correct in that the L2TP protocol creates a point-to-point connection through the Internet to establish the VPN tunnel. However, this term does not adequately describe the topology of the VPNs used in this scenario. **C** is incorrect because communications through the VPN tunnel could be client-to-server (such as a client accessing a share) or peer-to-peer (such as two servers synchronizing directory information).

11

Wide Area Network Technologies

QUESTIONS

As a network administrator, you will probably be focused primarily on managing local area networks (LANs) in your day-to-day work. However, in the modern networking world, LANs are commonly connected together using wide area network (WAN) links. These links may connect your LAN to another LAN somewhere else in the world. They are also used to connect your LAN to the Internet.

Therefore, as a network administrator you also need to be familiar with the technologies that are used to establish these WAN links. You need to be familiar with which part of the link is managed by a service provider and which parts you are responsible for managing within your organization.

In this chapter, you'll answer questions about common WAN technologies, their characteristics, and their applications.

1. A network is configured such that the data to be transferred from a source host to a destination host is divided up into pieces. Each piece of data travels from router to router through the network as it travels to its destination. Each piece of data may take a different route through the network than the other pieces. What kind of network is described in this scenario?

   A. Packet-switched
   B. Circuit-switched
   C. PSTN
   D. ISUP

2. Which of the following statements are true regarding a packet-switched network? (Choose two.)

   A. A dedicated connection is created between the sender and the receiver.
   B. All packets sent from the sender travel the same path through the network to the receiver.
   C. They generally use bandwidth more efficiently than circuit-switched networks.
   D. The various packets in a transmission may arrive at the destination out of sequence.
   E. If the path between the sender and the receiver fails, there is no way to redirect data through another path.

3. Which of the following statements are true regarding Asynchronous Transfer Mode (ATM)? (Choose two.)

   A. It uses a fixed-sized packet that is 53 bytes in size to transmit data.
   B. It can multiplex disparate network transmissions into a single data stream for transmission over one cable.
   C. It specifies bandwidths for transmissions sent over fiber-optic cables.
   D. It employs a splitter to split a single fiber-optic link to multiple customer locations.
   E. Using fiber-optic cabling, it can transfer data at speeds of 622 Mbps or faster.

4. Which WAN technologies allow multiple organizations to send packets created with different protocols onto a backbone and transmit them to a remote location using fiber-optic cabling? (Choose two.)

   A. ATM
   B. Synchronous Optical Network (SONET)
   C. Synchronous Digital Hierarchy (SDH)
   D. E-carrier
   E. Frame Relay

5. Given that SONET STS-1 runs at the base OC-1 data rate of 51.84 Mbps, how much data can STS-12 (OC-12) transfer in 1 second?

   A. 51.84 Mb
   B. 155.52 Mb
   C. 622.08 Mb
   D. 1244.16 Mb

6. Which WAN technology uses a Packet Assembler/Dissembler (PAD) device to connect a system to the network and is primarily implemented over analog voice lines with a maximum data rate of 2 Mbps?

   A. Frame Relay
   B. X.25
   C. T1
   D. T3

7. The Frame Relay WAN connection used by your organization has experienced temporary communication errors caused by an overheated hardware component. Given that several corrupted frames were transmitted on the WAN as a result, what happens next?

   A. Frame Relay detects the corrupted frames and requests that they be retransmitted.
   B. Frame Relay detects the corrupted frames and drops them.
   C. Frame Relay ignores the corrupted frames and relies on higher level protocols to detect them.
   D. Frame Relay uses CRC and parity information embedded in each frame to reconstruct the corrupted frames.

8. You are implementing Internet connectivity for a new start-up company that provides online storefronts for retailers. To do this, they have calculated that their Internet connection must provide a data rate of at least 20–30 Mbps. What should you do?

   A. Recommend they use an ISDN connection.
   B. Recommend they use a T1 connection.
   C. Recommend they use a T3 connection.
   D. Recommend they use a fractional T1 connection.

9. You are implementing a site-to-site VPN through the Internet for a large medical practice in Mexico City. After conducting a needs analysis, you have calculated that their WAN traffic during peak office hours will require a connection that provides a data rate of approximately 1.5 Mbps. What should you do?

   A. Recommend they use an ISDN connection.

   B. Recommend they use a T1 connection.

   C. Recommend they use a T3 connection.

   D. Recommend they use an E1 connection.

10. How many DS1 signals can be transported in a DS3 carrier?

    A. 3

    B. 28

    C. 168

    D. 240

11. You are troubleshooting a malfunctioning DSL modem. The device is experiencing connection problems with the DSL service provider. In addition, the client has complained of line noise on their analog telephone. Upon inspection, you notice that the WAN jack on the device is connected directly into an RJ-11 telephone wall jack. One of the RJ-45 jacks on the device is connected with a standard straight-through UTP cable to the WAN jack on an 802.11g wireless access point/router. What should you do?

    A. Install a DSL filter/splitter between the DLS modem and the RJ-11 wall jack.

    B. If the client is using a 2.4 GHz telephone, upgrade it to a 5 GHz phone.

    C. Replace the straight-through UTP cable with a crossover cable.

    D. Upgrade the WAP to an 802.11n device.

12. A client wants to connect her small business network to the Internet using the ADSL service provided by her local telephone company. Her network uses Gigabit Ethernet switches and network interfaces along with an 802.11n WAP. Her five employees will use the connection to manage the company's e-commerce web site and payment processing. Both of these services will be hosted by a third-party service provider. Her office is located in a rural area nearly 10 miles from the nearest phone company central office. Will this implementation work?

    A. Yes, this implementation will work as described in the scenario.

    B. No, a single ADSL line doesn't have sufficient bandwidth to support six concurrent users.

    C. No, ADSL lines are not compatible with Gigabit Ethernet networks.

    D. No, the office is physically located too far away from the phone company's central office.

13. Your home computer network is connected to the Internet using the cable Internet service provided by your local cable TV company. To which device is the cable modem in your home connected at the cable TV company? (Choose two.)

   A. Cable modem termination system

   B. Channel Service Unit /Data Service Unit (CSU/DSU)

   C. Cable TV headend

   D. Data termination equipment (DTE)

   E. WAN interface card (WIC)

14. You are the network administrator for a commercial real estate management company. Your company has built an office park containing 32 separate office buildings. The city has provided a single fiber-optic line to the property. You've been asked to recommend a technology for providing high-speed Internet access to the tenants in each building. What should you do?

   A. Work with the local phone company to provide ISDN connectivity to each building.

   B. Work with the local phone company to provide ADSL connectivity to each building.

   C. Work with the city to implement a PON to provide fiber to the premises of each building.

   D. Work with the local cable TV company to provide cable Internet connectivity to each building.

15. Which of the following components are required in a DWDM system? (Choose two.)

   A. Optical splitter

   B. Optical line terminal (OLT)

   C. Optical network units (ONUs)

   D. Terminal multiplexer

   E. Terminal demultiplexer

16. A municipal public safety department wants to implement its own wireless broadband network dedicated to mobile police, fire, and ambulance traffic. They want to be able to stream video from in-car and fixed surveillance cameras to dispatchers, officers, firefighters, and EMTs using a variety of devices. They also want to be able prioritize traffic to ensure that emergency data supersedes incidental data. For example, a video stream from cameras viewing a hostage situation should take priority over a user downloading a large e-mail attachment. As a consultant, you've been asked to recommend a wireless broadband technology. What should you do? (Choose two.)

   A. Recommend they implement a 3G wireless broadband network.

   B. Recommend they implement a Long Term Evolution (LTE) wireless broadband network.

   C. Recommend they implement a 2G wireless broadband network.

   D. Recommend an Evolved High Speed Packet Access (HSPA+) wireless broadband network.

   E. Recommend a WiMAX wireless broadband network.

17. Which of the following are disadvantages associated with using satellite-based Internet access? (Choose two.)

    A. Data rates that are not much faster than dial-up

    B. Lack of service in rural areas

    C. Weather interference

    D. Signal latency

    E. One-way data communication

18. A network is composed of multiple radio transceivers that each service a defined geographical area. Each transceiver incorporates a relay antenna to relay network connections from one area to the next. What type of network is in use?

    A. PON

    B. WiMAX

    C. Cellular

    D. DWDM

QUICK ANSWER KEY

1.	A	7.	B	13.	A, C
2.	C, D	8.	C	14.	C
3.	A, E	9.	D	15.	D, E
4.	B, C	10.	B	16.	B, D
5.	C	11.	A	17.	C, D
6.	B	12.	D	18.	C

IN-DEPTH ANSWERS

1. A network is configured such that the data to be transferred from a source host to a destination host is divided up into pieces. Each piece of data travels from router to router through the network as it travels to its destination. Each piece of data may take a different route through the network than the other pieces. What kind of network is described in this scenario?
   A. Packet-switched
   B. Circuit-switched
   C. PSTN
   D. ISUP

   ☑ **A.** The network described in this scenario is a packet-switched network. The data to be transmitted is divided up into blocks called *packets*. Each packet can take a different path through the network to the destination host.

   ☒ **B, C, and D** are incorrect. **B** is incorrect because circuit-switched networks establish a dedicated circuit between the sender and the receiver. All data sent from the sender to the receiver follows the same path through the network. The public telephone network is an example of a circuit-switched network. **C** is incorrect because the public-switched telephone network is an example of a circuit-switched network. **D** is incorrect because ISUP is a call setup protocol used on telephone circuit-switched networks to switch calls between phone exchanges.

2. Which of the following statements are true regarding a packet-switched network? (Choose two.)
   A. A dedicated connection is created between the sender and the receiver.
   B. All packets sent from the sender travel the same path through the network to the receiver.
   C. They generally use bandwidth more efficiently than circuit-switched networks.
   D. The various packets in a transmission may arrive at the destination out of sequence.
   E. If the path between the sender and the receiver fails, there is no way to redirect data through another path.

   ☑ **C and D.** Packet-switched networks are considered to be more efficient than circuit-switched networks because bandwidth is consumed only while data is being transmitted. In addition, the packets in a given transmission may arrive out of sequence. Therefore, each packet is assigned a sequence number so the original message can be reassembled correctly on the receiving host.

☒ **A, B,** and **E** are incorrect. **A** and **E** are incorrect because bandwidth is shared in a packet-switched network. Multiple hosts can use the medium at the same time. Congestion is managed by rerouting packets to use a different path through the network as needed. **B** is incorrect for the same reason.

3. Which of the following statements are true regarding Asynchronous Transfer Mode (ATM)? (Choose two.)
   A. It uses a fixed-sized packet that is 53 bytes in size to transmit data.
   B. It can multiplex disparate network transmissions into a single data stream for transmission over one cable.
   C. It specifies bandwidths for transmissions sent over fiber-optic cables.
   D. It employs a splitter to split a single fiber-optic link to multiple customer locations.
   E. Using fiber-optic cabling, it can transfer data at speeds of 622 Mbps or faster.

☑ **A** and **E.** ATM is a WAN technology that uses a fixed-sized packet called a *cell* that is 53 bytes in size to transmit data. It can be used with copper or fiber-optic cabling. Using fiber-optic cabling, it can transfer data at speeds of 622 Mbps or faster.

☒ **B, C,** and **D** are incorrect. **B** is incorrect because it describes the functionality of the Synchronous Optical Network (SONET) standard. **C** is incorrect because it describes the functionality of the Optical Carrier (OC) levels. **D** is incorrect because it describes the functionality of Passive Optical Network (PON) technology.

4. Which WAN technologies allow multiple organizations to send packets created with different protocols onto a backbone and transmit them to a remote location using fiber-optic cabling? (Choose two.)
   A. ATM
   B. Synchronous Optical Network (SONET)
   C. Synchronous Digital Hierarchy (SDH)
   D. E-carrier
   E. Frame Relay

☑ **B** and **C.** SONET and SDH are both WAN protocols that use multiplexing to combine and send multiple data streams over a fiber-optic cable. Different protocols can be used in each data stream. For example, ATM frames could be transmitted in one stream while Ethernet frames are transmitted in another.

☒ **A, D,** and **E** are incorrect. **A** is incorrect because ATM is a WAN technology that doesn't employ multiplexing. However, ATM is frequently implemented in conjunction with SONET and SDH. **D** is incorrect because E-carrier is a technology used throughout the world that uses multiplexing to send multiple data streams through copper cabling. **E** is incorrect because Frame Relay is a WAN technology that does not employ multiplexing.

5. Given that SONET STS-1 runs at the base OC-1 data rate of 51.84 Mbps, how much data can STS-12 (OC-12) transfer in 1 second?

   A. 51.84 Mb
   B. 155.52 Mb
   C. 622.08 Mb
   D. 1244.16 Mb

☑ **C.** The base rate for OC-1 is 51.84 Mbps. All other OC-*x* levels are multiples of this base rate. In this case, STS-12 (OC-12) is 12 times the base rate (51.84); which yields 622.08 Mbps.

☒ **A, B,** and **D** are incorrect. **A** is incorrect because 51.84 Mbps is the OC-1 data rate. **B** is incorrect because 155.52 Mbps is the data rate for OC-3 (three OC-1 channels). **D** is incorrect because 1244.16 Mbps is the data rate for OC-24 (24 OC-1 channels).

6. Which WAN technology uses a Packet Assembler/Dissembler (PAD) device to connect a system to the network and is primarily implemented over analog voice lines with a maximum data rate of 2 Mbps?

   A. Frame Relay
   B. X.25
   C. T1
   D. T3

☑ **B.** The X.25 WAN technology uses a PAD device to connect a system to an X.25 network. X.25 is implemented primarily using analog voice lines and supports a maximum data rate of 2 Mbps.

☒ **A, C,** and **D** are incorrect. **A** is incorrect because Frame Relay is a digital version of X.25 and can transfer data at a much faster rate (up to 50 Mbps). **C** and **D** are incorrect because both T1 and T3 technologies are part of the T-carrier system that uses digital signaling.

7. The Frame Relay WAN connection used by your organization has experienced temporary communication errors caused by an overheated hardware component. Given that several corrupted frames were transmitted on the WAN as a result, what happens next?
   A. Frame Relay detects the corrupted frames and requests that they be retransmitted.
   B. Frame Relay detects the corrupted frames and drops them.
   C. Frame Relay ignores the corrupted frames and relies on higher level protocols to detect them.
   D. Frame Relay uses CRC and parity information embedded in each frame to reconstruct the corrupted frames.

☑ **B.** Frame relay is capable of detecting corrupted frames, but it simply drops them. It does not request that they be retransmitted. Instead, it relies on upper layer protocols (such as TCP/IP) to request retransmission of corrupted information.

☒ **A, C,** and **D** are incorrect. **A** is incorrect because Frame Relay doesn't have the ability to request retransmission of corrupt frames. **C** is incorrect because Frame Relay detects the corrupted frames and drops them. It also relies on upper layer protocols to request retransmission. **D** is incorrect because Frame Relay frames do not contain parity information, and Frame Relay cannot reconstruct corrupt data from the CRC.

8. You are implementing Internet connectivity for a new start-up company that provides online storefronts for retailers. To do this, they have calculated that their Internet connection must provide a data rate of at least 20–30 Mbps. What should you do?
   A. Recommend they use an ISDN connection.
   B. Recommend they use a T1 connection.
   C. Recommend they use a T3 connection.
   D. Recommend they use a fractional T1 connection.

☑ **C.** The T3 carrier service is similar to T1; however, it is composed of 672, 64-Kbps channels (DS0 channels) that provide a total throughput of 44.736 Mbps. T3 is the only service listed that provides a data rate fast enough for the client in this scenario.

> ☒ **A, B,** and **D** are incorrect. **A** is incorrect because ISDN offers a maximum data rate of 1536 Kbps, which doesn't meet the client's requirements. **B** is incorrect because a T1 connection provides a data rate of 1.544 Mbps (DS1), which also doesn't meet the client's requirements. **D** is incorrect because a fractional T1 line would provide even less bandwidth than a standard T1 line.

9. You are implementing a site-to-site VPN through the Internet for a large medical practice in Mexico City. After conducting a needs analysis, you have calculated that their WAN traffic during peak office hours will require a connection that provides a data rate of approximately 1.5 Mbps. What should you do?

   A. Recommend they use an ISDN connection.
   B. Recommend they use a T1 connection.
   C. Recommend they use a T3 connection.
   D. Recommend they use an E1 connection.

> ☑ **D.** Because the medical practice is located in Mexico City, you can use an E-carrier connection. T-carrier connections are not widely used outside of the United States, Canada, and Japan. An E1-carrier is composed of 30, 64-Kbps data channels and 2, 64-Kbps signaling channels yielding a total bandwidth of 2.048 Mbps.
>
> ☒ **A, B,** and **C** are incorrect. **A** is incorrect because ISDN offers a maximum data rate of 1536 Kbps, which doesn't meet the client's requirements. **B** and **C** are incorrect because T-carrier connections are not widely available outside the United States.

10. How many DS1 signals can be transported in a DS3 carrier?
    A. 3
    B. 28
    C. 168
    D. 240

> ☑ **B.** A DS1 signal is composed of 24, 64-Kbps DS0 channels for a total of data rate of 1.544 Mbps. A DS3 carrier can transport 28 DS1-level signals (672 DS0 channels) for a total data rate of 44.736 Mbps.
>
> ☒ **A, C,** and **D** are incorrect. **A** is incorrect because DS3 carries 28 DS1 signals, not 3. **C** is incorrect because a DS4 carrier transports 168 DS1 signals. **D** is incorrect because a DS5 carrier transports 240 DS1 signals.

11. You are troubleshooting a malfunctioning DSL modem. The device is experiencing connection problems with the DSL service provider. In addition, the client has complained of line noise on their analog telephone. Upon inspection, you notice that the WAN jack on the device is connected directly into an RJ-11 telephone wall jack. One of the RJ-45 jacks on the device is connected with a standard straight-through UTP cable to the WAN jack on an 802.11g wireless access point/router. What should you do?

A. Install a DSL filter/splitter between the DLS modem and the RJ-11 wall jack.

B. If the client is using a 2.4 GHz telephone, upgrade it to a 5 GHz phone.

C. Replace the straight-through UTP cable with a crossover cable.

D. Upgrade the WAP to an 802.11n device.

☑ **A.** The DSL modem doesn't have an integrated DSL filter on its internal RJ-11 jack. Therefore, an external DSL filter/splitter needs to be installed between the DSL modem and the RJ-11 wall jack. Without the filter, high-frequency voice signals (above 3.4 KHz) interfere with the DSL signal while low-frequency DSL signals (below 3.4 KHz) are causing line noise on the analog phone service. With the filter, all signals above 3.4 KHz are sent to the DSL modem, while all signals below this frequency are sent to the analog telephone line.

☒ **B, C,** and **D** are incorrect. **B** is incorrect because the client's telephone is not the source of the DSL modem connection issues. It could, however, potentially cause interference with the client's wireless network. **C** is incorrect because the WAN port on most WAP/router devices is designed for uplink connections and already crosses the necessary pins, allowing you to use a standard straight-through UTP cable. **D** is incorrect because upgrading the WAP to an 802.11n device would not address the issue causing connection problems with the DSL modem.

---

12. A client wants to connect her small business network to the Internet using the ADSL service provided by her local telephone company. Her network uses Gigabit Ethernet switches and network interfaces along with an 802.11n WAP. Her five employees will use the connection to manage the company's e-commerce web site and payment processing. Both of these services will be hosted by a third-party service provider. Her office is located in a rural area nearly 10 miles from the nearest phone company central office. Will this implementation work?

A. Yes, this implementation will work as described in the scenario.

B. No, a single ADSL line doesn't have sufficient bandwidth to support six concurrent users.

C. No, ADSL lines are not compatible with Gigabit Ethernet networks.

D. No, the office is physically located too far away from the phone company's central office.

☑ **D.** The implementation of an ADSL line in this scenario will not work because the company's office is physically located too far away from the phone company's central office. Typically, your premise must be less than 4 km (2.5 miles) from the central office for ASDL service to work correctly. If the phone company has implemented higher quality copper wiring, it's possible to stretch this distance out to almost 8 km (5 miles). In any case, the office in this scenario is situated far beyond this limit.

☒ **A, B,** and **C** are incorrect. **A** is incorrect because the office is located too far away from the phone company's central office to support an ADSL line. **B** is incorrect because an ADSL line should provide more than adequate bandwidth for the business's requirements in this scenario. **C** is incorrect because the ADSL modem used to connect should provide one or more Ethernet ports that can be easily uplinked into just about any Ethernet network that uses UTP copper wiring.

13. Your home computer network is connected to the Internet using the cable Internet service provided by your local cable TV company. To which device is the cable modem in your home connected at the cable TV company? (Choose two.)

   A. Cable modem termination system
   B. Channel Service Unit /Data Service Unit (CSU/DSU)
   C. Cable TV headend
   D. Data termination equipment (DTE)
   E. WAN interface card (WIC)

☑ **A** and **C.** The cable modem in your home connects to a cable modem termination system (usually a cable TV headend) at the cable TV company using coaxial cable. Unlike ADSL technology, which requires you to be within a few miles of a phone company's central office, cable Internet technology allows cable runs of up to 100 miles.

☒ **B, D,** and **E** are incorrect. **B** is incorrect because a CSU/DSU is a T-carrier device used to convert frames from your internal LAN into frames that can be transmitted on a WAN (and vice versa). **D** is incorrect because a DTE is usually a router connected by a CSU/DSU to a T-carrier line. **E** is incorrect because a WIC is a specialized network interface that contains an integrated CSU/DSU that is used to connect a router to a T-carrier WAN.

14. You are the network administrator for a commercial real estate management company. Your company has built an office park containing 32 separate office buildings. The city has provided a single fiber-optic line to the property. You've been asked to recommend a technology for providing high-speed Internet access to the tenants in each building. What should you do?

  A. Work with the local phone company to provide ISDN connectivity to each building.

  B. Work with the local phone company to provide ADSL connectivity to each building.

  C. Work with the city to implement a PON to provide fiber to the premises of each building.

  D. Work with the local cable TV company to provide cable Internet connectivity to each building.

> ☑ **C.** You can work with the city to implement a passive optical network (PON). This technology uses unpowered optical splitters to allow a single optical fiber to serve multiple premises. This option would provide excellent uplink and downlink bandwidth to the tenants in each building.
>
> ☒ **A, B,** and **D** are incorrect. **A** is incorrect because ISDN provides limited bandwidth, which would not be attractive to potential tenants. **B** is incorrect because ADSL service providers usually throttle uplink speeds. Again, this may not be attractive to potential business tenants. **D** is incorrect because cable Internet uses a shared medium that could become congested during peak business hours. As with the prior options, this may prove to be unattractive to business tenants.

15. Which of the following components are required in a DWDM system? (Choose two.)

  A. Optical splitter

  B. Optical line terminal (OLT)

  C. Optical network units (ONUs)

  D. Terminal multiplexer

  E. Terminal demultiplexer

> ☑ **D** and **E.** Among other components, a DWDM system requires a terminal multiplexer and a terminal demultiplexer. The terminal multiplexer combines multiple optical carrier signals onto a single optical fiber at the transmitting end. It does this by using different light wavelengths for different signals. On the receiving end, the terminal demultiplexer divides the multiplexed signal back into separate signals and transmits each one on a separate fiber-optic cable.
>
> ☒ **A, B,** and **C** are incorrect. **A** is incorrect because optical splitters are used by a Passive Optical Network (PON) to enable a single fiber-optic cable to connect to multiple customer premises. **B** and **C** are incorrect because OLTs and ONUs are used to create a PON network.

16. A municipal public safety department wants to implement its own wireless broadband network dedicated to mobile police, fire, and ambulance traffic. They want to be able to stream video from in-car and fixed surveillance cameras to dispatchers, officers, firefighters, and EMTs using a variety of devices. They also want to be able prioritize traffic to ensure that emergency data supersedes incidental data. For example, a video stream from cameras viewing a hostage situation should take priority over a user downloading a large e-mail attachment. As a consultant, you've been asked to recommend a wireless broadband technology. What should you do? (Choose two.)

    A. Recommend they implement a 3G wireless broadband network.

    B. Recommend they implement a Long Term Evolution (LTE) wireless broadband network.

    C. Recommend they implement a 2G wireless broadband network.

    D. Recommend an Evolved High Speed Packet Access (HSPA+) wireless broadband network.

    E. Recommend a WiMAX wireless broadband network.

    ☑ **B** and **D.** An LTE wireless broadband network would be a good choice in this scenario. Under ideal conditions, LTE offers download speeds up to 100 Mbps and upload speeds up to 50 Mbps, which is enough to support high-quality streaming video. It also allows you to prioritize traffic based on application type and user. HSPA+ would be a viable alternative as it offers data prioritization as well. However, its maximum speed is considerable slower than LTE (about 20 Mbps compared to 100 Mbps offered by LTE). One advantage of HSPA+ over LTE is the fact that it can be used to upgrade an existing 3G network. Upgrading from 3G to LTE would require a complete retrofit of all equipment.

    ☒ **A, C,** and **E** are incorrect. **A** and **C** are incorrect because 2G and 3G networks don't provide enough bandwidth to support high-quality streaming video required by public safety. They also don't provide the high degree of prioritization control offered by LTE. **E** could be an option because WiMAX provides a reasonable amount of bandwidth (around 10 Mbps) and offers a certain degree of prioritization of network traffic. However, LTE and HSPA+ are better choices because they provide much more bandwidth and more granular prioritization.

17. Which of the following are disadvantages associated with using satellite-based Internet access? (Choose two.)

    A. Data rates that are not much faster than dial-up

    B. Lack of service in rural areas

    C. Weather interference

    D. Signal latency

    E. One-way data communication

☑ **C** and **D.** Satellite dishes are susceptible to interference from weather conditions. Heavy rain or snow can disrupt the signal. Satellite-based Internet access also experiences significant latency, because that the signal must travel around 20,000 miles into space to reach the satellite and then 20,000 miles back down to Earth. This can result in more than 1 second of round-trip latency on an IP network.

☒ **A, B,** and **E** are incorrect. **A** is incorrect because satellite-based Internet access provides data rates between 512 Kbps and 1 Mbps. While this rate is slower than ADSL or cable, it is still much faster than dial-up access. **B** is incorrect because satellites can provide Internet access to rural locations that cable or ASDL can't reach. **E** was true in the early days of satellite Internet access. Back then, you used the satellite dish for your downlink connection and a traditional PSTN modem for your uplink connection. Now, modern satellite service providers usually provide both uplinks and downlinks through the satellite dish.

18. A network is composed of multiple radio transceivers that each service a defined geographical area. Each transceiver incorporates a relay antenna to relay network connections from one area to the next. What type of network is in use?

A. PON

B. WiMAX

C. Cellular

D. DWDM

☑ **C.** The network described in this scenario is a cellular network. A cellular network is divided into specific geographical areas (cells) that are each serviced by a radio transceiver, called a *base station*, which is mounted on a radio tower. A relay antenna on each base station is used to move connections from one base station to the next as mobile devices move through the network.

☒ **A, B,** and **D** are incorrect. **A** is incorrect because a passive optical network (PON) is typically used to deliver fiber optic connectivity to the premises. **B** is incorrect because WiMAX is a microwave-based networking technology typically used to provide high-speed wireless Internet access to fixed sites. However, be aware that a mobile version of WiMAX has been developed that does function in a similar manner as a cellular network. **D** is incorrect because dense wavelength division multiplexing (DWDM) is a WAN technology used to multiplex multiple optical signals onto a single fiber-optic cable.

12

Implementing
a Network

❑   **2.6**   Given a set of requirements, plan and implement a basic SOHO network.

QUESTIONS

Network and system administrators are notorious for sharing a common set of traits, including the following:

■ They never read the documentation for anything.

■ They hate to plan out anything on paper, especially a hardware or software deployment.

■ They resist documenting anything.

If you're reading this, these characteristics probably describe you, too. However, when implementing a workstation, a server, or even an entire network, you must overcome these tendencies and do things the right way. If you don't, you'll probably spend a lot of time fixing your mistakes later on. These mistakes could lead to system outages, which cost your organization time and money.

Instead of deploying systems in a haphazard, unstructured manner, you should develop a deployment plan before you start buying hardware and installing software. Doing so will help you prevent costly errors and probably save your job. In this chapter, you'll answer questions about designing and implementing a network deployment.

1. You are designing an implementation plan for a new client/server network. Users in this network will use Windows 7 workstations. You need to implement a domain controller in the network that uses Server Message Block protocol that will be used for authentication, file sharing, and printer sharing. What can you do? (Choose two.)

    A. Install a Linux server system and configure it as a domain controller using the Samba package.

    B. Install a Windows 7 Enterprise system and configure it as a domain controller.

    C. Install a Windows Vista Business system and configure it as a domain controller.

    D. Install a Windows XP Professional system and configure it as a domain controller.

    E. Install a Windows Server 2008 R2 system and configure it as a domain controller.

2. If a Linux server has been configured to use local user accounts instead of directory user accounts, where is user account information stored? (Choose two.)

    A. /etc/group

    B. /etc/passwd

    C. /etc/shadow

    D. /etc/gshadow

    E. /etc/users

3. You are implementing a Linux network server that will store your organization's mission-critical files that users will access from their desktop client systems. You need to ensure that the files on the server are protected from hard disk failures and remain available 24/7. What should you do to accomplish this?

    A. Implement a RAID 0 hard disk array in the server.

    B. Implement a RAID 1 hard disk array in the server.

C. Implement a Fibre Channel controller and external Fibre Channel hard drive in the system.

D. Connect a tape drive to the server and configure daily backups of the file system.

4. You are planning the implementation of a new network server. This server will run Windows Server 2008 R2 and will be a domain controller. It will also host the Microsoft Exchange mail service. The server hardware you currently have on hand has a quad-core, 64-bit AMD processor running at 3.0 GHz. It has 2GB of RAM installed. It also has a three-drive RAID 5 array installed. The system has a 1000-watt power supply installed as well. What should you do to use this system in the deployment described in this scenario? (Choose two.)

A. Upgrade the system to use an Intel Core7 3.2 GHz quad-core processor.

B. Upgrade the system to a RAID 0+1 array.

C. Upgrade the system to a redundant dual power supply.

D. Upgrade the system to 8GB or more of RAM.

E. Upgrade the system to a 1200-watt power supply.

5. Which user account is created by default on a Linux system?

A. root

B. Admin

C. Administrator

D. Guest

6. A user called your help desk indicating she can't access a shared folder on a Windows server in the mycorp.com domain. The user logged into her Windows 7 workstation as the local JMarshall user, opened her e-mail client, and then tried to use Network Locations option to access the shared folder on the server. She was denied access. What should you do?

A. Verify that the JMarshall domain account has the necessary permissions to access the shared folder.

B. Instruct her to map a network drive to the shared folder instead of using Network Locations.

C. Instruct her log into her workstation as a domain user instead of a local user.

D. Instruct her to access the shared folder before starting her e-mail client.

7. You need to create a new user account for a user named Kimberly Sanders on your Linux system. You want to specify a user name of ksanders, a full name of Kimberly Sanders, and that a home directory be created. What should you do?

A. Enter **useradd -c "Kimberly Sanders" -m ksanders** at the shell prompt.

B. Enter **useradd -c "Kimberly Sanders" -m -u ksanders** at the shell prompt.

C. Enter **usermod -c "Kimberly Sanders" -m ksanders** at the shell prompt.

D. Enter **useradd -c "Kimberly Sanders" ksanders** at the shell prompt.

8. You need to delete a user account named jcarr from your Linux system and remove the contents of his home directory (/home/jcarr). What should you do?

   A. Enter **userdel jcarr** at the shell prompt.

   B. Enter **usermod --delete --rmhome jcarr** at the shell prompt.

   C. Enter **userdel -r jcarr** at the shell prompt.

   D. Enter **userdel --rmhome jcarr** at the shell prompt.

9. Which of the following is a strong password for a user account?

   A. Bob3

   B. TuxP3nguin

   C. penguin

   D. Castle

10. On a Linux system, you need to use the **chage** command to specify a minimum password age of 5 days, a maximum password age of 60 days, and 5 warning days prior to password expiration for a user named rtracy. What should you do?

   A. Enter **chage -m 5 -M 5 -W 60 rtracy** at the shell prompt.

   B. Enter **chage -m 60 -M 5 -W 5 rtracy** at the shell prompt.

   C. Enter **chage rtracy** at the shell prompt.

   D. Enter **chage -m 5 -M 60 -W 5 rtracy** at the shell prompt.

11. Which policy setting can be applied to Windows domain user accounts to prevent old passwords from being reused for a specified number of passwords changes?

   A. Enforce maximum password age.

   B. Passwords must meet complexity requirements.

   C. Enforce unique passwords.

   D. Enforce password history.

12. You need to delegate permission to complete a limited number of administrative tasks on your Windows server to a co-worker. You want her to be able to shut down the server, create and modify shares, back up and restore files, and change the system time. You do not want her to be able to complete any other administrative tasks on the server. What should you do?

   A. Make the user a member of the Backup Operators built-in group.

   B. Make the user a member of the Server Operators built-in group.

   C. Make the user a member of the Account Operators built-in group.

   D. Make the user a member of the Administrators built-in group.

13. Which type of Active Directory group can contain user accounts from any domain within the forest in which the group resides?

   A. Universal

   B. Global

C. Tree local

D. Forest

14. You need to add a group named editors to a Linux system. What should you do?

   A. Enter **newgroup -n editors** at the shell prompt.

   B. Enter **groupmod editors** at the shell prompt.

   C. Enter **groupadd editors** at the shell prompt.

   D. Enter **useradd -g editors** at the shell prompt.

15. You need to add the LEbbert user to the dbusers group on a Linux system. What should you do? (Choose two.)

   A. Enter **addtogroup dbusers LEbbert** at the shell prompt.

   B. Enter **usermod -G dbusers LEbbert** at the shell prompt.

   C. Enter **groupadd -A "LEbbert" dbusers** at the shell prompt.

   D. Enter **groupmod -A "LEbbert" dbusers** at the shell prompt.

16. Which NTFS permission allows a user to read, execute, delete, list folder contents, and write to the contents of the folder or file, but does not allow them to modify permissions assigned to files or folders?

   A. Full Control

   B. Modify

   C. Read & Execute

   D. List Folder Contents

17. The resources.odt file on your Linux system has a mode of 660. The file is owned by the LMorgan user and the users group. Your user account is VHammer on the system and is a member of the users group. What level of access do you have to the resources.odt file?

   A. Read, Write, and Execute

   B. Read and Execute

   C. Read only

   D. Read and Write

18. You need to change the permissions assigned of the contacts.odt file on a Linux system to rw–rw–r– –. Which commands can you use to do this? (Choose two.)

   A. **chmod u=rw,g=rw,o=r contacts.odt**

   B. **chmod 551 contacts.odt**

   C. **chmod u=rwx,g=rwx,o=r contacts.odt**

   D. **chmod g-rw contacts.odt**

   E. **chmod 664 contacts.odt**

19. You are designing a network implementation. Your office is composed of three suites. Suite A is within 10 meters of your server room. Suite B is about 50 meters from your server room. Suite C is about 150 meters from your server room. You plan to install a high-end managed Gigabit Ethernet switch in the server room and connect all of the Windows 7 workstations in each suite to the switch using CAT 6 cabling. Your network server will be implemented in the server room with the switch and will have Linux installed on it to provide file and print services. Will this implementation work?

    A. Yes, you can implement the network as planned.

    B. No, Windows workstations aren't compatible with Linux servers.

    C. No, the workstations in Suite C are too far away from the switch.

    D. No, you must replace the Cat 6 cabling with Cat 5e cabling to support Gigabit Ethernet speeds.

20. You are installing new server systems in your company's data center. The servers will be installed in three rows of racks with the front of each server in rows two and three facing the rear of the server in the preceding row. To prevent water damage in case of a fire, you have implemented a halon fire suppression system in the room. You have also installed an environmental monitoring system with sensors 2 feet and 6 feet from the floor. Will this implementation work?

    A. No, the servers in rows 2 and 3 might overheat.

    B. No, you should use a foam fire suppression system instead of halon.

    C. No, environmental monitors should be placed 3 feet from the floor.

    D. Yes, the implementation will work as designed.

21. You're planning to install Windows Server 2008 R2 on a system that you've built out of spare parts. Several components in the system aren't listed on the Server 2008 hardware compatibility list. This system will host a database application that will be used to track employee hours. What should you do?

    A. Install Server 2008 anyway and hope for the best.

    B. Install Server 2008 and then install the latest updates.

    C. Replace the incompatible parts with supported hardware.

    D. Download the appropriate drivers from the hardware manufacturer's web site on the Internet.

22. You are conducting a needs assessment to determine the requirements for a new network deployment. What questions should you ask? (Choose two.)

    A. What business problems will be fixed by this installation?

    B. Which server operating system should I use?

    C. Where can I get the best price on a new server?

    D. Who is requesting the new system?

    E. From which vendor should I buy switching equipment?

QUICK ANSWER KEY

1.	A, E	9.	B	17.	D
2.	B, C	10.	D	18.	A, E
3.	B	11.	D	19.	C
4.	C, D	12.	B	20.	A
5.	A	13.	A	21.	C
6.	C	14.	C	22.	A, D
7.	A	15.	B, D		
8.	C	16.	B		

IN-DEPTH ANSWERS

1. You are designing an implementation plan for a new client/server network. Users in this network will use Windows 7 workstations. You need to implement a domain controller in the network that uses Server Message Block protocol that will be used for authentication, file sharing, and printer sharing. What can you do? (Choose two.)
   A. Install a Linux server system and configure it as a domain controller using the Samba package.
   B. Install a Windows 7 Enterprise system and configure it as a domain controller.
   C. Install a Windows Vista Business system and configure it as a domain controller.
   D. Install a Windows XP Professional system and configure it as a domain controller.
   E. Install a Windows Server 2008 R2 system and configure it as a domain controller.

   ☑ **A** and **E.** You can install a Linux server and configure it as a domain controller using the Samba package. You can also install a Windows Server 2008 R2 server and configure it to function as a domain controller. In this configuration, you could use either server to store domain user accounts for authentication. Either server could also be used for file and printer sharing.

   ☒ **B, C,** and **D** are incorrect. **B, C,** and **D** are incorrect because Windows 7, Windows Vista, and Windows XP are all workstation operating systems and do not have the capability of functioning as a domain controller. However, they can join a domain hosted by a Windows or Linux server system.

2. If a Linux server has been configured to use local user accounts instead of directory user accounts, where is user account information stored? (Choose two.)
   A. /etc/group
   B. /etc/passwd
   C. /etc/shadow
   D. /etc/gshadow
   E. /etc/users

   ☑ **B** and **C.** Linux user accounts are stored in two files. General user information is stored in the /etc/passwd file. Encrypted user passwords are stored in the /etc/shadow file.

   ☒ **A, D,** and **E** are incorrect. **A** is incorrect because /etc/group contains group definitions on the system. **D** is incorrect because the /etc/gshadow file contains passwords assigned to groups. **E** is incorrect because the /etc/users file does not exist by default on a Linux system.

3. You are implementing a Linux network server that will store your organization's mission-critical files that users will access from their desktop client systems. You need to ensure that the files on the server are protected from hard disk failures and remain available 24/7. What should you do to accomplish this?

    A. Implement a RAID 0 hard disk array in the server.

    B. Implement a RAID 1 hard disk array in the server.

    C. Implement a Fibre Channel controller and external Fibre Channel hard drive in the system.

    D. Connect a tape drive to the server and configure daily backups of the file system.

    ☑ **B.** Implementing a RAID 1 array would be the best choice in this scenario. In a RAID 1 array, data is written redundantly to two or more hard disk drives in the array. If one disk in the array fails, the data remains instantly available from the other disks in the array.

    ☒ **A, C,** and **D** are incorrect. **A** is incorrect because RAID 0 arrays stripe data across multiple disks in the array without redundancy. This improves performance but does not protect data integrity. **C** is incorrect because a Fibre Channel controller and disk would also increase disk I/O performance, but it does not provide data redundancy in and of itself. Adding a Fibre Channel RAID 1 or RAID 5 array would provide redundancy with improved performance. **D** is incorrect as well. While using backups does provide data redundancy, they are also very slow to restore. It could take hours or even days to recover from a failed hard drive using backups alone. However, using backups in conjunction with a RAID 1 or RAID 5 array provides multiple layers of redundancy, which is a good strategy for protecting data.

4. You are planning the implementation of a new network server. This server will run Windows Server 2008 R2 and will be a domain controller. It will also host the Microsoft Exchange mail service. The server hardware you currently have on hand has a quad-core, 64-bit AMD processor running at 3.0 GHz. It has 2GB of RAM installed. It also has a three-drive RAID 5 array installed. The system has a 1000-watt power supply installed as well. What should you do to use this system in the deployment described in this scenario? (Choose two.)

    A. Upgrade the system to use an Intel Core7 3.2 GHz quad-core processor.

    B. Upgrade the system to a RAID 0+1 array.

    C. Upgrade the system to a redundant dual power supply.

    D. Upgrade the system to 8GB or more of RAM.

    E. Upgrade the system to a 1200-watt power supply.

☑ **C** and **D.** Running a domain controller and the Exchange e-mail service on the same system will require a lot of RAM to provide adequate performance. You should upgrade the system to 8GB (or more) of RAM, depending upon how many user accounts and mailboxes are configured on the system. In addition, you should upgrade the system to use a redundant power supply. This will allow the system to remain running should one of the power supplies fail, which happens relatively often.

☒ **A, B,** and **E** are incorrect. **A** is incorrect because switching to an Intel Core7 CPU wouldn't provide an appreciable increase in performance over a comparable AMD processor. **B** is incorrect because using a nested RAID 0+1 array wouldn't provide appreciably better protection or performance than a RAID 5 array and would increase complexity of the storage system. **E** is incorrect because the existing 1000-watt power supply should provide sufficient power for the server system. Very little would be gained by upgrading to a 1200-watt power supply.

5. Which user account is created by default on a Linux system?

A. root

B. Admin

C. Administrator

D. Guest

☑ **A.** The root user account is created by default on all Linux distributions. The root user is the super-user account on Linux, comparable to the Admin account on NetWare or the Administrator account on Windows systems.

☒ **B, C,** and **D** are incorrect. **B** is incorrect because Admin is the default super-user account created automatically on Novell NetWare/Open Enterprise Server systems. **C** is incorrect because Administrator is the default super-user account created automatically on Windows systems. **D** is incorrect because the guest user account is used to allow individuals to access a Windows system without requiring a user account. This account is disabled by default for security reasons.

6. A user called your help desk indicating she can't access a shared folder on a Windows server in the mycorp.com domain. The user logged into her Windows 7 workstation as the local JMarshall user, opened her e-mail client, and then tried to use Network Locations option to access the shared folder on the server. She was denied access. What should you do?

A. Verify that the JMarshall domain account has the necessary permissions to access the shared folder.

B. Instruct her to map a network drive to the shared folder instead of using Network Locations.

C. Instruct her log into her workstation as a domain user instead of a local user.

D. Instruct her to access the shared folder before starting her e-mail client.

☑ **C.** The key issue here is that the user logged into her workstation using a local Windows SAM account. You should instruct her to log in as a domain user. Assuming her domain user account has the necessary permissions, she should then be able to access the shared folder.

☒ **A, B,** and **D** are incorrect. **A** is incorrect because the user logged in as the local JMarshall user, not the domain JMarshall user. **B** is incorrect because domain credentials are required to enter the shared folder regardless of how it's accessed. **D** is incorrect because the e-mail client software is not preventing her from accessing the shared folder.

7. You need to create a new user account for a user named Kimberly Sanders on your Linux system. You want to specify a user name of ksanders, a full name of Kimberly Sanders, and that a home directory be created. What should you do?

A. Enter **useradd -c "Kimberly Sanders" -m ksanders** at the shell prompt.

B. Enter **useradd -c "Kimberly Sanders" -m -u ksanders** at the shell prompt.

C. Enter **usermod -c "Kimberly Sanders" -m ksanders** at the shell prompt.

D. Enter **useradd -c "Kimberly Sanders" ksanders** at the shell prompt.

☑ **A.** The **useradd -c "Kimberly Sanders" -m ksanders** command creates a new user account for a user named Kimberly Sanders with a user name of ksanders, a full name of Kimberly Sanders, and a home directory named /home/ksanders. Any user account parameters not explicitly configured in the command are assigned default values from the /etc/default/ useradd configuration file.

☒ **B, C,** and **D** are incorrect. **B** uses incorrect syntax for the **useradd** command. **C** uses an incorrect command (**usermod**). **D** omits the **-m** option, which is required to create a home directory for the user.

8. You need to delete a user account named jcarr from your Linux system and remove the contents of his home directory (/home/jcarr). What should you do?

A. Enter **userdel jcarr** at the shell prompt.

B. Enter **usermod --delete --rmhome jcarr** at the shell prompt.

C. Enter **userdel -r jcarr** at the shell prompt.

D. Enter **userdel --rmhome jcarr** at the shell prompt.

☑ **C.** Entering **userdel -r jcarr** will delete jcarr's account and remove his home directory.

☒ **A, B,** and **D** are incorrect. **A** deletes the jcarr user account, but it does not remove his home directory. **B** is incorrect because the **usermod** command is used to modify user accounts, not delete them. **D** is incorrect because it uses an incorrect option for removing the home directory (**--rmhome**).

9. Which of the following is a strong password for a user account?
   A. Bob3
   B. TuxP3nguin
   C. penguin
   D. Castle

☑ **B.** TuxP3nguin meets the specifications for a strong password because it has ten characters, uses upper- and lowercase characters, uses numbers and letters, and doesn't contain words that can be found in the dictionary.

☒ **A, C,** and **D** are incorrect. **A** is not a strong password because it contains only four characters. **C** is not a strong password because it doesn't contain numbers or uppercase letters. It is also a word found in the dictionary. **D** is not a strong password either because it is also a dictionary word. It's also somewhat short at only six characters, and it doesn't contain numbers.

10. On a Linux system, you need to use the **chage** command to specify a minimum password age of 5 days, a maximum password age of 60 days, and 5 warning days prior to password expiration for a user named rtracy. What should you do?
   A. Enter **chage -m 5 -M 5 -W 60 rtracy** at the shell prompt.
   B. Enter **chage -m 60 -M 5 -W 5 rtracy** at the shell prompt.
   C. Enter **chage rtracy** at the shell prompt.
   D. Enter **chage -m 5 -M 60 -W 5 rtracy** at the shell prompt.

☑ **D.** The **chage -m 5 -M 60 -W 5 rtracy** command specifies a minimum password age of 5 days (**-m**), a maximum password age of 60 days (**-M**), and 5 warning days (**-W**) for the rtracy user.

☒ **A, B,** and **C** are incorrect. **A** is incorrect because incorrect values are used for the **-M** and **-W** options in the command. **B** is incorrect because incorrect values are used for the **-m, -M,** and **-W** options in the command. **C** is incorrect because the command omits the options required to meet the password aging specifications of the scenario.

11. Which policy setting can be applied to Windows domain user accounts to prevent old passwords from being reused for a specified number of passwords changes?

    A. Enforce maximum password age.

    B. Passwords must meet complexity requirements.

    C. Enforce unique passwords.

    D. Enforce password history.

    ☑ **D.** The enforce password history policy setting prevents old passwords from being reused for a specified number of passwords changes. This policy should be used in conjunction with the minimum password age policy setting to prevent users from changing passwords repeatedly until they are allowed reuse their favorite password again.

    ☒ **A, B**, and **C** are incorrect. **A** is incorrect because the maximum password age policy setting specifies how long a password can be used before it must be changed. **B** is incorrect because the passwords must meet complexity requirements policy forces users to use strong passwords. **C** is incorrect because there is no enforce unique passwords password policy on a Windows system.

12. You need to delegate permission to complete a limited number of administrative tasks on your Windows server to a co-worker. You want her to be able to shut down the server, create and modify shares, back up and restore files, and change the system time. You do not want her to be able to complete any other administrative tasks on the server. What should you do?

    A. Make the user a member of the Backup Operators built-in group.

    B. Make the user a member of the Server Operators built-in group.

    C. Make the user a member of the Account Operators built-in group.

    D. Make the user a member of the Administrators built-in group.

    ☑ **B.** Users who are members of the Server Operators group can shut down servers, create and modify shares, lock and unlock the server, back up and restore files, and change the system time.

    ☒ **A, C**, and **D** are not correct. **A** is incorrect because members of the Backup Operators group are not allowed to modify shares or change the system time. **C** is incorrect members of the Account Operators group are allowed to manage user accounts. They are not allowed to complete the server maintenance tasks listed in this scenario. **D** is incorrect because making the user a member of the Administrators group would allow her full access to the server, which violates the specifications in this scenario.

13. Which type of Active Directory group can contain user accounts from any domain within the forest in which the group resides?

A. Universal

B. Global

C. Tree local

D. Forest

☑ **A.** Universal groups in Active Directory can contain user accounts from any domain within the forest in which the universal group resides.

☒ **B, C,** and **D** are incorrect. **B** is incorrect because global groups can contain user accounts only from the same domain where global group resides. **C** and **D** are incorrect because there is no such thing as a tree local or forest group in Active Directory.

14. You need to add a group named editors to a Linux system. What should you do?

A. Enter **newgroup -n editors** at the shell prompt.

B. Enter **groupmod editors** at the shell prompt.

C. Enter **groupadd editors** at the shell prompt.

D. Enter **useradd -g editors** at the shell prompt.

☑ **C.** The **groupadd** command is used to add new groups to a Linux system. In this example, the **groupadd editors** command creates a new group named editors.

☒ **A, B,** and **D** are incorrect. **A** is incorrect because the **newgroup** command doesn't exist by default on a Linux system. **B** and **D** are incorrect because the **groupmod** and **useradd** commands can't be used to create a new group on a Linux system.

15. You need to add the LEbbert user to the dbusers group on a Linux system. What should you do? (Choose two.)

A. Enter **addtogroup dbusers LEbbert** at the shell prompt.

B. Enter **usermod -G dbusers LEbbert** at the shell prompt.

C. Enter **groupadd -A "LEbbert" dbusers** at the shell prompt.

D. Enter **groupmod -A "LEbbert" dbusers** at the shell prompt.

☑ **B and D.** You can enter **usermod -G dbusers LEbbert** at the shell prompt to add the LEbbert user account to the dbusers group on a Linux system. The **groupmod -A "LEbbert" dbusers** command can also be used. Both of these commands assume the dbusers group already exists on the system.

☒ **A and C** are incorrect. **A** is incorrect because the **addtogroup** command doesn't exist by default on Linux **C** is incorrect because the **groupadd** command can't be used to add users to a group.

16. Which NTFS permission allows a user to read, execute, delete, list folder contents, and write to the contents of the folder or file, but does not allow them to modify permissions assigned to files or folders?
    A. Full Control
    B. Modify
    C. Read & Execute
    D. List Folder Contents

☑ **B.** The Modify NTFS permission allows a user to read, execute, delete, list folder contents, and write to the contents of the folder or file. However, it does not allow users to modify permissions assigned to files or folders.

☒ **A, C, and D** are incorrect. **A** is incorrect because the Full Control NTFS permission allows the user to modify permissions assigned to files and folders. **C** is incorrect because the Read & Execute NTFS permission allows users only to read the contents of files and to execute an executable. **D** is incorrect because the List Folder Contents NTFS permission allows users only to view the contents of a folder.

17. The resources.odt file on your Linux system has a mode of 660. The file is owned by the LMorgan user and the users group. Your user account is VHammer on the system and is a member of the users group. What level of access do you have to the resources.odt file?
    A. Read, Write, and Execute
    B. Read and Execute
    C. Read only
    D. Read and Write

☑ **D.** In Linux file systems, the Read permission has a numeric value of 4. The Write permission has a numeric value of 2. The Execute permission has a numeric value of 1. A file or folder's mode consists of three values. The first value is the sum of the permissions assigned to the file or folder's owner. The second value is the sum of the permissions assigned to the file's or folder's owning group. The third value is the sum of the permissions assigned to all other authenticated users on the system. In this example, VHammer is a member of the users group, which is the owning group of the file. Group is assigned a value of 6 in the mode. Therefore, all users who are members of the users group have Read (4) and Write (2) permissions to the file.

☒ **A, B,** and **C** are incorrect. **A** is incorrect because Read, Write, and Execute permissions would require a value of 7 in the second number in the file's mode. **B** is incorrect because Read and Execute permissions would require a value of 5 in the second number in the file's mode. **C** is incorrect because Read only permissions would require a value of 4 in the second number in the file's mode.

18. You need to change the permissions assigned of the contacts.odt file on a Linux system to rw–rw–r– –. Which commands can you use to do this? (Choose two.)

A. chmod u=rw,g=rw,o=r contacts.odt
B. chmod 551 contacts.odt
C. chmod u=rwx,g=rwx,o=r contacts.odt
D. chmod g-rw contacts.odt
E. chmod 664 contacts.odt

☑ **A** and **E.** Either the **chmod u=rw,g=rw,o=r contacts.odt** or the **chmod 664 contacts.odt** command sets the mode of the contacts.odt file to rw–rw–r– –. This mode grants read and write permissions to the file owner and the owning group. It also grants read permission to all other authenticated users on the system.

☒ **B, C,** and **D** are incorrect. **B** is incorrect because the command sets the file's mode to r-xr-x--x. **C** is incorrect because the command sets the file's mode to rwxrwxr--. **D** removes read and write permissions from the owning group.

19. You are designing a network implementation. Your office is composed of three suites. Suite A is within 10 meters of your server room. Suite B is about 50 meters from your server room. Suite C is about 150 meters from your server room. You plan to install a high-end managed Gigabit Ethernet switch in the server room and connect all of the Windows 7 workstations in each suite to the switch using CAT 6 cabling. Your network server will be implemented in the server room with the switch and will have Linux installed on it to provide file and print services. Will this implementation work?

A. Yes, you can implement the network as planned.

B. No, Windows workstations aren't compatible with Linux servers.

C. No, the workstations in Suite C are too far away from the switch.

D. No, you must replace the Cat 6 cabling with Cat 5e cabling to support Gigabit Ethernet speeds.

☑ **C.** In this scenario, the workstations in Suite C are too far away from the switch. The maximum cable length for a Gigabit Ethernet network using CAT 6 cabling is 100 meters.

☒ **A, B,** and **D** are incorrect. **A** is incorrect because the maximum cable length specification is exceeded for the cable runs to Suite C. **B** is incorrect because Linux servers can be configured with the Samba service to provide domain services, file sharing, and printer sharing for Windows workstations. **D** is incorrect because Gigabit Ethernet is compatible with either CAT 5e or CAT 6 UTP. Using CAT 6 UTP would be a better choice because it allows for expansion and upgrades in the future.

20. You are installing new server systems in your company's data center. The servers will be installed in three rows of racks with the front of each server in rows two and three facing the rear of the server in the preceding row. To prevent water damage in case of a fire, you have implemented a halon fire suppression system in the room. You have also installed an environmental monitoring system with sensors 2 feet and 6 feet from the floor. Will this implementation work?

A. No, the servers in rows 2 and 3 might overheat.

B. No, you should use a foam fire suppression system instead of halon.

C. No, environmental monitors should be placed 3 feet from the floor.

D. Yes, the implementation will work as designed.

☑ **A.** Because the front of the servers in rows 2 and 3 face the rear of the servers in the row ahead of them, they will likely draw hot exhaust air from those other servers and might overheat. A better approach would be to create hot and cold aisles. This involves lining up server racks in alternating rows with cold air intakes facing one way and hot air exhausts facing the other. The rows composed of rack fronts are called cold aisles and typically face air conditioner output ducts. The rows the heated air exhausts into are called hot aisles and typically face air conditioner return ducts.

☒ **B, C,** and **D** are incorrect. **B** is incorrect because halon and foam fire suppression systems are both viable alternatives to using water-based sprinklers. **C** is incorrect because environmental monitoring equipment should be placed at multiple levels in the server room to detect hot zones. **D** is incorrect because the cooling configuration of the room has not been designed correctly.

21. You're planning to install Windows Server 2008 R2 on a system that you've built out of spare parts. Several components in the system aren't listed on the Server 2008 hardware compatibility list. This system will host a database application that will be used to track employee hours. What should you do?

A. Install Server 2008 anyway and hope for the best.

B. Install Server 2008 and then install the latest updates.

C. Replace the incompatible parts with supported hardware.

D. Download the appropriate drivers from the hardware manufacturer's web site on the Internet.

> ☑ **C.** The best approach is to use supported hardware. The HCLs for most operating systems, including Windows servers, Windows workstations, and most Linux distributions, are available on the Internet. Using supported hardware ensures that the hardware will be compatible with your operating system software.
>
> ☒ **A, B,** and **D** are incorrect. **A** is incorrect because using unsupported hardware may cause significant instability in the system. **B** and **D** are also incorrect for the same reason, unless the drivers have been tested by the operating system vendor and verified to work correctly.

22. You are conducting a needs assessment to determine the requirements for a new network deployment. What questions should you ask? (Choose two.)

A. What business problems will be fixed by this installation?

B. Which server operating system should I use?

C. Where can I get the best price on a new server?

D. Who is requesting the new system?

E. From which vendor should I buy switching equipment?

> ☑ **A and D.** To determine the requirements for a network deployment, you should conduct a formal needs assessment. Part of this process involves determining why the new the new deployment is needed and who will be using it. You should also be concerned with who will maintain the deployment when you're done, who will pay for the deployment, and who will actually perform the deployment.
>
> ☒ **B, C,** and **E** are incorrect. **B** is incorrect because a needs assessment should focus on goals, outcomes, requirements, and resources. The results of your needs assessment will dictate answers to questions such as what OS to use. **C** and **E** are incorrect because purchasing decisions should not be included in the needs assessment. Again, the results of your needs assessment will dictate answers to questions such as what hardware devices and software will be needed. You can use this information to determine the best vendors from which equipment can be purchased.

13

Maintaining and Supporting a Network

QUESTIONS

Being a technical wizard is only part of the skill set you'll need to be a network administrator. You also need to have excellent management skills. Specifically, you need to be able to organize and document the physical and logical network in your organization. A common mistake made by network administrators is thinking that they can keep their networks organized "in their heads." When the network is small, this might be possible. However, as the network grows, this organizational technique fails as the complexity of the network quickly exceeds their ability to organize it all.

Documenting the network correctly ensures that the person who takes your place someday will have the information he or she needs to manage the system effectively. In addition to documenting the physical and logical network, you need to be able to establish policies for how your network will be managed. For example, you can implement an asset management policy that dictates how equipment will be purchased and how long it will stay in service. You should also implement a change management policy to ensure that changes in the network are made cleanly and don't cause more problems than they solve.

You should also use baselining to track the performance of your key systems. You take an initial baseline when your systems are in a pristine "out of the box" condition. Then you take subsequent baselines as time passes and compare them to the original baseline. By doing this, you can identify conditions that are impacting performance.

To monitor your network systems effectively, you need to be familiar with how they store their log files. You should also be familiar with monitoring solutions such as the Simple Network Management Protocol (SNMP). You should also understand how to capture data from your network and analyze it.

In this chapter, you will answer questions that test your knowledge about these topics.

1. You have been hired as the IT manager for a midsized company. Upon inspection of the data center and wiring closet, you find the company's network infrastructure to be in a state of chaotic disorganization. What should you do? (Choose two.)
   A. Rebuild the network from scratch to be sure you understand what each device does and where each wire goes.
   B. Document the purpose of each network device, such as switches and routers.
   C. Leave the infrastructure as is and learn over time by trial and error the function of each device and wire.
   D. Group related wires together and document their purpose.
   E. Implement VLANs and group departments together on the same VLAN.

2. You need to implement a cable management plan in your server room and wiring closet. What should you do? (Choose two.)
   A. Tag each of your network devices and identify the associated connectors on your patch panel.
   B. Using colored cables, implement a color-code scheme to categorize network devices.
   C. Implement network management software to create an inventory of your network devices.
   D. Use Microsoft Visio to diagram the location of all devices in your network.
   E. Standardize on a single color for all network cabling in your network.

3. You need to create a physical map of your network. What should you do? (Choose two.)
   A. Create a database of all the workstations in your network along with their asset tag number, purchase date, and replacement cost.
   B. Determine which servers can be virtualized.
   C. Identify all WAN links and note their type and speed.
   D. Group wires in your wiring closet together by color or purpose.
   E. Identify all workstations and note their location.

4. You are creating a logical map of your network. What information should you include? (Choose two.)
   A. Domain controllers
   B. Switch locations
   C. WIC locations
   D. IP address assignments
   E. Cable runs

5. Your company uses a network server running Novell Open Enterprise Server to manage network authentication, file sharing, printer sharing, and file archiving services. All of your network users and resources are represented by objects in your organization's eDirectory tree. Documenting the tree structure and the objects it contains is part of which network documentation process?
   A. Wiring schematics
   B. Asset management
   C. Physical network map
   D. Logical network map

6. Which of the following processes or policies should be included in your organization's asset management plan? (Choose two.)
   A. Strong password policy
   B. Social engineering response process
   C. Equipment purchase approval process
   D. Equipment disposal process
   E. Cable color-coding standards

7. You've just installed several new Linux servers for a client and have installed a new Novell eDirectory tree to manage user authentication as well as rights to shared network resources. Now what should you do?
   A. Document the rights you granted to users in the eDirectory tree.
   B. Destroy all receipts for your hardware and software purchases.
   C. Create a hidden admin user in the tree in case you need to access the tree at a later date.
   D. Install any available operating system updates.

8. You've just finished the implementation of a new network for a small startup business. What should you do? (Choose two.)
   A. Make a pitch to the business owner to upgrade his network hardware.
   B. Document the firewall configuration.
   C. Specify what applications are allowed to run on each server.
   D. Document the procedure for gaining an access badge to the office complex.
   E. Install operating system updates on each network host.

9. Which of the following processes should be included in a network's change management plan? (Choose two.)
   A. A procedure for verifying the state of the system after a change has been implemented
   B. A procedure for tracking the life cycle of a new network component
   C. A procedure for approving vendors from whom new network equipment will be purchased
   D. A procedure for determining when a network component has become obsolete
   E. A procedure for testing proposed changes in a test environment

10. You are replacing a SCSI RAID 1 array in your network server with an external Fibre Channel RAID 5 storage device. As a part of your organization's change management plan, you have already identified the need for the change and have tested the upgrade in a lab environment. What should you do next?
    A. Prepare a backout plan.
    B. Schedule a time for the upgrade.
    C. Implement the new hardware.
    D. Add the new hardware to your asset database.

11. Which utilities can you use on a Linux server or workstation to develop a system baseline? (Choose two.)
    A. nmap
    B. tcpdump
    C. top
    D. netstat
    E. sar

12. You created a server baseline when your Windows Server 2008 system was initially deployed. Nine months later, you notice in your latest baselines that the server's page file utilization is increasing dramatically. What should you do?
    A. Do nothing. The system is operating perfectly.
    B. Add storage space.
    C. Upgrade to a faster CPU.
    D. Add more memory.

13. To which file do most Linux services write their log entries by default?

   A. /var/log/messages

   B. /var/log

   C. /dev/log

   D. /var/log/lastlog

14. Which SNMP component runs on your network devices to monitor their performance and send status updates?

   A. SNMP Agents

   B. SNMP Manager

   C. SNMP Management Information Base (MIB)

   D. SNMP Managed Devices

15. Which of the following are default community names used for SNMP versions 1 and 2? (Choose two.)

   A. Administrator community name: **snmpadmin**

   B. Read-Only community name: **public**

   C. Read/Write community name: **private**

   D. Trap community name: **snmptrap**

16. You need to implement an SNMP system to monitor the servers, switches, routers, firewalls, and printers in your network. However, you're concerned about potential security holes that could be opened by implementing such a system. What should you do?

   A. Implement SNMP version 1

   B. Implement SNMP version 2

   C. Implement SNMP version 3

   D. Implement SNMP version 4

17. You need to check your IIS Web Server log files on your Windows server for suspicious activity. What should you do?

   A. Review the files in the C:\windows\system32\logfiles\w3svc1 directory.

   B. Review the files in the C:\windows\system32\logfiles\msftpsvc1 directory.

   C. Review the files in the C:\windows\system32\logfiles\cluster directory.

   D. Review the files in the C:\windows\system32\config directory.

18. Which general log file on a Linux system contains log entries from most applications and services running on the system?

   A. /var/log/faillog

   B. /var/log/boot.msg

   C. /var/log/messages

   D. /var/log/wtmp

19. You need to use the **tcpdump** command on a Linux system to capture packet headers on your network for analysis. Given that the name of the network interface on the Linux system is eth0, what should you do?
    A. Enter **tcpdump --headers** at the shell prompt.
    B. Enter **tcpdump eth0** at the shell prompt.
    C. Enter **tcpdump eth0 --headers** at the shell prompt.
    D. Enter **tcpdump -i eth0** at the shell prompt.

20. You need to implement a network traffic analysis package on your network. However, your network uses a Gigabit Ethernet switch, so your management system can't see all of the traffic being transmitted on the switch. What can you do to expose all the traffic on the switch to the management system running your traffic analysis software?
    A. Replace the switch with an Ethernet hub.
    B. Configure port mirroring on the switch.
    C. Implement VLANs on the switch.
    D. Configure the Spanning Tree Protocol on the switch.

QUICK ANSWER KEY

1.	B, D	8.	B, C	15.	B, C
2.	A, B	9.	A, E	16.	C
3.	C, E	10.	A	17.	A
4.	A, D	11.	C, E	18.	C
5.	D	12.	D	19.	D
6.	C, D	13.	C	20.	B
7.	A	14.	A		

IN-DEPTH ANSWERS

1. You have been hired as the IT manager for a midsized company. Upon inspection of the data center and wiring closet, you find the company's network infrastructure to be in a state of chaotic disorganization. What should you do? (Choose two.)
    A. Rebuild the network from scratch to be sure you understand what each device does and where each wire goes.
    B. Document the purpose of each network device, such as switches and routers.
    C. Leave the infrastructure as is and learn over time by trial and error the function of each device and wire.
    D. Group related wires together and document their purpose.
    E. Implement VLANs and group departments together on the same VLAN.

    ☑ **B** and **D.** The network in this scenario needs to be organized and documented with a wiring diagram. Among other tasks, you should document the purpose of each network device, such as switches and routers. You should also group related wires together and document their purpose.

    ☒ **A, C,** and **E** are incorrect. **A** is incorrect because this would result in a tremendous amount of downtime and, frankly, isn't necessary. Documenting what's already there is a more efficient approach. **C** is incorrect because you will likely experience a serious error at some point and will not have the information required to fix the problem. A network crisis is not the time to begin learning how your network works. **E** is a great idea, but you really should learn and document the existing network before making significant changes such as implementing new VLANs.

2. You need to implement a cable management plan in your server room and wiring closet. What should you do? (Choose two.)
    A. Tag each of your network devices and identify the associated connectors on your patch panel.
    B. Using colored cables, implement a color-code scheme to categorize network devices.
    C. Implement network management software to create an inventory of your network devices.
    D. Use Microsoft Visio to diagram the location of all devices in your network.
    E. Standardize on a single color for all network cabling in your network.

☑ **A** and **B.** You can do several things to implement a cable management plan for your network. For example, you can tag each of your network devices and identify the associated connectors on your patch panel. This helps you know how your network devices are connected. You can also use colored cables to implement a color-coding scheme to categorize network devices. For example, cross-over cables could be red, servers could be gray, workstations could be blue, and printers could be orange.

☒ **C, D,** and **E** are incorrect. **C** and **D** are good ideas, but they are part of the network mapping process, not cable management. **E** is incorrect because using the same color of cable for all systems can make it more difficult to manage your cabling.

3. You need to create a physical map of your network. What should you do? (Choose two.)
- **A.** Create a database of all the workstations in your network along with their asset tag number, purchase date, and replacement cost.
- **B.** Determine which servers can be virtualized.
- **C.** Identify all WAN links and note their type and speed.
- **D.** Group wires in your wiring closet together by color or purpose.
- **E.** Identify all workstations and note their location.

☑ **C** and **E.** Creating a network map involves documenting your physical network infrastructure, such as the location of network servers, workstations, switches, routers, and firewalls. You should note the make and model of each device along with any other device-specific information, such as MAC addresses. You should also identify all WAN links and document their type and speed.

☒ **A, B,** and **D** are incorrect. **A** is incorrect because inventorying workstations in a database is part of the asset management process. **B** is incorrect because identifying servers that can be virtualized isn't a process that would be included in network mapping. However, the information gained while creating your network map could be used later on to help you decide which servers can be virtualized. **D** is incorrect because grouping wires in the wiring closet is part of the cable management process.

4. You are creating a logical map of your network. What information should you include? (Choose two.)
   A. Domain controllers
   B. Switch locations
   C. WIC locations
   D. IP address assignments
   E. Cable runs

   ☑ **A and D.** Your logical network map should document logical network information, such as the location of domain controllers, IP address assignments, the location of DHCP and DNS servers, services running on network servers, and so on.

   ☒ **B, C,** and **E** are incorrect. These choices are incorrect because they represent networking hardware components that should be included on a physical network map.

5. Your company uses a network server running Novell Open Enterprise Server to manage network authentication, file sharing, printer sharing, and file archiving services. All of your network users and resources are represented by objects in your organization's eDirectory tree. Documenting the tree structure and the objects it contains is part of which network documentation process?
   A. Wiring schematics
   B. Asset management
   C. Physical network map
   D. Logical network map

   ☑ **D.** The structure of the eDirectory tree and the objects it contains represents logical network information. Therefore, documenting the tree is part of the logical network mapping process.

   ☒ **A, B,** and **C** are incorrect. **A** is incorrect because your wiring map documents each of your cable runs along with cable connections in the wiring closet. **B** is incorrect because asset management is the process of tracking your network devices' life spans and replacement costs. **C** is incorrect because the physical network map documents the physical location of your network hardware, such as routers, servers, switches, and workstations.

6. Which of the following processes or policies should be included in your organization's asset management plan? (Choose two.)

- A. Strong password policy
- B. Social engineering response process
- C. Equipment purchase approval process
- D. Equipment disposal process
- E. Cable color-coding standards

☑ **C and D.** Your organization's asset management plan should include a process or policy for approving new network equipment requests and purchases. It should also include processes for disposing of obsolete or malfunctioning network equipment. You should also consider implementing procedures for approving vendors and life cycle management.

☒ **A, B, and E are incorrect.** A and **B** are incorrect because strong password and social engineering policies should be included in your organization's security policy. **E** is incorrect because color-coding network cables is part of your cable management plan.

7. You've just installed several new Linux servers for a client and have installed a new Novell eDirectory tree to manage user authentication as well as rights to shared network resources. Now what should you do?

- A. Document the rights you granted to users in the eDirectory tree.
- B. Destroy all receipts for your hardware and software purchases.
- C. Create a hidden admin user in the tree in case you need to access the tree at a later date.
- D. Install any available operating system updates.

☑ **A.** After installing the new servers, you should document the user accounts you created in the tree. You should also document the rights you granted to each user to files in the file system as well as to other objects in the eDirectory tree.

☒ **B, C, and D are incorrect.** **B** is incorrect because you should keep a copy of all receipts related to the project in your records. **C** is incorrect because it creates a gaping security hole in the network. It also violates the relationship of trust between you and your client. **D** is incorrect because any operating system updates should have been tested and then installed before the eDirectory tree was installed on the servers.

8. You've just finished the implementation of a new network for a small startup business. What should you do? (Choose two.)
   A. Make a pitch to the business owner to upgrade his network hardware.
   B. Document the firewall configuration.
   C. Specify what applications are allowed to run on each server.
   D. Document the procedure for gaining an access badge to the office complex.
   E. Install operating system updates on each network host.

   ☑ **B** and **C.** After completing the implementation, you should document all aspects of the network deployment. For example, you should document the rules you configured in the network firewall. You should also create a software restriction policy that specifies what applications are allowed to run on each server.

   ☒ **A, D,** and **E** are incorrect. **A** may or may not be appropriate in any given situation. At any rate, it really isn't a part of the network documentation process. **D** may be useful for your personal records if you plan to continue providing services for the organization. However, it's not a necessary component in the network documentation. **E** is incorrect because testing and applying operating system updates should have been included in the network deployment plan.

9. Which of the following processes should be included in a network's change management plan? (Choose two.)
   A. A procedure for verifying the state of the system after a change has been implemented
   B. A procedure for tracking the life cycle of a new network component
   C. A procedure for approving vendors from whom new network equipment will be purchased
   D. A procedure for determining when a network component has become obsolete
   E. A procedure for testing proposed changes in a test environment

   ☑ **A** and **E.** A network change management plan should include a procedure for verifying the state of the system after a change has been implemented. It should also include a procedure for testing proposed changes in a test environment prior to rolling out the change in the production environment.

   ☒ **B, C,** and **D** are incorrect. **B, C,** and **D** are all components of an asset management plan.

10. You are replacing a SCSI RAID 1 array in your network server with an external Fibre Channel RAID 5 storage device. As a part of your organization's change management plan, you have already identified the need for the change and have tested the upgrade in a lab environment. What should you do next?

    A. Prepare a backout plan.

    B. Schedule a time for the upgrade.

    C. Implement the new hardware.

    D. Add the new hardware to your asset database.

    ☑ **A.** After identifying the need for the change and testing the new upgrade procedure in your lab, you should next prepare a backout plan before going any farther in the process. The backout plan specifies how you will get the system back to a functional state should the hardware upgrade fail for some reason.

    ☒ **B, C,** and **D** are incorrect. **B** is incorrect because you should schedule the upgrade only after a backout plan has been created and tested. **C** is incorrect because you should proceed with the upgrade in this scenario only after a backout plan has been created and the data on the existing RAID array has been backed up. **D** is incorrect because this process is part of the asset management process, not the change management process.

11. Which utilities can you use on a Linux server or workstation to develop a system baseline? (Choose two.)

    A. nmap

    B. tcpdump

    C. top

    D. netstat

    E. sar

    ☑ **C** and **E.** You can use top and sar to develop a system baseline on a Linux system. The top utility displays display system performance information along with a list of processes currently being run by the Linux kernel. The sar utility can be used to monitor specific aspects of the system and write the output to a file for review.

    ☒ **A, B,** and **D** are incorrect. **A** is incorrect because the nmap utility is used to scan a network host for security vulnerabilities. However, it could be used as a part of a basic system baselining process to generate a list of open network ports. **B** is incorrect because the tcpdump utility is used to capture and analyze packets on the network. **D** is incorrect because the **netstat** command is used to view information about the network interfaces in a Linux system. However, like the **nmap** command, **netstat** could be used to generate a limited amount of information that could be used in the baseline, such as a list of open ports on the system.

12. You created a server baseline when your Windows Server 2008 system was initially deployed. Nine months later, you notice in your latest baselines that the server's page file utilization is increasing dramatically. What should you do?

   A. Do nothing. The system is operating perfectly.

   B. Add storage space.

   C. Upgrade to a faster CPU.

   D. Add more memory.

> ☑ **D.** A steady increase in page file utilization is an indication that the system is moving more and more data from RAM to virtual memory and probably needs more physical memory.
>
> ☒ **A, B,** and **C** are incorrect. **A** is incorrect because if you choose to do nothing, your server's performance will degrade as it spends more and more time moving information in and out of the page file instead of providing services. **B** and **C** are incorrect because adding storage space or a faster CPU will not address the problem of insufficient server RAM.

13. To which file do most Linux services write their log entries by default?

   A. /var/log/messages

   B. /var/log

   C. /dev/log

   D. /var/log/lastlog

> ☑ **C.** Most Linux services write their log entries to /dev/log device file. The syslog daemon (syslogd or syslog-ng) captures entries sent to /dev/log and writes them to the appropriate log files based on the settings contained in the /etc/syslog.conf file.
>
> ☒ **A, B,** and **D** are incorrect. **A** is partially correct because log messages from most Linux services end up in /var/log/messages by default. However, they don't write directly to the /var/log/messages file. Instead, they use the process described in the correct answer to let the syslog daemon determine to which log file the messages are written. **B** is incorrect because /var/log is a directory, not a file, on Linux. **D** is incorrect because the /var/log/lastlog file contains information about user logins.

14. Which SNMP component runs on your network devices to monitor their performance and send status updates?
   A. SNMP Agents
   B. SNMP Manager
   C. SNMP Management Information Base (MIB)
   D. SNMP Managed Devices

   ☑ **A.** SNMP Agents are small software applications that run on a variety of network devices, including servers, workstations, printers, routers, and switches. The agents monitor their respective devices and provide status information to the SNMP Manager.

   ☒ **B, C,** and **D** are incorrect. **B** is incorrect because the SNMP Manager collects data from network hosts that are being monitored via the SNMP protocol by SNMP Agents. **C** is incorrect because the MIB defines the parameters that the SNMP Agents will monitor on their respective devices. **D** is incorrect because SNMP Managed Devices are the physical devices on your network that are being monitored by SNMP Agents.

15. Which of the following are default community names used for SNMP versions 1 and 2? (Choose two.)
   A. Administrator community name: **snmpadmin**
   B. Read-Only community name: **public**
   C. Read/Write community name: **private**
   D. Trap community name: **snmptrap**

   ☑ **B** and **C.** Many SNMP systems use by default a Read-Only community name of **public** and a Read/Write community name of **private**. You should change these default community names to different values as they are used to control access to SNMP agents. SNMP versions 1 and 2 transmit community names as clear-text, allowing anyone running a sniffer to capture them easily.

   ☒ **A** and **D** are incorrect. **A** is incorrect because there is no Administrator community name in SNMP. **D** is incorrect because the Trap community name does not have a default value.

16. You need to implement an SNMP system to monitor the servers, switches, routers, firewalls, and printers in your network. However, you're concerned about potential security holes that could be opened by implementing such a system. What should you do?

    A. Implement SNMP version 1

    B. Implement SNMP version 2

    C. Implement SNMP version 3

    D. Implement SNMP version 4

    ☑ **C.** SNMP version 3 offers a much higher degree of security than earlier versions offered. Version 3 implements encryption of packets passed between the SNMP Manager and the managed devices. It requires SNMP Agents to authenticate with the SNMP Manager. It also implements mechanisms that check to see if an SNMP packet has been tampered with.

    ☒ **A, B,** and **D** are incorrect. **A** and **B** are incorrect because SNMP versions 1 and 2 are notoriously unsecure. The only authentication mechanism they provide is the community name string, which is transmitted as clear-text on the network. **D** is incorrect because there is no such thing as SNMP version 4 at this time.

17. You need to check your IIS Web Server log files on your Windows server for suspicious activity. What should you do?

    A. Review the files in the C:\windows\system32\logfiles\w3svc1 directory.

    B. Review the files in the C:\windows\system32\logfiles\msftpsvc1 directory.

    C. Review the files in the C:\windows\system32\logfiles\cluster directory.

    D. Review the files in the C:\windows\system32\config directory.

    ☑ **A.** The Microsoft IIS Web Server stores its log files in the C:\windows\system32\logfiles\w3svc1 directory. The log files in this directory are standard text files and can be viewed with a text editor.

    ☒ **B, C,** and **D** are incorrect. **B** is incorrect because the C:\windows\system32\logfiles\msftpsvc1 directory contains log files for the Microsoft FTP server. **C** is incorrect because the C:\windows\system32\logfiles\cluster directory contains log files for the Microsoft clustering service. **D** is incorrect because the C:\windows\system32\config directory contains the Microsoft Event Viewer log files. These files should be viewed with Event Viewer instead of a text editor.

18. Which general log file on a Linux system contains log entries from most applications and services running on the system?

   A. /var/log/faillog

   B. /var/log/boot.msg

   C. /var/log/messages

   D. /var/log/wtmp

   ☑ **C.** The /var/log/messages file is the general log file on a Linux system. The log messages from most Linux applications and services, with some exceptions, are written to this file by the syslog daemon. Because of this, the /var/log/messages file can become quite large. A common practice is to use the **tail** command to display the last few lines of the file, which contain the most recent entries.

   ☒ **A, B,** and **D** are incorrect. **A** is incorrect because the /var/log/faillog file contains a list of failed login attempts. This file would be viewed with the **faillog** command. **B** is incorrect because the /var/log/boot.msg file contains messages generated by the system during system startup. **D** is incorrect because the /var/log/wtmp file contains system login information. It is accessed using the **who** and **last** commands.

19. You need to use the **tcpdump** command on a Linux system to capture packet headers on your network for analysis. Given that the name of the network interface on the Linux system is eth0, what should you do?

   A. Enter **tcpdump --headers** at the shell prompt.

   B. Enter **tcpdump eth0** at the shell prompt.

   C. Enter **tcpdump eth0 --headers** at the shell prompt.

   D. Enter **tcpdump -i eth0** at the shell prompt.

   ☑ **D.** The **tcpdump -i eth0** command will capture the headers of all packets the eth0 interface can see on the network. To capture the contents of the packets, you can use the **-w** option with the command to save the packet contents to a specified file.

   ☒ **A, B,** and **C** are incorrect. **A** is incorrect because it uses an incorrect option (**--headers** is invalid). **B** is incorrect because you need to use the **-i** option with the command to specify a specific interface. If you were to enter just **tcpdump** at the shell prompt, it will use the first network interface in the system by default to capture packets. **C** is incorrect because it specifies an invalid option (**--headers**) and it omits the **-i** option, which is required to specify on which interface to capture packets.

20. You need to implement a network traffic analysis package on your network. However, your network uses a Gigabit Ethernet switch, so your management system can't see all of the traffic being transmitted on the switch. What can you do to expose all the traffic on the switch to the management system running your traffic analysis software?

A. Replace the switch with an Ethernet hub.

B. Configure port mirroring on the switch.

C. Implement VLANs on the switch.

D. Configure the Spanning Tree Protocol on the switch.

☑ **B.** Most higher end network switches provide port mirroring technology. Port mirroring allows traffic from one or more ports on the switch to be "mirrored" to the port where your management system is connected. This allows the management system to capture and analyze all of the traffic on the switch.

☒ **A, C,** and **D** are incorrect. **A** would work because using a hub would allow the management system to see all traffic on the network. However, it would also dramatically increase the amount of traffic on the network, so it isn't a viable option. **C** is incorrect because implementing VLANs would not expose traffic on the switch to the management system. **D** is incorrect because the Spanning Tree Protocol is used to prevent switching loops. It, likewise, would not expose traffic on the switch to the management workstation.

14

Network Security

QUESTIONS

In the early days of networking, network security was somewhat of a side issue. System administrators and software developers seemed to be more concerned with making the network function than they were with making sure it was secure. Today, the role of security in the network has changed radically. Due to a rash of break-ins and data thefts over the last decade, network security is of paramount importance today.

Modern information security is focused on protecting an organization or user's electronic information. Current information security challenges are becoming increasingly sophisticated and correspondingly difficult to detect. As a result, the demand for IT professionals who know how to secure networks and computers is at an all-time high.

The goals of information security are frequently summarized by the acronym *CIA*, which stands for the following:

- **Confidentiality**   Only authorized persons should be able to access information.
- **Integrity**   We need to be assured the information has not been tampered with.
- **Availability**   The information must be accessible to persons authorized to use it.

In this chapter, you answer questions that test your knowledge of basic network security principles and practices.

1. You are concerned that your organization could become the victim of a social engineering attack. What should you do to mitigate the risk?
   A. Implement a border firewall to filter inbound network traffic.
   B. Establish a written security policy.
   C. Train managers to monitor user activity.
   D. Teach users how to recognize and respond to social engineering attacks.

2. Several users have forwarded you an e-mail purporting that your company's benefits provider has just launched a new benefits management web site for all employees. To access the site, they are told in the e-mail to click a link and provide their personal information. Upon investigation, you discover that your company's benefits provider did not send this e-mail. What kind of attack just occurred?
   A. Piggybacking
   B. Phishing
   C. Denial of service
   D. Smurf

3. Which of the following scenarios best depict a man-in-the-middle attack?
   A. An attacker connects to an unsecured wireless network posing as a valid network host and intercepts network communications and tampers with their contents.
   B. An attacker connects to an unsecured wireless network and monitors the traffic being transmitted on the network without modifying it in any way.
   C. An attacker sets up a wireless access point (WAP) using the same SSID as an organization's legitimate WAP, causing users to connect to her WAP instead of their company's WAP.
   D. A user within an organization installs a WAP and connects it to the company's network without the permission or knowledge of the IT department.

4. An attacker has written an exploit that overwrites the return memory address in a stack frame of a legitimate running program on a server. As a result, the legitimate program's execution resumes at the wrong address, allowing the attacker's exploit code to be run. What kind of attack is this?
   A. Buffer overflow
   B. Virus
   C. Worm
   D. Password attack

5. You are responsible for managing your organization's public FTP server and are concerned that the server could be used to facilitate an FTP bounce attack. What should you do to prevent this?
   A. Configure the FTP server not to allow **OPEN** commands that try to connect to any host other than the originating host.
   B. Configure the FTP server not to allow **BINARY** commands that try to connect to any host other than the originating host.
   C. Configure the FTP server not to allow **PORT** commands that try to connect to any host other than the originating host.
   D. Configure the FTP server not to allow **GET** commands that try to connect to any host other than the originating host.

6. Which type of DoS attack sends a flood of TCP connection requests with spoofed source addresses, resulting in the target system being overloaded with half-open TCP connections that never get completed?
   A. Smurf
   B. ICMP Flood
   C. Teardrop
   D. SYN Flood

7. Which of the following identify the key differences between a worm and a virus? (Choose two.)
    A. Worms can independently replicate themselves.
    B. A virus relies on a host for replication.
    C. Worms must be launched by some other process on the system.
    D. Viruses must be launched by some other process on the system.
    E. Worms are usually geared toward destroying data while viruses tend to focus on gathering sensitive information.

8. An IT staffer employed by your organization wrote a database application several years ago for your human resources department to manage employee time-off requests. He was recently terminated by the company. When that happened, a latent virus that he had hidden within his application executed and destroyed all of the data in the employee time-off database. What kind of malware is described in this scenario?
    A. Keylogger
    B. Logic bomb
    C. Trojan
    D. Spyware

9. You want to implement a network monitoring host in your network that will capture data for analysis. Your network consists of a switched Gigabit Ethernet network that is also connected to a wireless 802.11n network. What should you do to accomplish this? (Choose two.)
    A. Configure the wireless interface to use a different wireless channel than the 802.11n network is configured to use.
    B. Configure the wireless interface to use an SSID different from the SSID configured on the 802.11n network.
    C. Install an 802.11n wireless network interface that is capable of operating in monitor mode.
    D. Configure a VLAN dedicated to the monitoring station and connect the host to the appropriate port in the switch.
    E. Install a Gigabit Ethernet interface in the workstation that is capable of operating in promiscuous mode.

10. Which Kerberos component is responsible for issuing tickets?
    A. Authentication Server (AS)
    B. Ticket-Granting Ticket (TGT)
    C. Key Distribution Center (KDC)
    D. Realm

11. You need to select an authentication protocol for use with a VPN tunnel. Your organization manages retirement accounts for small and medium-sized businesses, so security is critical. Which authentication protocol transmits passwords as clear-text and should *not* be used in this scenario?

   A. Password Authentication Protocol (PAP)

   B. Challenge Handshake Authentication Protocol (CHAP)

   C. Microsoft Challenge Handshake Authentication Protocol (MS-CHAP)

   D. Microsoft Challenge Handshake Authentication Protocol version 2 (MS-CHAPv2)

12. Which protocol encapsulates the Extensible Authentication Protocol (EAP) within an encrypted Transport Layer Security (TLS) tunnel?

   A. LEAP

   B. EAP-MD5

   C. PEAP

   D. EAP-PSK

13. You've been asked to implement a two-factor authentication scheme for your organization's network. What should you do? (Choose two.)

   A. Require users to supply a username and a password to log in.

   B. Require users to supply a smartcard to log in.

   C. Require users to supply a fingerprint scan to log in.

   D. Require users to supply a username, password, and fingerprint scan to log in.

   E. Require users to supply a fingerprint scan and a retina scan to log in.

14. You are designing a network deployment. One of the requirements your client has specified is that users authenticate once to the network to gain access to network resources. What should you do? (Choose two possibilities.)

   A. Recommend they implement NetWare 3.12 on their network servers using the bindery for storing user and group information.

   B. Recommend they implement Linux on their network servers using local /etc/passwd, /etc/shadow, and /etc/group files to store user and group information.

   C. Recommend they implement Microsoft Windows Server 2008 on their network servers using Active Directory to store user and group information.

   D. Recommend they implement Novell Open Enterprise Server on their network servers using eDirectory to store user and group information.

   E. Recommend they implement Microsoft Windows Server 2008 on their network servers using a workgroup to store user and group information.

15. You are using a web browser to purchase items from the www.mytechstuff.com e-commerce web site and need to submit your credit card number to the site using the Public Key Infrastructure (PKI). Your browser has requested the public key for the web server from a trusted third-party certificate authority (CA). What happens next?

    A. The browser uses the server's public key for encryption.

    B. The browser uses the server's private key for encryption.

    C. The browser uses your workstation's public key for encryption.

    D. The browser uses your workstation's private key for encryption.

16. Which of the following describe the TACACS+ protocol? (Choose two.)

    A. It uses the UDP protocol on port 49.

    B. It allows you to use up to three separate servers: one for authentication, one for authorization, and one for accounting.

    C. It encrypts only the password that is transmitted from the client to the server.

    D. It uses the TCP protocol on port 49.

    E. It is backward-compatible with RADIUS servers and clients.

17. Which of the following are entities in the network access control (NAC) mechanism defined by the 802.1x specification? (Choose two.)

    A. VPN tunnel

    B. Authenticator

    C. Certificate authority

    D. Digital signatures

    E. Supplicant

18. A small architectural consulting firm needs you to set up a firewall for its Internet connection. The firewall will be placed between its internal network and its Internet connection. The firewall needs to filter traffic based on source IP address, destination IP address, and port number. What should you do?

    A. Recommend the firm implement an application-level gateway.

    B. Recommend the firm implement a stateful firewall.

    C. Recommend the firm implement a packet-filtering firewall.

    D. Recommend the firm implement a circuit-level gateway.

19. Your organization has recently implemented a customer-facing KnowledgeBase application on a web server in your DMZ. You need to configure the boundary firewall protecting the DMZ such that traffic destined for ports 80 (HTTP) or 443 (HTTPS) on the web server is allowed through, but traffic destined for other services, such as FTP, SSH, POP3, and SMTP, is blocked. What should you do?

A. Create a rule that denies all traffic and then add two allow rules that permit traffic destined for ports 80 and 443.

B. Create deny rules for traffic destined for ports 20, 21, 22, 25, and 110; then create allow rules for traffic destined for ports 80 and 443.

C. Create a rule that allows all traffic, and then add deny rules for traffic destined for ports 20, 21, 22, 25, and 110.

D. Create a rule that allows all traffic; then create allow rules for traffic destined for ports 80 and 443.

20. By which parameter does the Standard Access Control List (ACL) on Cisco routers allow you to filter network traffic?

A. TCP three-way handshake state

B. Destination IP address

C. Source IP address

D. Protocol

21. Your organization is frequently visited by salespeople from vendors' companies. When they come into your facility, they frequently plug their laptops into any available wall jack, hoping to get Internet connectivity. You are concerned that allowing them to do this could result in the spread of malware throughout your network. What should you do?

A. Implement SNMP traps on your Cisco switch.

B. Configure port security on your Cisco switch.

C. Configure aliases on your Cisco switch.

D. Enable port analysis on your Cisco switch.

22. A small startup business has hired you to implement its network. The company is using a fractional T1 connection for Internet access. Its service provider provided a single registered IP address for the company's connection. The company currently has 11 employees. What should you do?

A. Recommend that they configure a dedicated system in the organization that provides Internet access.

B. Recommend they implement internal private IP addressing with a Network Address Translation (NAT) router facing the Internet.

C. Recommend they purchase additional registered addresses from the service provider for each employee.

D. Recommend they switch to an ADSL connection for Internet access.

23. You are helping a small startup business design its network. The business's main server will host a mission-critical database application. This database will store highly sensitive proprietary information. The business will also provide a web server that customers can access to download evaluation software, view company information, and access support documents. Where should the web server in this scenario be placed?

    A. On the internal network

    B. In the public zone

    C. On the internal network behind a NAT router configured to forward ports 80 and 443

    D. In the demilitarized zone (DMZ)

24. Which mechanism is used by host-based intrusion detection systems (HIDS) to detect intrusions?

    A. Network traffic monitoring

    B. Host log files

    C. SNMP traps

    D. Port monitoring

25. Which type of IDS captures activity and compares it against a file containing known exploits?

    A. Signature-based

    B. Anomaly-based

    C. Heuristic

    D. Host-based

26. Your organization's network is connected to the Internet using a T1 connection. Users use the Internet for competitive research. The connection is also used to provide remote users with a client-to-site VPN connection into the network. You've implemented a boundary firewall and a DMZ firewall, but you are still concerned that an intruder could find a way through and compromise sensitive data in your internal network. What could you do to prevent this from happening? (Choose two.)

    A. Delay the intruder by implementing a honeypot in the DMZ and implement a host-based IDS on the system to gather intelligence about the attacker.

    B. Delay the intruder by implementing a honeynet in the DMZ and implement a network-based IDS on the system to gather intelligence about the attacker.

    C. Isolate the internal network by disconnecting it from the DMZ.

    D. Implement an application-level gateway in the internal network facing the DMZ.

27. You've been hired to manage a mid-sized organization's network. On your first day, you notice that your predecessor has installed Microsoft Security Essentials on the Windows 7 workstations in the network. She also configured a host-based IDS on each of your Windows Server 2008 servers. The Automatic Updates feature has been disabled on all Windows servers and workstations. What should you do?

A. Upgrade Microsoft Security Essentials to an antivirus package from a company such as Symantec or Trendnet.

B. Replace the HIDS on the servers with a network-based IDS (NIDS).

C. Enable the Automatic Updates feature on all Windows hosts.

D. Implement an update server in the network, and then configure all Windows hosts to get their updates from this server.

28. Which of the following components should be included in your organization's overall security policy? (Choose two.)

A. Acceptable Use Policy (AUP)

B. Cable Management Policy (CMP)

C. Vendor Approval Process (VAP)

D. Lifecycle Management Policy (LMP)

E. An Incident Response Policy (IRP)

29. You want to conduct a vulnerability scan of a server in your network. Which tools would be most appropriate for this purpose? (Choose two.)

A. nmap

B. nessus

C. netstat

D. iperf

E. iptables

QUICK ANSWER KEY

1.	D	11.	A	21.	B
2.	B	12.	C	22.	B
3.	A	13.	B, D	23.	D
4.	A	14.	C, D	24.	B
5.	C	15.	A	25.	A
6.	D	16.	B, D	26.	A, B
7.	A, B	17.	B, E	27.	D
8.	B	18.	C	28.	A, E
9.	C, E	19.	A	29.	A, B
10.	C	20.	C		

IN-DEPTH ANSWERS

1. You are concerned that your organization could become the victim of a social engineering attack. What should you do to mitigate the risk?
   A. Implement a border firewall to filter inbound network traffic.
   B. Establish a written security policy.
   C. Train managers to monitor user activity.
   D. Teach users how to recognize and respond to social engineering attacks.

   ☑ **D.** The best way to combat social engineering is to train your users how to recognize and respond to social engineering attacks. For example, many organizations train employees to forward any calls or e-mails requesting a password or other network information to their help desk.

   ☒ **A, B,** and **C** are incorrect. **A** is incorrect because filtering network traffic with a firewall fails to address the human element involved in social engineering. **B** is incorrect because, although a written security policy is a necessary measure, it will do little to defend your network if your users don't know how to recognize social engineering attempts. **C** is incorrect because management oversight is expensive and unlikely to detect a social engineering attempt until it is too late. Raising user awareness of the issue tends to be much more effective.

2. Several users have forwarded you an e-mail purporting that your company's benefits provider has just launched a new benefits management web site for all employees. To access the site, they are told in the e-mail to click a link and provide their personal information. Upon investigation, you discover that your company's benefits provider did not send this e-mail. What kind of attack just occurred?
   A. Piggybacking
   B. Phishing
   C. Denial of service
   D. Smurf

   ☑ **B.** A phishing attack has occurred in this scenario. In a phishing attack, a spoofed e-mail containing a link to a fake web site is used to trick users into revealing sensitive information, such as a username, password, bank account number, or credit card number. Both the e-mail and the web site used in the attack appear on the surface to be legitimate.

☒ **A, C, and D are incorrect. A** is incorrect because piggybacking occurs when an unauthorized person follows behind an authorized person to enter a secured building or area within a building. Piggybacking is also sometimes called *tailgating*. **C** is incorrect because a denial of service (DoS) attack involves using network mechanisms to flood a particular host with so many bogus requests that it can no longer respond to legitimate network requests. **D** is incorrect because a Smurf attack is a distributed type of DoS attack that inserts a target system's IP address for the source address of ICMP echo request packets, causing a flood of ICMP echo response packets to be sent to a victim system.

---

3. Which of the following scenarios best depict a man-in-the-middle attack?

A. An attacker connects to an unsecured wireless network posing as a valid network host and intercepts network communications and tampers with their contents.

B. An attacker connects to an unsecured wireless network and monitors the traffic being transmitted on the network without modifying it in any way.

C. An attacker sets up a wireless access point (WAP) using the same SSID as an organization's legitimate WAP, causing users to connect to her WAP instead of their company's WAP.

D. A user within an organization installs a WAP and connects it to the company's network without the permission or knowledge of the IT department.

☑ **A.** A man-in-the-middle attack occurs when the attacker intercepts legitimate network traffic and then poses as one of the parties involved in the network communications. The best way to defend against this type of attack is to use some type of authentication protocol that requires mutual authentication.

☒ **B, C, and D are incorrect. B** is incorrect because it describes a passive logging attack. **C** is incorrect because it describes an evil twin attack. **D** is incorrect because it describes a rogue WAP security issue.

---

4. An attacker has written an exploit that overwrites the return memory address in a stack frame of a legitimate running program on a server. As a result, the legitimate program's execution resumes at the wrong address, allowing the attacker's exploit code to be run. What kind of attack is this?

A. Buffer overflow

B. Virus

C. Worm

D. Password attack

☑ **A.** Because the exploit overwrites the return address in the stack frame of a legitimate running program, this is a buffer overflow attack. This allows whatever instructions are stored at the return address to be run without your knowledge or permission.

☒ **B, C,** and **D** are incorrect. **B** is partially correct in that the buffer overflow may be used as an insertion vector for a virus. **C** is incorrect because a worm is a self-replicating type of virus. **D** is incorrect because a password attack attempts to identify the password used by a user account.

5. You are responsible for managing your organization's public FTP server and are concerned that the server could be used to facilitate an FTP bounce attack. What should you do to prevent this?

   A. Configure the FTP server not to allow **OPEN** commands that try to connect to any host other than the originating host.

   B. Configure the FTP server not to allow **BINARY** commands that try to connect to any host other than the originating host.

   C. Configure the FTP server not to allow **PORT** commands that try to connect to any host other than the originating host.

   D. Configure the FTP server not to allow **GET** commands that try to connect to any host other than the originating host.

☑ **C.** Typically, the **PORT** command is used to configure the data connection between the FTP server and the FTP client to use a high port (above 1024) instead of the default port 20. The FTP bounce attack occurs when an attacker issues the **PORT** command but directs it to a host other than the FTP server or client. The **PORT** command attempts to establish a connection with the target host on the specified port. To keep this from happening, you need to configure your FTP server not to allow **PORT** commands that try to connect to any host other than the originating host.

☒ **A, B,** and **D** are incorrect. **A** is incorrect because the **OPEN** command is used to establish an FTP connection with an FTP server. **B** is incorrect because the **BINARY** command is used to tell the FTP server what type of file is to be downloaded. Text files can be downloaded using the ASCII command. **D** is incorrect because the **GET** command is used to download a file from the FTP server to the FTP client.

6. Which type of DoS attack sends a flood of TCP connection requests with spoofed source addresses, resulting in the target system being overloaded with half-open TCP connections that never get completed?

   A. Smurf

   B. ICMP Flood

   C. Teardrop

   D. SYN Flood

☑ **D.** A SYN Flood DoS attack sends a flood of TCP SYN messages with an invalid source address to a target system. The target responds with the appropriate SYN/ACK responses, but because the source address is invalid, the target never receives the final ACK messages that complete the connections. The target must then wait for the half-open connections to timeout before it can accept new connection requests. As a result, the target becomes unavailable for legitimate TCP connections.

☒ **A, B,** and **C** are incorrect. **A** and **B** are incorrect because Smurf and ICMP Flood attacks send ICMP echo requests to the broadcast address of a network segment, causing all hosts on the network to respond with an ICMP echo reply. The source address of the ICMP echo request packets is spoofed with the IP address of the target system, causing all ICMP echo response packets to be sent to the target system and potentially overloading it. **C** is incorrect because the Teardrop attack is an older DoS attack that sends IP fragments with oversized payloads to the target host, which can cause some older operating systems to crash.

---

7. Which of the following identify the key differences between a worm and a virus? (Choose two.)

   A. Worms can independently replicate themselves.

   B. A virus relies on a host for replication.

   C. Worms must be launched by some other process on the system.

   D. Viruses must be launched by some other process on the system.

   E. Worms are usually geared toward destroying data while viruses tend to focus on gathering sensitive information.

☑ **A** and **B.** By definition, a worm is capable of independently replicating itself. It uses an available network connection to send copies of itself to other computers. A virus, on the other hand, must infect a host, such as a file, for it to be replicated. The virus is replicated when the infected file is copied to another computer.

☒ C, D, and E are incorrect. C and D are incorrect because both worms and viruses are not always dependent upon other processes to launch them. E is incorrect because both worms and virus can destroy data or gather sensitive information, among other nefarious deeds.

8. An IT staffer employed by your organization wrote a database application several years ago for your human resources department to manage employee time-off requests. He was recently terminated by the company. When that happened, a latent virus that he had hidden within his application executed and destroyed all of the data in the employee time-off database. What kind of malware is described in this scenario?

   A. Keylogger
   B. Logic bomb
   C. Trojan
   D. Spyware

☑ **B.** The malware in this scenario is a logic bomb. With a logic bomb, malware is hidden within what appears to be a legitimate application. The application functions normally until a certain event occurs—in this case, its programmer being fired. When the predetermined event occurs, the latent malware within the application becomes active.

☒ A, D, and E are incorrect. A is incorrect because a keylogger records user keystrokes (which may include usernames and passwords) and sends them to a specified network location or e-mail address. C is nearly correct in that a Trojan tricks you into installing what you think to be a legitimate application, only to find that you installed a virus instead. The key difference between a Trojan and a logic bomb is the latency of the malware. The malware in a Trojan goes active immediately and the application you thought you were installing rarely actually works. D is incorrect because spyware is hidden malware that quietly monitors and collects information about you as you work on the computer.

9. You want to implement a network monitoring host in your network that will capture data for analysis. Your network consists of a switched Gigabit Ethernet network that is also connected to a wireless 802.11n network. What should you do to accomplish this? (Choose two.)

    A. Configure the wireless interface to use a different wireless channel than the 802.11n network is configured to use.

    B. Configure the wireless interface to use an SSID different from the SSID configured on the 802.11n network.

    C. Install an 802.11n wireless network interface that is capable of operating in monitor mode.

    D. Configure a VLAN dedicated to the monitoring station and connect the host to the appropriate port in the switch.

    E. Install a Gigabit Ethernet interface in the workstation that is capable of operating in promiscuous mode.

    ☑ **C and E.** To monitor network traffic on the wired network, the network board in the management system must be able to operate in promiscuous mode. In addition, it should be connected to the monitor port on the switch. To capture wireless traffic, you must implement a wireless interface that is capable of operating in monitor mode.

    ☒ **A, B,** and **D** are incorrect. **A** and **B** are incorrect because you should configure the wireless interface in the monitoring workstation to use the same SSID and channel as the 802.11n network. **D** is incorrect because connecting the monitoring station to a dedicated VLAN would further isolate the host from traffic on the switch.

10. Which Kerberos component is responsible for issuing tickets?

    A. Authentication Server (AS)

    B. Ticket-Granting Ticket (TGT)

    C. Key Distribution Center (KDC)

    D. Realm

    ☑ **C.** The Kerberos Key Distribution Center (KDC) is responsible for issuing tickets to network hosts. A ticket is needed for a host to request a service from another other host on the network.

    ☒ **A, B,** and **D** are incorrect. **A** is incorrect because the Authentication Server (AS) is a component within the KDC that grants the requesting host a Ticket-Granting Ticket (TGT). **B** is incorrect because a TGT gives the host permission to request a service ticket. **D** is incorrect because a realm is the administrative domain for the Kerberos service.

11. You need to select an authentication protocol for use with a VPN tunnel. Your organization manages retirement accounts for small and medium-sized businesses, so security is critical. Which authentication protocol transmits passwords as clear-text and should *not* be used in this scenario?

   A. Password Authentication Protocol (PAP)

   B. Challenge Handshake Authentication Protocol (CHAP)

   C. Microsoft Challenge Handshake Authentication Protocol (MS-CHAP)

   D. Microsoft Challenge Handshake Authentication Protocol version 2 (MS-CHAPv2)

   ☑ **A.** The Password Authentication Protocol (PAP) is considered too unsecure for most modern networks because it transmits passwords as clear-text. A hacker using a packet sniffer could capture passwords as they are transmitted on the network, which would compromise the security of the link.

   ☒ **B, C,** and **D** are incorrect because CHAP, MS-CHAP, andMS-CHAPv2 each create an MD5 (CHAP) or an MD4 (MS-CHAP and MS-CHAPv2) password hash that is transmitted from the client to the server. If the hashes for the password are the same on the client and the server, then the client is authenticated. The key advantage of using these authentication mechanisms is the fact that the actual password itself is never transmitted on the network. However, you should be aware that the hashes can still be compromised if they are captured and compared against a rainbow table, which could potentially reveal the password that was used to create the hash.

12. Which protocol encapsulates the Extensible Authentication Protocol (EAP) within an encrypted Transport Layer Security (TLS) tunnel?

   A. LEAP

   B. EAP-MD5

   C. PEAP

   D. EAP-PSK

   ☑ **C.** One of the shortcomings of EAP is the fact that it assumes that security is being provided by another protocol, which may or may not be the case. If the assumed security component is missing, the EAP authentication information could potentially be exposed on the network. To address this issue, the Protected Extensible Authentication Protocol (PEAP) encapsulates EAP within an encrypted TLS tunnel.

   ☒ **A, B,** and **D** are incorrect. **A** and **B** are incorrect because the Lightweight Extensible Authentication Protocol (LEAP) and EAP-MD5 both protect authentication information using MD5 hashes, which are much less secure than TLS. **D** is incorrect because EAP-PSK uses preshared keys for authentication and encryption instead of TLS.

13. You've been asked to implement a two-factor authentication scheme for your organization's network. What should you do? (Choose two.)
    A. Require users to supply a username and a password to log in.
    B. Require users to supply a smartcard to log in.
    C. Require users to supply a fingerprint scan to log in.
    D. Require users to supply a username, password, and fingerprint scan to log in.
    E. Require users to supply a fingerprint scan and a retina scan to log in.

> ☑ **B** and **D.** Multifactor authentication requires the user to supply two or more authentication factors from the three categories of authentication factors: 1) Something they know, 2) Something they have, and 3) Something they are. A smartcard is an example of two-factor authentication because it requires the user to supply something they have (the smartcard) and something they know (the PIN number assigned to the smartcard). Requiring users to supply a username, password, and fingerprint scan is also an example of two-factor authentication because users must supply something they know (the username and password) along with something they are (the fingerprint scan).
>
> ☒ **A, C,** and **E** are incorrect. **A** is incorrect because usernames and passwords come from only one authentication factor category (what the user knows). **C** is incorrect because requiring a fingerprint scan also only utilizes one authentication factor category (what the user is). **E** is incorrect because retina scans and fingerprint scans also utilize only one authentication factor category (what the user is).

14. You are designing a network deployment. One of the requirements your client has specified is that users authenticate once to the network to gain access to network resources. What should you do? (Choose two possibilities.)
    A. Recommend they implement NetWare 3.12 on their network servers using the bindery for storing user and group information.
    B. Recommend they implement Linux on their network servers using local /etc/passwd, /etc/shadow, and /etc/group files to store user and group information.
    C. Recommend they implement Microsoft Windows Server 2008 on their network servers using Active Directory to store user and group information.
    D. Recommend they implement Novell Open Enterprise Server on their network servers using eDirectory to store user and group information.
    E. Recommend they implement Microsoft Windows Server 2008 on their network servers using a workgroup to store user and group information.

☑ **C** and **D.** Using Windows servers and Active Directory will allow your users to log into the network once and have access to all network resources to which they have been assigned permissions. Likewise, using Open Enterprise Servers with eDirectory will also allow users to log into the network once and have access to all network resources to which they have been assigned rights. This is possible because both Active Directory and eDirectory are composed of objects within a single database that represent users, groups, and network resources.

☒ **A, B,** and **E** are incorrect. **A** is incorrect because older NetWare servers maintain a local user and group database called the *bindery* on each individual server. To enable single sign-on, you would have to implement some type of bindery synchronization solution to ensure each bindery database contained the same user and group accounts. **B** is incorrect because Linux servers that use local authentication also maintain separate user and group accounts on each system. To enable single sign-on, you could implement the Network Information Service (NIS) to enable each Linux server in the network to use a common set of user and group accounts. **E** is incorrect because Windows servers in a workgroup maintain a set of user and group accounts in the local SAM database. To enable single sign-on, you would need to convert one of the servers to a domain controller and join all of the other systems in the network to the domain.

15. You are using a web browser to purchase items from the www.mytechstuff.com e-commerce web site and need to submit your credit card number to the site using the Public Key Infrastructure (PKI). Your browser has requested the public key for the web server from a trusted third-party certificate authority (CA). What happens next?

A. The browser uses the server's public key for encryption.

B. The browser uses the server's private key for encryption.

C. The browser uses your workstation's public key for encryption.

D. The browser uses your workstation's private key for encryption.

☑ **A.** When using PKI to encrypt messages, your browser will first request the public key for a given web site from a CA (either internal or external). The CA sends the public key to your browser, which will then use it to encrypt the message and then send it to the web server. The server uses its private key to decrypt the message that was encrypted with its public key by your web browser. The important thing to remember about PKI is that a message encrypted with a public key can be decrypted only with the corresponding private key. The public key can't be used to decrypt a message encrypted with the same public key.

☒ **B, C,** and **D** are incorrect. **B** is incorrect because the server's private key is kept securely on the server. It is never sent to client systems. **C** is incorrect because a message encrypted by the workstation's public key could be decrypted only with the workstation's private key, which the server doesn't have. **D** is incorrect because workstation uses the server's public key to encrypt the message, not its own private key (if it has one).

16. Which of the following describe the TACACS+ protocol? (Choose two.)
    A. It uses the UDP protocol on port 49.
    B. It allows you to use up to three separate servers: one for authentication, one for authorization, and one for accounting.
    C. It encrypts only the password that is transmitted from the client to the server.
    D. It uses the TCP protocol on port 49.
    E. It is backward-compatible with RADIUS servers and clients.

☑ **B** and **D.** The TACACS+ protocol is an AAA protocol originally developed by Cisco to provide a centralized remote access system. TACACS+ provides three protocols for authentication, authorization, and accounting, which potentially allows each one to be configured on a different server in your network. Unlike RADIUS, which uses the UDP protocol, TACACS+ uses the TCP protocol on port 49.

☒ **A, C,** and **E** are incorrect. **A** is incorrect because TACACS+ uses the TCP protocol. **C** is incorrect because TACACS+ encrypts all transmissions between the client and the server, unlike RADIUS, which encrypts only passwords. **E** is incorrect because the TACACS+ protocol is completely different from RADIUS and is not backward-compatible with it.

17. Which of the following are entities in the network access control (NAC) mechanism defined by the 802.1x specification? (Choose two.)
    A. VPN tunnel
    B. Authenticator
    C. Certificate authority
    D. Digital signatures
    E. Supplicant

☑ **B** and **E.** The 802.1x specification defines three entities that participate in the network access control mechanism. The *supplicant* is a client device (such as a workstation) that needs to connect to the network. The *authenticator* is a network device that the supplicant uses to connect to the network, such as a wireless access point or a switch. The *authentication server* receives the supplicant's authentication credentials from the authenticator and determines whether or not the supplicant is allowed to access the network.

☒ **A, C,** and **D** are incorrect. **A** is incorrect because the 802.1x specification applies to many types of networks, including LANs, WANs, and wireless LANs. **C** and **D** are incorrect because certificate authorities and digital signatures are associated with the Public Key Infrastructure (PKI).

18. A small architectural consulting firm needs you to set up a firewall for its Internet connection. The firewall will be placed between its internal network and its Internet connection. The firewall needs to filter traffic based on source IP address, destination IP address, and port number. What should you do?

A. Recommend the firm implement an application-level gateway.

B. Recommend the firm implement a stateful firewall.

C. Recommend the firm implement a packet-filtering firewall.

D. Recommend the firm implement a circuit-level gateway.

☑ **C.** A packet-filtering firewall captures all packets passing through it and compares them against a set of rules you define that specifies what type of traffic is allowed and what type isn't. A packet-filtering firewall can filter traffic based on the source address, destination address, source port, destination port, and protocol type. As such, a packet-filtering firewall operates at the network and transport layers of the OSI model. Packet-filtering firewalls are frequently implemented as dedicated hardware appliances. However, you can also build your own by installing multiple network boards in a system and configuring a software firewall. For example, you can use **iptables** to implement a software-based packet-filtering firewall on Linux hosts.

☒ **A, B,** and **D** are incorrect. **A** is incorrect because an application-level gateway is a type of firewall that operates at the application layer of the OSI model and is usually designed to manage traffic for a specific network application, such as HTTP traffic. **B** is incorrect because a stateful firewall operates at the transport layer of the OSI model. A stateful firewall monitors protocol sessions instead of individual packets. **D** is incorrect because a circuit-level gateway is a type of firewall that monitors the status of the three-way TCP handshake used to establish a TCP session.

19. Your organization has recently implemented a customer-facing KnowledgeBase application on a web server in your DMZ. You need to configure the boundary firewall protecting the DMZ such that traffic destined for ports 80 (HTTP) or 443 (HTTPS) on the web server is allowed through, but traffic destined for other services, such as FTP, SSH, POP3, and SMTP, is blocked. What should you do?

    A.   Create a rule that denies all traffic and then add two allow rules that permit traffic destined for ports 80 and 443.

    B.   Create deny rules for traffic destined for ports 20, 21, 22, 25, and 110; then create allow rules for traffic destined for ports 80 and 443.

    C.   Create a rule that allows all traffic, and then add deny rules for traffic destined for ports 20, 21, 22, 25, and 110.

    D.   Create a rule that allows all traffic; then create allow rules for traffic destined for ports 80 and 443.

    ☑   **A.** A guideline you should follow when configuring firewalls is to create an implicit deny rule first that blocks all traffic, and then add allow rules for the specific traffic you want to allow through. In this scenario, you should first create a rule that denies all traffic and then add two allow rules that permit traffic destined for ports 80 and 443.

    ☒   **B, C,** and **D** are incorrect. **B** is incorrect because it uses only explicit deny rules. Depending on the default rules used by the firewall, this configuration will block traffic to the services specified while allowing traffic to the web server, but it could potentially allow all other traffic not explicitly denied through as well. **C** is incorrect because it allows all traffic through except for that explicitly denied by the deny rules. **D** is incorrect because it also allows all traffic through using an implicit allow rule.

20. By which parameter does the Standard Access Control List (ACL) on Cisco routers allow you to filter network traffic?

    A.   TCP three-way handshake state

    B.   Destination IP address

    C.   Source IP address

    D.   Protocol

    ☑   **C.** The Standard ACL on Cisco routers allows you to configure a packet-filtering firewall that filters network traffic based on source IP address. You configure ACLs using the **access-list** command.

☒ **A, B**, and **D** are incorrect. **A** is incorrect because Standard ACLs are not capable of configure a stateful or circuit-level firewall. **B** is incorrect because Extended ACLs are required to filter based on destination IP address on a Cisco router. **D** is incorrect because Standard ACLs are not capable of filtering traffic by protocol.

21. Your organization is frequently visited by salespeople from vendors' companies. When they come into your facility, they frequently plug their laptops into any available wall jack, hoping to get Internet connectivity. You are concerned that allowing them to do this could result in the spread of malware throughout your network. What should you do?

A. Implement SNMP traps on your Cisco switch.

B. Configure port security on your Cisco switch.

C. Configure aliases on your Cisco switch.

D. Enable port analysis on your Cisco switch.

☑ **B.** The port security feature on a Cisco switch allows you to configure the switch such that only network hosts that have a specific MAC address are allowed to connect to a switch port. In this scenario, port security would prevent external salespeople from connecting their laptops to your network.

☒ **A, C,** and **D** are incorrect. **A** is incorrect because SNMP traps would not prevent unauthorized users from connecting to the LAN. **C** is incorrect because aliases on a Cisco switch simply allow you to configure shorthand aliases for long commands. **D** is incorrect because port analysis enables port monitoring, but it doesn't prevent port use by unauthorized users.

22. A small startup business has hired you to implement its network. The company is using a fractional T1 connection for Internet access. Its service provider provided a single registered IP address for the company's connection. The company currently has 11 employees. What should you do?

A. Recommend that they configure a dedicated system in the organization that provides Internet access.

B. Recommend they implement internal private IP addressing with a Network Address Translation (NAT) router facing the Internet.

C. Recommend they purchase additional registered addresses from the service provider for each employee.

D. Recommend they switch to an ADSL connection for Internet access.

☑ **B.** You should recommend that they implement a private IP addressing scheme, such as 10.*x.x.x*, on their internal network and use a NAT router to connect to the Internet. The NAT router will translate the private IP addresses into the single registered IP address whenever an internal host accesses an Internet resource. You usually also implement Port Address Translation (PAT) in conjunction with NAT to translate port numbers as well as IP addresses.

☒ **A, C,** and **D** are incorrect. **A** is incorrect because it would be unfeasible (and unnecessary) to require all employees to share a workstation when they need Internet access. **C** would work, but it would increase the cost of the network and isn't necessary. It also increases complexity because you must ensure you have enough registered addresses to accommodate growth within the organization. **D** is incorrect because ADSL connections usually provide only a single registered IP address, just as was provided with the T1 line in this scenario.

23. You are helping a small startup business design its network. The business's main server will host a mission-critical database application. This database will store highly sensitive proprietary information. The business will also provide a web server that customers can access to download evaluation software, view company information, and access support documents. Where should the web server in this scenario be placed?

A. On the internal network

B. In the public zone

C. On the internal network behind a NAT router configured to forward ports 80 and 443

D. In the demilitarized zone (DMZ)

☑ **D.** The best place for a web server in this scenario that contains customer-facing information would be behind the organization's boundary firewall in the DMZ. This isolates the web server from the internal network. An attack that exploits a vulnerability in the web server would affect other systems only in the DMZ. The internal database server would be protected by the DMZ firewall, which has a high level of security.

☒ **A, B,** and **C** are incorrect. **A** and **C** are incorrect because placing the web server on the internal network would require you to allow incoming traffic from the Internet onto the internal network. Doing so would represent a significant security risk. **B** is incorrect because placing the web server in the public zone would place it outside the administrator's direct control and expose it to every hacker in the world.

24. Which mechanism is used by host-based intrusion detection systems (HIDS) to detect intrusions?
  A. Network traffic monitoring
  B. Host log files
  C. SNMP traps
  D. Port monitoring

  ☑ **B.** Host-based IDS usually use the log files created by the operating system and applications on the host it is protecting to detect intrusion attempts.

  ☒ **A, C,** and **D** are incorrect. **A** is incorrect because HIDS do not monitor network traffic to detect intrusions. This is typically done by network-based intrusion detection systems (NIDS). **C** and **D** are incorrect because HIDS don't use SNMP traps or port monitoring to detect intrusions.

25. Which type of IDS captures activity and compares it against a file containing known exploits?
  A. Signature-based
  B. Anomaly-based
  C. Heuristic
  D. Host-based

  ☑ **A.** Signature-based IDS captures system activity and compares it against a file containing known exploits. If it finds a match, it sends out notification of an intrusion. An active IDS (also called an intrusion *prevention* system or IPS) may also take steps to stop the intrusion.

  ☒ **B, C,** and **D** are incorrect. **B** and **C** are incorrect because neither anomaly-based nor heuristic IDS use a signature file to detect intrusions. Instead, they both analyze the behavior of the system looking for activities that are out of the ordinary. These two types of IDS are capable of detecting new types of intrusions where signature-based IDS can detect only intrusion methods contained in the signature file. **D** is incorrect because a HIDS can be signature-based, anomaly-based, or heuristic.

26. Your organization's network is connected to the Internet using a T1 connection. Users use the Internet for competitive research. The connection is also used to provide remote users with a client-to-site VPN connection into the network. You've implemented a boundary firewall and a DMZ firewall, but you are still concerned that an intruder could find a way through and compromise sensitive data in your internal network. What could you do to prevent this from happening? (Choose two.)

A. Delay the intruder by implementing a honeypot in the DMZ and implement a host-based IDS on the system to gather intelligence about the attacker.

B. Delay the intruder by implementing a honeynet in the DMZ and implement a network-based IDS on the system to gather intelligence about the attacker.

C. Isolate the internal network by disconnecting it from the DMZ.

D. Implement an application-level gateway in the internal network facing the DMZ.

☑   **A and B.** You can delay (and possibly catch) an intruder by implementing a honeypot system or a honeynet network as a decoy in the DMZ. With the appropriate IDS system in place, you can monitor attackers as they try to break into these tempting, yet worthless, systems.

☒   **C and D** are incorrect. C is incorrect because isolating the internal network would prevent internal users from using the Internet for competitive research. It would also prevent remote users from using the VPN to access the network. **D** is incorrect because application-level gateways are used to manage traffic for a specific application, such as a web server. They do not provide the type of protection required in this scenario.

27. You've been hired to manage a mid-sized organization's network. On your first day, you notice that your predecessor has installed Microsoft Security Essentials on the Windows 7 workstations in the network. She also configured a host-based IDS on each of your Windows Server 2008 servers. The Automatic Updates feature has been disabled on all Windows servers and workstations. What should you do?

A. Upgrade Microsoft Security Essentials to an antivirus package from a company such as Symantec or Trendnet.

B. Replace the HIDS on the servers with a network-based IDS (NIDS).

C. Enable the Automatic Updates feature on all Windows hosts.

D. Implement an update server in the network, and then configure all Windows hosts to get their updates from this server.

☑ **D.** The best solution in this scenario would be to implement an update server in the network and then configure your Windows hosts to get their updates from this server. This setup will allow you to test all updates in a lab environment before rolling them out into production.

☒ **A, B,** and **C** are incorrect. **A** is incorrect because switching to a different antivirus package isn't necessary in this scenario. **B** is incorrect because NIDS aren't necessarily better than HIDS. Each type of IDS plays a specific role in the overall security of the network. **C** is partially correct. Enabling Automatic Updates would ensure that your Windows hosts are updated regularly. However, using an update server would allow you to test all updates before rolling them out to your production environment. It would also eliminate redundant downloads of the same update files from the Internet to multiple Windows hosts.

28. Which of the following components should be included in your organization's overall security policy? (Choose two.)
   A. Acceptable Use Policy (AUP)
   B. Cable Management Policy (CMP)
   C. Vendor Approval Process (VAP)
   D. Lifecycle Management Policy (LMP)
   E. An Incident Response Policy (IRP)

☑ **A** and **E.** Your overall security policy should include, among other things, an Acceptable Use Policy and an Incident Response Policy. The AUP defines the purposes for which the organization's computer equipment and network can and cannot be used. The IRP defines specific procedures that should be taken when a security incident occurs.

☒ **B, C,** and **D** are incorrect. **B** is incorrect because a Cable Management Policy is part of your physical network management plan. **C** and **D** are incorrect because the Vendor Approval Process and Lifecycle Management Policy are part of your asset management plan.

29. You want to conduct a vulnerability scan of a server in your network. Which tools would be most appropriate for this purpose? (Choose two.)

    A. nmap

    B. nessus

    C. netstat

    D. iperf

    E. iptables

    ☑   **A** and **B.** The nmap and nessus tools provide excellent security scanning abilities. The nessus tool can check for misconfigured hardware or software that opens security holes, verify that default or blank passwords have not been used, and see if the system is susceptible to mangled IP packets. The nmap tool can discover network hosts, scan for open ports, and report operating system types and versions.

    ☒   **C, D** and **E** are incorrect. **C** is partially correct in that netstat provides some vulnerability testing functions, such as scanning for open ports. However, it is much less powerful than nmap or nessus. **D** is incorrect because iperf is used to test network bandwith between two hosts. **E** is incorrect because iptables is used to configure software-based firewalls on Linux systems.

15

Troubleshooting the Network

QUESTIONS

It's often been said that life as a network administrator involves hour after hour of boredom followed by a few minutes of sheer terror. The day-to-day work of a network admin is fairly routine. However, when problems happen on the network, mass panic can ensue. The key to surviving these times is in knowing how to troubleshoot network issues effectively and efficiently. Much like a doctor, you must first do no harm; then you must fix what ails the network.

The key is to use a standardized troubleshooting model. By using a standardized process, you can adapt to, confront, and resolve a broad range of network problems. Instead of using a methodical troubleshooting approach, many new network administrators go off half-cocked and start trying to implement fixes before they really understand the problem. They try one fix after another, hoping that one of them will repair the issue. But this is a very dangerous practice that can (and will) cause more problems than it solves.

Instead, you should use a standardized troubleshooting model. The goal of a troubleshooting model is to identify concretely the source of the problem before you start fixing things. In this chapter, you answer questions that test your knowledge of the troubleshooting process. You also are presented with several troubleshooting scenarios and are asked to determine the most appropriate course of action to take.

1. Several users have called to complain that print jobs sent to a shared network printer are not being printed. What should you do to determine the scope of the problem? (Choose two.)
   A. Identify which users are affected by the problem and where they are located.
   B. Establish a theory of probable cause.
   C. Question the users experiencing the problem to determine exactly what symptoms they are experiencing.
   D. Establish a plan of action to resolve the problem and identify potential effects.
   E. Escalate this issue to a network printing specialist.

2. A user called to complain that she is unable to access the Internet from her Windows 7 workstation. You are in the first stage of troubleshooting the issue. What should you do?
   A. Use the **IPCONFIG /RELEASE** and **IPCONFIG /RENEW** commands on her workstation to renew her DHCP lease.
   B. Install the latest updates from Microsoft on the workstation.
   C. Turn off the Windows firewall on the workstation.
   D. Use the **IPCONFIG /ALL** command on her workstation to view her current networking configuration.

3. You've discovered that the eDirectory partition replication process is failing between three of your Novell servers. You are in the first stage of troubleshooting the issue. What key question should you ask?

   A. Will promoting a Read/Write replica to a Master replica fix the issue?

   B. What has changed in the system since eDirectory last replicated correctly?

   C. Will installing a second network interface dedicated to replication traffic fix the issue?

   D. Should the Read/Write replicas be removed from the replica ring?

4. A small business client has called indicating that they have lost Internet connectivity through their DSL connection. You've gathered all information you can about the issue, which appears to be affecting all users on the network. The outage began sometime between midnight on Thursday and 8:00 A.M. on Friday when the owner opened the office for the day. You now need to establish a theory of probably cause. Which hypothesis should you test first?

   A. The company needs to switch to a different service provider.

   B. The DSL modem needs to be upgraded to a newer model that supports faster connection speeds.

   C. The company needs to upgrade to a T1 line.

   D. The DSL modem needs to be restarted.

5. You are troubleshooting an issue with a user's Windows 7 workstation. After gathering information, you have arrived at a theory of probable cause that the installation of a recent application overwrote several key system .DLL files. You suspect that this change is causing instability with other applications on the system that worked correctly before this application was installed. What should you do next?

   A. Uninstall the application in question.

   B. Escalate the issue to an administrator who has expertise with Windows 7.

   C. Test the theory to determine cause.

   D. Establish a plan of action to resolve the problem and identify potential effects.

6. You've just finished fixing a problem with the backup service on a Linux server in the marketing department in your organization. A recent operating system update overwrote your cron configuration files, causing your backup service to fail to run. You've gone through the troubleshooting process to identify the problem, establish a theory, test the theory, plan a course of action, and implement the resolution. What should you do next? (Choose two.)

   A. Contact the organization that supports the Linux distribution and inform them of what happened.

   B. Implement a new backup daemon and storage device on the server.

   C. Document what happened and how the incident was resolved.

   D. Verify that everything is working correctly and move the command to start the backup service to a crontab file that won't be overwritten during a system update.

   E. Post a description of what happened and how you resolved the issue to several Linux community forums.

7. Your organization has recently hired a large number of new sales reps. To support the new workstations these employees will use, you've purchased an additional network switch and installed it in the data center. You uplinked your existing switch to the new switch using a standard UTP patch cable that is about 18 inches in length. However, during testing, you've found that none of the workstations on the new switch are able to contact your organization's domain controller, which is connected to the original switch. What should you do?

A. Use a shorter patch cable. Uplink cables should be 12 inches long or less.

B. Replace the straight-through UTP patch cable with a crossover cable.

C. Connect the domain controller to the new switch.

D. Check the patch cable for open shorts.

8. You're troubleshooting connectivity problems on your Fast Ethernet network between a bank of office cubicles and your server room. Each workstation in each cubicle is connected to the network switch in the server room with a CAT 5e cable. Each cable run is approximately 160 feet long and runs through the ceiling plenum between fluorescent light fixtures. The connectivity problems are intermittent. You ran several tests over the weekend while everyone was gone and found no issues at all. However, during the workday, the issue becomes very apparent. What can you do to fix the issue?

A. Route the cables away from the fluorescent light ballasts.

B. Shorten the cable runs to a maximum of 100 feet, including drop cables.

C. Upgrade the network cabling to CAT 6 UTP to accommodate Fast Ethernet speeds.

D. Upgrade to a higher end network switch that can accommodate more traffic.

9. Which aspect of UTP cabling determines how immune it is to crosstalk?

A. The thickness of the plastic sheathing around the wires

B. The thickness of the plastic insulator around each wire

C. The gauge of the copper wire itself

D. The number of twists per inch

10. You suspect that you have a bad cable in a run between an RJ-45 wall jack and the server room where your switch is located. What tools can you use to test the continuity of each wire in the cable and verify that it is connected correctly to the jacks at each end of the run? (Choose two.)

A. Cable crimper or punch down tool

B. Cable tester

C. Butt set

D. Tone generator

E. Cable certifier

11. The cable TV coaxial cable coming into your house has multiple splitters installed. The first two-way splitter, which has –3.5 db loss, divides the signal between your first and second floors. On the first floor, you have installed another three-way splitter downstream from the first. This splitter, which has –5.5 db loss, provides cable TV to your family room, home office, and master bedroom. You have installed a third two-way splitter, which has –3.5 db loss, in your home office so you can connect the cable line to a TV set and your cable modem. Will this configuration work?

    A. Yes, this configuration will provide adequate signal strength.

    B. No, the signal won't propagate past the second splitter.

    C. No, the cumulative db loss will result in a very weak signal for the cable modem and TV set in the home office.

    D. No, the signal won't propagate past the third splitter.

12. You need to locate a specific UTP cable among nearly 30 cables running through the ceiling plenum. What should you do?

    A. Use a multimeter to identify the correct cable.

    B. Use a toner probe to identify the correct cable.

    C. Use a TDR to identify the correct cable.

    D. Use an OTDR to identify the correct cable.

13. Which type of network testing device can be configured to send a test pattern of bits to an interface and then test the reception of these bits by connecting the interface's output to its own input?

    A. Loopback plug

    B. TDR

    C. OTDR

    D. Fox and hound

14. The training department in your organization wants to use the 802.11g wireless network to stream training videos to employees. You are worried that the wireless network may not have enough bandwidth to handle this load. How can you find out? (Choose two.)

    A. Use iperf to test the throughput of the wireless network.

    B. Use nmap to test the throughput of the wireless network.

    C. Use netstat to test the throughput of the wireless network.

    D. Upgrade the wireless network to 802.11n.

    E. Use netcat to test the throughput of the wireless network.

15. Which of the following utilities are examples of connectivity testing software? (Choose two.)

    A. ifconfig

    B. RPC ping

    C. ipconfig

    D. traceroute

    E. dig

16. As a result of a recent server overheating, you are implementing an environmental monitoring system in your server room so you can keep better track of the temperature. Where should you place the sensors in the server room? (Choose two.)

    A. 2 feet from the floor

    B. 5 feet from the floor

    C. In the ceiling

    D. Next to the door

    E. Near the air conditioning vents

17. You are responsible for managing a public safety system that streams video from surveillance cameras to laptops in police and fire vehicles using a 4G wireless broadband connection. It is absolutely critical that the video traffic on the network be given higher priority than other traffic, such as officers checking their e-mail. What network mechanisms can be used to do this? (Choose two.)

    A. Caching engine

    B. QoS

    C. Buffering

    D. Traffic shaping

18. To maximize uptime, a company has configured its data center with duplicate hardware for each server. The duplicate hardware is constantly updated with mirrored information from the production server. The mirrored server is always on but dormant while the production server handles all network requests. However, if the production server goes down, the mirrored server instantly goes active and processes network requests using the same data and services that were hosted by the production server. What type of redundancy is being used in this scenario?

    A. Fault tolerance

    B. High availability

    C. Load balancing

    D. Cold spare

19. Which protocol allows multiple hosts on the same network to share IP addresses to provide failover redundancy?

   A. Spanning Tree Protocol

   B. Simple Network Management Protocol

   C. Common Address Redundancy Protocol

   D. Round Robin DNS

20. Which of the following network applications would be most sensitive to latency in the network?

   A. Streaming video

   B. Voice over IP (VoIP)

   C. SMB-based file and printer sharing

   D. NTP time synchronization

QUICK ANSWER KEY

1.	A, C	8.	A	15.	B, D
2.	D	9.	D	16.	A, B
3.	B	10.	B, E	17.	B, D
4.	D	11.	C	18.	A
5.	C	12.	B	19.	C
6.	C, D	13.	A	20.	B
7.	B	14.	A, E		

IN-DEPTH ANSWERS

1. Several users have called to complain that print jobs sent to a shared network printer are not being printed. What should you do to determine the scope of the problem? (Choose two.)

A. Identify which users are affected by the problem and where they are located.

B. Establish a theory of probable cause.

C. Question the users experiencing the problem to determine exactly what symptoms they are experiencing.

D. Establish a plan of action to resolve the problem and identify potential effects.

E. Escalate this issue to a network printing specialist.

> ☑ **A and C.** The first step in troubleshooting a network issue is to gather as much information as you can about the problem before implementing any fixes. First you should identify which users are affected by the problem and where they are located. This will help you determine whether the printing issue is localized or general in nature. You should also question the users who are having trouble printing to determine exactly what they are doing and what symptoms they are experiencing. Are they sending print jobs incorrectly? Are any error messages displayed when they try to print? Doing this will help you determine the scope of the issue.
>
> ☒ **B, D, and E are incorrect.** B and D are incorrect because you should avoid forming a hypothesis and establishing a plan of action until you have gathered as much information as you can about the issue. Otherwise, you risk fixing "problems" that don't exist and potentially introducing new problems in the network. E is incorrect because escalation should not occur until you have concretely identified the problem and determined that it involves issues you aren't authorized to fix. For example, the source of the printing problem might be a simple paper jam, which is a relatively easy problem to fix and doesn't require escalation.

2. A user called to complain that she is unable to access the Internet from her Windows 7 workstation. You are in the first stage of troubleshooting the issue. What should you do?

A. Use the **IPCONFIG /RELEASE** and **IPCONFIG /RENEW** commands on her workstation to renew her DHCP lease.

B. Install the latest updates from Microsoft on the workstation.

C. Turn off the Windows firewall on the workstation.

D. Use the **IPCONFIG /ALL** command on her workstation to view her current networking configuration.

☑ **D.** The first phase of troubleshooting a network issue involves gathering as much information as possible about the problem. In this scenario, using the **IPCONFIG /ALL** command on the workstation will provide you with IP configuration information that you can use later on to formulate a hypothesis.

☒ **A, B,** and **C** are incorrect because each of these answers involves implementing a fix. This shouldn't be done until you have gathered as much information as possible about the problem and formed a solid hypothesis as to what is causing it. Implementing fixes without first fully understanding the problem is unlikely to fix the real issue and can introduce additional issues.

3. You've discovered that the eDirectory partition replication process is failing between three of your Novell servers. You are in the first stage of troubleshooting the issue. What key question should you ask?

A. Will promoting a Read/Write replica to a Master replica fix the issue?

B. What has changed in the system since eDirectory last replicated correctly?

C. Will installing a second network interface dedicated to replication traffic fix the issue?

D. Should the Read/Write replicas be removed from the replica ring?

☑ **B.** Because you are in the first stage of troubleshooting the issue, you should gather as much information as you can before you start implementing fixes. You should investigate what has changed in the system since the last time eDirectory replicated correctly. Doing this may help you identify a causal factor for the problem.

☒ **A, C,** and **D** are incorrect because each of these answers focuses on testing a theory to determine the cause of the problem. This process should not be attempted until you have gathered all information possible.

4. A small business client has called indicating that they have lost Internet connectivity through their DSL connection. You've gathered all information you can about the issue, which appears to be affecting all users on the network. The outage began sometime between midnight on Thursday and 8:00 A.M. on Friday when the owner opened the office for the day. You now need to establish a theory of probably cause. Which hypothesis should you test first?

A. The company needs to switch to a different service provider.

B. The DSL modem needs to be upgraded to a newer model that supports faster connection speeds.

C. The company needs to upgrade to a T1 line.

D. The DSL modem needs to be restarted.

☑ **D.** When establishing a theory of probable cause, be careful that you don't overlook the obvious. Network administrators sometimes go after the most complex solutions first before investigating simpler ones that carry less risk. In this scenario, you should see if the DSL modem simply needs to be restarted, a common issue with DSL devices. The risk associated with restarting the modem is negligible. The impact on the organization is minimal, because the restart should take only about a minute.

☒ **A, B,** and **C** are incorrect. **A** is incorrect because switching providers could result in extended downtime, as they will likely have to wait for the new provider to activate the service. **B** is incorrect because upgrading the modem will result in downtime while the new device is purchased, installed, and configured to work with the service provider. Depending on the provider, this could take anywhere from a few hours to a few days. **C** is incorrect because upgrading to a T1 line is expensive and will require extensive changes to the network.

5. You are troubleshooting an issue with a user's Windows 7 workstation. After gathering information, you have arrived at a theory of probable cause that the installation of a recent application overwrote several key system .DLL files. You suspect that this change is causing instability with other applications on the system that worked correctly before this application was installed. What should you do next?

   A. Uninstall the application in question.
   B. Escalate the issue to an administrator who has expertise with Windows 7.
   C. Test the theory to determine cause.
   D. Establish a plan of action to resolve the problem and identify potential effects.

☑ **C.** At this point, you have determined a theory of probable cause. The next logical step in the troubleshooting process is to test the theory to determine the actual cause of the problem. For example, in this scenario, you could image the workstation to a virtual machine in a lab environment and then uninstall the application. If your theory is confirmed, you can then determine the next actions required to resolve problem. If your theory is not confirmed, you may need to establish a new theory or escalate the problem to someone with more expertise.

☒ **A, B,** and **D** are incorrect. **A** is incorrect because the fix is being implemented without first verifying the cause. It also fails to account for potential side effects of the fix before implementing it. **B** is incorrect because it isn't necessary to escalate the issue until you are sure of the problem. **D** is incorrect because you should first test your theory before establishing a plan of action to resolve the problem.

6. You've just finished fixing a problem with the backup service on a Linux server in the marketing department in your organization. A recent operating system update overwrote your cron configuration files, causing your backup service to fail to run. You've gone through the troubleshooting process to identify the problem, establish a theory, test the theory, plan a course of action, and implement the resolution. What should you do next? (Choose two.)

   A. Contact the organization that supports the Linux distribution and inform them of what happened.

   B. Implement a new backup daemon and storage device on the server.

   C. Document what happened and how the incident was resolved.

   D. Verify that everything is working correctly and move the command to start the backup service to a crontab file that won't be overwritten during a system update.

   E. Post a description of what happened and how you resolved the issue to several Linux community forums.

   ☑ **C** and **D.** After implementing a solution to a problem identified during the troubleshooting process, you should then verify full system functionality and implement preventative measures to keep the issue from reoccurring. In this scenario, you could move the command to start the backup service to a crontab file that won't be affected by a system update. You should also document your findings, actions, and outcomes in a log book or file. That way, if the issue ever occurs again, you can simply consult your troubleshooting log instead of going through the entire troubleshooting process.

   ☒ **A, B,** and **E** are incorrect. **A** is a good idea, but it's unlikely that the distro will change its OS update process to fit your specific Linux implementation. **B** is incorrect because making a change like this should have been addressed when you formulated an action plan to fix the issue in question. **E** is a good idea that may help others avoid the problems you encountered, but it isn't a necessary component of the troubleshooting process. In fact, your organization's security policy may prohibit you from posting information such as this to a public forum.

7. Your organization has recently hired a large number of new sales reps. To support the new workstations these employees will use, you've purchased an addition network switch and installed it in the data center. You uplinked your existing switch to the new switch using a standard UTP patch cable that is about 18 inches in length. However, during testing, you've found that none of the workstations on the new switch are able to contact your organization's domain controller, which is connected to the original switch. What should you do?

   A. Use a shorter patch cable. Uplink cables should be 12 inches long or less.

   B. Replace the straight-through UTP patch cable with a crossover cable.

   C. Connect the domain controller to the new switch.

   D. Check the patch cable for open shorts.

☑ **B.** Depending on the switch, you may need to use a crossover cable to cascade two switches together. Some switches provide a dedicated uplink port that crosses the Tx and Rx pins for you, allowing you to use a standard straight-through cable. However, many lower end switches do not, and you must use a crossover to match the Tx pins on one switch with the Rx pins on the other, and vice versa.

☒ **A, C,** and **D** are incorrect. **A** is incorrect because 18 inches is an acceptable length for a switch-to-switch patch cable. **C** is incorrect because the workstations connected to the original switch will not be able to communicate with the domain controller. **D** is possible, but it's unlikely that an 18-inch patch cable will have an open short.

8. You're troubleshooting connectivity problems on your Fast Ethernet network between a bank of office cubicles and your server room. Each workstation in each cubicle is connected to the network switch in the server room with a CAT 5e cable. Each cable run is approximately 160 feet long and runs through the ceiling plenum between fluorescent light fixtures. The connectivity problems are intermittent. You ran several tests over the weekend while everyone was gone and found no issues at all. However, during the workday, the issue becomes very apparent. What can you do to fix the issue?

A. Route the cables away from the fluorescent light ballasts.

B. Shorten the cable runs to a maximum of 100 feet, including drop cables.

C. Upgrade the network cabling to CAT 6 UTP to accommodate Fast Ethernet speeds.

D. Upgrade to a higher end network switch that can accommodate more traffic.

☑ **A.** The cable runs have been routed between fluorescent light ballasts, which are notorious EMI emitters and are a likely cause of the problem. This is borne out by the fact that no connectivity problems occurred on the weekend when everyone was gone and the lights were off. Rerouting the cables or shielding them will likely fix the problem.

☒ **B, C,** and **D** are incorrect. **B** is incorrect because 100Base-T networks support a maximum cable length of up to 100 meters. Cable runs of 160 feet are only about 50 meters long. **C** isn't necessary as 100Base-T networks are compatible with CAT 5e UTP. **D** is incorrect because the source of the problem is not the switch, but the cabling leading up to the switch.

9. Which aspect of UTP cabling determines how immune it is to crosstalk?
   A. The thickness of the plastic sheathing around the wires.
   B. The thickness of the plastic insulator around each wire.
   C. The gauge of the copper wire itself.
   D. The number of twists per inch.

   ☑ **D.** The twisting of wire pairs together in UTP cabling is responsible for cancelling out crosstalk between wires. The tighter the twists, the more the crosstalk is cancelled out. For example, CAT 6 cabling is twisted much more tightly than CAT 5 cabling, allowing it to transfer data at higher speeds.

   ☒ **A, B,** and **C** are incorrect. **A** and **B** are incorrect because the plastic cable sheath and insulation do very little to prevent crosstalk. In fact, this is why UTP cable is so susceptible to EMI. **C** is incorrect because the gauge of the copper wire has no impact on crosstalk.

10. You suspect that you have a bad cable in a run between an RJ-45 wall jack and the server room where your switch is located. What tools can you use to test the continuity of each wire in the cable and verify that it is connected correctly to the jacks at each end of the run? (Choose two.)
    A. Cable crimper or punch down tool
    B. Cable tester
    C. Butt set
    D. Tone generator
    E. Cable certifier

    ☑ **B** and **E.** Either a cable tester or a cable certifier can be used in this scenario. Both types of devices have components that connect to each end of the cable run. A cable tester tests each wire in the cable for continuity and verifies each one is connected to the right pin in the jack or plug. A cable certifier does the same thing, but it also tests the bandwidth of the cable.

    ☒ **A, C,** and **D** are incorrect. **A** is incorrect because a cable crimper is used to attach a plug to the end of a UTP cable and a punch down tool is used to connect UTP cable to a patch panel. **C** is incorrect because a butt set is used to test telephone wiring. **D** is partially correct because a tone generator tells you whether or not you have connectivity through the wire. However, a tone generator is less useful if you need to determine whether the cable is connected to the wall jack correctly.

11. The cable TV coaxial cable coming into your house has multiple splitters installed. The first two-way splitter, which has –3.5 db loss, divides the signal between your first and second floors. On the first floor, you have installed another three-way splitter downstream from the first. This splitter, which has –5.5 db loss, provides cable TV to your family room, home office, and master bedroom. You have installed a third two-way splitter, which has –3.5 db loss, in your home office so you can connect the cable line to a TV set and your cable modem. Will this configuration work?

   A. Yes, this configuration will provide adequate signal strength.

   B. No, the signal won't propagate past the second splitter.

   C. No, the cumulative db loss will result in a very weak signal for the cable modem and TV set in the home office.

   D. No, the signal won't propagate past the third splitter.

   ☑   **C.** It is very likely that the cumulative db loss (–12.5 db) caused by the splitting the cable multiple times will result in a very weak signal by the time it reaches the cable modem and the TV set in the home office. To remedy this, you could reduce the number of devices sharing the same line. You could also install a signal amplifier on the run leading to the home office to boost the signal strength.

   ☒   **A, B,** and **D** are incorrect. **A** is incorrect because a –12 db loss will result in a lower quality TV picture and less performance by the cable modem. **B** and **D** are incorrect because the signal can be split multiple times, although the signal strength will experience db loss each time it does.

---

12. You need to locate a specific UTP cable among nearly 30 cables running through the ceiling plenum. What should you do?

   A. Use a multimeter to identify the correct cable.

   B. Use a toner probe to identify the correct cable.

   C. Use a TDR to identify the correct cable.

   D. Use an OTDR to identify the correct cable.

   ☑   **B.** A toner probe would be the best tool in this scenario. You connect a tone generator to one end of the cable you want to locate in the plenum, and then pass the tone probe over each cable. When the probe detects the tone from the generator, you know you've found the right cable.

☒ **A, C, and D are incorrect. A** is incorrect because, although a multimeter can be used to detect a signal on a UTP cable, it requires penetrating the cable sheath and wire insulation with a metal probe. This isn't the best idea. **C** is incorrect because a TDR sends a signal down a cable and measures the amount of time it takes for the signal to return. Using this information, it calculates the distance to the end of the cable. If this distance is less than the physical length of the cable, then you know the cable is broken (or *open*) at that distance. **D** is incorrect because an OTDR performs the same function as a TDR but on fiber-optic cables instead of UTP.

13. Which type of network testing device can be configured to send a test pattern of bits to an interface and then test the reception of these bits by connecting the interface's output to its own input?
    A. Loopback plug
    B. TDR
    C. OTDR
    D. Fox and hound

☑ **A.** A loopback plug is a testing device that sends a test pattern of bits on an interface and then tests the reception of these bits by connecting the interface's output to its own input. This helps you determine whether the interface itself is working correctly.

☒ **B, C, and D are incorrect. B** and **C** are incorrect because TDRs and OTDRs rely on electrical or optical signals reflecting back down the medium on which they were originally transmitted. They do not connect input to output. **D** is incorrect because a fox and hound transmits a tone on one end of a cable segment that can be detected on the other end, allowing you to identify which cable segment runs where.

14. The training department in your organization wants to use the 802.11g wireless network to stream training videos to employees. You are worried that the wireless network may not have enough bandwidth to handle this load. How can you find out? (Choose two.)
    A. Use iperf to test the throughput of the wireless network.
    B. Use nmap to test the throughput of the wireless network.
    C. Use netstat to test the throughput of the wireless network.
    D. Upgrade the wireless network to 802.11n.
    E. Use netcat to test the throughput of the wireless network.

☑ **A and E.** The commonly used iperf (Windows) and netcat (Linux) utilities test throughput on a network. They can be very useful when testing wireless networks where bandwidth varies with distance and environmental conditions. In this scenario, you'd probably find that wireless clients near the WAP have adequate bandwidth to handle the streaming video while clients farther away may not.

☒ **B, C, and D** are incorrect. **B** is incorrect because nmap is a powerful network tool that is used to detect rogue hosts (as a network scanner), analyze network packets (as a protocol analyzer), and scan hosts for open ports (as a vulnerability analyzer). The one thing it can't do is test network bandwidth. **C** is incorrect because the netstat utility is used to view stats for network interfaces, check for open ports, and view routing tables. Like nmap, it can't test network bandwidth. **D** is incorrect because a variety of factors affect the bandwidth available on wireless connection. Upgrading to 802.11n may help clients that are located close to the WAP, but clients that are farther away or have sources of interference nearby may still not have enough bandwidth. A better (and less expensive) approach would be to test the network first with a throughput tester.

15. Which of the following utilities are examples of connectivity software? (Choose two.)
   A. ifconfig
   B. RPC ping
   C. ipconfig
   D. traceroute
   E. dig

☑ **B and D.** You can use the RPC ping utility to test connectivity between a Microsoft Exchange Server and a workstation running the Microsoft Exchange Client software. The **traceroute** Linux command uses the ICMP protocol to trace the route an IP packet takes through various network to its destination host.

☒ **A, C, and E** are incorrect. **A** is incorrect because the **ifconfig** command is used on Linux systems to view statistics about network interfaces and to configure IP addressing information. **C** is incorrect because the **ipconfig** command is used on Windows systems to manage network interfaces. **E** is incorrect because dig is used to send name resolution requests to DNS servers.

16. As a result of a recent server overheating, you are implementing an environmental monitoring system in your server room so you can keep better track of the temperature. Where should you placed the sensors in the server room? (Choose two.)

A. 2 feet from the floor

B. 5 feet from the floor

C. In the ceiling

D. Next to the door

E. Near the air conditioning vents

☑ **A and B.** Rack-mounted servers are typically implemented between 2 and 5 feet from the floor. Even tower server systems are typically installed within this height range in a server room. Therefore, you should monitor the temperatures within this range. You'll likely see that the 5 foot sensors read considerably hotter than the 2 foot sensors. In fact, if there is more than a 10 degree (Fahrenheit) difference between these two levels, you should consider increasing airflow in your server room or add cooling capacity to the server room's air conditioning unit.

☒ **C, D, and E** are incorrect. **C** is incorrect because servers don't operate next to the ceiling; therefore, the temperature at this location is less relevant. **D** is incorrect because the opening and closing of the door will cause sensors to provide inaccurate readings. **E** is incorrect because the air at this location will be considerably cooler than that throughout the rest of the room.

17. You are responsible for managing a public safety system that streams video from surveillance cameras to laptops in police and fire vehicles using a 4G wireless broadband connection. It is absolutely critical that the video traffic on the network be given higher priority than other traffic, such as officers checking their e-mail. What network mechanisms can be used to do this? (Choose two.)

A. Caching engine

B. QoS

C. Buffering

D. Traffic shaping

☑ **B and D.** You can use quality of service (QoS) in this scenario to prioritize video traffic on the broadband network over other types of traffic. This ensures that bandwidth will always be available for the video streams, which could be the difference between life and death in an emergency situation. Traffic shaping also allows you to delay certain types of network packets, such as mail traffic, to reserve bandwidth for video streaming. Both of these mechanisms are also frequently used to manage voice over IP (VoIP) traffic as well as streaming video.

☒ **A and C are incorrect. A** is incorrect because a caching engine stores frequently accessed content from the Internet locally. This can be beneficial in many types of networks, but it really isn't useful in this scenario. **C** is incorrect because the use of buffering in this scenario could be disastrous. Buffering involves predownloading a video stream before starting playback. Video streams from public safety surveillance cameras must be as close to real-time as possible.

18. To maximize uptime, a company has configured its data center with duplicate hardware for each server. The duplicate hardware is constantly updated with mirrored information from the production server. The mirrored server is always on but dormant while the production server handles all network requests. However, if the production server goes down, the mirrored server instantly goes active and processes network requests using the same data and services that were hosted by the production server. What type of redundancy is being used in this scenario?
    A. Fault tolerance
    B. High availability
    C. Load balancing
    D. Cold spare

☑ **A.** There is a fine line between the concepts of fault tolerance and high availability, resulting in frequent confusion. However, the generally accepted industry usage is to refer to a system as fault tolerant when no service interruption occurs during a failover event. In this scenario, the duplicated hardware, data, and services are kept "hot" so that when the production server goes down, the mirrored server can immediately take over processing with no interruption. Be aware that this high degree of redundancy is very expensive, because you must implement twice the equipment and hire extra administrators to manage it.

☒ **B, C, and D are incorrect. B** is incorrect because a high availability environment is generally considered to have an element of delay during the failover process. As a result, there is a minimal amount of service interruption. **C** is incorrect because load balancing usually involves sharing the workload among multiple systems in the network. In this scenario, the redundant system is on, but dormant until needed. **D** is incorrect because a cold spare is kept in a powered off state until needed.

19. Which protocol allows multiple hosts on the same network to share IP addresses to provide failover redundancy?

A. Spanning Tree Protocol

B. Simple Network Management Protocol

C. Common Address Redundancy Protocol

D. Round Robin DNS

☑ **C.** The Common Address Redundancy Protocol (CARP) allows you to group multiple hosts on the same network together and share IP addresses to provide failover redundancy. Within this group, one host is designated as the *master* while the other group members are *slaves*. The master answers and processes all requests sent to the shared IP address. If the master goes down for some reason, one of the slaves in the group takes over for the master by processing requests sent to the shared IP address.

☒ **A, B, and D are incorrect. A** is incorrect because the Spanning Tree Protocol is used to prevent switching loops with cascaded Ethernet switches. **B** is incorrect because SNMP is used to monitor network hosts. **D** is incorrect because Round Robin DNS is used to balance the network processing load between multiple servers (for example, balancing HTTP requests between multiple web servers).

20. Which of the following network applications would be most sensitive to latency in the network?

A. Streaming video

B. Voice over IP (VoIP)

C. SMB-based file and printer sharing

D. NTP time synchronization

☑ **B.** In most circumstances, VoIP traffic would be the most sensitive to network latency due to the two-way nature of the application and the fact that it runs on UDP, which doesn't retransmit late or missing packets. Excessive latency could disrupt conversations and quickly cause users to become frustrated.

☒ **A, C, and D are incorrect. A** is a close second place behind VoIP for latency sensitivity. Video streams can absorb a certain amount of network latency; however, video and audio quality begins to suffer once latency passes a certain threshold. This is because streaming video, like VoIP, uses UDP and late or missing packets aren't retransmitted. **C** is incorrect because file and printer sharing use the TCP protocol, which uses acknowledgements to retransmit late or missing packets. Unless the latency is excessive, the end user probably won't notice a second or two of delay when saving files or sending print jobs. **D** is incorrect because the Network Time Protocol is designed to accommodate networks with variable latency.

A

Pre-Assessment Test

INSTRUCTIONS

Prior to completing the practice items in the chapters of this book, you should first complete this pre-assessment test to identify key areas that you need to focus on as you study for your Network+ exam.

In this activity, you will be presented with 50 assessment items that mirror the type of items you are likely to see on the real Network+ exam. The weighting of CompTIA Network+ objective domains used in the real Network+ exam is also mirrored in this activity, as shown in the following table:

Domain	Number of Pre-Assessment Items
1.0 Network Technologies	11
2.0 Network Installation and Configuration	12
3.0 Network Media and Topologies	8
4.0 Network Management	10
5.0 Network Security	9
Total:	50

To make this activity as realistic and accurate as possible, you should allocate 45 minutes of uninterrupted time to complete these items. Turn off your phone, computer, TV, and music player; then find a comfortable place to work. Then set a timer for 45 minutes and begin this activity. This is very important. Allowing more than 45 minutes will yield inaccurate results.

Be sure you work through all of the questions in this activity before you check your answers. Again, this pre-assessment should mimic a real testing environment as much as possible. Wait until you have answered every question before checking the answers.

When you are done, you can use the "Quick Answer Key" along with the "In-Depth Answers" sections to evaluate your responses. Keep track of the number of questions you answer correctly and compare this number with the table found in the "Analyzing Your Pre-Assessment Results" section at the end of this activity. This table will give you valuable feedback based on the number of correct answers you gave. You should also compare the answers you missed with the objective map at the end of this activity to identify areas that you need to focus on as you study.

Ready? Set your timer for 45 minutes and begin!

QUESTIONS

1. Which protocols function at the Internet layer of the TCP/IP model? (Choose two.)
   A. Internet Group Management Protocol
   B. Sequenced Packet Exchange Protocol
   C. Address Resolution Protocol
   D. Internet Control Message Protocol
   E. Transmission Control Protocol

2. Which of the following are functions of the of the data link layer in the OSI model? (Choose two.)
   A. Retransmits missing or corrupted frames
   B. Transmits electrical signals between hosts
   C. Manages access to a shared network medium
   D. Establishes connection-oriented communication sessions
   E. Determines the route a packet should take to reach its destination

3. You've decided to use a subnet mask of 255.192.0.0 with your 10.0.0.0 network to create four separate subnets. The network ID for one of the subnets is 10.64.0.0. You are installing a router on this subnet and want to assign the highest numbered IP address possible to this system. What should you do?
   A. Assign the system an IP address of 10.127.255.254.
   B. Assign the system an IP address of 10.63.255.254.
   C. Assign the system an IP address of 10.191.255.254.
   D. Assign the system an IP address of 10.255.255.254.

4. Which of the following are true concerning the Interior Gateway Routing Protocol (IGRP)? (Choose two.)
   A. It uses bandwidth as a routing metric.
   B. It uses hop count as a routing metric.
   C. It uses delay as a routing metric.
   D. It supports a maximum hop count of 15.
   E. It supports a maximum hop count of 64.

5. You need to configure an interface in your Cisco router. What should you do to specify that you want to configure the first Ethernet adapter on the device?
   A. Enter **configure interface 0/0** at the router command prompt.
   B. Enter **interface 0** at the router command prompt.
   C. Enter **ifconfig eth0** at the router command prompt.
   D. Enter **interface f0/0** at the router command prompt.

6. You have just configured and enabled the Secure Shell (SSH) and Network Time Protocol (NTP) daemons on a Linux server. What should you do to allow network traffic for these daemons through the server's firewall? (Choose two.)
   A. Open port 23 in the server's firewall.
   B. Open port 443 in the server's firewall.
   C. Open port 123 in the server's firewall.
   D. Open port 22 in the server's firewall.
   E. Open port 161 in the server's firewall.

7. Which application layer protocols are used to deliver audio and video over IP networks? (Choose two.)
   A. SAP
   B. RDP
   C. RTP
   D. RTCP
   E. LDAP

8. Your workstation needs to copy a file to a server on the same network segment with an IP address of 192.168.1.1. Part of this process involves resolving the server's IP address into its MAC address using the ARP protocol. What happens first in this process?
   A. An ARP request packet is broadcast to all the machines on the network segment to determine the MAC address of the host with an IP address of 192.168.1.1.
   B. ARP sends a unicast ARP request packet to the host with an IP address of 192.168.1.1 requesting its MAC address.
   C. An ARP request packet is broadcast to all the machines on the network segment to determine the MAC address of the default gateway router.
   D. The workstation looks in its local ARP cache to see if an entry already exists for 192.168.1.1.

9. The server hosting your organization's intranet web server has gone down and you've migrated the site to a different web server. Your want to allow employees to be able to access the site on the new server without extensive reconfiguration or retraining. To do this, you decide to modify the IP address assigned to the A record for original web server and change it to point to the new server's IP address. Because your DNS server is a Windows system, you've opened the zone in DNS manager on the primary DNS server to make the change. Will this strategy work?
   A. Yes, the DNS record change will take effect and users will be able to access the web site on the new server.
   B. No, the change should be made on a secondary DNS server for the zone.

    C. No, you must create an alias (CNAME) record in the zone that points to the existing record for the new web server.

    D. No, you must leave the DNS servers as they are and retrain users to access the intranet web site using the new web server's URL.

10. A user called to complain that she is unable to send print jobs to the shared workgroup printer near her cubicle from her Windows 7 workstation. You are in the first stage of troubleshooting the issue. What should you do?

    A. Use the **IPCONFIG /RELEASE** and **IPCONFIG /RENEW** commands on her workstation to renew her DHCP lease.

    B. Install the latest updates from Microsoft on the workstation.

    C. Reinstall the printer driver for the printer on the workstation.

    D. Use the **PING** command on her workstation to test communications with the printer.

11. You have installed four servers as virtual machines on a VMware ESX hypervisor host. Each virtual server is connected to a virtual port on the same virtual switch within the hypervisor. The virtual switch is connected to a physical Ethernet interface in the hypervisor host through an uplink port. This physical interface is connected to a physical multilayer switch in your server room that also functions as a router for the network segment to which the hypervisor host is connected. One of the virtual servers needs to send information to one of the other virtual servers. How does the data get there?

    A. The data goes through the virtual switch to the physical interface, then to the physical switch, and then back through the same path to the destination host.

    B. The data goes directly through the physical interface to the physical switch and then back through the same path to the destination host.

    C. The virtual servers are isolated from each other and data cannot be shared between them.

    D. The data is transferred directly from one virtual host to the other through the virtual switch.

12. You need to add a static route to the 172.18.0.0 network in the routing table of a Linux router. This network uses the default subnet mask for its address class. The next hop to reach this network is 172.17.255.254 and is reached through the first Ethernet interface in the Linux router. What should you do?

    A. Enter **route add −net 172.18.0.0 netmask 255.255.0.0 gw 172.17.255.254 eth0** at the shell prompt.

    B. Enter **route add 172.18.0.0 MASK 255.255.0.0 172.17.255.254** at the shell prompt.

    C. Enter **ip route 172.18.0.0 255.255.0.0 172.17.255.254** at the shell prompt.

    D. Enter **route add −net 172.18.0.0 netmask 255.255.0.0 gw 172.17.255.254 eth1** at the shell prompt.

13. A private network uses a dynamic NAT router to connect to the Internet. A workstation on the private network behind the NAT router sends a packet to the Internet. What happens first?
    A. The NAT router adds an entry to its translation table listing the packet's private IP address, source port, and translated port.
    B. The destination host receives the translated packet and establishes a connection to the port and IP address contained in the translated packet's header.
    C. PAT assigns the connection a port number from a pool of available ports, inserting this port number in the source port field.
    D. The NAT router replaces the private IP address of the sender in the source field of the packet header with the NAT router's public IP address.

14. You need to make configuration changes to your Cisco router. You are currently in privilege exec mode. What should you do next?
    A. Enter **enable** at the command prompt.
    B. Enter **disable** at the command prompt.
    C. Enter **config term** at the command prompt.
    D. Enter **exit** at the command prompt.

15. You are implementing a wireless network in an office of a large call center. The work space is rectangular in shape with an open floor plan. Employees work in pods of cubicles in the center of the open plan. You need to implement wireless access points such that each employee receives adequate signal strength. However, the office manager is concerned about signal emanation outside the facility. What should you do? (Choose two.)
    A. Implement a WAP with a highly directional antenna in the center of the office complex.
    B. Implement a WAP with a semi-directional antenna in the center of the office complex.
    C. Implement a WAP with an omni-directional antenna in each corner of the office complex.
    D. Implement a WAP with an omni-directional antenna in the center of the office complex.
    E. Implement a WAP with a semi-directional antenna in each corner of the office complex.

16. You've discovered that the 802.11n wireless network signal from your building is emanating some distance into neighboring businesses. What can you do to stop this? (Choose two.)
    A. Implement wireless repeaters at strategic locations within your building.
    B. Replace omni-directional WAPs with semi-directional WAPs strategically located around the perimeter of the building.
    C. Increase the gain on the WAP antenna.
    D. Reduce the power level of the WAP.
    E. Implement a directional WAP in the center of the building.

17. Many users have called to complain that they can't log into the network server, nor can they access the Internet. The symptoms appear to be affecting all workstations on the same network segment. Upon inspection, you find that the affected hosts are being assigned IP addresses in the 169.254.*x.x* range, but they should be using the 172.17.*x.x* address range. Given that your network uses DHCP for IP address assignments, what should you do?

    A. Configure a DHCP relay agent to forward DHCPDISCOVER messages to your DHCP server.

    B. Reboot all affected workstations.

    C. Check the network for a rogue DHCP server.

    D. Check the status of your DHCP server because the affected workstations are using Automatic Private IP Addressing (APIPA).

18. The wireless users located in a remote corner of your office suite are complaining of dropped connections and slow data transfers over the wireless network. Given that your organization uses an 802.11g wireless network with WAPs implemented in the center of the office suite, what should you do?

    A. Implement MAC address filtering.

    B. Upgrade the users' computers to 802.11g network interfaces.

    C. Implement an additional WAP in the location where the users work.

    D. Change the channel used by the WAP nearest the users to a higher numbered channel.

19. A new employee has reported that she can't connect to your organization's 802.11n wireless network from her new laptop. None of the other employees that work near her have reported any trouble connecting to the wireless network. Given that your wireless network uses WPA-2 for security, what should you do? (Choose two.)

    A. Verify the user has configured the connection with the correct SSID.

    B. Install an 802.11n wireless USB adapter in the laptop.

    C. Verify the user has configured the connection with the correct WEP key.

    D. Change the channel used by the WAP to eliminate interference from other 2.4 GHz devices.

    E. Verify that the wireless interface in the laptop is enabled.

20. You are experiencing errors caused by an MTU black hole. TCP connections between hosts on different network segments frequently hang after successfully completing the three-way handshake. What is causing this? (Choose two.)

    A. Network security devices are configured to disallow ICMP messages.

    B. The stateful firewall isn't monitoring the state of TCP connections correctly.

    C. The sender and receiver are on different network segments.

    D. VLANs have been configured that subdivide each physical network segment.

    E. Senders are configured with an MTU that is larger than the MTU size supported by a router in the path to the receiver.

21. The workstations on one segment of your network are unable to reach a Windows domain controller located on a different network segment. You've checked, and the server has been assigned a static IP address of 192.168.0.1. Your workstations are assigned IP addresses via DHCP in the 192.168.1.10–192.168.1.253 range with a subnet mask of 255.255.255.0. You are unable to ping the server from any workstation, yet the workstations are able to ping each other. What should you do?

    A. Assign the Linux server an IP address of 195.168.1.1.

    B. Verify that the network switch has power and is turned on.

    C. Create an IP address reservation for 192.168.0.1 in the DHCP server configuration.

    D. Verify that the workstations have the correct default gateway router address assigned.

22. You are implementing a Windows network server to store your organization's mission-critical files that users will access from their desktop client systems. You need to ensure that the files on the server are protected from hard disk failures and remain available 24/7. What should you do to accomplish this? (Choose two.)

    A. Implement a RAID 0 hard disk array in the server.

    B. Implement a RAID 5 hard disk array in the server.

    C. Synchronize data and services on the server to a hot backup system.

    D. Connect a tape drive to the server and configure daily backups of the file system.

    E. Implement bonded network interfaces in the system and load balance between them.

23. You need to delegate permission to complete a limited number of administrative tasks on your Windows server to a co-worker. You want her to be able to back up and restore all files on the server, regardless of who owns them and what permissions have been assigned to them. You also want her to be able to shut down the server, if necessary. You do not want her to be able to complete any other administrative tasks on the server. What should you do?

    A. Make the user a member of the Backup Operators built-in group.

    B. Make the user a member of the Server Operators built-in group.

    C. Make the user a member of the Account Operators built-in group.

    D. Make the user a member of the Administrators built-in group.

24. Which of the following is true about multimode fiber-optic network cabling?

    A. The sheathing of multimode fiber-optic cabling is yellow.

    B. The central core is larger than that of singlemode fiber-optic cabling.

    C. It transmits a single ray of light.

    D. It supports longer segment lengths than singlemode fiber-optic cabling.

25. Which type of connector is typically used to connect Category 6 UTP cabling to a network interface card?
   A. RJ-45
   B. AUI
   C. RJ-11
   D. BNC

26. Which wireless networking standard runs at a frequency of 2.4 GHz with a maximum data transmission rate of 11 Mbps?
   A. 802.11a
   B. 802.11b
   C. 802.11g
   D. 802.11n

27. You are troubleshooting a malfunctioning DSL modem for a client. The device is experiencing connection problems with the DSL service provider. In addition, the client has complained of line noise on the analog telephone connected to the same line that is used for the DSL connection. You notice that the WAN jack on the device is connected into an RJ-11 telephone wall jack through a DSL filter/splitter device. Two of the RJ-45 jacks on the device are connected with standard straight-through UTP cable to desktop PC systems. What should you do?
   A. Connect the DSL modem to a single desktop PC system only.
   B. Replace the DSL filter/splitter.
   C. Cascade the DSL modem to a separate Ethernet switch and connect the desktop PCs to the new switch.
   D. Replace the straight-through UTP cables with crossover cables.

28. You are responsible for managing a 10Base-T Ethernet network. Each host on this network is connected to a central Ethernet hub by a dedicated run of UTP cable. What type of logical topology does this network use?
   A. Ring
   B. Star
   C. Bus
   D. Mesh

29. You are troubleshooting connectivity problems on your Gigabit Ethernet network between a pod of cubicles and your server room. Each workstation in each cubicle is connected to the network switch in the server room with a CAT 6a cable. Each cable run is approximately 325 feet long and runs through the ceiling plenum. Each workstation's drop cable that connects it to the RJ-45 wall jack is 10 feet long. What can you do to fix the issue?

    A. Shorten the cable runs to a maximum of 328 feet, including drop cables.

    B. Route the cables through the walls instead of through the ceiling plenum.

    C. Upgrade the network cabling to CAT 7 UTP to accommodate Gigabit Ethernet speeds.

    D. Upgrade to a higher end network switch that can accommodate more traffic.

30. You need to expand an existing switched Ethernet network to accommodate additional network hosts by adding a second switch to the network segment. What should you do? (Choose two.)

    A. Connect the cascaded port on the existing switch to an available port on the new switch with a straight-through cable.

    B. Connect the ring out port from the new switch to the ring in port on the existing switch.

    C. Connect the ring in port from the new switch to the ring out port on the existing switch.

    D. Connect the cascaded port on the existing switch to an available port on the new switch with a crossover cable.

    E. Connect an open port on the existing switch to an open port on the new switch with a crossover cable.

31. Which term refers to point at which the telecom network ends and connects with your organization's wiring?

    A. MDF

    B. Demarc

    C. IDF

    D. CDF

32. Your organization has remote employees who work from home. They frequently need to access information on the Windows servers in your company's home office. To provide secure remote access for these users, you have decided to implement a virtual private network (VPN) with a VPN concentrator. Which encryption methods can be used by the VPN? (Choose two.)

    A. Internet Protocol Security (IPSec)

    B. Layer 2 Tunneling Protocol (L2TP)

    C. Point-to-Point Tunneling Protocol (PPTP)

    D. Data Encryption Standard (DES)

    E. Secure Socket Layer/Transport Layer Security (SSL/TLS)

33. Which type of network testing device transmits a tone on one end of a cable segment that can be detected on the other end, allowing you to identify which cable segment runs where?

A. Fox and hound

B. Loopback plug

C. TDR

D. OTDR

34. Human Resources wants to use your Fast Ethernet network to stream motivational videos to the company's employees. You are worried that the network might not have enough bandwidth to handle streaming videos on top of its normal network traffic. What can you do to find out?

A. Use iperf to test the throughput of the network.

B. Upgrade the network to Gigabit Ethernet.

C. Use netstat to test the throughput of the network.

D. Use nmap to test the throughput of the network.

35. You suspect a run of fiber-optic cable is broken somewhere in the ceiling plenum. What can you do to test this hypothesis?

A. Use a multimeter to test the cable.

B. Use an OTDR to test the cable.

C. Use a toner probe to test the cable.

D. Use a TDR to test the cable.

36. You need to use the **dig** command to query your DNS server for a list of all authoritative DNS servers for the nebo-tech.com domain. Which command will do this?

A. `dig nebo-tech.com ns`

B. `dig nebo-tech.com mx`

C. `dig nebo-tech.com +short`

D. `dig nebo-tech.com SOA`

37. Which SNMP component runs on a server and collects data from network hosts that are being monitored using the SNMP protocol?

A. SNMP Agent

B. SNMP Manager

C. SNMP Management Information Base (MIB)

D. SNMP Managed Devices

38. You need to create a physical map of your network. What should you do? (Choose two.)

   A. Create a database of all the workstations in your network along with their asset tag number, purchase date, and replacement cost.

   B. Identify the IP addresses assigned to each network device.

   C. Identify the location of all network switches, along with their type and speed.

   D. Identify the location of all servers.

   E. Group wires in your wiring closet together by color or purpose.

39. Which of the following processes or policies should be included in your organization's asset management plan? (Choose two.)

   A. Acceptable use policy

   B. Vendor approval process

   C. Social engineering response process

   D. Equipment lifecycle management process

   E. Password aging policy

40. Your company provides outsourced call center services to large clients. It is absolutely critical that the Voice over IP (VoIP) traffic on the network be given higher priority than other traffic, such as employees browsing the Internet. What network mechanisms can be used to do this?

   A. Caching

   B. Buffering

   C. Traffic shaping

   D. Virtualization

41. Which of the following network applications would be least sensitive to latency in the network?

   A. Streaming video

   B. SMB-based file and printer sharing

   C. Voice over IP (VoIP)

   D. Streaming music

42. You are implementing a new wireless network for a financial services firm. You need to ensure that the network is as secure as possible. What should you do?

   A. Implement WEP encryption.

   B. Implement WPA with TKIP encryption.

   C. Implement WPA2 with AES encryption.

   D. Implement WPA encryption using preshared keys (PSK).

43. An individual has configured Kismet on her Linux netbook to capture information about wireless networks. She is walking around the downtown commercial district of your city with Kismet running, gathering information about all of the wireless networks she encounters. When she finds an unencrypted network, she draws a)(symbol on a nearby wall along with the SSID of the network. What kind of wireless exploit is in use in this scenario?

A. War chalking

B. Evil twin

C. WPA cracking

D. War driving

44. You need to configure a site-to-site L2TP VPN tunnel through the Internet to connect a branch office to your main company headquarters. Which security mechanism can you use to protect the data in the tunnel as it is transmitted through the Internet?

A. Internet Protocol Security (IPSec)

B. Microsoft Point-to-Point Encryption (MPPE)

C. Point-to-Point Tunneling Protocol (PPTP)

D. Secure Shell (SSH)

45. You've been asked to implement a two-factor authentication scheme for your organization's network. What should you do?

A. Require that users supply a username and a password to log in.

B. Require that users supply a username, password, and passphrase to log in.

C. Require that users supply fingerprint and retina scans to log in.

D. Require that users supply a username, password, and fingerprint scan to log in.

46. Which component of WEP encryption enables hackers to crack the encryption and compromise wireless data?

A. Keystream

B. CRC-32 checksum

C. Payload

D. Initialization vector

47. You are concerned that users in your organization are using weak passwords. What should you do to mitigate the risk? (Choose two.)

A. Disable broadcast forwarding on your routers.

B. Establish a written password policy and post it on the company intranet site.

C. Implement strong password policies on workstation and server operating systems.

D. Require users to give their passwords to their managers for verification of password strength.

E. Implement password aging policies on workstation and server operating systems.

48. Your organization has recently implemented a customer-facing FTP server containing software updates in your DMZ. You need to configure the boundary firewall protecting the DMZ such that traffic destined for ports 20 and 21on the FTP server is allowed through, but traffic destined for other services, such as HTTP, POP3, IMAP, and SMTP, is blocked. What should you do?

    A. Create a rule that allows all traffic, and then add deny rules for traffic destined for ports 25, 80, 110, 143, and 443.

    B. Create a rule that denies all traffic, and then add two allow rules that permit traffic destined for ports 20 and 21.

    C. Create deny rules for traffic destined for ports 25, 80, 110, 143, and 443; then create allow rules for traffic destined for ports 20 and 21.

    D. Create a rule that allows all traffic; then create allow rules for traffic destined for ports 20 and 21.

49. You are helping a small startup business design its network. The business's main server will store research and development files as well as a human resources database application that utilizes Microsoft SQL Server. The business will also provide a web server that customers can use to access a knowledge base application for self-support. Where should you place the main server in this scenario?

    A. On the internal network

    B. In the public zone

    C. On the internal network behind a NAT router configured to forward port 1433 to the database service.

    D. In the demilitarized zone (DMZ)

50. You want to conduct a vulnerability scan of a server in your network. You need to check for misconfigured hardware or software that opens security holes and verify that blank user passwords have not been used. Which tool would be most appropriate for this purpose?

    A. nmap

    B. netstat

    C. iperf

    D. iptables

    E. nessus

QUICK ANSWER KEY

1.	A, D	**18.**	C	**35.**	B
2.	A, C	**19.**	A, E	**36.**	A
3.	A	**20.**	A, E	**37.**	B
4.	A, C	**21.**	D	**38.**	C, D
5.	D	**22.**	B, C	**39.**	B, D
6.	C, D	**23.**	A	**40.**	C
7.	C, D	**24.**	B	**41.**	B
8.	D	**25.**	A	**42.**	C
9.	A	**26.**	B	**43.**	A
10.	D	**27.**	B	**44.**	A
11.	D	**28.**	C	**45.**	D
12.	A	**29.**	A	**46.**	D
13.	D	**30.**	A, E	**47.**	C, E
14.	C	**31.**	B	**48.**	B
15.	D, E	**32.**	A, E	**49.**	A
16.	B, D	**33.**	A	**50.**	E
17.	D	**34.**	A		

IN-DEPTH ANSWERS

1. ☑ **A and D.** The Internet Group Management Protocol (IGMP) and the Internet Control Message Protocol (ICMP) are the two protocols used at the Internet layer of the TCP/IP model. IGMP is used to establish multicast group membership. ICMP is used to communicate error and status information.

☒ **B, C, and E are incorrect. B** is incorrect because SPX is routing connection-oriented protocol that functions at the Transport layer of the OSI model. However, it is not categorized within the TCP/IP model. **C** is incorrect because ARP is used to resolve IP addresses into MAC addresses. It functions at the link layer of the TCP/IP model. **E** is incorrect because TCP is used to establish connection-oriented sessions at the transport layer of the TCP/IP model.

2. ☑ **A and C.** Two of the functions performed by the data link layer of the OSI model are to retransmit missing or corrupted frames (provided by the LLC sublayer) and to manage access to a shared network medium (provided by the MAC sublayer). For example, the CSMA/CD media access protocol is used on Ethernet networks to allow multiple hosts to use the same network bus at the same time while detecting collision at the data link layer.

☒ **B, D, and E are not correct. B** is incorrect because transmitting electrical signals between hosts is the function of the physical layer. **D** is incorrect because establishing communication sessions is the function of the transport layer. **E** is incorrect because routing is the function of the network layer.

3. ☑ **A.** Using a subnet mask of 255.192.0.0 on the 10.0.0.0 network creates four subnets: 10.0.0.0, 10.64.0.0, 10.128.0.0, and 10.192.00. The highest available IP address on the 10.64.0.0 subnet is 10.127.255.254.

☒ **B, C, and D are incorrect. B** is incorrect because 10.63.255.254 is the highest available IP address on the 10.0.0.0 subnet. **C** is incorrect because 10.191.255.254 is the highest available IP address on the 10.128.0.0 subnet. **D** is incorrect because 10.255.255.254 is the highest available IP address on the 10.192.0.0 subnet.

4. ☑ **A and C.** IGRP can use multiple metrics for calculating the best route, including bandwidth and delay. It can also use MTU and reliability to calculate the best route.

☒ **B, D, and E are incorrect. B** is incorrect because the RIP routing protocol uses hop count as a routing metric. **D and E** are incorrect because IGRP supports a maximum hop count of 255. The older RIP routing protocol is limited to a hop count of 15.

5. ☑ **D.** You must enter **interface f0/0** at the command prompt of the Cisco router to tell the operating system that you want to configure the first Ethernet interface installed in it. Then you can enter commands to configure the interface.

☒ **A, B,** and **C** are incorrect. **A** and **B** use invalid Cisco router commands. **C** is incorrect because **ifconfig eth0** is a command used on a Linux system to manage network interfaces.

6. ☑ **C** and **D.** The NTP daemon requires that port 123 be open in the firewall to allow it to synchronize time with other network hosts. The SSH daemon requires port 22 to be open in the firewall to allow users to establish secure remote sessions with the server using.

☒ **A, B,** and **E** are incorrect. **A** is incorrect because port 23 is used by Telnet to allow remote access to the host. **B** is incorrect because port 443 is the port used for secure HTTPS communications. **E** is incorrect because port 161 is used by the SNMP protocol to monitor network hosts.

7. ☑ **C** and **D.** The Real-time Transport Protocol (RTP) protocol and the RTP Control Protocol (RTCP) are used to deliver media such as audio and video over an IP network. The RTP protocol delivers the actual media content. The RTCP protocol is used to deliver control information for the media being delivered by RTP, such as QoS information.

☒ **A, B,** and **E** are incorrect. **A** is incorrect because the SAP protocol is an older network advertisement protocol used in conjunction with the IPX/SPX protocol to identify hosts on the network. **B** is incorrect because the RDP protocol is used to provide remote desktop sessions to network clients. **E** is incorrect because the LDAP protocol is used to access information in an LDAP-compliant directory service, such as Microsoft Active Directory or Novell eDirectory.

8. ☑ **D.** When a host needs to resolve an IP address to a MAC address, the sending system will first look in its local ARP cache to see if an entry already exists for the IP address in question. If an entry exists, the host will use the MAC address from the table and transmit. If an entry for the destination system's IP address doesn't exist in the ARP cache, an ARP request packet is broadcast to all the machines on the network segment to determine the MAC address of the host.

☒ **A, B,** and **C** are incorrect. **A** is incorrect because the sender will first check its local ARP cache before sending a broadcast to try to resolve the IP address. **B** is incorrect because ARP uses broadcasts to resolve IP addresses into MAC addresses. **C** is incorrect because the sending and destination systems reside on the same network segment.

9. ☑ **A.** This strategy will work. The change will be transparent from the end user's perspective. Employees will be able to use the same URL they are accustomed to using to access the intranet web site on the new web server.

    ☒ **B, C,** and **D** are incorrect. **B** is incorrect because the change should be made on the primary server for the DNS zone, not on the secondary. **C** is incorrect because using a CNAME record will require you to retrain every employee to use the new hostname in the URL used to access the intranet web site. **D** will work but could represent a significant amount of work. Simply editing the existing A record will allow all employees to use the same URL to access the intranet site on the new web server; eliminating the need for retraining.

10. ☑ **D.** The first phase of troubleshooting a network issue involves gathering as much information as possible about the problem. In this scenario, using the **PING** command to test communications between the workstation and the printer will provide you with network communication information that you can use later on to formulate a hypothesis.

    ☒ **A, B,** and **C** are incorrect because each of these answers involves implementing a fix. This shouldn't be done until you have gathered as much information as possible about the problem and formed a solid hypothesis as to what is causing it. Implementing fixes without first fully understanding the problem is unlikely to fix the real issue and could possibly introduce new issues that will complicate your troubleshooting efforts.

11. ☑ **D.** A virtual switch functions in exactly the same manner as a real switch. In fact, the virtual servers probably can't tell the difference between them. Therefore, the data is transferred directly from one virtual server to the other through the virtual switch.

    ☒ **A, B,** and **C** are incorrect. **A** and **B** are incorrect because the virtual switch within the hypervisor functions just like a physical switch. It isn't necessary for data being transferred between virtual servers to go out on the physical network. **C** is incorrect because virtual hosts can communication with each other through the virtual switch in this scenario unless they have been specifically configured to be isolated, which isn't the case.

12 ☑ **A.** Entering **route add –net 172.18.0.0 netmask 255.255.0.0 gw 172.17.255.254 eth0** at the shell prompt of the Linux router will add a route to the 172.18.0.0 network through the gateway with an IP address of 172.17.255.254. This router will then know where to send packets destined for a host on the 172.18.0.0 network.

    ☒ **B, C,** and **D** are incorrect. **B** is incorrect because is specifies the command to add this route to a Windows-based router. **C** is the correct command for adding the route to a Cisco router, but not to a Linux-based router. **D** is incorrect because it specifies the wrong network interface in the router (eth1).

13 ☑ **D.** The NAT router first replaces the private IP address of the sender in the source field of the packet header with the NAT router's public IP address. After translating the private IP address to the public IP address, the NAT router uses Port Address Translation (PAT) to assign the connection a port number from a pool of available ports, inserting this port number in the source port field. This allows the NAT router to keep track of which external requests originated from which internal hosts and ensures the information sent in response makes it back to the appropriate system on the private network.

☒ **A, B,** and **C** are incorrect. **A** is incorrect because NAT and PAT must occur before the connection is added to the NAT router's translation table. **B** is incorrect because an entry must be added to the NAT router's translation table before the packet can be transmitted to the destination host and a connection established. **C** is incorrect because the private IP address must be translated to the public address before the port can be translated.

14 ☑ **C.** To make changes to the configuration of a Cisco router, you must change to global configuration mode, which allows you to make actual configuration changes to the router. In this scenario, you are already in privilege exec mode, so you can enter global configuration mode by entering **config term** at the command prompt.

☒ **A, B,** and **D** are incorrect. **A** is incorrect because the **enable** command is used to switch from user exec mode to privilege exec mode, which has already been done in this scenario. **B** is incorrect because the **disable** command is used to switch from privilege exec mode to user exec mode. **D** is incorrect because the **exit** command is used to switch from global configuration mode to privilege exec mode.

15 ☑ **D** and **E.** The goal of antenna placement for the wireless network in this scenario is to achieve the adequate coverage without excessive signal emanation outside the facility. An omni-directional antenna in the center of the open rectangular work area would provide the best coverage. Using semi-directional antennae in each corner would fill in the dead spots left by the omni-directional antenna but reduce signal emanation outside the facility.

☒ **A, B,** and **C** are incorrect. **A** and **B** are incorrect because using a semi- or highly directional antenna in the center of the complex would provide poor coverage in a rectangular work space. **C** is incorrect because using omni-directional antennae in each corner of the office would emanate the wireless signal outside the facility.

16 ☑ **B and D.** You could employ several strategies to reduce signal emanation. One is to replace omni-directional WAPs with semi-directional WAPs located along the perimeter of the building with the signal aimed toward the center of the facility. Another is to reduce the power level of your WAP. However, depending upon the layout of your building, you may need to implement additional directional WAPs to cover dead spots created by the reduced signal strength.

☒ **A, C, and E are incorrect.** **A** is incorrect because wireless repeaters would likely increase signal emanation unless they used directional antennae. **C** is incorrect because increasing the gain on the antenna would both likely increase signal emanation rather than reduce it. **E** is incorrect because it would result in wireless signal dead spots.

17 ☑ **D.** The most likely cause of this issue is a down or malfunctioning DHCP server. The workstations are using APIPA addresses, which indicates they could not contact your DHCP server to establish an address lease when the booted up. You should check the status of your DHCP server to see if it is down. You should also verify network connectivity to ensure that DHCPDISCOVER broadcasts can reach the DHCP server.

☒ **A, B, and C are incorrect.** **A** is incorrect because broadcast filtering is not an issue in this scenario, so a DHCP relay agent won't solve the problem. **B** is incorrect because rebooting the workstations will not enable them to get an IP address from a DHCP server that is down or malfunctioning. **C** is incorrect because a rogue DHCP server would most likely not hand out IP addresses in the range reserved for APIPA.

18 ☑ **C.** The bandwidth available to wireless network client decreases as the distance from the WAP increases. In this scenario, the users are probably too far away to get a good signal or perhaps physical barriers lie between them and the WAP that are degrading the signal. Implementing an additional WAP in the location near these users will probably fix the issue.

☒ **A, B, and D are incorrect.** **A** is incorrect because MAC address filtering controls who can and who can't connect to the wireless network. It does not improve signal strength. **B** is incorrect because upgrading users' computers to 802.11g interfaces will not improve the weak signal issue in this scenario. **D** could be correct in some circumstances; however, channel interference would probably affect a larger number of wireless users, not just those working in a remote corner of the office suite.

19. ☑ **A and E.** You should first verify that the wireless interface in the laptop is enabled. Some manufactures ship laptops with the wireless interface disabled. You should also verify the user is using the correct SSID when trying to connect to the wireless network.

☒ **B, C, and D are incorrect.** **B** is incorrect because 802.11n WAPs are backward-compatible with 802.11g and 802.11b network interfaces. Installing a new wireless interface probably isn't necessary. **C** is incorrect because WEP is not used to secure wireless communications in this scenario. **D** is incorrect because interference issues would affect all wireless users in the location, not just one user.

20. ☑ **A** and **E.** MTU black holes occur when the sending host is configured with an MTU that is larger than the MTU size on a router in a path to the recipient and network devices are configured not to allow ICMP messages. In this situation, the router is unable to send "ICMP Fragmentation Needed" messages to the sender to tell it to reduce the MTU size. As a result, TCP connections are set up correctly, but then oversized packets are lost when the ICMP notification messages are blocked. Many network security devices are configured by default to block ICMP traffic. Allowing ICMP messages will fix the issue.

☒ **B**, **C**, and **D** are incorrect. **B** is incorrect because the size of the MTU is causing the issue in this scenario, not the state of the TCP connection. **C** is incorrect because routing data between networks from sender to receiver doesn't itself cause a black hole. It is caused by a router with a small MTU size somewhere in the route. **D** is incorrect because the use of VLANs doesn't cause over- or under-sized MTUs.

21. ☑ **D.** Most likely, the workstations in this scenario have been configured with the wrong default gateway router address. The fact that the workstations can ping each other indicates that the basic network infrastructure is functioning. A misconfigured gateway address will allow hosts on the same segment to communicate with each other but will not allow them to communicate with hosts on other network segments. In this scenario, it's possible that the DHCP option that delivers the gateway address has been misconfigured with the wrong IP address.

☒ **A**, **B**, and **C** are incorrect. **A** is incorrect because changing the IP address of the server to 192.168.1.1 won't fix the issue, because the domain controller and the workstations are on different network segments. **B** is incorrect because workstations on the segment can ping each other, indicating the network switch is functioning correctly. **C** is incorrect because 192.168.0.1 is not within the IP address range being distributed by the DHCP server, nor is the domain controller even on the same segment as the DHCP server.

22. ☑ **B** and **C.** Implementing a RAID 5 array and synchronizing the server to a hot backup would be the best choices in this scenario. In a RAID 5 array, data is striped among multiple disks with parity information distributed among all of the disks in the array. If one disk in the array fails, data can be recalculated using the parity information from the other disks in the array. Synchronizing data to a hot backup system ensures that if the original system goes down, service and data can be restored almost instantly.

☒ **A**, **D**, and **E** are incorrect. **A** is incorrect because RAID 0 arrays stripe data across multiple disks in the array without redundancy. This improves performance but does not protect data integrity. **D** is incorrect as well. While running backups provides a degree of data protection, they are very slow to restore. It could take hours or even days to recover from a failed hard drive using backups alone. **E** is incorrect because bonded network adapters do not contribute to data protection and disaster recovery.

23. ☑ **A.** Users who are members of the Backup Operators group can back up and restore all files on the server, regardless of who owns them and what permissions have been assigned to them. They are also allowed to shut down the server.

    ☒ **B, C, and D** are not correct. **B** is incorrect because members of the Server Operators group are allowed a higher degree of administrative access than members of the Backup Operators group. For example, they can manage network shares and network services. **C** is incorrect because members of the Account Operators group are only allowed to manage user accounts. They are not allowed to complete the server backup tasks listed in this scenario. **D** is incorrect because making the user a member of the Administrators group would allow her full access to the server, which violates the specifications in this scenario.

24. ☑ **B.** Multimode fiber-optic cabling has a central core that is much larger than that of singlemode fiber-optic cabling. It's designed to carry multiple light rays (modes) concurrently for short distances.

    ☒ **A, C, and D** are incorrect. **A** is incorrect because the sheath around most multimode fiber-optic cables is orange; singlemode cables are usually yellow. **C** is incorrect because singlemode fiber-optic cabling transmits a single ray (or mode) of light through glass or plastic fiber. **D** is incorrect because singlemode fiber-optic cabling supports longer transmission distances than multimode fiber-optic cable and is also more expensive.

25. ☑ **A.** An RJ-45 connector is used to connect a host's network interface card to Category 6 UTP cabling. Be aware that there are different grades of RJ-45 connectors, and the one you choose must match the grade of cable you are using. For example, if you are use Category 6 cabling, then you should use a Category 6 compatible RG-45 connector.

    ☒ **B, C, and D** are incorrect. **B** is incorrect because an AUI connector is typically used to connect thicknet (RG-8) coaxial cable to a network interface board. **C** is incorrect because RJ-11 connectors are used for telephone jacks, not network connections. **D** is incorrect because BNC connectors are used to connect thinnet coaxial cables to a network interface boards.

26. ☑ **B.** 802.11b is an older wireless networking standard that operates in the 2.4 GHz frequency range and transmits data at maximum of 11 Mbps. 802.11b devices are compatible with 802.11g and 802.11n devices, as these standards all operate in the 2.4 GHz frequency range. However, 802.11a devices are incompatible with 802.11b devices because the 802.11a standard operates at 5 GHz.

    ☒ **A, C, and D** are incorrect. **A** is incorrect because 802.11a devices operate at 5 GHz and have a maximum data rate of 54 Mbps. **C** and **D** are incorrect because the 802.11g and 802.11n standards support data rates higher than 11 Mbps.

27. ☑ **B.** The external DSL filter/splitter is the most likely culprit in this scenario and probably needs to be replaced. When the filter is malfunctioning, high-frequency voice signals (above 3.4 KHz) interfere with the DSL signal while low-frequency DSL signals (below 3.4 KHz) cause line noise on the analog phone. When the filter is working correctly, all signals above 3.4 KHz are sent to the DSL modem, while all signals below this frequency are sent to the analog telephone line.

☒ **A, C,** and **D** are incorrect because the DSL modem includes an integrated Ethernet switch that can provide network connectivity to multiple hosts, just like any other switch. It uses standard straight-through UTP cables just as would be used with a standard switch as well.

28. ☑ **C.** Even though this network is wired as a *physical* star, it still operates as a *logical* bus due to the fact it uses a hub for the central connecting point. All data transmitted on the network is sent to all hosts on the network. Only the host to whom the data is addressed actually accepts it. All other hosts ignore the data. In this way, this network functions logically in exactly the same manner as a 10Base-2 network that uses a single run of coaxial cable to connect all hosts.

☒ **A, B,** and **D** are incorrect. **A** is incorrect because a logical ring topology would require data to be passed from host to host in a ring. **B** is incorrect because a logical star topology would require the use of a switch instead of a hub. **D** is incorrect because a physical mesh topology would require a dedicated link from each host to every other host on the network.

29. ☑ **A.** The cable runs are too long in this scenario. 1000Base-T Ethernet supports a maximum cable length of 100 meters, including any drop cables. In this scenario, the total cable length is over 102 meters. Shortening the drop cables will likely fix the problem.

☒ **B, C,** and **D** are incorrect. **B** is incorrect because running cabling through the ceiling plenum is a very common practice and doesn't cause issues unless the cables are run too close to EMI emitters such as high voltage lines or other electrical equipment. **C** isn't necessary as 1000Base-T networks are compatible with CAT 6a UTP. **D** is incorrect because the source of the problem is not the switch, but the cabling leading up to the switch.

30. ☑ **A** and **E.** To uplink two switches, you can connect the cascade port on one switch to a standard port on the second switch. Alternatively, you can also connect any port on the first switch to any open port on the second switch using a crossover cable.

☒ **B, C,** and **D** are incorrect. **B** and **C** are incorrect because ring in and ring out ports are used to connect Token Ring MSAUs together, not Ethernet switches. **D** is incorrect because the cascade port on a switch is already crossed-over and doesn't require a crossover cable to cascade it with another switch.

31. ☑ **B.** The term "demarc" refers to the demarcation point at which the telecom network ends and connects with your organization's wiring. Typically, this is the network interface device (NID) in a modern network, which is usually owned by the telephone company.

☒ **A, C, and D** are incorrect. **A** is incorrect because a main distribution frame (MDF) is a signal distribution frame for connecting your internal network equipment to external cabling and subscriber carrier equipment. **C** is incorrect because intermediate distribution frame (IDF) is a frame that serves as a distribution point for cables from the MDF. **D** is incorrect because a combined distribution frame (CDF) combines the functionality of an MDF and an IDF into a single distribution frame.

32. ☑ **A and E.** Internet Protocol Security (IPSec) is commonly used to encrypt remote access sessions with a VPN concentrator. This isn't the only option, however. You can also use other protocols, such as SSL/TLS, to encrypt the data in VPN tunnel. Either configuration would allow the remote employees to connect to your home office network securely over the Internet.

☒ **B, C, and D** are incorrect. **B and C** are incorrect because L2TP and PPTP are protocols that can be used to establish the point-to-point VPN tunnel, but neither protocol is capable of securing the tunnel once created. **D** is incorrect because DES is an older (and weaker) encryption standard that is unlikely to be used in a modern VPN solution.

33. ☑ **A.** A fox and hound transmits a tone on one end of a cable segment that can be detected on the other end, allowing you to identify which cable segment runs where. The hound can read the tone through the wire's insulation. A quality unit can even detect the signal through a wall.

☒ **B, C, and D** are incorrect. **B** is incorrect because a loopback plug is a testing device that sends a test pattern of bits on an interface and then tests the reception of these bits by connecting the interface's output to its own input. **C and D** are incorrect because TDRs and OTDRs rely on electrical or optical signals reflecting back down the medium on which they were originally transmitted. They do not connect input to output.

34. ☑ **A.** The iperf utility can be used on Windows systems to test throughput on a network. In this scenario, you'd probably find that the network bandwidth would be adequate prior to 9:00 in the morning and after 4:00 in the afternoon. However, you may find your network over-utilized during peak work hours for streaming video traffic. You can also use utilities such as ttcp on UNIX/Linux systems to accomplish the same task.

☒ **B, C,** and **D** are incorrect. **B** is incorrect because a variety of factors affect the bandwidth available on the network. Upgrading to Gigabit Ethernet would be very expensive, depending upon the size of the network. A less expensive approach would be to test the network first with a throughput tester and make infrastructure decisions from there. **C** is incorrect because the netstat utility is used to view stats for network interfaces, check for open ports, and view routing tables. It can't test network bandwidth. **D** is incorrect because nmap is a powerful network tool that can be used to analyze network packets and scan hosts for open ports, but it can't be used to test network bandwidth.

35. ☑ **B.** An OTDR sends a light signal down a cable and measures the amount of time it takes for the signal to return. Using this information, it calculates the distance to the end of the cable. If this distance is less than the physical length of the cable, then you know the cable is broken (or *open*) at that distance.

☒ **A, C,** and **D** are incorrect. **A** is incorrect because a multimeter works only with copper cable. **C** is incorrect because toner probe is also used only with copper cable. **D** is incorrect because a TDR performs the same function as an OTDR, but with copper cable instead of fiber.

36. ☑ **A.** The **dig nebo-tech.com ns** command will query your DNS server for a list of all authoritative name servers for the nebo-tech.com domain.

☒ **B, C,** and **D** are incorrect. **B** is incorrect because the command returns a list of all mail server records for the nebo-tech.com zone. **C** is incorrect because this command performs an A record lookup of the nebo-tech.com domain. **D** is incorrect because this command displays start of authority information for the nebo-tech.com zone.

37. ☑ **B.** The SNMP Manager collects data from network hosts that are being monitored using the SNMP protocol by SNMP Agents installed on each host. The agents monitor their respective devices and provide status updates to the SNMP Manager.

☒ **A, C,** and **D** are incorrect. **A** is incorrect because SNMP Agents are small software applications that run on a variety of network devices, including servers, workstations, printers, routers, and switches. SNMP Agents send information to the SNMP Manager. **C** is incorrect because the SNMP MIB defines the information that SNMP Agents will monitor on their respective devices. **D** is incorrect because SNMP Managed Devices are the physical devices on your network that are being monitored by SNMP Agents.

38. ☑ **C and D.** Creating a network map involves documenting your physical network infrastructure, such as the location of network servers, workstations, switches, routers, and firewalls. You should note the make and model of each device along with any other device-specific information, such as MAC addresses.

☒ **A, B,** and **E** are incorrect. **A** is incorrect because inventorying workstation lifecycle information in a database is part of the asset management process. **B** is incorrect because device IP address information should be documented in your logical network map. **E** is incorrect because grouping wires in the wiring closet is part of the cable management process.

39. ☑ **B and D.** Your organization's asset management plan should include a process or policy for approving vendors from whom networking equipment can be purchased. This will ensure that you will receive adequate service and support from the vendor. It should also include processes for tracking the lifecycle of your networking equipment. This will help you more accurately forecast future replacement costs.

☒ **A, C,** and **E** are incorrect because an acceptable use policy, a social engineering response policy, and a password aging policy should be included in your organization's security plan.

40. ☑ **C.** You can use traffic shaping in this scenario to delay certain types of network packets, such as web or email packets, to reserve bandwidth for VoIP traffic. This will help ensure that your customer service representatives experience an acceptable audio quality level during their calls.

☒ **A, B,** and **D** are incorrect. **A** is incorrect because caching stores frequently accessed content from the Internet locally. This can be beneficial in many types of networks, but it really isn't useful in this scenario. **B** is incorrect because the use of buffering in this scenario could wreak havoc on real-time, two-way conversations using VoIP. **D** is incorrect because virtualization is used to consolidate network hosts onto fewer hardware platforms. Again, this technology doesn't address the issue in this scenario.

41. ☑ **B.** In most circumstances, SMB-based file and printer sharing would be the least sensitive to network latency. File and printer sharing use the TCP protocol, which uses acknowledgements to retransmit late or missing packets. Unless the latency is excessive, the end user probably won't notice a millisecond or two of delay when saving files or sending print jobs.

☒ **A, C,** and **D** are incorrect. **A** and **D** are incorrect because audio and video streams can absorb a certain amount of network latency; however, video and audio quality begins to suffer once latency passes a certain threshold. This is because streaming video uses UDP and late or missing packets aren't retransmitted. **C** is incorrect because VoIP traffic is quite sensitive to network latency due to the two-way nature of the traffic and the fact that it runs on UDP, which doesn't retransmit late or missing packets.

42. ☑ **C.** You should implement WPA2 with AES (sometimes referred to as CCMP) encryption on your wireless access points and on all client systems that will connect to them. The AES encryption used with WPA2 provides stronger security than the other options listed in this scenario. The security of this system could be increased further by implementing WPA2 in Enterprise mode, which integrates a RADIUS authentication server along with an Extensible Authentication Protocol (EAP) into the wireless network.

☒ **A, B,** and **D** are incorrect. **A** is incorrect because WEP encryption is notoriously weak and can be compromised with relative ease. **B** and **D** are incorrect because WPA is weaker than WPA2. WPA-TKIP is vulnerable to attacks that exploit weak passphrases. WPA-PSK requires all devices to authenticate to the WAP using the same encryption key.

43. ☑ **A.** This is an example of war chalking. A variety of symbols are used by war chalkers to identify the type and strength of wireless networks they identify. For example, the symbol)(is used to identify an unencrypted network. Sometimes they will also record the SSID of the network with the symbol. An encrypted network may be identified by the () symbol.

☒ **B, C,** and **D** are incorrect. **B** is incorrect because an evil twin wireless exploit involves a rogue WAP configured with the same SSID as a legitimate WAP that is connected to a rogue web server hosting web pages that look like legitimate bank or credit card web sites. Victims connect to the rogue WAP thinking it is the legitimate WAP and send their confidential information to the criminal's web server. **C** is incorrect because WPA cracking involves using software to capture packets transmitted on the wireless network and crack the WPA encryption used to secure them. **D** is incorrect because war driving involves driving around to search for wireless network signals and marking their location on a map.

44. ☑ **A.** The L2TP protocol establishes the VPN tunnel, but it doesn't provide security. The IPSec protocol is commonly used with an L2TP VPN tunnel to protect data within the tunnel.

☒ **B, C,** and **D** are incorrect. **B** is incorrect because MPPE is used to protect data within a VPN tunnel created by the PPTP protocol. **C** is incorrect because PPTP is used to create a VPN tunnel. Much like L2TP, it only creates the tunnel; it doesn't secure the data. **D** is incorrect because SSH can be used both to create and encrypt a VPN tunnel. It doesn't require the use of L2TP to set up the tunnel.

45. ☑ **D.** Multifactor authentication requires the user to supply two or more authentication factors from the three categories of authentication factors: something they know, something they have, and something they are. Requiring users to supply a username, password, and fingerprint scan is an example of two-factor authentication because users must supply something they know (the username and password) along with something they are (the fingerprint scan).

    ☒ **A, B,** and **C** are incorrect. **A** and **B** are incorrect because usernames, passphrases, and passwords come from only one authentication factor category (what the user knows). **C** is incorrect because requiring fingerprint and retina scans also utilizes only one authentication factor category (what the user is).

46. ☑ **D.** One of the key weaknesses of WEP is the fact that it reuses the same 24-bit initialization vectors (IVs) and transmits them as clear-text in the header of packets containing a WEP-encrypted payload. If enough packets are captured, the complete encryption key can be reconstructed from this information.

    ☒ **A, B,** and **C** are incorrect. **A** is partially correct, because the keystream in WEP is composed of the IV and the WEP key. The resulting keystream is combined with the clear-text payload to create a stream cipher. **B** is incorrect because the WEP CRC-32 checksum is used to check for errors during transmission. **C** is incorrect because the payload is simply the data being transmitted on the wireless network.

47. ☑ **C** and **E.** The best way to eliminate weak passwords is to implement strong password policies and password aging policies on the workstation and server operating systems in your network. For example, you could configure a strong password policy that requires a minimum length of 8 characters, uppercase and lowercase characters, and numbers. You could also implement a password aging policy that requires passwords to be changed every 30 days with minimum password change interval of 5 days, for example.

    ☒ **A, B,** and **D** are incorrect. **A** is a good way to prevent denial-of-service attacks, but will do little to mitigate the risk from weak passwords. **B** is incorrect because, although a written password policy is a necessary measure, it alone will do little to defend your network because users will probably not read it. **D** is incorrect because requiring users to give their passwords to their managers opens huge security holes in your network.

48. ☑ **B.** A guideline you should follow when configuring firewalls is to create an implicit deny rule first that blocks all traffic, and then add allow rules for the specific traffic you want to allow through. In this scenario, you should first create a rule that denies all traffic, and then add two allow rules that permit traffic destined for ports 20 and 21.

☒ **A, C, and D are incorrect. A** is incorrect because it uses only explicit deny rules. This configuration will block traffic to the services specified, but it will allow all other traffic not explicitly denied. **C** is incorrect because it allows all traffic through except for that explicitly denied by the deny rules. **D** is incorrect because it also allows all traffic through using an implicit allow rule.

49. ☑ **A.** The best place for the main server in this scenario that contains proprietary information would be behind the organization's boundary and DMZ firewalls on the internal network. This isolates the server from the external public network.

☒ **B, C, and D are incorrect. B** is incorrect because placing the main server in the public zone would place it outside the administrator's direct control and expose it to every hacker in the world. **C** is incorrect because placing the main server on the internal network with port forwarding enabled for port 1433 would expose the Microsoft SQL Server to the DMZ, which represents an unacceptable security risk. **D** is incorrect because placing the main server in the DMZ would also expose proprietary information on the server to the DMZ, which also represents an unacceptable security risk.

50. ☑ **E.** The nessus tool is the only option presented in this scenario that can check for misconfigured hardware or software that opens security holes and verify that default or blank passwords have not been used.

☒ **A, B, C, and D are incorrect** because none of these utilities can check for misconfigured hardware or software that opens security holes and verify that blank user passwords have not been used.

ANALYZING YOUR PRE-ASSESSMENT RESULTS

Now that you're done, let's analyze your pre-assessment results! You can use this information to identify two things:

- What resources you should use to prepare for your Network+ exam
- Objectives that you might need to spend some extra time studying

With the recommendations in the previous table in mind, you can now use the following objective mapping table to determine which objectives need your focus:

Number of Answers Correct	Recommended Course of Study
1–12	If this had been the actual Network+ exam, you probably wouldn't have passed. You need considerable study time before taking the Network+ exam. It is recommended that you thoroughly review an in-depth study aid, such as *CompTIA Network+ Certification Study Guide, Fifth Edition* before proceeding with use of this book.
13–25	If this had been the actual Network+ exam, you probably wouldn't have passed. Additional study is necessary before taking the Network+ exam. It is recommended that you review an in-depth study aid, such as *CompTIA Network+ Certification Study Guide, Fifth Edition* before proceeding with use of this book.
26–37	If this had been the actual Network+ exam, you probably wouldn't have passed. Additional study and targeted review is recommended. At this level it will be helpful to know which exam objectives are points of weakness so you can tailor your studies based on your needs. Use the Objective Map shown next to determine which objectives are targets for further study, and allocate extra time to review the questions related to these objectives and the in-depth answer explanations that accompany them.
38–50	Congratulations! If this was the actual Network+ exam, you probably would have passed. However, it is still recommended that you work through all of the questions included in this book to ensure that you are familiar with all of the content that may appear on the actual exam.

With the recommendations in the previous table in mind, you can now use the following objective mapping table to determine which objectives need your focus:

Domain	Weight	Objective	Chapter	Question No. in Pretest
1.0 Network Technologies	21%	1.1 Compare the layers of the OSI and TCP/IP models.	2, 4	1
		1.2 Classify how applications, devices, and protocols relate to the OSI model layers.	2, 3	2
		1.3 Explain the purpose and properties of IP addressing.	4, 7	3
		1.4 Explain the purpose and properties of routing and switching.	3, 6, 7	4, 5
		1.5 Identify common TCP and UDP default ports.	4	6
		1.6 Explain the function of common networking protocols.	4, 5	7, 8
		1.7 Summarize DNS concepts and its components.	8	9
		1.8 Given a scenario, implement the following network troubleshooting methodology.	15	10
		1.9 Identify virtual network components.	3	11
2.0 Network Installation and Configuration	23%	2.1 Given a scenario, install and configure routers and switches.	6, 7, 8	12, 13, 14
		2.2 Given a scenario, install and configure a wireless network.	9	15, 16
		2.3 Explain the purpose and properties of DHCP.	8	17
		2.4 Given a scenario, troubleshoot common wireless problems.	9	18, 19
		2.5 Given a scenario, troubleshoot common router and switch problems.	6	20, 21
		2.6 Given a set of requirements, plan and implement a basic SOHO network.	12	22, 23

Domain	Weight	Objective	Chapter	Question No. in Pretest
3.0 Network Media and Topologies	17%	3.1 Categorize standard media types and associated properties.	1, 3	24
		3.2 Categorize standard connector types based on network media.	1, 3	25
		3.3 Compare and contrast different wireless standards.	9	26
		3.4 Categorize WAN technology types and properties.	10, 11	27
		3.5 Describe different network topologies.	1	28
		3.6 Given a scenario, troubleshoot common physical connectivity problems.	15	29
		3.7 Compare and contrast different LAN technologies.	1, 3	30
		3.8 Identify components of wiring distribution.	3	31
4.0 Network Management	20%	4.1 Explain the purpose and features of various network appliances.	3	32
		4.2 Given a scenario, use appropriate hardware tools to troubleshoot connectivity issues.	15	33, 35
		4.3 Given a scenario, use appropriate software tools to troubleshoot connectivity issues.	5, 15	34, 36
		4.4 Given a scenario, use the appropriate network monitoring resource to analyze traffic.	13	37
		4.5 Describe the purpose of configuration management documentation.	13	38, 39
		4.6 Explain different methods and rationales for network performance optimization.	15	40, 41

Domain	Weight	Objective	Chapter	Question No. in Pretest
5.0 Network Security	19%	5.1 Given a scenario, implement appropriate wireless security measures.	9	42, 43
		5.2 Explain the methods of network access security.	10	44
		5.3 Explain methods of user authentication.	14	45
		5.4 Explain common threats, vulnerabilities, and mitigation techniques.	9, 14	46, 47
		5.5 Given a scenario, install and configure a basic firewall.	14	48, 49
		5.6 Categorize different types of network security appliances and methods.	14	50

B

Practice Exam

1. You are designing a geographically dispersed network implementation for a client. Routers provide interconnectivity between the network segments. You need to specify the network protocols that will be used to enable communications between hosts. What should you do? (Choose two possibilities.)
    A.   Recommend the client use IP.
    B.   Recommend the client use NetBIOS.
    C.   Recommend the client use IPX.
    D.   Recommend the client use DLC.
    E.   Recommend the client use NetBEUI.

2. Which NetBIOS mode is used for connection-oriented communications?
    A.   Datagram
    B.   Session
    C.   Connectionless
    D.   Stateless

3. Which protocols are application layer protocols? (Choose two.)
    A.   FTP
    B.   IPX
    C.   NetBIOS
    D.   SMTP
    E.   UDP

4. Which layer of the OSI model is responsible for managing logical addressing and routing of packets using information stored in a routing table?
    A.   Application
    B.   Presentation
    C.   Network
    D.   Physical

5. Which data link sublayer of the OSI model defines rules for accessing the network media?
    A.   Logical Link Control
    B.   Media Access Control
    C.   Network Access Control
    D.   Transport Control

6. A financial services firm has asked you to implement a wireless network for its office. To keep its financial advisers informed of the latest trends, the firm uses a 2.4 GHz wireless distribution system to transmit television news channels to TV sets in each work area. To eliminate interference, they have requested a wireless network using the 5.725 GHz to 5.850 GHz frequency range and a maximum data rate of 54 Mbps. What should you do?

   A. Recommend the client implement a 802.11a network.

   B. Recommend the client implement a 802.11b network.

   C. Recommend the client implement a 802.11g network.

   D. Recommend the client implement a 802.11n network.

7. You've been hired by a medium-sized non-profit to manage its Ethernet network. Upon inspection, you notice that the network uses fiber-optic cable. What type of network could this be? (Choose two.)

   A. 10Base-2

   B. 10Base-5

   C. 10Base-T

   D. 10Base-FL

   E. 1000Base-LX

8. Which protocols are transport layer protocols? (Choose two.)

   A. IP

   B. TCP

   C. UDP

   D. IGMP

   E. FTP

9. You need to assign NetBIOS computer names to several new Windows workstations on your network. What should you do? (Choose two.)

   A. Name a system WS1.

   B. Name a system WORKGROUPWORKSTATION1.

   C. Name a system WS:1.

   D. Name a system WORKSTATION1.

   E. Name a system WS?1.

10. You've opened a web browser on your workstation and have entered a URL in the Location field. Which layer of the OSI model ensures the data is formatted correctly for transmission to the web server?

   A. Presentation

   B. Session

   C. Transport

   D. Network

11. Which layer of the OSI model is responsible for logically addressing data prior to placing signals on the network medium?

   A. Data link

   B. Session

   C. Network

   D. Physical

12. You need to assign an IPv4 address to a Macintosh workstation on your network. What should you do?

   A. Assign an IP address of 10.0.0.0.

   B. Assign an IP address of 10.255.255.255.

   C. Assign an IP address of 10.0.0.0.287.

   D. Assign an IP address of 10.0.2.1.

13. Which protocols are session layer protocols in the OSI model? (Choose two.)

   A. HTTP

   B. IP

   C. NetBIOS

   D. RPC

   E. TCP

14. Which setting configures a network interface to both send and receive data, but not at the same time?

   A. Simplex

   B. Half duplex

   C. Full duplex

   D. Time-division duplexing

15. After entering the **ifconfig** command at the command prompt of a Linux workstation, you see that the following 48-bit MAC address has been assigned to the network board: 00-17-08-3B-06-3B. What is the manufacturer ID contained in this MAC address?

A. 00-17

B. 00-17-08

C. 00

D. 3B-06-3B

16. Which of the following is a valid EUI-64 MAC address?

A. 00-00-AA-AA-BB-CC-DD-EE

B. 00-14-A5-FD-42-A1

C. 00:00:1B:EF:0B:AD:D3:HC

D. 00-50-56-C0-00-01-AC-DD-01

17. A network is composed of seven systems connected by four cascaded Ethernet switches. One host is a Windows server (FS1), and the rest are Windows workstations (WS1, WS2, WS3, WS4, WS5, and WS6). FS1, WS1, and WS2 are connected to the first switch, WS3 and WS4 are connected to the second switch, WS5 is connected to the third switch, and WS6 is connected to the fourth switch. If a user on WS3 sends a request for a service to the FS1 server, which hosts will receive a copy of the Ethernet frames that make up the request?

A. WS3 and FS1 only

B. FS1 only

C. WS1, WS2, WS3, WS4, and FS1 only

D. All hosts connected to all switches

18. You manage networks for a legal consulting firm that has four separate Ethernet networks, one in each building in its campus. You want to connect all of these networks together, but you're concerned about overwhelming the network with unnecessary traffic. You want to manage traffic such that data addressed to hosts on the same local segment remain on that segment, while data addressed to hosts on a different segment are forwarded. What should you do?

A. Implement bridges or hubs.

B. Implement hubs or repeaters.

C. Implement switches or hubs.

D. Implement routers or bridges.

19. You are working with a 24-port layer 1 switch and want to use it to create three separate VLANs. What should you do?

  A. Assign specific physical ports on the switch to VLANs that you define.

  B. Assign the MAC addresses of the systems connected to the switch to VLANs you define.

  C. Use the network layer logical address assigned to individual network packets to define VLAN membership.

  D. Purchase a layer 2 switch. Layer 1 switches can't be used to create VLANs.

20. A 24-port layer 2 switch has been configured with two separate VLANs using the MAC addresses of hosts connected to it. The FS1 server as well as workstations WS1, WS2, and WS3 are associated with VLAN1 on the switch. The FS2 server as well as workstations WS4, WS5, and WS6 are associated with VLAN2 on the same switch. If FS2 sends a network broadcast, which hosts will receive it?

  A. FS1 and FS2

  B. FS1, FS2, WS4, WS5, WS6

  C. FS2, WS4, WS5, WS6

  D. All hosts will receive it

21. You manage a network for a financial services firm. The network is composed of three Ethernet hubs that have been cascaded together. FS1, WS1, and WS2 are connected to Hub1; WS3, WS4, and FS2 are connected to Hub2; and WS5, WS6, and WS7 are connected to Hub3. What is the collision domain for the FS1 host?

  A. The network port to which the FS1 server is connected on the hub

  B. All hosts connected to Hub1

  C. All hosts connected to Hub1, Hub2, and Hub3

  D. All hosts connected to Hub1 and Hub2

22. Which of the following hardware devices operate at the physical and data link layers in the OSI model?

  A. Firewall

  B. Router

  C. Switch

  D. Hub

23. You have been asked by a client to manage a legacy 10Base-5 Ethernet network. You need to connect a new PC system to the thicknet (RG-8) coaxial network. The network interface card you purchased has three different connections from which you can choose to connect to the network. What should you do?

  A. Use a BNC connector.

  B. Use an AUI connector.

  C. Use an RJ-11 connector.

  D. Use an RJ-45 connector.

24. You are working with a network that has a dedicated link from each host to every other host on the network. What type of physical topology does this network use?

    A. Ring

    B. Star

    C. Bus

    D. Mesh

25. You are responsible for managing a 100Base-T Ethernet network. Each host has its own network cable that connects to a switch. What type of physical topology does this network use?

    A. Ring

    B. Star

    C. Bus

    D. Mesh

26. Which category of network cable supports a maximum data rate of 100 Mbps?

    A. Category 2

    B. Category 3

    C. Category 5

    D. Category 5e

    E. Category 6

27. You are creating a T1 crossover cable and need to make sure the wires are crossed correctly. What should you do?

    A. Connect pins 1, 2, 3, and 4 to pins 4, 3, 2, and 1.

    B. Connect pins 1, 3, 4, and 5 to pins 4, 3, 1, and 5.

    C. Connect pins 1, 2, 3, and 5 to pins 3, 5, 1, and 2.

    D. Connect pins 1, 2, 4, and 5 to pins 4, 5, 1, and 2.

28. You are planning the implementation of a new Ethernet network. The client has requested that the network be capable of 100 Mbps or faster data transfers. What should you do? (Choose three possibilities.)

    A. Recommend a 10Base-5 network.

    B. Recommend a 10Base-T network.

    C. Recommend a 1000Base-CX network.

    D. Recommend a 1000Base-T network.

    E. Recommend a Fast Ethernet network.

    F. Recommend a 10Base-2 network.

29. Which type of network typically uses RG-8 coaxial cabling?

    A. Token Ring

    B. 10Base-T

    C. 10Base-5

    D. 10GBase-T

30. Which protocol is frequently used to transfer streaming media over IP networks?

    A. IGMP

    B. SSH

    C. HTTP

    D. HTTPS

    E. RTP

31. You need to access the console of a Linux server in the data center remotely from your cubicle to add a new user account to the system. What should you do?

    A. Establish an SSH connection.

    B. Establish a Telnet connection.

    C. Establish a VNC connection.

    D. Establish an SNMP connection.

32. You have just implemented the Internet Information Server (IIS) on a Windows Server 2008 system. The server must be configured to allow traffic through for this service. What should you do? (Choose two.)

    A. Open port 123 in the server's firewall.

    B. Open port 119 in the server's firewall.

    C. Open port 143 in the server's firewall.

    D. Open port 80 in the server's firewall.

    E. Open port 443 in the server's firewall.

33. You have just implemented an FTP server on your Windows Server 2008 system to allow users to upload and download files using the FTP protocol. Which port is used for the FTP control connection by this service?

    A. 20

    B. 53

    C. 80

    D. 21

    E. 443

34. You need to clear the entire ARP cache on your Windows 7 workstation. What should you do?

A. Enter **arp −n** at the command prompt.

B. Enter **arp −a** at the command prompt.

C. Enter **arp −s** at the command prompt.

D. Enter **arp −g** at the command prompt.

E. Enter **arp −d *** at the command prompt.

35. You need to add an entry manually to your Linux server's ARP cache that maps the 10.0.0.1 IP address to the 00-14-A5-FD-42-A1 MAC address. What should you do?

A. Enter **arp −a 10.0.0.1 00-14-A5-FD-42-A1** at the shell prompt.

B. Enter **arp −s 10.0.0.1 00-14-A5-FD-42-A1** at the shell prompt.

C. Enter **arp −d 10.0.0.1 00-14-A5-FD-42-A1** at the shell prompt.

D. Enter **arp −H 10.0.0.1 00-14-A5-FD-42-A1** at the shell prompt.

36. Which command was used at the Command prompt of a Windows system to generate the following output?

```
Wireless Network Connection:
Node IpAddress: [192.168.1.100] Scope Id: []
    No names in cache
```

A. netstat −e

B. nbtstat −n

C. netstat −a

D. nbtstat −c

37. Based upon the output of the **tracert** command shown here, what is the average response time for the router with an IP address of 63.146.27.230?

```
Tracing route to ns.novell.com [137.65.1.1]
over a maximum of 30 hops:

    1     1 ms    <1 ms     <1 ms    192.168.1.1
    2     2 ms     1 ms      1 ms    192.168.0.1
    3    41 ms    40 ms     40 ms    slkc-dsl-gw10-202.slkc.qwest.net [67.41.239.202]
    4    42 ms    41 ms     41 ms    slkc-agw1.inet.qwest.net [67.41.238.73]
    5    59 ms    61 ms     68 ms    sjp-brdr-03.inet.qwest.net [67.14.34.10]
    6    59 ms    59 ms     61 ms    63.146.27.230
    7    79 ms    59 ms     58 ms    0.ae1.XL4.SJC7.ALTER.NET [152.63.51.41]
    8   122 ms    92 ms     91 ms    0.so-7-0-0.XT2.DEN4.ALTER.NET [152.63.1.118]
    9    92 ms    92 ms     91 ms    POS7-0.GW3.DEN4.ALTER.NET [152.63.72.73]
   10   101 ms   101 ms    101 ms    unknown.customer.alter.net [65.206.183.22]
```

```
11   164 ms   163 ms   182 ms   192.94.118.247
12   450 ms   105 ms   105 ms   137.65.2.66
13   104 ms   105 ms   105 ms   ns.novell.com [137.65.1.1]
```

Trace complete.

A. 62.66

B. 41.33

C. 61

D. 59.66

38. While monitoring a Linux server system using the **netstat** command, you notice that a new port has been opened on the system. You are concerned and want to find out which process opened the port. What should you do?

A. Enter **netstat –p** at the shell prompt.

B. Enter **netstat –e** at the shell prompt.

C. Enter **netstat –a** at the shell prompt.

D. Enter **netstat –o** at the shell prompt.

39. You've connected to the ftp.mycorp.com FTP server using the **ftp** command at the shell prompt of a Linux workstation. You need to upload an executable file to the FTP server. What should you do? (Choose two.)

A. Enter **upload** at the FTP prompt.

B. Enter **put** at the FTP prompt.

C. Enter **get** at the FTP prompt.

D. Enter **binary** at the FTP prompt.

E. Enter **ls** at the FTP prompt.

40. Which of the following is true regarding the TFTP protocol?

A. It utilizes a connection-oriented TCP session.

B. It utilizes a connectionless UDP session.

C. It supports user authentication to control access.

D. It allows you to generate a listing of files available for download on the TFTP server.

41. You've just enabled routing on a Cisco router. You need to verify that the appropriate routes exist in the routing table. What should you do?

A. Enter **route view** at the command prompt of the router.

B. Enter **ip routing** at the command prompt of the router.

C. Enter **route print** at the command prompt of the router.

D. Enter **show ip route** at the command prompt of the router.

42. You need to view the routing table on a Linux system configured to function as a router. What should you do?

   A. Enter **show ip route** at the shell prompt.

   B. Enter **route** at the shell prompt.

   C. Enter **ip routing** at the shell prompt.

   D. Enter **route view** at the shell prompt.

43. Which routing protocols run directly over the IP protocol? (Choose two.)

   A. Routing Information Protocol (RIP)

   B. Open Shortest Path First (OSPF)

   C. Intermediate System to Intermediate System (IS-IS)

   D. Enhanced Interior Gateway Routing Protocol (EIGRP)

   E. Border Gateway Protocol (BGP)

44. Which routing metric measures how long it takes a packet to travel from one network to another?

   A. Hop count

   B. MTU

   C. Latency

   D. Distance vector

   E. Link state

45. The Windows server hosting your Microsoft LiveMeeting services is named fs1.mycorp.com. You want to create an alias in the mycorp.com zone on your DNS server named livemeeting that points to the existing fs1 record. What should you do?

   A. Create an A record.

   B. Create a CNAME record.

   C. Create an NS record.

   D. Create an MX record.

46. You've discovered an older laptop in your equipment closet that has in integrated 802.11b wireless network adapter. Your organization uses 802.11a wireless access points to provide wireless connectivity to your network. What can you do to connect this device to the wireless network?

   A. Connect the integrated 802.11b adapter directly to the 802.11a wireless network.

   B. Disable the integrated 802.11b adapter and install an 802.11g USB wireless network adapter.

   C. Install a wireless bridge and connect the integrated 802.11b adapter to the 802.11b side of the bridge.

   D. Disable the integrated 802.11b adapter and install an 802.11a USB wireless network adapter.

47. You just implemented an 802.11n wireless network for a retail business in a strip mall. However, you are experiencing significant interference in the wireless network, causing dropped connections. You've discovered that that neighboring businesses in the mall are using channels 1, 6, and 11 for their 802.11x wireless networks. What should you do?

    A. Set your wireless access point to use channel 2.

    B. Set your wireless access point to use channel 5.

    C. Set your wireless access point to use channel 10.

    D. Set your wireless access point to use channel 9.

48. Which mechanism can be used with WPA security to provide dynamic key generation and rotation, ensuring each packet gets a unique encryption key?

    A. Lightweight Extensible Authentication Protocol (LEAP)

    B. Protected Extensible Authentication Protocol (PEAP)

    C. Temporal Key Integrity Protocol (TKIP)

    D. Extensible Authentication Protocol-MD5 (EAP-MD5)

49. Given optimal wireless conditions, which wireless networking standard provides the shortest range?

    A. 802.11a

    B. 802.11b

    C. 802.11g

    D. 802.11n

50. Your company uses work-from-home employees to answer customer service calls. These employees access your company's network through a VPN each night to update the company's customer service database. Some of these employees are located in Europe and use Basic Rate Interface (BRI) ISDN connections to access the company VPN. What's the fastest data rate these users can achieve?

    A. 56 Kbps

    B. 128 Kbps

    C. 256 Kbps

    D. 512 Mbps

51. Which type of ISDN device connects TE2 devices to an ISDN network?

    A. Terminal adapter (TA)

    B. Terminal equipment 1 (TE1)

    C. Network terminator 2 (NT2)

    D. Network terminator 1 (NT1)

52. You need to establish a remote connection to a Linux server from a Linux workstation using the Secure Shell (SSH) protocol. You are currently logged into your workstation as the root user and need to access the Linux server as root on that system. Given that the hostname of the Linux server is fs1, what should you do? (Choose two.)

    A. Enter **ssh fs1** at the shell prompt of your Linux workstation.

    B. Enter **ssh –l root fs1** at the shell prompt of your Linux workstation.

    C. Enter **ssh –u root fs1** at the shell prompt of your Linux workstation.

    D. Enter **ssh root fs1** at the shell prompt of your Linux workstation.

    E. Enter **ssh --user root fs1** at the shell prompt of your Linux workstation.

53. You need to access an application running in a Citrix server farm from a Windows workstation. You need to configure your workstation's firewall to allow traffic from the Independent Computing Architecture (ICA) thin client protocol. What should you do? (Choose two.)

    A. Open port 47 in the firewall.

    B. Open port 80 in the firewall.

    C. Open port 1293 in the firewall.

    D. Open port 1494 in the firewall.

    E. Open port 1723 in the firewall.

54. You are configuring a PPP connection and want to use an authentication protocol that authenticates both the client and the server when setting up the connection. What should you do?

    A. Use MS-CHAPv2 for authentication.

    B. Use CHAP for authentication.

    C. Use MS-CHAP for authentication.

    D. Use PAP for authentication.

55. You are a consultant working for a financial services firm. The firm allows you to work remotely from your home office using a VPN connection through the Internet. The firm's VPN server uses the L2TP protocol to create the encrypted tunnel. You need to configure your home computer's firewall to allow VPN traffic. What must you do? (Choose two.)

    A. Open port TCP port 23 in the firewall.

    B. Open TCP port 80 in the firewall.

    C. Open TCP port 389 in the firewall.

    D. Open UDP port 1701 in the firewall

    E. Open UDP port 5500 in the firewall.

56. What security protocol uses Encapsulation Security Payloads (ESP) to encrypt traffic and the Authentication Header (AH) protocol for message integrity and authentication?
    A. Internet Protocol Security (IPsec)
    B. Transport Layer Security (TLS)
    C. Internet Security Association and Key Management Protocol (ISAKMP)
    D. Secure Shell (SSH)

57. A network is configured such that when data is transferred, a dedicated connection is established. All data sent from the sender to the receiver follows the same path through the network. What kind of network is described in this scenario?
    A. Packet-switched
    B. Circuit-switched
    C. Messaged-switched
    D. Connectionless

58. Which of the following statements are true regarding a packet-switched network? (Choose two.)
    A. A dedicated connection is created between the sender and the receiver.
    B. All packets sent from the sender can potentially travel a different path through the network to the receiver.
    C. They generally use bandwidth more efficiently than circuit-switched networks.
    D. Data always arrives at the destination in the sequence in which they were sent.
    E. If the path between the sender and the receiver fails, there is no way to redirect data through another path.

59. Given that SONET STS-1 runs at the base OC-1 data rate of 51.84 Mbps, how much data can STS-24 (OC-24) transfer in 1 second?
    A. 155.52 Mb
    B. 2488.32 Mb
    C. 622.08 Mb
    D. 1244.16 Mb

60. You are implementing a VPN for a U.S.-based medical transcription firm. Home-based employees of the firm will use the VPN through the Internet to access the data and applications needed to process transcription jobs. After conducting a needs analysis, you have calculated that their WAN traffic during peak office hours will require a connection that provides a data rate of approximately 35 Mbps. What should you do?
    A. Recommend they use an ISDN connection.
    B. Recommend they use a T1 connection.

    C. Recommend they use a T3 connection.

    D. Recommend they use an E1 connection.

61. You need to implement a cable management plan in your server room and wiring closet. What should you do? (Choose two.)

    A. Create a logical network diagram.

    B. Create a physical network diagram.

    C. Standardize on a single color for all network cabling in your network.

    D. Use colored cables to implement a color-code scheme to categorize network devices.

    E. Avoid using overly long patch cables in the wiring closet room.

62. You are creating a logical map of your network. What information should you include? (Choose two.)

    A. DHCP servers

    B. Repeater locations

    C. WIC locations

    D. VLANs

    E. Cable runs

63. Your company uses a Windows Server 2008 domain controller to manage network authentication, file sharing, printer sharing, and database services. All of your network users and resources are represented by objects in your domain. Documenting the domain structure and the objects it contains is part of which network documentation process?

    A. Asset management plan

    B. Cable management plan

    C. Physical network map

    D. Logical network map

64. Which of the following processes should be included in a network's change management plan? (Choose two.)

    A. A procedure for verifying the state of the system after a change has been implemented.

    B. A procedure for implementing a backup strategy.

    C. A procedure for approving vendors from whom new network equipment will be purchased.

    D. A procedure for determining when a network component has become obsolete.

    E. A procedure for testing proposed changes in a test environment.

65. You just received an e-mail indicating your company's Human Resources department has partnered with a company that provides employees with substantial discounts at many large national retailers. To take advantage of this benefit, employees must access a web site by clicking a link in the message. After checking with Human Resources, you find that they didn't send the e-mail. What should you do?

A. Warn users that a spoofing attack has occurred.

B. Warn users that a phishing attack has occurred.

C. Configure your routers and firewalls to prevent a Denial of Service (DoS) attack.

D. Warn Human Resources that an eavesdropping attack has occurred.

66. Which of the following scenarios best describe a buffer overflow attack?

A. An attacker connects to an unsecured wireless network posing as a valid network host and intercepts network communications and tampers with their contents.

B. An attacker uses a sniffer to capture and analyze network traffic to try and read confidential data.

C. An attacker floods a host with thousands of responses to illegitimate ping requests, making it impossible for it to respond to normal network requests.

D. An attacker tries to gain administrative access to the system by sending more data to an application than is expected.

67. An attacker has written an exploit that sends mangled IP fragments with overlapping and oversized payloads to the target host. What kind of Denial of Service attack is this?

A. Teardrop

B. SYN flood

C. Ping of Death

D. Nuke

68. A programmer wrote what appears to be a gaming application. However, when it is installed, an exploit is launched that logs all the information transferred using the HTTP protocol and uploads it to the programmer's FTP server. What kind of malware is described in this scenario?

A. Keylogger

B. Trojan

C. Logic bomb

D. Worm

69. You are concerned that your organization's e-mail server could be used by spammers to send spam messages without your permission. You are also concerned that it could be used by worms to propagate themselves. What can you do to prevent this? (Choose two.)

A. Require SMTP authentication.

B. Restrict outbound e-mail only to source hosts within your network.

C. Turn off forwarding of network broadcasts on your routers.

D. Turn on forwarding of network broadcasts on your routers.

E. Allow outbound e-mail from hosts outside your network.

70. Which Kerberos component gives the host permission to request a service ticket?

A. Authentication Server (AS)

B. Ticket-Granting Ticket (TGT)

C. Key Distribution Center (KDC)

D. Realm

71. You are configuring a PPP connection for a modem that will be used to establish a connection with a remote access server at your company's main office. Which authentication protocol transmits passwords as clear-text and should *not* be used in this scenario?

A. Password Authentication Protocol (PAP)

B. Challenge Handshake Authentication Protocol (CHAP)

C. Microsoft Challenge Handshake Authentication Protocol (MS-CHAP)

D. Microsoft Challenge Handshake Authentication Protocol version 2 (MS-CHAPv2)

72. Which protocol uses preshared keys for authentication?

A. LEAP

B. EAP-MD5

C. PEAP

D. EAP-PSK

73. You've been asked to implement a two-factor authentication scheme for your organization's network. What should you do? (Choose two.)

A. Require users to supply a username and a password to log in.

B. Require users to supply a username, password, and PIN number to log in.

C. Require users to supply a username and password as well as a number from a hardware authenticator to log in.

D. Require users to supply a smartcard and a PIN number.

E. Require users to connect a security hardware device (dongle) to log in.

74. Which is an entity in the network access control (NAC) mechanism (defined by the 802.1x specification), such as a workstation, that needs to connect to the network?

A. Authentication server

B. Supplicant

C. Certificate authority

D. Authenticator

75. A small financial consulting firm needs you to set up a firewall for its Internet connection. The firewall will be placed between the internal network and the Internet. The firewall must monitor the status of the three-way TCP handshake used to establish a TCP session between hosts inside and outside the firewall. Hosts inside the firewall should be allowed to establish TCP connections with hosts outside the firewall, but not vice versa. What should you do?

    A. Implement an application-level gateway.

    B. Implement a proxy server.

    C. Implement a packet-filtering firewall.

    D. Implement a circuit-level gateway.

76. A client needs an Intrusion Detection System (IDS) that is able to "learn" what network traffic is normal on her network and use this information to classify anything outside the norm as suspicious. What should you do?

    A. Implement a signature-based IDS.

    B. Implement a heuristic IDS.

    C. Implement a network-based IDS.

    D. Implement a host-based IDS.

77. You've just arrived at work only to discover that no one is able to log in through your Windows Server 2008 domain controllers. You are in the first stage of troubleshooting the issue. What key question should you ask?

    A. Will configuring one domain controller to seize the PDC Emulator role from the malfunctioning domain controller fix the issue?

    B. What has changed in the system since users were able to authenticate correctly?

    C. Are the latest updates installed on each server?

    D. Is time synchronizing between the servers?

78. You are troubleshooting an issue with a user's Linux workstation. After gathering information, you have arrived at a theory of probable cause that the installation of a recent update overwrote several key configuration files and populated them with default values. You suspect that this change is causing services that worked correctly before this update was installed not to start on system boot. What should you do next?

    A. Uninstall the update in question.

    B. Call the Linux vendor's technical support number.

    C. Test the theory to determine cause.

    D. Establish a plan of action to resolve the problem and identify potential effects.

79. You suspect that you have a bad cable in a run between an RJ-45 wall jack and the server room where your switch is located. What should you do?

    A. Use a cable crimper or punch down tool to verify connections are secure.

    B. Use a cable tester to test the continuity of the cable and that the jack is wired correctly.

    C. Use a toner probe to test the continuity of the cable and that the jack is wired correctly.

    D. Use a multimeter to test the continuity of the cable and that the jack is wired correctly.

80. You need to determine whether a run of UTP cable has an open short somewhere between the RJ-45 wall jack and the switch in the server room and how far away the break is from the wall jack. What should you do?

    A. Use a cable tester to test the cable.

    B. Use a TDR to test the cable.

    C. Use a toner probe to test the cable.

    D. Use an OTDR to test the cable.

81. You recently experienced a catastrophic server failure in your server room due to overheating, even though the thermostat was set to 68 degrees Fahrenheit. What can you do to prevent this from happening again? (Choose two.)

    A. Aim the air conditioning diffuser vent in the server room at the rear of your server systems.

    B. Prop the door to the server room open to vent excess heat.

    C. Rearrange the systems in the server room to form hot and cold aisles.

    D. Install temperature monitoring equipment in the server room.

    E. Reduce the thermostat in the server room to 62 degrees Fahrenheit.

82. A company has configured its ecommerce web site to be installed on multiple servers so the requests sent to the site will be distributed among all servers. What type of redundancy is being used in this scenario?

    A. Fault tolerance

    B. High availability

    C. Load balancing

    D. Cold spare

83. A client's web server is frequently bogged down with client requests during peak hours. You have been hired to balance HTTP requests for the heavily utilized web site among multiple web servers. What should you do?

    A. Implement the Spanning Tree Protocol.

    B. Implement the Simple Network Management Protocol.

    C. Implement the Common Address Redundancy Protocol.

    D. Implement Round Robin DNS.

84. You have just made global configuration changes to your Cisco router and want to put it back into read-only mode. What must you do? (Choose two.)
    A. Enter **enable** at the command prompt.
    B. Enter **disable** at the command prompt.
    C. Enter **config term** at the command prompt.
    D. Enter **exit** at the command prompt.
    E. Enter **configure** at the command prompt.

85. You need to configure an Ethernet interface in a Cisco router with an IP address of 10.0.0.1 using the default Class A subnet mask. What should you do?
    A. Enter **ip address 10.0.0.1 255.0.0.0** at the router's command prompt.
    B. Enter **ip address 10.0.0.1 255.255.255.0** at the router's command prompt.
    C. Enter **ipaddr 10.0.0.1 255.0.0.0** at the router's command prompt
    D. Enter **ifconfig eth0 10.0.0.1 netmask 255.0.0.0** at the router's command prompt.

86. Which VLAN feature is used by switches to prevent switching loops that could occur if multiple switches were wired together incorrectly?
    A. Trunking
    B. Spanning Tree Protocol
    C. Port Mirroring
    D. QoS

87. A user has called the help desk indicating that his Windows workstation is displaying a "Duplicate IP address..." error message. You're curious because your network uses DHCP to assign IP addresses. You check the workstation and find that it has been assigned a static IP address. What should you do to fix this issue?
    A. Check the network for another workstation that has been statically assigned the duplicated IP address and assign that host a different address.
    B. Reconfigure the workstation to use DHCP to get its IP addressing information.
    C. Type **ipconfig /renew** at the workstation's command prompt.
    D. Statically assign the workstation a different IP address.

88. The workstations on your network are unable to reach a Linux-based file and print server on a different network segment. You've checked and the server is up and running with a static IP address assignment of 172.18.0.1. Your workstations have been assigned IP addresses from your DHCP server using addresses in the 172.17.8.100 to 172.17.8.253 range with a subnet mask of 255.255.0.0. You are unable to ping the server from any workstation, yet the workstations are able to ping each other. What should you do?
    A. Assign the Linux server an IP address that is not being used in the range of 172.17.8.100 to 172.17.8.253.
    B. Verify that the network switch has power and is turned on.

    C. Check the subnet mask assigned to the Linux server.

    D. Verify that the workstations have the correct default gateway router address assigned.

89. Which interior gateway protocols are distance vector routing protocols? (Choose two.)

    A. Border Gateway Protocol (BGP)

    B. Routing Information Protocol (RIP)

    C. Open Shortest Path First (OSPF)

    D. Interior Gateway Routing Protocol (IGRP)

    E. Intermediate System–to–Intermediate System (IS-IS)

90. Which routing protocol is an Exterior Gateway Protocol that can be used on global public networks such as the Internet?

    A. Enhanced Interior Gateway Routing Protocol (EIGRP)

    B. Interior Gateway Routing Protocol (IGRP)

    C. Routing Information Protocol (RIP)

    D. Border Gateway Protocol (BGP)

91. Some routing protocols determine the best route to take based on how many routers a packet must traverse to reach its destination. Which metric measures this?

    A. Hop count

    B. MTU

    C. Latency

    D. Link state

92. Which routing protocols are Interior Gateway Protocols (IGP)? (Choose two.)

    A. Intermediate System–to–Intermediate System (IS-IS)

    B. Exterior Gateway Protocol 3 (EGP3)

    C. Spanning Tree Protocol (STP)

    D. Border Gateway Protocol (BGP)

    E. Enhanced Interior Gateway Routing Protocol (EIGRP)

93. In your network, the routers know about your network topology and monitor the state of the link between the routers. What types of dynamic routing protocols are in use in this network? (Choose two.)

    A. Hybrid routing protocol

    B. Link state routing protocol

    C. Distance vector routing protocol

    D. Exterior Gateway Protocol

94. Which standard allows VLANs to span multiple network switches?

    A. 802.8

    B. 802.11

    C. 802.1q

    D. 802.14

95. Your workstation is configured to use DHCP to get its IP addressing information. When you boot the system and the operating system loads, it sends out a DHCPDISCOVER broadcast on the network. The DHCP server receives the message and responds with a DHCPOFFER to the workstation. What happens next?

    A. The DHCP server immediately follows the DHCPOFFER with a DHCPACK message.

    B. The workstation receives the DHCPOFFER message and responds with a DHCPACK to the server.

    C. The workstation broadcasts a DHCPREQUEST message on the network.

    D. The workstation sends a DHCPAPPROVE or DHCPDENY message.

96. Which mechanism can be used by DHCP servers to define the IP addresses that the server can hand out to clients?

    A. DHCP scope

    B. DHCP subnet address range

    C. DHCP option

    D. DHCP address exclusion

97. Your organization's network is composed of two segments connected by routers. Your DHCP server is on segment A, while your DNS server is on segment B. Workstations are connected to all segments; however, you've discovered that only the workstations on segment A are able to get IP addresses from the DHCP server. What should you do?

    A. Configure a DHCP relay agent on segment B.

    B. Configure your routers to forward broadcasts.

    C. Configure a DHCP relay agent on segment A.

    D. Install a separate DHCP server on segment B.

98. Your security team discovered a rogue WAP that was configured with the same SSID as a legitimate WAP. Which term best describes the security risk in this scenario?

    A. Rogue access point

    B. Evil twin

    C. War driving

    D. Data emanation

99. You want to establish a VPN connection from your laptop at home to your company's internal network through the Internet. Your company's VPN server uses the PPTP protocol to create the encrypted tunnel. You need to configure your workstation's firewall to allow the VPN traffic through. What must you do?

    A. Open port TCP port 25 in the firewall.

    B. Open UDP port 1701 in the firewall.

    C. Open TCP port 1723 in the firewall

    D. Open UDP port 5500 in the firewall.

100. You are configuring a VPN for a client that employs remote workers. The client has specified that the VPN be created using the L2TP protocol. However, you are aware that a VPN tunnel created with L2TP is inherently insecure. What should you do?

    A. Secure the tunnel with IPSec.

    B. Secure the tunnel with MPPE.

    C. Secure the tunnel with TLS.

    D. Secure the tunnel with MS-CHAP.

QUICK ANSWER KEY

1.	A, C	22.	C	43.	B, D
2.	B	23.	B	44.	C
3.	A, D	24.	D	45.	B
4.	C	25.	B	46.	D
5.	B	26.	C	47.	D
6.	A	27.	D	48.	C
7.	D, E	28.	C, D, E	49.	A
8.	B, C	29.	C	50.	B
9.	A, D	30.	E	51.	A
10.	A	31.	A	52.	A, B
11.	C	32.	D, E	53.	B, D
12.	D	33.	D	54.	A
13.	C, D	34.	E	55.	D, E
14.	B	35.	B	56.	A
15.	B	36.	D	57.	B
16.	A	37.	D	58.	B, C
17.	B	38.	A	59.	D
18.	D	39.	B, D	60.	C
19.	A	40.	B	61.	D, E
20.	C	41.	D	62.	A, D
21.	C	42.	B	63.	D

64.	A, E	**77.**	B	**90.**	D
65.	B	**78.**	C	**91.**	A
66.	D	**79.**	B	**92.**	A, E
67.	A	**80.**	B	**93.**	A, B
68.	B	**81.**	C, D	**94.**	C
69.	A, B	**82.**	C	**95.**	C
70.	B	**83.**	D	**96.**	B
71.	A	**84.**	B, D	**97.**	A
72.	D	**85.**	A	**98.**	B
73.	C, D	**86.**	B	**99.**	C
74.	B	**87.**	B	**100.**	A
75.	D	**88.**	D		
76.	B	**89.**	B, D		

IN-DEPTH ANSWERS

1. You are designing a geographically dispersed network implementation for a client. Routers provide interconnectivity between the network segments. You need to specify the network protocols that will be used to enable communications between hosts. What should you do? (Choose two possibilities.)
   A. Recommend the client use IP.
   B. Recommend the client use NetBIOS.
   C. Recommend the client use IPX.
   D. Recommend the client use DLC.
   E. Recommend the client use NetBEUI.

   ☑ **A and C are correct.** Both the IP and IPX protocols are designed to be routed between network segments by routers.

   ☒ **B, D, and E are incorrect.** B and E are incorrect because the NetBIOS and NetBEUI protocols are LAN protocols and can't be natively routed to different networks. However, together they can be piggybacked with other routable protocols, such as IP, to enable internetworking. **D** is incorrect because the Data Link Control (DLC) protocol, used by IBM SNA mainframe computers to communicate with peripheral devices, is also not routable.

2. Which NetBIOS mode is used for connection-oriented communications?
   A. Datagram
   B. Session
   C. Connectionless
   D. Stateless

   ☑ **B.** In Session mode, the NetBIOS protocol uses connection-oriented communications where data transmissions are acknowledged by the recipient.

   ☒ **A, C, and D are incorrect.** A is incorrect because in Datagram mode data is sent from the sender to the receiver without acknowledgments. **C** and **D** are incorrect because connectionless connections and stateless connections both refer to unacknowledged data transmissions.

3. Which protocols are application layer protocols? (Choose two.)
   A. FTP
   B. IPX
   C. NetBIOS
   D. SMTP
   E. UDP

> ☑ **A** and **D.** FTP and SMTP are both application layer protocols.
>
> ☒ **B, C,** and **E** are incorrect. **B** is incorrect because IPX is a network layer protocol. **C** is incorrect because NetBIOS is a session layer protocol. **E** is incorrect because UDP is a transport layer protocol.

4. Which layer of the OSI model is responsible for managing logical addressing and routing of packets using information stored in a routing table?
   A. Application
   B. Presentation
   C. Network
   D. Physical

> ☑ **C.** The network layer is responsible for managing logical addressing information; the delivery (or routing) of those packets using information stored in a routing table. The IP and IPX protocols function at this layer.
>
> ☒ **A, B,** and **D** are incorrect. **A** is incorrect because the application layer provides services such as web or FTP servers. **B** is incorrect because the presentation layer is responsible for formatting data correctly. **D** is incorrect because the physical layer is responsible for converting data to a pattern of electrical signals that will be sent on the network medium.

5. Which data link sublayer of the OSI model defines rules for accessing the network media?
   A. Logical Link Control
   B. Media Access Control
   C. Network Access Control
   D. Transport Control

☑ **B.** The Media Access Control sublayer of the data link layer defines rules for hosts that need to access the network media. Access control schemes such as CSMA/CD, CSMA/CA, and token passing are defined here.

☒ **A, C,** and **D** are incorrect. **A** is incorrect because the Logical Link Control sublayer of the data link layer provides error control and flow control functions. **C** and **D** are incorrect because there are no sublayers named Network Access Control or Transport Control within the data link layer of the OSI model.

6. A financial services firm has asked you to implement a wireless network for its office. To keep its financial advisers informed of the latest trends, the firm uses a 2.4 GHz wireless distribution system to transmit television news channels to TV sets in each work area. To eliminate interference, they have requested a wireless network using the 5.725 GHz to 5.850 GHz frequency range and a maximum data rate of 54 Mbps. What should you do?

A. Recommend the client implement a 802.11a network.

B. Recommend the client implement a 802.11b network.

C. Recommend the client implement a 802.11g network.

D. Recommend the client implement a 802.11n network.

☑ **A.** The 802.11a standard transfers data at 54 Mbps and uses frequencies ranging from 5.725 GHz to 5.850 GHz. This wireless standard has not been widely adopted by consumers but has been used to a degree in the enterprise.

☒ **B, C,** and **D** are incorrect. **B** is incorrect because the 802.11b standard uses frequency ranges of 2.4 GHz to 2.4835 GHz, but transfers data at only 11 Mbps. **C** is incorrect because the 802.11g standard transfers data at 54 Mbps, but uses frequency ranges of 2.4 GHz to 2.4835 GHz. **D** is incorrect because the 802.11n standard transfers data at 5 GHz or 2.4 GHz, but increases data transfer rates to 150 Mbps or more.

7. You've been hired by a medium-sized non-profit to manage its Ethernet network. Upon inspection, you notice that the network uses fiber-optic cable. What type of network could this be? (Choose two.)

A. 10Base-2

B. 10Base-5

C. 10Base-T

D. 10Base-FL

E. 1000Base-LX

☑ **D** and **E**. 10Base-FL and 1000Base-LX both utilize fiber-optic cabling. 10Base-FL is an older standard that is limited to 10 Mbps data transfers over fiber, while 1000Base-LX is a newer Gigabit Ethernet standard that can transfer data at 1000 Mbps over fiber.

☒ **A**, **B**, and **C** are incorrect. **A** and **B** are incorrect because the 10Base-2 and 10Base-5 standards utilize coaxial cabling. 1000Base-CX also uses a type of coaxial cabling called "Twinax." **C** is incorrect because 10Base-T uses UTP wiring.

8. Which protocols are transport layer protocols? (Choose two.)

A. IP
B. TCP
C. UDP
D. IGMP
E. FTP

☑ **B** and **C**. The TCP and UDP protocols are transport layer protocols in the OSI model. The TCP protocol is used to set up connection-oriented sessions that require packets to be acknowledged by the recipient. It is used by applications that require a high degree of data integrity, such as file sharing. The UDP protocol sets up connectionless sessions that do not require acknowledgments. It is used by applications that can tolerate a degree of data loss, such as streaming audio and video.

☒ **A**, **D**, and **E** are incorrect. **A** and **E** are incorrect because the IP and IGMP protocols are network layer protocols. **D** is incorrect because the NFS protocol functions at the application layer.

9. You need to assign NetBIOS computer names to several new Windows workstations on your network. What should you do? (Choose two.)

A. Name a system WS1.
B. Name a system WORKGROUPWORKSTATION1.
C. Name a system WS:1.
D. Name a system WORKSTATION1.
E. Name a system WS?1.

☑ **A** and **D**. NetBIOS computer names on a Microsoft network can have a maximum of 15 characters. Computer names may not use characters such as : * ? |. Therefore, WS1 and WORKSTATION1 are both valid NetBIOS computer names.

☒ **B, C,** and **E** are incorrect. **B** is incorrect because the name is longer than 15 characters. **C** and **E** are incorrect because they use illegal characters (: and ?).

10. You've opened a web browser on your workstation and have entered a URL in the Location field. Which layer of the OSI model ensures the data is formatted correctly for transmission to the web server?
    A. Presentation
    B. Session
    C. Transport
    D. Network

☑ **A.** The presentation layer of the OSI model is responsible for ensuring that the data being sent from the application layer by the web browser is formatted correctly for transmission to the web server.

☒ **B, C,** and **D** are incorrect. **B** is incorrect because the session layer is concerned only with managing network sessions between hosts. **C** is incorrect because the transport layer is responsible for breaking data into packets and ensuring delivery. **D** is incorrect because the network layer provides for the routing of data between networks.

11. Which layer of the OSI model is responsible for logically addressing data prior to placing signals on the network medium?
    A. Data link
    B. Session
    C. Network
    D. Physical

☑ **C.** The network layer is responsible for logically addressing data prior to transmitting signals on the network medium. For example, on an IP network, each host is logically assigned an IP address that is used to identify it uniquely. Each packet transmitted on the network contains the IP address of the sender as well as the IP address of the recipient.

☒ **A, B,** and **D** are incorrect. **A** is incorrect because the data link layer of the OSI model is responsible for physical addressing using MAC addresses, not logical addressing. **B** is incorrect because the session layer is concerned only with managing network sessions between hosts. **D** is incorrect because the physical layer is responsible for actually transmitting the data as electrical signals on the network medium.

12. You need to assign an IPv4 address to a Macintosh workstation on your network. What should you do?
    A. Assign an IP address of 10.0.0.0.
    B. Assign an IP address of 10.255.255.255.
    C. Assign an IP address of 10.0.0.0.287.
    D. Assign an IP address of 10.0.2.1.

☑ **D.** The maximum decimal value that can be assigned to any octet in an IP address is 255. In addition, 0 is reserved for network addresses. Accordingly, 10.0.2.1 is the only address in this scenario that could be assigned to a network host.

☒ **A, B,** and **C** are incorrect. **A** is incorrect because 10.0.0.0 is a network address that cannot be assigned to a host. **B** is incorrect because 10.255.255.255 is a broadcast address that cannot be assigned to a network host. **C** is incorrect because 287 exceeds the maximum value (of 255) for an 8-bit octet.

13. Which protocols are session layer protocols in the OSI model? (Choose two.)
    A. HTTP
    B. IP
    C. NetBIOS
    D. RPC
    E. TCP

☑ **C** and **D.** The NetBIOS and Remote Procedure Call (RPC) protocols function at the session layer of the OSI model. NetBIOS is used to configure session layer LAN communications on Server Message Block (SMB)–compatible networks (such as Windows and Samba). RPC allows commands to be run on a different computer system on the network.

☒ **A**, **B**, and **E** are incorrect. **A** is incorrect because HTTP is an application layer protocol. **B** is incorrect because IP is a network layer protocol. **E** is incorrect because TCP is a transport layer protocol.

14. Which setting configures a network interface to both send and receive data, but not at the same time?

A. Simplex
B. Half duplex
C. Full duplex
D. Time-division duplexing

☑ **B.** When set to half duplex, a network interface can send and receive data, but not at the same time. It's similar to talking to someone on a two-way radio. You can receive only if you're not currently talking. Because of this, it's important that the duplex setting on your switch port is the same as the duplex setting on the network interface to which it is connected.

☒ **A**, **C**, and **D** are incorrect. **A** is incorrect because simplex communications are unidirectional, comparable to listening to a radio station. **C** is incorrect because full-duplex communications allow bidirectional communications at the same time. **D** is incorrect because time-division duplexing is a scheme used to emulate full-duplex communications on a half-duplex communication channel.

15. After entering the **ifconfig** command at the command prompt of a Linux workstation, you see that the following 48-bit MAC address has been assigned to the network board: 00-17-08-3B-06-3B. What is the manufacturer ID contained in this MAC address?

A. 00-17
B. 00-17-08
C. 00
D. 3B-06-3B

☑ **B.** The first three octets of any MAC address (48-bit or 64-bit) make up the Organizationally Unique Identifier (OUI) and are unique to the manufacturer that made the network board. In this example, 00-17-08 indicates the network interface was made by Hewlett-Packard.

☒ **A, C,** and **D** are incorrect. **A** doesn't include the third octet of the OUI. **C** includes only one of the three octets included in the OUI. **D** includes the last three octets of the MAC address, which are assigned by the device manufacturer in any manner it wants.

16. Which of the following is a valid EUI-64 MAC address?
   A. 00-00-AA-AA-BB-CC-DD-EE
   B. 00-14-A5-FD-42-A1
   C. 00:00:1B:EF:0B:AD:D3:HC
   D. 00-50-56-C0-00-01-AC-DD-01

☑ **A.** 00-00-AA-AA-BB-CC-DD-EE is an example of an EUI-64 MAC address. EUI-64 MAC addresses are 64-bits long, composed of 8 octets represented with hexadecimal numbers.

☒ **B, C,** and **D** are incorrect. **B** is a valid 48-bit MAC addresses, but is too short for an EUI-64 MAC address. **C** is 64-bits long, but contains invalid hexadecimal characters (H). **D** is 72-bits long and is, therefore, not a valid 64-bit MAC address.

17. A network is composed of seven systems connected by four cascaded Ethernet switches. One host is a Windows server (FS1), and the rest are Windows workstations (WS1, WS2, WS3, WS4, WS5, and WS6). FS1, WS1, and WS2 are connected to the first switch, WS3 and WS4 are connected to the second switch, WS5 is connected to the third switch, and WS6 is connected to the fourth switch. If a user on WS3 sends a request for a service to the FS1 server, which hosts will receive a copy of the Ethernet frames that make up the request?
   A. WS3 and FS1 only
   B. FS1 only
   C. WS1, WS2, WS3, WS4, and FS1 only
   D. All hosts connected to all switches

☑ **B.** An Ethernet switch learns which network hosts are connected to each switch port using their MAC addresses. Using this information, the switch forwards data only to the switch port where the system to which the data is addressed is connected.

☒ **A, C,** and **D** are incorrect. **A** and **C** are incorrect because only FS1 will receive a copy of the frames in this scenario. **D** would be correct if this network used hubs instead of switches.

18. You manage networks for a legal consulting firm that has four separate Ethernet networks, one in each building in its campus. You want to connect all of these networks together, but you're concerned about overwhelming the network with unnecessary traffic. You want to manage traffic such that data addressed to hosts on the same local segment remain on that segment, while data addressed to hosts on a different segment are forwarded. What should you do?

    A. Implement bridges or hubs.

    B. Implement hubs or repeaters.

    C. Implement switches or hubs.

    D. Implement routers or bridges.

    ☑ **D.** Bridges are data link layer devices and can manage traffic based on the MAC addresses contained within Ethernet frames. For example, a bridge can learn which hosts are connected to each segment. If a frame is addressed to a host on the same LAN segment, the bridge won't forward it to the other connected segments. If a frame is addressed to a host on a different segment, the bridge will forward it to that segment only. Routers are network layer devices that can accomplish the same task using logical network addresses (such as IP addresses). If data is logically addressed to a host on the same segment, it is delivered directly. If it is addressed to a host on a different network, it is automatically delivered to the default gateway router, which then uses routing protocols to determine how to get the data to the correct network.

    ☒ **A, B** and **C** are incorrect. **A** is partially correct in that a bridge would work. However, hubs are physical layer devices and forward all frames to all connected hosts, which would create excess traffic and collisions. **B** is incorrect because repeaters and hubs are physical layer devices that forward all frames to all connected hosts. **C** is partially correct because switches can be used to forward data only to the port to which the destination host is connected. However, as noted, hubs are physical layer devices and forward all frames to all connected hosts.

19. You are working with a 24-port layer 1 switch and want to use it to create three separate VLANs. What should you do?

    A. Assign specific physical ports on the switch to VLANs that you define.

    B. Assign the MAC addresses of the systems connected to the switch to VLANs you define.

    C. Use the network layer logical address assigned to individual network packets to define VLAN membership.

    D. Purchase a layer 2 switch. Layer 1 switches can't be used to create VLANs.

☑ **A.** A layer 1 switch assigns specific ports to specific VLANs. For example, you could specify that the hosts connected to ports 1, 2, and 3 are members of one VLAN while hosts connected to ports 4, 5, and 6 are members of a different VLAN.

☒ **B, C,** and **D** are not correct. **B** is incorrect because a layer 2 switch uses the MAC addresses of the systems connected to the switch to define VLANs. **C** is incorrect because layer 3 switches base VLAN membership on the logical address (such as IP address) of individual network packets, not on physical hosts or physical ports. **D** is incorrect because layer 1, 2, and 3 switches can each be used to create VLANs; it's just done using different mechanisms.

20. A 24-port layer 2 switch has been configured with two separate VLANs using the MAC addresses of hosts connected to it. The FS1 server as well as workstations WS1, WS2, and WS3 are associated with VLAN1 on the switch. The FS2 server as well as workstations WS4, WS5, and WS6 are associated with VLAN2 on the same switch. If FS2 sends a network broadcast, which hosts will receive it?

A. FS1 and FS2

B. FS1, FS2, WS4, WS5, WS6

C. FS2, WS4, WS5, WS6

D. All hosts will receive it

☑ **C.** Because FS2, WS4, WS5, and WS6 are members of the same VLAN, they are members of the same broadcast domain.

☒ **A, B,** and **D** are incorrect. **A** is incorrect because FS1 is a member of different VLAN and, therefore, not a member of the same broadcast domain. **B** and **D** are incorrect because FS1, WS1, WS2, and WS3 are members of different VLANs and are, therefore, not members of the same broadcast domain.

21. You manage a network for a financial services firm. The network is composed of three Ethernet hubs that have been cascaded together. FS1, WS1, and WS2 are connected to Hub1; WS3, WS4, and FS2 are connected to Hub2; and WS5, WS6, and WS7 are connected to Hub3. What is the collision domain for the FS1 host?

A. The network port to which the FS1 server is connected on the hub

B. All hosts connected to Hub1

C. All hosts connected to Hub1, Hub2, and Hub3

D. All hosts connected to Hub1 and Hub2

> ☑ **C.** Since this network uses cascading hubs, all hosts connected to the hubs are part of the same collision domain.
>
> ☒ **A, B,** and **D** are incorrect. **A** would be correct if the network used Ethernet switches. **B** is partially correct; however, because the three hubs are cascaded together, Hub2 and Hub3 are also part of the collision domain. **D** is incorrect because devices plugged into Hub3 are also part of the same collision domain.

22. Which of the following hardware devices operate at the physical and data link layers in the OSI model?

   A.   Firewall

   B.   Router

   C.   Switch

   D.   Hub

> ☑ **C.** Switches operate at both the physical and data link layers. They transmit signals directly on the network media like a hub, but they also manage traffic based on layer 2 MAC addresses.
>
> ☒ **A, B,** and **D** are incorrect. **A** is incorrect because firewalls function at the network, transport, and application layers of the OSI model (depending upon the type of firewall). **B** is incorrect because routers operate at the network layer. **D** is incorrect because hubs are physical layer devices in the OSI model.

23. You have been asked by a client to manage a legacy 10Base-5 Ethernet network. You need to connect a new PC system to the thicknet (RG-8) coaxial network. The network interface card you purchased has three different connections from which you can choose to connect to the network. What should you do?

   A.   Use a BNC connector.

   B.   Use an AUI connector.

   C.   Use an RJ-11 connector.

   D.   Use an RJ-45 connector.

☑ **B.** A 15-pin AUI connector is used to connect thicknet (RG-8) coaxial cable to a 10Base-5 network interface board. Unless you manage a legacy Ethernet network, it is unlikely that you will work much with this type of connector.

☒ **A, C,** and **D** are incorrect. **A** is incorrect because a BNC connector is typically used to connect a host's 10Base-2 network interface card to an RG-58 coaxial cable segment. **C** is incorrect because RJ-11 connectors are used for telephone jacks, not Ethernet network connections. **D** is incorrect because RJ-45 connectors are used to connect unshielded twisted-pair cables to Ethernet network interface boards.

24. You are working with a network that has a dedicated link from each host to every other host on the network. What type of physical topology does this network use?
    A. Ring
    B. Star
    C. Bus
    D. Mesh

☑ **D.** A physical mesh topology requires that a dedicated link be established from each host to every other host on the network. This type of topology is not frequently implemented. When it is, it is usually done using wireless radio signals instead of physical wires.

☒ **A, B,** and **C** are incorrect. **A** is incorrect because a ring topology requires that each host be connected to one upstream and one downstream neighbor, forming a ring. **B** is incorrect because a star topology requires each host to connect to a central connecting point. **C** is incorrect because a bus topology connects all network hosts to the same network cable segment.

25. You are responsible for managing a 100Base-T Ethernet network. Each host has its own network cable that connects to a switch. What type of physical topology does this network use?
    A. Ring
    B. Star
    C. Bus
    D. Mesh

☑ **B.** This network uses a physical star topology. A physical star topology requires that each host have its own network cable that connects to a central hub or switch.

☒ **A, C,** and **D** are incorrect. **A** is incorrect because a physical ring topology requires the network media to be connected from host, to host, to host in a ring without terminators on each end. **C** is incorrect because a bus topology requires that all network hosts be connected to the same physical network cable segment without a central connecting point. **D** is incorrect because a physical mesh topology would require a dedicated link from each host to every other host on the network.

26. Which category of network cable supports a maximum data rate of 100 Mbps?
    A. Category 2
    B. Category 3
    C. Category 5
    D. Category 5e
    E. Category 6

☑ **C.** CAT 5 UTP is rated for data rates up to 100 Mbps. If you are implementing a new network, you should consider using CAT 5e or CAT 6 cabling to avoid limiting your network to this speed.

☒ **A, B, D,** and **E** are incorrect. **A** is incorrect because CAT 2 UTP is rated only to 4 Mbps. **B** is incorrect because CAT 3 UTP is rated only to 10 Mbps. **D** and **E** are incorrect because Category 5e and Category 6 support speeds up to 1000 Mbps.

27. You are creating a T1 crossover cable and need to make sure the wires are crossed correctly. What should you do?
    A. Connect pins 1, 2, 3, and 4 to pins 4, 3, 2, and 1.
    B. Connect pins 1, 3, 4, and 5 to pins 4, 3, 1, and 5.
    C. Connect pins 1, 2, 3, and 5 to pins 3, 5, 1, and 2.
    D. Connect pins 1, 2, 4, and 5 to pins 4, 5, 1, and 2.

☑ **D.** T1 cabling follows T568B standards, so a T1 crossover cable should connect pins 1, 2, 4, and 5 to pins 4, 5, 1, and 2.

☒ **A, B,** and **C** are incorrect. **A** is incorrect because it does not connect the TX+/– pins to the RX+/– pins, so the transmit signals will never reach the reception pins. **B** is incorrect because it also fails to connect the TX+/– pins to the RX+/– pins. **C** is incorrect because it also does not connect the TX+/– pins to the RX+/– pins.

28. You are planning the implementation of a new Ethernet network. The client has requested that the network be capable of 100 Mbps or faster data transfers. What should you do? (Choose three possibilities.)

    A. Recommend a 10Base-5 network.

    B. Recommend a 10Base-T network.

    C. Recommend a 1000Base-CX network.

    D. Recommend a 1000Base-T network.

    E. Recommend a Fast Ethernet network.

    F. Recommend a 10Base-2 network.

☑ **C, D,** and **E.** Both 1000Base-CX and 1000Base-T are capable of transferring data at 1000 Mbps. Fast Ethernet can transfer data at 100 Mbps. Given a choice, you should opt for the fastest data rate that is feasible given your project and budget constraints. No one ever complains that the network transfers data too quickly.

☒ **A, B,** and **F** are incorrect. **A** and **F** are incorrect because 10Base-5 and 10Base-2 are older Ethernet standards that use coaxial cabling and are limited to 10 Mbps transfers. **B** is incorrect because 10Base-T is also an older Ethernet standard that uses UTP cabling and is limited to 10 Mbps transfers.

29. Which type of network typically uses RG-8 coaxial cabling?

    A. Token Ring

    B. 10Base-T

    C. 10Base-5

    D. 10GBase-T

☑ **C.** 10Base-5 uses RG-8 coaxial cabling. 10Base-5 is an older Ethernet standard that was popular for a time in commercial and industrial environments, where its heavier shielding helped protect data transmitted on the network from electromagnetic interference (EMI).

☒ **A, B,** and **D** are incorrect. **A** is incorrect because most Token Ring implementations use IBM Type-1 shielded twisted-pair (STP) network cabling. **B** is incorrect because 10Base-T uses Category 3 or better UTP. **D** is incorrect because 10GBase-T requires the use of Category 6a UTP.

30. Which protocol is frequently used to transfer streaming media over IP networks?
  A. IGMP
  B. SSH
  C. HTTP
  D. HTTPS
  E. RTP

☑ **E.** The RTP protocol is used frequently to transfer streaming media over IP networks. For example, it is commonly used to transmit voice data over IP networks. It's also used to transmit video over IP networks.

☒ **A, B, C,** and **D** are incorrect. **A** is incorrect because IGMP is used by network hosts and routers to define multicast group membership. **B** is incorrect because the SSH protocol is used to establish remote access sessions with network hosts. **C** and **D** are incorrect because HTTP and HTTPS are used to transfer HTML documents from web servers to web browsers. HTTPS accomplishes the same task as HTTP, but uses encryption to scramble the contents of the transmission.

31. You need to access the console of a Linux server in the data center remotely from your cubicle to add a new user account to the system. What should you do?
  A. Establish an SSH connection.
  B. Establish a Telnet connection.
  C. Establish a VNC connection.
  D. Establish an SNMP connection.

☑ **A.** Because you will need to authenticate to the Linux server as an administrative user and then use the connection to create a new username and password, you should use a remote access protocol that encrypts data as it is being transferred over the network. In this scenario, the Secure Shell protocol (SSH) would be the best choice.

☒ **B, C,** and **D** are incorrect. **B** is incorrect because the Telnet protocol does not encrypt data. Using Telnet in this scenario could expose usernames, passwords, and all data being transferred to network packet sniffers. **C** is incorrect because most VNC implementations use relatively weak security mechanisms. However, if you prefer the graphical user interface provided by VNC, you can tunnel the VNC traffic through an SSH tunnel to add a higher degree of protection. **D** is incorrect because SNMP is used to monitor network hosts. It can't be used to access them remotely.

32. You have just implemented the Internet Information Server (IIS) on a Windows Server 2008 system. The server must be configured to allow traffic through for this service. What should you do? (Choose two.)

A. Open port 123 in the server's firewall.
B. Open port 119 in the server's firewall.
C. Open port 143 in the server's firewall.
D. Open port 80 in the server's firewall.
E. Open port 443 in the server's firewall.

☑ **D** and **E.** IIS is a Microsoft web server service. Therefore, it uses HTTP to transfer clear-text (unencrypted) data on port 80. It also uses port 443 to transmit secure data that has been encrypted using the TLS or SSL protocol.

☒ **A, B,** and **C** are incorrect. **A** is incorrect because 123 is used by NTP to synchronize time among hosts on the network. **B** is incorrect because port 119 is used by NNTP to download messages from a newsgroup server. **C** is incorrect because port 143 is used by IMAP4 to manage messages on an e-mail server.

33. You have just implemented an FTP server on your Windows Server 2008 system to allow users to upload and download files using the FTP protocol. Which port is used for the FTP control connection by this service?

A. 20
B. 53
C. 80
D. 21
E. 443

☑ **D.** FTP uses port 21 for a control connection that is used to manage the FTP session. In this scenario, ports 20 (data) and 21 (control) must be opened in the server's firewall for the FTP service to work.

☒ **A, B, C,** and **E** are incorrect. **A** is incorrect because port 20 is used by FTP to transfer data. **B** is incorrect because port 53 is used by DNS servers to handle name resolution requests. **C** is incorrect because port 80 is used by the HTTP protocol used by web servers and web browsers to transfer clear-text (unencrypted) data. **E** is incorrect because port 443 is used by HTTPS for secure data that has been encrypted using the TLS or SSL protocols.

34. You need to clear the entire ARP cache on your Windows 7 workstation. What should you do?
    A. Enter **arp −n** at the command prompt.
    B. Enter **arp −a** at the command prompt.
    C. Enter **arp −s** at the command prompt.
    D. Enter **arp −g** at the command prompt.
    E. Enter **arp −d *** at the command prompt.

☑ **E.** The **arp** command used with the **−d *** option will clear the entire ARP cache. You can replace * in the command with a specific host to delete just that host from the ARP cache.

☒ **A, B, C,** and **D** are incorrect. **A** is incorrect because the **−n** option is used to display the ARP cache entries for a specific network interface. **B** and **D** are incorrect because the **−a** and **−g** options are used with the **arp** command to view the local ARP cache. **C** is incorrect because the **−s** option is used to add an entry to the ARP cache.

35. You need to add an entry manually to your Linux server's ARP cache that maps the 10.0.0.1 IP address to the 00-14-A5-FD-42-A1 MAC address. What should you do?
    A. Enter **arp −a 10.0.0.1 00-14-A5-FD-42-A1** at the shell prompt.
    B. Enter **arp −s 10.0.0.1 00-14-A5-FD-42-A1** at the shell prompt.
    C. Enter **arp −d 10.0.0.1 00-14-A5-FD-42-A1** at the shell prompt.
    D. Enter **arp −H 10.0.0.1 00-14-A5-FD-42-A1** at the shell prompt.

☑ **B.** The **arp –s 10.0.0.1 00-14-A5-FD-42-A1**command at the shell prompt will add this mapping into the ARP cache of the Linux server. Once entered into the cache, the ARP protocol will use this mapping when the local system needs to contact the host with 10.0.0.1 IP address. It will no longer need to send broadcasts to resolve the IP address into a MAC address.

☒ **A, C, and D** are incorrect. **A** is incorrect because the **–a** option causes the **arp** command to display the ARP cache, not add entries to it. **C** is incorrect because the **–d** option causes the **arp** command to delete the ARP cache, not add entries to it. **D** is incorrect because the **–H** option is used to specific the type of ARP entry to work with, such as ether, arcnet, and so on.

36. Which command was used at the Command prompt of a Windows system to generate the following output?

```
Wireless Network Connection:
Node IpAddress: [192.168.1.100] Scope Id: []
    No names in cache
```

A. netstat –e

B. nbtstat –n

C. netstat –a

D. nbtstat –c

☑ **D.** The **nbtstat –c** command was used to generate the output shown in this question. The **–c** option is used to display the local NetBIOS cache.

☒ **A, B, and C** are incorrect. **A** is incorrect because the **netstat –e** command is used to display Ethernet statistics. **B** is incorrect because the **nbtstat –n** command lists NetBIOS names for the local machine. **C** is incorrect because the **netstat –a** command displays all connections and ports.

37. Based upon the output of the **tracert** command shown here, what is the average response time for the router with an IP address of 63.146.27.230?

```
Tracing route to ns.novell.com [137.65.1.1]
over a maximum of 30 hops:

  1     1 ms    <1 ms    <1 ms  192.168.1.1
  2     2 ms     1 ms     1 ms  192.168.0.1
  3    41 ms    40 ms    40 ms  slkc-dsl-gw10-202.slkc.qwest.net [67.41.239.202]
  4    42 ms    41 ms    41 ms  slkc-agw1.inet.qwest.net [67.41.238.73]
  5    59 ms    61 ms    68 ms  sjp-brdr-03.inet.qwest.net [67.14.34.10]
  6    59 ms    59 ms    61 ms  63.146.27.230
  7    79 ms    59 ms    58 ms  0.ae1.XL4.SJC7.ALTER.NET [152.63.51.41]
  8   122 ms    92 ms    91 ms  0.so-7-0-0.XT2.DEN4.ALTER.NET [152.63.1.118]
  9    92 ms    92 ms    91 ms  POS7-0.GW3.DEN4.ALTER.NET [152.63.72.73]
 10   101 ms   101 ms   101 ms  unknown.customer.alter.net [65.206.183.22]
 11   164 ms   163 ms   182 ms  192.94.118.247
 12   450 ms   105 ms   105 ms  137.65.2.66
 13   104 ms   105 ms   105 ms  ns.novell.com [137.65.1.1]

Trace complete.
```

A. 62.66

B. 41.33

C. 61

D. 59.66

☑ **D.** The **tracert** command sent three ICMP echo request packets to the router with an IP address of 63.146.27.230 and the response times for these packets were 59, 59, and 61 milliseconds. Therefore, the average response time for this router was 59.66 ms.

☒ **A, B,** and **C** are incorrect. A is incorrect because 62.66 ms is the average response time for the router with an IP address of 67.14.34.10. **B** is incorrect because 62.66 ms is the average response time for the router with an IP address of 67.41.238. **C** is incorrect because this metric doesn't match the response times for any of the routers in the output of this command.

38. While monitoring a Linux server system using the **netstat** command, you notice that a new port has been opened on the system. You are concerned and want to find out which process opened the port. What should you do?

A. Enter **netstat –p** at the shell prompt.

B. Enter **netstat –e** at the shell prompt.

C. Enter **netstat –a** at the shell prompt.

D. Enter **netstat –o** at the shell prompt.

☑ **A.** The **–p** option causes the **netstat** command on Linux to display the PID of the process that opened each port on the system. You can then use this information to determine which process is responsible and decide if it is a legitimate process or some form of malware.

☒ **B, C,** and **D** are incorrect. **B** is incorrect because the **–e** option causes the Linux **netstat** command to display extended information. **C** is incorrect because the **–a** option causes **netstat** on Linux to display both listening and nonlistening sockets. **D** is incorrect because the **–o** option is used by the **netstat** command on Windows to display PID numbers for processes that open ports.

39. You've connected to the ftp.mycorp.com FTP server using the **ftp** command at the shell prompt of a Linux workstation. You need to upload an executable file to the FTP server. What should you do? (Choose two.)

A. Enter **upload** at the FTP prompt.

B. Enter **put** at the FTP prompt.

C. Enter **get** at the FTP prompt.

D. Enter **binary** at the FTP prompt.

E. Enter **ls** at the FTP prompt.

☑ **B** and **D.** Because the file is an executable, you should first use the **binary** command to tell the FTP client and server that you are uploading a binary file. Then you use the **put** command to upload the file.

☒ **A, C,** and **E** are incorrect. **A** is incorrect because **upload** is an invalid FTP client command. **C** is incorrect because the **get** command is used to download files from the FTP server. **E** is incorrect because the **ls** command displays a list of files and subdirectories in the current directory.

40. Which of the following is true regarding the TFTP protocol?

A. It utilizes a connection-oriented TCP session.

B. It utilizes a connectionless UDP session.

C. It supports user authentication to control access.

D. It allows you to generate a listing of files available for download on the TFTP server.

☑ **B.** The TFTP protocol runs on UDP port 69. Packets are sent unacknowledged from the TFTP server to the client.

☒ **A, C,** and **D** are incorrect. **A** is incorrect because the TFTP protocol uses the UDP protocol, not TCP. **C** is incorrect because TFTP does not provide a mechanism to authenticate users. **D** is incorrect because TFTP does not allow the client to generate a listing of files and directories available on the TFTP server.

41. You've just enabled routing on a Cisco router. You need to verify that the appropriate routes exist in the routing table. What should you do?

A. Enter **route view** at the command prompt of the router.

B. Enter **ip routing** at the command prompt of the router.

C. Enter **route print** at the command prompt of the router.

D. Enter **show ip route** at the command prompt of the router.

☑ **D.** Entering **show ip route** at the command prompt of the router will cause the router to display its routing table. A route should have been automatically added for each of the networks to which it is connected.

☒ **A, B,** and **C** are incorrect. **A** is incorrect because the **route view** command is invalid. **B** is incorrect because the **ip routing** command is used to enable routing; it doesn't display the routing table. **C** is incorrect because **route print** is used at the command prompt of a Windows server, not the command prompt of the router.

42. You need to view the routing table on a Linux system configured to function as a router. What should you do?

A. Enter **show ip route** at the shell prompt.

B. Enter **route** at the shell prompt.

C. Enter **ip routing** at the shell prompt.

D. Enter **route view** at the shell prompt.

☑ **B.** Entering **route** at the shell prompt of a Linux router will display the system's routing table. You can use the **add** option with the route command to add routes manually, including the default route.

☒ **A, C,** and **D** are incorrect. **A** is incorrect because the **show ip route** command is used to display the system's routing table from a Cisco router command prompt. **C** is incorrect because the **ip routing** command is used to enable routing on a Cisco router. **D** is incorrect because the **route view** command is invalid on Linux.

43. Which routing protocols run directly over the IP protocol? (Choose two.)
   A. Routing Information Protocol (RIP)
   B. Open Shortest Path First (OSPF)
   C. Intermediate System to Intermediate System (IS-IS)
   D. Enhanced Interior Gateway Routing Protocol (EIGRP)
   E. Border Gateway Protocol (BGP)

☑ **B** and **D.** The OSPF and EIGRP routing protocols run directly over IP.

☒ **A, C,** and **E** are incorrect. **A** is incorrect because RIP runs over UDP. **C** is incorrect because IS-IS functions at the data link layer of the OSI model. **E** is incorrect because the BGP protocol runs over TCP.

44. Which routing metric measures how long it takes a packet to travel from one network to another?
   A. Hop count
   B. MTU
   C. Latency
   D. Distance vector
   E. Link state

☑ **C.** Latency is used to measure how long it takes for a packet to travel from one network to another. Using this metric, some routing protocols choose routes with the least latency.

☒ **A, B, D,** and **E** are incorrect. **A** is incorrect because the hop count metric measures how many routers a packet must traverse to reach its destination. **B** is incorrect because the maximum transmission unit (MTU) metric determines the maximum packet size sent through an interface. **D** and **E** are incorrect because the terms "distance vector" and "link state" are used to categorize different types of routing protocols. They are not routing metrics.

45. The Windows server hosting your Microsoft LiveMeeting services is named fs1.mycorp.com. You want to create an alias in the mycorp.com zone on your DNS server named livemeeting that points to the existing fs1 record. What should you do?

A. Create an A record.

B. Create a CNAME record.

C. Create an NS record.

D. Create an MX record.

☑ **B.** CNAME records create aliases that point to existing records in the DNS zone. In this example, you could create a CNAME record named livemeeting that points to the fs1 record in the zone. This would result in the livemeeting.mycorp.com DNS name resolving to the fs1 server's IP address.

☒ **A, C,** and **D** are incorrect. **A** is partially correct because you could create an A record for the livemeeting hostname and configure it to resolve to the same IP address as fs1. However, this isn't the best practice, because it creates multiple DNS records that must be managed for the same IP address. Using CNAME records simplifies management. **C** is incorrect because NS records point to the host records for the hosts that are DNS servers for the zone. **D** is incorrect because MX records are used for e-mail server host records.

46. You've discovered an older laptop in your equipment closet that has in integrated 802.11b wireless network adapter. Your organization uses 802.11a wireless access points to provide wireless connectivity to your network. What can you do to connect this device to the wireless network?

A. Connect the integrated 802.11b adapter directly to the 802.11a wireless network.

B. Disable the integrated 802.11b adapter and install an 802.11g USB wireless network adapter.

C. Install a wireless bridge and connect the integrated 802.11b adapter to the 802.11b side of the bridge.

D. Disable the integrated 802.11b adapter and install an 802.11a USB wireless network adapter.

☑ **D.** 802.11a devices run at 5 GHz instead of 2.4 GHz as 802.11b/g/n wireless standards do. Therefore, the most effective way to connect this laptop to the wireless network is to install an 802.11a network adapter in the system.

☒ **A, B,** and **C** are incorrect. **A** is incorrect because the integrated 802.11b wireless network interface is not compatible with 802.11a wireless networks. **B** is incorrect because 802.11g devices are not compatible with 802.11a wireless networks. **C** is incorrect because installing a bridge isn't necessary to connect the laptop to the 802.11a network.

47. You just implemented an 802.11n wireless network for a retail business in a strip mall. However, you are experiencing significant interference in the wireless network, causing dropped connections. You've discovered that that neighboring businesses in the mall are using channels 1, 6, and 11 for their 802.11x wireless networks. What should you do?

   A. Set your wireless access point to use channel 2.

   B. Set your wireless access point to use channel 5.

   C. Set your wireless access point to use channel 10.

   D. Set your wireless access point to use channel 9.

☑ **D.** Because there is frequency overlap between channels within the 2.4 GHz range, you need to select a channel far away from those already in use. In this example, channels 1, 6, and 11 are used by nearby equipment. Therefore setting your WAP to use channel 9 should eliminate interference from these devices.

☒ **A, B,** and **C** are incorrect. **A** is incorrect because there is overlap between the frequencies used by channels 1 (2.3995–2.4245 GHz) and 2 (2.4045–2.4295 GHz) in the 2.4 GHz range. **B** is incorrect because there is also overlap between the frequencies used by channels 5 and 6 in the 2.4 GHz range. **C** is incorrect because there is overlap between the frequencies used by channels 10 and 11 in the 2.4 GHz range.

48. Which mechanism can be used with WPA security to provide dynamic key generation and rotation, ensuring each packet gets a unique encryption key?

   A. Lightweight Extensible Authentication Protocol (LEAP)

   B. Protected Extensible Authentication Protocol (PEAP)

   C. Temporal Key Integrity Protocol (TKIP)

   D. Extensible Authentication Protocol-MD5 (EAP-MD5)

☑ **C.** TKIP is designed to address WEP's key-based flaws. It provides dynamic key generation and rotation, ensuring that each packet gets a unique encryption key.

☒ **A, B,** and **D** are incorrect. **A** is incorrect because LEAP uses passwords only. No digital certificates or any other type of PKI mechanism is used, so some information is sent as clear-text. **B** is incorrect because PEAP encapsulates EAP authentication information within an encrypted SSL/TLS tunnel. **D** is incorrect because EAP-MD5 is an early authentication mechanism that offers very little security. It uses an MD5 hash to secure data, which is vulnerable to a variety of attacks.

49. Given optimal wireless conditions, which wireless networking standard provides the shortest range?

- **A.** 802.11a
- **B.** 802.11b
- **C.** 802.11g
- **D.** 802.11n

☑ **A.** Under ideal conditions, an 802.11a wireless network has a maximum outdoor range of less than 400 feet, with a maximum indoor range of around 120 feet. Other wireless network standards can reach out as far as 800 feet.

☒ **B, C,** and **D** are incorrect. **B** and **C** are incorrect because the 802.11b and 802.11g standards are limited to a maximum outdoor range of more than 450 feet and a maximum indoor range of around 125 feet. **D** is incorrect because the 802.11n standard offers the longest wireless range. It can extend the wireless signal out to around 800 feet outdoors. Under indoor conditions, it has a maximum range of around 230 feet.

50. Your company uses work-from-home employees to answer customer service calls. These employees access your company's network through a VPN each night to update the company's customer service database. Some of these employees are located in Europe and use Basic Rate Interface (BRI) ISDN connections to access the company VPN. What's the fastest data rate these users can achieve?

- **A.** 56 Kbps
- **B.** 128 Kbps
- **C.** 256 Kbps
- **D.** 512 Mbps

☑ **B.** The fastest data rate the remote users will be able to achieve is 128 Kbps. A BRI ISDN connection uses two, 64-Kbps B channels for data and one, 16-Kbps D channel for signaling.

☒ **A, C,** and **D** are incorrect. **A** is incorrect because the entry-level BRI ISDN interface provides speeds up to 128 Kbps. **C** and **D** are incorrect because speeds over 128 Kbps can be achieved only by Primary Rate Interface ISDN or an alternative technology such as DSL, cable, or satellite.

51. Which type of ISDN device connects TE2 devices to an ISDN network?
- A. Terminal adapter (TA)
- B. Terminal equipment 1 (TE1)
- C. Network terminator 2 (NT2)
- D. Network terminator 1 (NT1)

☑ **A.** A terminal adapter (TA) connects TE2 devices to an ISDN network. For example, the ISDN interface in a computer is an example of a TA.

☒ **B, C,** and **D** are incorrect. **B** is incorrect because terminal equipment 1 (TE1) devices can be directly connected to the NT1 or NT2 devices. An example is an ISDN telephone. **C** is incorrect because network terminator 2 (NT2) devices manage data link and network layer functions in networks with multiple devices. **D** is incorrect because network terminator 1 devices communicate directly with the ISDN service provider's central office switch.

52. You need to establish a remote connection to a Linux server from a Linux workstation using the Secure Shell (SSH) protocol. You are currently logged into your workstation as the root user and need to access the Linux server as root on that system. Given that the hostname of the Linux server is fs1, what should you do? (Choose two.)
- A. Enter **ssh fs1** at the shell prompt of your Linux workstation.
- B. Enter **ssh –l root fs1** at the shell prompt of your Linux workstation.
- C. Enter **ssh –u root fs1** at the shell prompt of your Linux workstation.
- D. Enter **ssh root fs1** at the shell prompt of your Linux workstation.
- E. Enter **ssh --user root fs1** at the shell prompt of your Linux workstation.

☑ **A** and **B.** You can enter **ssh –l root fs1** at the shell prompt of your Linux workstation to establish an SSH connection between your workstation and the SSH server. You will be prompted to enter the password of the root user on the fs1 server. Because you need to connect to the fs1 server as the same user account you're using currently using on the local system, you could also just enter **ssh fs1** at the shell prompt. Because no username is specified in the command, the SSH utility will automatically authenticate you to the remote system using the same username you used to log into the local system (in this case, the root user). Be aware, however, that many Linux distributions are preconfigured not to allow root-level access through the SSH server daemon for security reasons.

⊠ C, D, and E are incorrect. C and E are incorrect because these commands use incorrect options to specify the username (**–u** and **--user**). D is incorrect because it does not include the **–l** option to specify the username.

53. You need to access an application running in a Citrix server farm from a Windows workstation. You need to configure your workstation's firewall to allow traffic from the Independent Computing Architecture (ICA) thin client protocol. What should you do? (Choose two.)
    A. Open port 47 in the firewall.
    B. Open port 80 in the firewall.
    C. Open port 1293 in the firewall.
    D. Open port 1494 in the firewall.
    E. Open port 1723 in the firewall.

☑ **B** and **D**. Citrix systems use ICA to provide remote access to applications running in the server farm. ICA runs on IP port 1494, so this port must be open in your workstation's firewall. The ICA browsing port (80) must also be open to allow browsing of available applications in the server farm.

⊠ **A**, **C**, and **E** are incorrect. **A** and **E** are incorrect because protocol ID 47 and port 1723 are used to allow PPTP traffic to pass through the firewall. **C** is incorrect because port 1293 is used for IPSec.

54. You are configuring a PPP connection and want to use an authentication protocol that authenticates both the client and the server when setting up the connection. What should you do?
    A. Use MS-CHAPv2 for authentication.
    B. Use CHAP for authentication.
    C. Use MS-CHAP for authentication.
    D. Use PAP for authentication.

☑ **A**. MS-CHAPv2 authenticates both the client and the server when setting up a PPP connection. MS-CHAP2 uses the MD4 hashing algorithm instead of MD5 used by CHAP.

⊠ **B**, **C** and **D** are incorrect. **B** and **C** are incorrect because both CHAP and MS-CHAP use a challenge-response mechanism for authentication, but they authenticate only the client end of the connection. **D** is incorrect because PAP authenticates only the client end of the remote session. It is considered insecure because the client credentials are sent in clear-text.

55. You are a consultant working for a financial services firm. The firm allows you to work remotely from your home office using a VPN connection through the Internet. The firm's VPN server uses the L2TP protocol to create the encrypted tunnel. You need to configure your home computer's firewall to allow VPN traffic. What must you do? (Choose two.)

A. Open port TCP port 23 in the firewall.

B. Open TCP port 80 in the firewall.

C. Open TCP port 389 in the firewall.

D. Open UDP port 1701 in the firewall

E. Open UDP port 5500 in the firewall.

☑ **D and E.** To allow traffic from a VPN tunnel created with the L2TP protocol, you need to open UDP port 1701 in your workstation's firewall. You must also open UDP port 5500 (for IPSec) and UDP port 500 (for key exchange via ISAKMP).

☒ **A, B,** and **C** are incorrect. **A** is incorrect because TCP port 23 is used typically used by Telnet for remote access. **B** is incorrect because TCP port 80 is typically used for web servers using the HTTP protocol. **C** is incorrect because TCP port 389 is used by the LDAP protocol.

56. What security protocol uses Encapsulation Security Payloads (ESP) to encrypt traffic and the Authentication Header (AH) protocol for message integrity and authentication?

A. Internet Protocol Security (IPsec)

B. Transport Layer Security (TLS)

C. Internet Security Association and Key Management Protocol (ISAKMP)

D. Secure Shell (SSH)

☑ **A.** The IPSec protocol uses Encapsulation Security Payload (ESP) to encrypt traffic and the Authentication Header (AH) protocol for message integrity and authentication. It can also use the Internet Key Exchange (IKE) to exchange encryption keys between systems.

☒ **B, C,** and **D** are incorrect. **B** is incorrect because TLS is an alternative security mechanism to IPSec. **C** is incorrect because the ISAKMP security protocol is used by IKE to establish a security association between endpoints during the setup of an L2TP/IPSec VPN connection. **D** is incorrect because SSH is used to establish encrypted remote connections between systems running the SSH server and SSH client. SSH can be used, however, to create an encrypted tunnel through which network traffic can pass, essentially creating a very basic VPN.

57. A network is configured such that when data is transferred, a dedicated connection is established. All data sent from the sender to the receiver follows the same path through the network. What kind of network is described in this scenario?

A. Packet-switched

B. Circuit-switched

C. Messaged-switched

D. Connectionless

☑ **B.** The network described in this scenario is a circuit-switched network. This kind of network establishes a dedicated circuit between the sender and the receiver. All data sent from the sender to the receiver follows the same path through the network. The public telephone network is an example of a circuit switched network.

☒ **A, C,** and **D** are incorrect. **A** is incorrect because in packet-switched networks, the data to be transmitted is divided up into blocks called *packets*. Each packet can take a different path through the network to the destination host. **C** is incorrect because message-switching was an early form of packet switching. The key difference is that message-switched networks didn't fragment data into packets. **D** is incorrect because connectionless sessions transmit unacknowledged data on packet-switched networks.

58. Which of the following statements are true regarding a packet-switched network? (Choose two.)

A. A dedicated connection is created between the sender and the receiver.

B. All packets sent from the sender can potentially travel a different path through the network to the receiver.

C. They generally use bandwidth more efficiently than circuit-switched networks.

D. Data always arrives at the destination in the sequence in which they were sent.

E. If the path between the sender and the receiver fails, there is no way to redirect data through another path.

☑ **B and C.** Bandwidth is shared in a packet-switched network, allowing multiple hosts to use the medium at the same time. Congestion is managed by rerouting packets to use different paths through the network as needed. Packet-switched networks are considered to be more efficient than circuit-switched networks because bandwidth is consumed only while data is being transmitted.

☒   **A, D**, and **E** are incorrect. **A** is incorrect because bandwidth is shared in a packet-switched network. Multiple hosts can use the medium at the same time. **D** is incorrect because the packets in a given transmission can arrive out of sequence. Therefore, each packet is assigned a sequence number so the original message can be reassembled correctly on the receiving host. **E** is incorrect because congestion is managed in a packet-switched network by rerouting packets to use a different path through the network as needed.

59. Given that SONET STS-1 runs at the base OC-1 data rate of 51.84 Mbps, how much data can STS-24 (OC-24) transfer in 1 second?
   A. 155.52 Mb
   B. 2488.32 Mb
   C. 622.08 Mb
   D. 1244.16 Mb

☑   **D.** The base rate for OC-1 is 51.84 Mbps. All other OC-*x* levels are multiples of this base rate. In this case, STS-24 (OC-24) is 24 times the base rate (51.84), which yields 1244.16 Mbps.

☒   **A, B**, and **C** are incorrect. **A** is incorrect because 155.52 Mbps is the OC-3 data rate. **B** is incorrect because 2488.32 Mbps is the data rate for OC-48. **C** is incorrect because 622.08 Mbps is the data rate for OC-12.

60. You are implementing a VPN for a U.S.-based medical transcription firm. Home-based employees of the firm will use the VPN through the Internet to access the data and applications needed to process transcription jobs. After conducting a needs analysis, you have calculated that their WAN traffic during peak office hours will require a connection that provides a data rate of approximately 35 Mbps. What should you do?
   A. Recommend they use an ISDN connection.
   B. Recommend they use a T1 connection.
   C. Recommend they use a T3 connection.
   D. Recommend they use an E1 connection.

☑ **C.** The T3 carrier service is similar to T1; however, it is composed of 672 64-Kbps channels (DS0 channels) that provide a total throughput of 44.736 Mbps. T3 is the only service listed in this scenario that provides a data rate fast enough for the client.

☒ **A, B,** and **D** are incorrect **A** is incorrect because ISDN offers a maximum data rate of 1536 Kbps, which doesn't meet the client's requirements. **B** is incorrect because a T1 connection provides a data rate of 1.544 Mbps (DS1), which also doesn't meet the client's requirements. **D** is incorrect because T-carrier connections are used in the United States, while E-carrier connections are used elsewhere in the world.

61. You need to implement a cable management plan in your server room and wiring closet. What should you do? (Choose two.)
   A. Create a logical network diagram.
   B. Create a physical network diagram.
   C. Standardize on a single color for all network cabling in your network.
   D. Use colored cables to implement a color-code scheme to categorize network devices.
   E. Avoid using overly long patch cables in the wiring closet room.

☑ **D and E.** There are several things you can do to implement a cable management plan for your network. You can also use colored cables to implement a color-coding scheme to categorize network devices. For example, crossover cables could be red, servers could be gray, workstations could be blue, and printers could be orange. You should also avoid using overly long patch cables in the wiring closet. Overly long cables make it more difficult to organize and arrange the cables.

☒ **A, B,** and **C** are incorrect. **A** and **B** are good ideas, but they are part of the network mapping process, not cable management. **C** is incorrect because using the same color of cable for all systems can make it more difficult to manage your cabling.

62. You are creating a logical map of your network. What information should you include? (Choose two.)
   A. DHCP servers
   B. Repeater locations
   C. WIC locations
   D. VLANs
   E. Cable runs

☑ **A and D.** Your logical network map should document logical network information, such as the location of domain controllers, IP address assignments, the location of DHCP and DNS servers, services running on network servers, VLANs and computers that belong to VLANs, and so on.

☒ **B, C**, and **E** are incorrect because they represent networking hardware components that should be included on a physical network map.

63. Your company uses a Windows Server 2008 domain controller to manage network authentication, file sharing, printer sharing, and database services. All of your network users and resources are represented by objects in your domain. Documenting the domain structure and the objects it contains is part of which network documentation process?
    A. Asset management plan
    B. Cable management plan
    C. Physical network map
    D. Logical network map

☑ **D.** The structure of the domain and the objects it contains represents logical network information. Therefore, documenting the tree is part of the logical network mapping process.

☒ **A, B**, and **C** are incorrect. **A** is incorrect because your asset management plan tracks the life span and replacement cost of your network devices. **B** is incorrect because a cable management plan specifies how network cabling is organized and managed. **C** is incorrect because the physical network map documents the physical location of your network hardware, such as routers, servers, switches, and workstations.

64. Which of the following processes should be included in a network's change management plan? (Choose two.)
    A. A procedure for verifying the state of the system after a change has been implemented.
    B. A procedure for implementing a backup strategy.
    C. A procedure for approving vendors from whom new network equipment will be purchased.
    D. A procedure for determining when a network component has become obsolete.
    E. A procedure for testing proposed changes in a test environment.

☑ **A and E.** A network change management plan should include a procedure for verifying the state of the system after a change has been implemented. It should also include a procedure for testing proposed changes in a test environment prior to rolling out the change in the production environment.

☒ **B, C, and D are incorrect. B** is a component of a network disaster recovery plan. **C** and **D** are components of an asset management plan.

65. You just received an e-mail indicating your company's Human Resources department has partnered with a company that provides employees with substantial discounts at many large national retailers. To take advantage of this benefit, employees must access a web site by clicking a link in the message. After checking with Human Resources, you find that they didn't send the e-mail. What should you do?

A. Warn users that a spoofing attack has occurred.

B. Warn users that a phishing attack has occurred.

C. Configure your routers and firewalls to prevent a Denial of Service (DoS) attack.

D. Warn Human Resources that an eavesdropping attack has occurred.

☑ **B.** A phishing attack has occurred in this scenario, and users need to be warned not to click the link in the e-mail. In a phishing attack, an e-mail containing a link to a fake web site is used to trick users to reveal sensitive information, such as a username, password, bank account number, or credit card number. Both the e-mail and the web site used in the attack appear on the surface to be legitimate.

☒ **A, C, and D are incorrect. A** is partially correct because spoofing occurs when a hacker modifies the source address of the packets he or she is sending so that they appear to be coming from someone else. Hackers can spoof the IP address, MAC address, or e-mail address to make the message appear as if it is coming from someone else. Spoofing is a common method to bypass access controls placed on switches, routers, or firewalls. **C** is incorrect because a DoS attack floods a particular host with so many bogus requests that it can no longer respond to legitimate network requests. **D** is incorrect because an eavesdropping attack involves using a sniffer to capture and analyze network traffic.

66. Which of the following scenarios best describe a buffer overflow attack?

A. An attacker connects to an unsecured wireless network posing as a valid network host and intercepts network communications and tampers with their contents.

B. An attacker uses a sniffer to capture and analyze network traffic to try and read confidential data.

C. An attacker floods a host with thousands of responses to illegitimate ping requests, making it impossible for it to respond to normal network requests.

D. An attacker tries to gain administrative access to the system by sending more data to an application than is expected.

☑ **D.** A buffer overflow occurs when an exploit writes data beyond the buffer's memory boundary, writing information to memory where it should not. Depending upon the exploit and the operating system, this could cause security vulnerabilities to be exposed, such as providing administrative access to the system.

☒ **A, B,** and **C** are incorrect. A is incorrect because it describes a man-in-the-middle attack, where an attacker intercepts legitimate network traffic and then poses as one of the parties involved in the network communications. **B** is incorrect because it describes an eavesdropping attack, where data is "lifted" from the network medium. C is incorrect because it describes a Denial of Service attack.

67. An attacker has written an exploit that sends mangled IP fragments with overlapping and oversized payloads to the target host. What kind of Denial of Service attack is this?

A. Teardrop

B. SYN flood

C. Ping of Death

D. Nuke

☑ **A.** A teardrop attack involves sending mangled IP fragments with overlapping and oversized payloads to the target host. Most newer operating systems are immune to this attack, but many older operating systems will crash when they try to reassemble the original message from the mangled fragments.

☒ **B, C,** and **D** are incorrect. B is incorrect because a SYN flood sends a flood of packets to the target host, causing it to be unable to respond to legitimate network requests. C is incorrect because a Ping of Death attack sends an oversized ICMP Echo Request packet to a target host. **D** is incorrect because a nuke attack sends corrupt ICMP packets to the target host.

68. A programmer wrote what appears to be a gaming application. However, when it is installed, an exploit is launched that logs all the information transferred using the HTTP protocol and uploads it to the programmer's FTP server. What kind of malware is described in this scenario?

A. Keylogger

B. Trojan

C. Logic bomb

D. Worm

☑ **B.** The malware in this scenario is a Trojan. A Trojan tricks you into installing what you think to be a legitimate application, only to find that you installed malware instead.

☒ **A, C, and D are incorrect. A** is incorrect because a keylogger captures user keystrokes (which can include usernames and passwords) and sends them to a specified network location or e-mail address. **C** is incorrect because a logic bomb contains malware hidden within what appears to be a legitimate application. The application functions normally until a certain event occurs, when the latent malware within the application becomes active. The key difference between a Trojan and a logic bomb is the latency of the malware. The malware in a Trojan goes active immediately and the application you thought you were installing rarely actually works. **D** is incorrect because a worm is a self-replicating type of malware.

69. You are concerned that your organization's e-mail server could be used by spammers to send spam messages without your permission. You are also concerned that it could be used by worms to propagate themselves. What can you do to prevent this? (Choose two.)

A. Require SMTP authentication.

B. Restrict outbound e-mail only to source hosts within your network.

C. Turn off forwarding of network broadcasts on your routers.

D. Turn on forwarding of network broadcasts on your routers.

E. Allow outbound e-mail from hosts outside your network.

☑ **A and B.** You can shut down open relay by configuring your e-mail server to require users to authenticate before sending messages. You can also restrict outbound mail only to source hosts within your network.

☒ **C, D, and E are incorrect. C** is incorrect because disabling forwarding of broadcasts by your routers will help prevent some types of DoS attacks, but it will not prevent spammers and worms from using your mail server for relay. **D** is incorrect because enabling forwarding of broadcasts by your routers will not prevent spammers and worms from using your mail server for relay, and it will make your network susceptible to DoS attacks. **E** is incorrect because allowing outbound e-mail from hosts outside your network is the definition of open relay.

70. Which Kerberos component gives the host permission to request a service ticket?
  A. Authentication Server (AS)
  B. Ticket-Granting Ticket (TGT)
  C. Key Distribution Center (KDC)
  D. Realm

  ☑ **B.** TGT gives a host permission to request a service ticket. A ticket is needed for a host to request a service from another other host on the network.

  ☒ **A, C,** and **D** are incorrect. **A** is incorrect because the Authentication Server (AS) is a component within the Kerberos Key Distribution Center (KDC) that grants the requesting host a Ticket-Granting Ticket (TGT). **C** is incorrect because the KDC is responsible for issuing tickets to network hosts. **D** is incorrect because a Realm is the administrative domain for the Kerberos service.

71. You are configuring a PPP connection for a modem that will be used to establish a connection with a remote access server at your company's main office. Which authentication protocol transmits passwords as clear-text and should *not* be used in this scenario?
  A. Password Authentication Protocol (PAP)
  B. Challenge Handshake Authentication Protocol (CHAP)
  C. Microsoft Challenge Handshake Authentication Protocol (MS-CHAP)
  D. Microsoft Challenge Handshake Authentication Protocol version 2 (MS-CHAPv2)

  ☑ **A.** The Password Authentication Protocol (PAP) is considered too unsecure for most modern networks because it transmits passwords as clear-text. A hacker using a packet sniffer could capture passwords as they are transmitted on the network, which would compromise the security of the link.

  ☒ **B, C,** and **D** are incorrect because CHAP, MS-CHAP, and MS-CHAPv2 each create an MD5 (CHAP) or an MD4 (MS-CHAP and MS-CHAPv2) password hash that is transmitted from the client to the server. If the hashes for the password are the same on the client and the server, then the client is authenticated. The key advantage of using these authentication mechanisms is the fact that the actual password itself is never transmitted on the network. However, you should be aware that the hashes can still be compromised if they are captured and compared against a rainbow table, which could potentially reveal the password that was used to create the hash.

72. Which protocol uses preshared keys for authentication?
   A. LEAP
   B. EAP-MD5
   C. PEAP
   D. EAP-PSK

☑ **D. EAP-PSK** uses preshared keys for authentication and encryption.

☒ **A, B,** and **C** are incorrect. **A** and **B** are incorrect because the Lightweight Extensible Authentication Protocol (LEAP) and EAP-MD5 both protect authentication information using MD5 hashes. **C** is incorrect because the Protected Extensible Authentication Protocol (PEAP) encapsulates EAP within an encrypted TLS tunnel.

73. You've been asked to implement a two-factor authentication scheme for your organization's network. What should you do? (Choose two.)
   A. Require users to supply a username and a password to log in.
   B. Require users to supply a username, password, and PIN number to log in.
   C. Require users to supply a username and password as well as a number from a hardware authenticator to log in.
   D. Require users to supply a smartcard and a PIN number.
   E. Require users to connect a security hardware device (dongle) to log in.

☑ **C** and **D.** Multifactor authentication requires the user to supply two or more authentication factors from the three categories of authentication factors: something they know, something they have, and something they are. A smartcard is an example of two-factor authentication, because it requires the user to supply something they have (the smartcard) and something they know (the PIN number assigned to the smartcard). Requiring users to supply a username, password, and a number from a hardware authenticator is also an example of two-factor authentication, because users must supply something they know (the username and password) along with something they have (the number from the authenticator).

☒ **A, B,** and **E** are incorrect. **A** and **B** are incorrect because usernames, passwords, and PIN numbers come from only one authentication factor category (what the user knows). **E** is incorrect because a security dongle requires only one factor category (something the user has).

74. Which is an entity in the network access control (NAC) mechanism (defined by the 802.1x specification), such as a workstation, that needs to connect to the network?

  A. Authentication server

  B. Supplicant

  C. Certificate authority

  D. Authenticator

> ☑ **B.** The 802.1x specification defines three entities that participate in the network access control mechanism. The supplicant is a client device (such as a workstation) that needs to connect to the network.
>
> ☒ **A, C,** and **D** are incorrect. **A** is incorrect because the authentication server receives the supplicant's authentication credentials from the authenticator and determines whether or not the supplicant is allowed to access the network. **C** is incorrect because certificate authorities are components associated with the Public Key Infrastructure (PKI), not with the 802.1x specification. **D** is incorrect because the authenticator is a network device the supplicant uses to connect to the network, such as a wireless access point or a switch.

75. A small financial consulting firm needs you to set up a firewall for its Internet connection. The firewall will be placed between the internal network and the Internet. The firewall must monitor the status of the three-way TCP handshake used to establish a TCP session between hosts inside and outside the firewall. Hosts inside the firewall should be allowed to establish TCP connections with hosts outside the firewall, but not vice versa. What should you do?

  A. Implement an application-level gateway.

  B. Implement a proxy server.

  C. Implement a packet-filtering firewall.

  D. Implement a circuit-level gateway.

> ☑ **D.** A circuit-level gateway is a type of firewall that monitors the status of the three-way TCP handshake used to establish a TCP session. Circuit-level gateways do not filter individual packets. Instead, they monitor TCP connections at the session layer of the OSI model to determine whether a network session is legitimate or not.

☒ **A**, **B**, and **C** are incorrect. **A** is incorrect because an application-level gateway is a type of firewall that operates at the application layer of the OSI model. These gateways are usually designed to manage traffic for a specific network application, such as HTTP traffic. **B** is incorrect because a proxy server acts as an intermediary between clients and servers (particularly web servers). **C** is incorrect because a packet-filtering firewall captures all packets passing through it and compares them against a set of rules you define that specifies what type of traffic is allowed and what type isn't. A packet-filtering firewall can filter traffic based on the source address, destination address, source port, destination port, and protocol type.

76. A client needs an Intrusion Detection System (IDS) that is able to "learn" what network traffic is normal on her network and use this information to classify anything outside the norm as suspicious. What should you do?
    A. Implement a signature-based IDS.
    B. Implement a heuristic IDS.
    C. Implement a network-based IDS.
    D. Implement a host-based IDS.

☑ **B.** A heuristic IDS understands what is considered normal activity (a baseline) and then considers anything outside that normal activity to be suspicious. There is some ambiguity in the industry as to what constitutes an anomaly-based IDS versus a heuristic IDS, as both work on similar principles.

☒ **A**, **C**, and **D** are incorrect. **A** is incorrect because a signature-based IDS captures system activity and compares it against a file containing known exploits. If there is a match, it sends out notification of an intrusion. An active IDS (also called an intrusion prevention system, or IPS) may also take steps to stop the intrusion. **C** is incorrect because NIDS can be signature-based, anomaly-based, or heuristic. **D** is also incorrect because a HIDS can be signature-based, anomaly-based, or heuristic.

77. You've just arrived at work only to discover that no one is able to log in through your Windows Server 2008 domain controllers. You are in the first stage of troubleshooting the issue. What key question should you ask?
    A. Will configuring one domain controller to seize the PDC Emulator role from the malfunctioning domain controller fix the issue?
    B. What has changed in the system since users were able to authenticate correctly?

    C. Are the latest updates installed on each server?

    D. Is time synchronizing between the servers?

    ☑ **B.** Because you are in the first stage of troubleshooting the issue, you should gather as much information as you can before you start implementing fixes. You should investigate what has changed in the system since the last time users were able to log in correctly. Doing this may help you identify a causal factor for the problem.

    ☒ **A, C,** and **D** are incorrect because each of these answers focuses on testing a theory to determine the cause of the problem. This process should not be attempted until you have gathered all information possible.

78. You are troubleshooting an issue with a user's Linux workstation. After gathering information, you have arrived at a theory of probable cause that the installation of a recent update overwrote several key configuration files and populated them with default values. You suspect that this change is causing services that worked correctly before this update was installed not to start on system boot. What should you do next?

    A. Uninstall the update in question.

    B. Call the Linux vendor's technical support number.

    C. Test the theory to determine cause.

    D. Establish a plan of action to resolve the problem and identify potential effects.

    ☑ **C.** At this point, you have determined a theory of probable cause. The next logical step in the troubleshooting process is to test the theory to determine the actual cause of the problem. For example, in this scenario you could set up a virtual machine in a lab environment, install the same Linux distribution on it, and then customize the configuration files in question. Then install the update and observe what happens to the configuration files. If the theory is confirmed, you can then determine the next action required to resolve problem. If the theory is not confirmed, you may need to establish a new theory or escalate the problem to someone with more expertise.

    ☒ **A, B,** and **D** are incorrect. **A** is incorrect because a fix is being implemented without verifying the cause first. It also fails to account for potential side effects of the fix before implementing it. **B** is incorrect because you should first test the theory to identify the problem before calling technical support. **D** is incorrect because it is best to test the theory and identify the problem before making changes to the system.

79. You suspect that you have a bad cable in a run between an RJ-45 wall jack and the server room where your switch is located. What should you do?

    A. Use a cable crimper or punch down tool to verify connections are secure.

    B. Use a cable tester to test the continuity of the cable and that the jack is wired correctly.

    C. Use a toner probe to test the continuity of the cable and that the jack is wired correctly.

    D. Use a multimeter to test the continuity of the cable and that the jack is wired correctly.

> ☑ **B.** Either a cable tester or a cable certifier can be used in this scenario. Both types of devices have components that connect to each end of the cable run. A cable tester tests each wire in the cable for continuity and verifies that each one is connected to the right pin in the jack or plug. A cable certifier does the same thing, but it also tests the bandwidth of the cable.
>
> ☒ **A, C,** and **D** are incorrect. **A** is incorrect because a cable crimper is used to attach a plug to the end of a UTP cable, while a punch down tool is used to connect UTP cable to a patch panel. **C** is incorrect because a toner probe is used to locate a specific UTP cable among many cables in a bundle. **D** is partially correct because it could be used to test each wire in a UTP cable; however, it would require two multimeters (and probably two people), one on each end, to accomplish this. A cable tester or certifier is a much more efficient tool for testing cables.

80. You need to determine whether a run of UTP cable has an open short somewhere between the RJ-45 wall jack and the switch in the server room and how far away the break is from the wall jack. What should you do?

    A. Use a cable tester to test the cable.

    B. Use a TDR to test the cable.

    C. Use a toner probe to test the cable.

    D. Use an OTDR to test the cable.

> ☑ **B.** A time-domain reflectometer (TDR) would be the best tool with which to test the cable. A TDR sends a signal down a cable and measures the amount of time it takes for the signal to return. Using this information, it calculates the distance to the end of the cable. If this distance is less than the physical length of the cable, you know the cable is broken (or *open*) at that distance.

☒ **A**, **C**, and **D** are incorrect. **A** is partially correct because a cable tester tests each wire in the cable for continuity and verifies that each one is connected to the right pin in the jack or plug. However, it isn't capable of telling you where in the run the cable is open. **C** is incorrect because a toner probe is used to identify a specific cable within a cable bundle. **D** is incorrect because an OTDR performs the same function as a TDR, but on fiber-optic cables instead of UTP.

81. You recently experienced a catastrophic server failure in your server room due to overheating, even though the thermostat was set to 68 degrees Fahrenheit. What can you do to prevent this from happening again? (Choose two.)

    A. Aim the air conditioning diffuser vent in the server room at the rear of your server systems.
    B. Prop the door to the server room open to vent excess heat.
    C. Rearrange the systems in the server room to form hot and cold aisles.
    D. Install temperature monitoring equipment in the server room.
    E. Reduce the thermostat in the server room to 62 degrees Fahrenheit.

    ☑ **C** and **D.** You should consider rearranging the systems in the server room to form hot and cold aisles. The hot exhaust from all systems should be oriented toward each other, forming the hot aisle. The intakes of all systems should be oriented away from the hot aisle, forming a cold aisle. You should also consider implementing temperature monitoring equipment in the server room. This will help you identify hot spots and temperature spikes.

    ☒ **A**, **B**, and **E** are incorrect. **A** is incorrect because cool air from your air conditioning system should be directed toward the intakes of your server systems, not to the rear where hot exhaust is typically vented. **B** is incorrect because propping the door open introduces a security risk for your systems. It also may interfere with the normal operation of the server room cooling system. **E** is incorrect because reducing the temperature on the thermostat may or may not help cool the room. If the air conditioning system has additional capacity, this will definitely help. However, if the air conditioning system is already at capacity, reducing the temperature on the thermostat will not cool the room any further.

82. A company has configured its ecommerce web site to be installed on multiple servers so the requests sent to the site will be distributed among all servers. What type of redundancy is being used in this scenario?

    A. Fault tolerance

    B. High availability

    C. Load balancing

    D. Cold spare

> ☑ **C.** Load balancing usually involves sharing the workload among multiple systems. If one server becomes overloaded, other servers can still handle new requests. This sharing of workloads is completely transparent to the end user.
>
> ☒ **A, B,** and **D** are incorrect. **A** is incorrect because fault tolerance ensures that the data is available through data redundancy. **B** is incorrect because high availability involves configuring redundancy in the system such that if one system fails, another immediately takes it place. For example, you could configure two or more servers (nodes) in a cluster. The primary node services requests while the secondary node remains in a standby state unless the primary server becomes unavailable. **D** is incorrect because a cold spare provides hardware redundancy and is kept in a powered off state until needed.

83. A client's web server is frequently bogged down with client requests during peak hours. You have been hired to balance HTTP requests for the heavily utilized web site among multiple web servers. What should you do?

    A. Implement the Spanning Tree Protocol.

    B. Implement the Simple Network Management Protocol.

    C. Implement the Common Address Redundancy Protocol.

    D. Implement Round Robin DNS.

> ☑ **D.** Round Robin DNS is used to balance the network processing load among multiple servers (for example, balancing HTTP requests among multiple web servers). This is done by configuring a single domain name with multiple IP addresses. The DNS server returns the list of IP addresses associated with the domain name in random order between clients. The client systems usually attempt to connect to the first IP address received from the DNS server. In this way, the server that services clients is randomized for each request.

☒ **A**, **B**, and **C** are incorrect. **A** is incorrect because the Spanning Tree Protocol is used to prevent switching loops with cascaded Ethernet switches. **B** is incorrect because Simple Network Management Protocol (SNMP) is used to monitor network hosts. **C** is incorrect because the Common Address Redundancy Protocol (CARP) allows you to group multiple hosts on the same network together and share IP addresses to provide failover redundancy.

84. You have just made global configuration changes to your Cisco router and want to put it back into read-only mode. What must you do? (Choose two.)

A. Enter **enable** at the command prompt.

B. Enter **disable** at the command prompt.

C. Enter **config term** at the command prompt.

D. Enter **exit** at the command prompt.

E. Enter **configure** at the command prompt.

☑ **B** and **D.** The **disable** command is used to switch from privilege exec mode to user exec mode (which is a read-only mode). The **exit** command is used to switch from global configuration mode to privilege exec mode.

☒ **A**, **C** and **E** are incorrect. **A** is incorrect because the **enable** command is used on a Cisco router to switch from user exec mode to privilege exec mode. **C** is incorrect because the **config term** command enables global configuration mode, which allows you to make configuration changes to the router. **E** is incorrect because **configure** is not a valid command on a Cisco router.

85. You need to configure an Ethernet interface in a Cisco router with an IP address of 10.0.0.1 using the default Class A subnet mask. What should you do?

A. Enter **ip address 10.0.0.1 255.0.0.0** at the router's command prompt.

B. Enter **ip address 10.0.0.1 255.255.255.0** at the router's command prompt.

C. Enter **ipaddr 10.0.0.1 255.0.0.0** at the router's command prompt

D. Enter **ifconfig eth0 10.0.0.1 netmask 255.0.0.0** at the router's command prompt.

☑ **A.** To set the IP address used by an interface in a Cisco router, you first enter **interface f0/0** at the command prompt of the Cisco router to tell the operating system that you want to configure the first Ethernet interface installed in it. Then you enter **ip address 10.0.0.1 255.0.0.0** at the router's command prompt.

☒ **B, C,** and **D** are incorrect. **B** is incorrect because the command specifies the wrong subnet mask (Class C). **C** is incorrect because it uses an invalid command (**ipaddr**) for a Cisco router. **D** is incorrect because it uses the **ifconfig** command, which is used to set the IP address on a Linux system, not a Cisco router.

86. Which VLAN feature is used by switches to prevent switching loops that could occur if multiple switches were wired together incorrectly?

A. Trunking

B. Spanning Tree Protocol

C. Port Mirroring

D. QoS

☑ **B.** The Spanning Tree Protocol is used by switches to prevent switching loops that could occur if multiple switches are wired together incorrectly.

☒ **A, C,** and **D** are incorrect. **A** is incorrect because trunking allows you to carry VLAN traffic between network switches. **C** is incorrect because port mirroring allows the switch to send a copy of data that reaches certain ports to a monitored port, which allows you to monitor network traffic. **D** is incorrect because QoS settings allow you to prioritize certain types of network traffic over other types.

87. A user has called the help desk indicating that his Windows workstation is displaying a "Duplicate IP address…" error message. You're curious because your network uses DHCP to assign IP addresses. You check the workstation and find that it has been assigned a static IP address. What should you do to fix this issue?

A. Check the network for another workstation that has been statically assigned the duplicated IP address and assign that host a different address.

B. Reconfigure the workstation to use DHCP to get its IP addressing information.

C. Type **ipconfig /renew** at the workstation's command prompt.

D. Statically assign the workstation a different IP address.

☑ **B.** The most efficient way to fix this issue is to reconfigure the workstation to get its IP addressing information from the DHCP server on your network. This will prevent IP address conflicts as DHCP servers use lease information to keep track of which IP addresses have been handed out and which ones are available.

☒ **A, C,** and **D** are incorrect. **A** and **D** would work temporarily; however, the problem will likely surface again. As a general rule, you can prevent IP address conflicts by limiting static IP address assignments only to infrastructure systems on your network, such as servers and routers. All workstations should get their IP addressing information dynamically from a DHCP server. **C** is incorrect because the host has a static IP address assignment. Therefore, the **ipconfig /renew** command can't be used renew its DHCP lease.

88. The workstations on your network are unable to reach a Linux-based file and print server on a different network segment. You've checked and the server is up and running with a static IP address assignment of 172.18.0.1. Your workstations have been assigned IP addresses from your DHCP server using addresses in the 172.17.8.100 to 172.17.8.253 range with a subnet mask of 255.255.0.0. You are unable to ping the server from any workstation, yet the workstations are able to ping each other. What should you do?

A. Assign the Linux server an IP address that is not being used in the range of 172.17.8.100 to 172.17.8.253.

B. Verify that the network switch has power and is turned on.

C. Check the subnet mask assigned to the Linux server.

D. Verify that the workstations have the correct default gateway router address assigned.

☑ **D.** The most likely cause of the issue in the scenario is a misconfigured default gateway router address (or the gateway router itself is down). The fact that the workstations can ping each other indicates the basic network infrastructure is functioning on the local segment. Because the server is on a different physical network segment, a router is required for the workstations to reach it.

☒ **A, B,** and **C** are incorrect. **A** is incorrect because changing the IP address of the server to something in the 172.17.8.100 to 172.17.8.253 range won't fix the issue. **B** is incorrect because network connectivity on the local segment is not an issue, as evidenced by the fact that the workstations can ping each other. **C** could be a possible cause of the problem. However, it's much more likely that the wrong gateway router IP address is being delivered to the workstations from the DHCP server.

89. Which interior gateway protocols are distance vector routing protocols? (Choose two.)

A. Border Gateway Protocol (BGP)

B. Routing Information Protocol (RIP)

C. Open Shortest Path First (OSPF)

D. Interior Gateway Routing Protocol (IGRP)

E. Intermediate System–to–Intermediate System (IS-IS)

☑ **B and D.** RIP and IGRP are both distance vector routing protocols. Distance vector routing protocols require a router to keep all of its neighboring routers updated with any changes discovered in the networks to which it is connected.

☒ **A, C,** and **E** are incorrect. **A** is incorrect because BGP is an exterior gateway routing protocol. **C** and **E** are incorrect because both OSPF and IS-IS are link state interior gateway protocols.

90. Which routing protocol is an Exterior Gateway Protocol that can be used on global public networks such as the Internet?

A. Enhanced Interior Gateway Routing Protocol (EIGRP)

B. Interior Gateway Routing Protocol (IGRP)

C. Routing Information Protocol (RIP)

D. Border Gateway Protocol (BGP)

☑ **D.** The Border Gateway Protocol (BGP) is an Exterior Gateway Protocol. BGP is used on the Internet to route data around the world. BGP does not use interior gateway protocol metrics to make routing decisions (such as hop count, MTU, and latency). Instead, it uses network path information along with network rules to determine the best route to use.

☒ **A, B,** and **C** are incorrect. **A** is incorrect because EIGRP is an interior gateway protocol designed by Cisco to replace IGRP. **B** is incorrect because IGRP is a distance vector interior gateway protocol. **C** is incorrect because RIP is a distance vector interior gateway protocol.

91. Some routing protocols determine the best route to take based on how many routers a packet must traverse to reach its destination. Which metric measures this?

- **A.** Hop count
- **B.** MTU
- **C.** Latency
- **D.** Link state

☑ **A.** The hop count metric measures how many routers a packet must traverse to reach its destination. Some routing protocols use this metric instead of the MTU or latency to determine the best route to take.

☒ **B, C,** and **D** are incorrect. **B** is incorrect because the maximum transmission unit (MTU) metric determines the largest single transmission unit size. **C** is incorrect because latency measures how long it takes for data to cross a network from router to router. **D** is incorrect because the term "link state" is used to categorize a type of routing protocol. It is not a routing metric.

92. Which routing protocols are Interior Gateway Protocols (IGP)? (Choose two.)

- **A.** Intermediate System–to–Intermediate System (IS-IS)
- **B.** Exterior Gateway Protocol 3 (EGP3)
- **C.** Spanning Tree Protocol (STP)
- **D.** Border Gateway Protocol (BGP)
- **E.** Enhanced Interior Gateway Routing Protocol (EIGRP)

☑ **A** and **E.** The Intermediate System–to–Intermediate System (IS-IS) and Enhanced Interior Gateway Routing Protocol (EIGRP) protocols are examples of Interior Gateway Protocols. IGPs are used to exchange routing information within an autonomous system.

☒ **B, C,** and **D** are incorrect. **B** and **D** are incorrect because the EGP3 and BGP protocols are examples of Exterior Gateway Protocols (EGPs). **C** is incorrect because the Spanning Tree Protocol is a switching protocol used to prevent switching loops.

93. In your network, the routers know about your network topology and monitor the state of the link between the routers. What types of dynamic routing protocols are in use in this network? (Choose two.)

A. Hybrid routing protocol

B. Link state routing protocol

C. Distance vector routing protocol

D. Exterior Gateway Protocol

☑ **A and B.** In a link state routing protocol environment, your routers know about the network topology and monitor the state of the links between the routers. If a link is down, that information is stored in the routing table and that pathway will not be used. Hybrid routing protocols include features of both distance vector and link state protocols.

☒ **C and D are incorrect. C** is incorrect because distance vector routing protocol routers use hop counts to determine the best route without taking into account the speed or state of the link. Link state routing protocols choose the best route beyond a simple hop count by taking into account, for example, the speed of a link, or whether a link is up or down. **D** is incorrect because distance vector routing protocols are types of Interior Gateway Protocol, not Exterior Gateway Protocol.

94. Which standard allows VLANs to span multiple network switches?

A. 802.8

B. 802.11

C. 802.1q

D. 802.14

☑ **C.** The IEEE 802.1q standard defines a method for adding VLAN tags to Ethernet frames. By doing this, you can extend a VLAN beyond a single network switch.

☒ **A, B, and D are incorrect. A** is incorrect because the IEEE 802.8 standard defines fiber-optic token passing network technology. **B** is incorrect because the IEEE 802.11 standard defines wireless network technology. **D** is incorrect because the IEEE 802.14 standard defines how cable modems function.

95. Your workstation is configured to use DHCP to get its IP addressing information. When you boot the system and the operating system loads, it sends out a DHCPDISCOVER broadcast on the network. The DHCP server receives the message and responds with a DHCPOFFER to the workstation. What happens next?
  A. The DHCP server immediately follows the DHCPOFFER with a DHCPACK message.
  B. The workstation receives the DHCPOFFER message and responds with a DHCPACK to the server.
  C. The workstation broadcasts a DHCPREQUEST message on the network.
  D. The workstation sends a DHCPAPPROVE or DHCPDENY message.

☑ **C.** Once a client receives one or more DHCP offers, it broadcasts a DHCPREQUEST message indicating it has decided which offer to accept. The DHCP server whose offer was accepted will respond with a DHCPACK to finalize the IP address assignment. DHCP servers whose offers were not accepted withdraw their offers.

☒ **A, B,** and **D** are incorrect. **A** is incorrect because the DHCP server does not immediately send a DHCPACK until it receives a DHCPREQUEST from the client. **B** is incorrect because the client sends a DHCPREQUEST message after it receives a DHCPOFFER from the server. **D** is incorrect because there is no such thing as a DHCPAPPROVE or DHCPDENY message in the DHCP protocol.

96. Which mechanism can be used by DHCP servers to define the IP addresses that the server can hand out to clients?
  A. DHCP scope
  B. DHCP subnet address range
  C. DHCP option
  D. DHCP address exclusion

☑ **B.** DHCP servers use a subnet address range to define the IP addresses that the DHCP server can hand out to clients. For example, a subnet address range may be defined as 192.168.1.100 to 192.168.1.253. Only IP addresses within this range can be handed out to clients by the DHCP server.

☒ **A, C,** and **D** are incorrect. **A** is incorrect because a DHCP scope is a logical grouping of IP addresses and options. **C** is incorrect because you use DHCP options to deliver additional IP configuration parameters to DHCP clients, such as the default gateway router and DNS server addresses. **D** is incorrect because address exclusions are used to reserve IP addresses within a range so that they will not be distributed by the DHCP server.

97. Your organization's network is composed of two segments connected by routers. Your DHCP server is on segment A, while your DNS server is on segment B. Workstations are connected to all segments; however, you've discovered that only the workstations on segment A are able to get IP addresses from the DHCP server. What should you do?

A. Configure a DHCP relay agent on segment B.

B. Configure your routers to forward broadcasts.

C. Configure a DHCP relay agent on segment A.

D. Install a separate DHCP server on segment B.

☑ **A.** Most routers are configured by default not to forward broadcast messages. This is done to reduce network traffic and prevent DoS attacks. Therefore, the DHCPDISCOVER broadcasts sent from clients on segment B can't reach the DHCP server on segment A. To fix this, you can configure a DHCP relay agent on segment B that manages DHCP messages between the clients on this segment and the DHCP server on segment A.

☒ **B, C,** and **D** are incorrect. **B** is incorrect because configuring routers to forward broadcasts would increase network traffic and could expose your network to certain DoS exploits. **C** is incorrect because a relay agent on segment A would not be able service DHCP clients on segment B. **D** would work, but it isn't necessary and would increase your administrative workload.

98. Your security team discovered a rogue WAP that was configured with the same SSID as a legitimate WAP. Which term best describes the security risk in this scenario?

A. Rogue access point

B. Evil twin

C. War driving

D. Data emanation

☑ **B.** The WAP in this scenario is an evil twin. This exploit is commonly used in conjunction with a rogue web server connected to the evil twin that mimics commonly used banking, e-commerce, and credit card web sites to trick users who attach to the WAP into revealing personal information.

☒ **A, C,** and **D** are incorrect. **A** is incorrect because a rogue access point is typically a WAP installed and connected to the wired network without the permission of knowledge of the IT department. **C** refers to the practice of driving around looking for open wireless networks. **D** is incorrect because data emanation refers to the "leaking" of your wireless network signal beyond your physical facility.

99. You want to establish a VPN connection from your laptop at home to your company's internal network through the Internet. Your company's VPN server uses the PPTP protocol to create the encrypted tunnel. You need to configure your workstation's firewall to allow the VPN traffic through. What must you do?

A. Open port TCP port 25 in the firewall.

B. Open UDP port 1701 in the firewall.

C. Open TCP port 1723 in the firewall

D. Open UDP port 5500 in the firewall.

☑ **C.** TCP port 1723 is used by VPN tunnels created using the PPTP protocol. This port must be opened in the firewall of the workstation in this scenario to allow VPN traffic through.

☒ **A, B,** and **D** are incorrect. **A** is incorrect because TCP port 25 is used by SMTP servers to accept and forward e-mail messages. **B** and **D** are incorrect because UDP port 1701, UDP port 5500 (for IPSec), and UDP port 500 (for key exchange via ISAKMP) are used to allow traffic from a VPN tunnel using the L2TP protocol.

100. You are configuring a VPN for a client that employs remote workers. The client has specified that the VPN be created using the L2TP protocol. However, you are aware that a VPN tunnel created with L2TP is inherently insecure. What should you do?

A. Secure the tunnel with IPSec.

B. Secure the tunnel with MPPE.

C. Secure the tunnel with TLS.

D. Secure the tunnel with MS-CHAP.

☑ **A.** The IPSec protocol is commonly used to secure L2TP/IPSec VPNs.

☒ **B, C,** and **D** are incorrect. **B** is incorrect because The PPTP protocol is responsible for establishing the VPN tunnel (like L2TP), but it doesn't encrypt the contents of the tunnel. Instead, it relies on the Microsoft Point-to-Point Encryption (MPPE) protocol to secure the tunnel. **C** is incorrect because TLS or SSL can be used to secure SSL VPNs, but neither is used to secure an L2TP VPN. **D** is incorrect because MS-CHAP is an authentication protocol. It can be used to authenticate users in a VPN tunnel, but it isn't capable of encrypting data transmissions.

C

About the CD

The CD-ROM included with this book comes complete with MasterExam practice exam software and a link to download a Secure PDF copy of the book. The software is easy to install on any Windows 2000/XP/Vista/7 computer and must be installed to access the MasterExam feature. To register for the bonus MasterExam, simply click the Bonus MasterExam link on the main launch page and follow the directions to the free online registration.

SYSTEM REQUIREMENTS

The software requires Windows 2000 or later and Internet Explorer 6.0 or later and 20 MB of hard disk space for full installation. The Secure PDF copy of the book requires Adobe Digital Editions.

INSTALLING AND RUNNING MASTEREXAM

If your computer's CD-ROM drive is configured to auto run, the CD-ROM will automatically start up upon inserting the disk. From the opening screen you may install MasterExam by clicking the MasterExam link. This will begin the installation process and create a program group named LearnKey. To run MasterExam, choose Start | All Programs | LearnKey | MasterExam. If the auto run feature did not launch your CD, browse to the CD and click the LaunchTraining.exe icon.

MasterExam

MasterExam provides you with a simulation of the actual exam. The number of questions, the type of questions, and the time allowed are intended to be an accurate representation of the exam environment. You have the option to take an open book exam, including hints, references, and answers; a closed book exam; or the timed MasterExam simulation.

When you launch MasterExam, a digital clock display will appear in the bottom-right corner of your screen. The clock will continue to count down to zero unless you choose to end the exam before the time expires.

SECURE PDF COPY OF THE BOOK

The contents of this book are available as a free download in Adobe Digital Editions Secure PDF format. To download your copy, please visit http://books.mcgraw-hill.com/ebookdownloads/9780071788809. You will be required to provide your name, email address, and unique access code. The unique access code can be found on the label that is adhered to the flap of the CD envelope bound into the sleeve in the back of this book. Upon submitting this information, an email will be sent to the address you provided. Follow the instructions included in the email to download your Secure PDF.

Note *The unique access code entitles you to download one copy of the Secure PDF to one personal computer. The unique access code can only be used once, and the Secure PDF is only usable on the computer on which it was downloaded. Be sure to download the Secure PDF to the computer you intend to use.*

Adobe Digital Editions is required to open, view, and navigate the Secure PDF. It is available as a free download from Adobe's website, www.adobe.com, and is also included on the CD. It is highly recommended that you download and install Adobe Digital Editions before attempting to download the Secure PDF.

HELP

A help file is provided through the help button on the main page in the lower-left corner. An individual help feature is also available through MasterExam.

REMOVING MASTEREXAM INSTALLATION

MasterExam is installed to your hard drive. For best results removing this program, use the Start | All Programs | LearnKey | Uninstall option.

TECHNICAL SUPPORT

For questions regarding the content of the Secure PDF or MasterExam, please visit www.mhprofessional.com or email customer.service@mcgraw-hill.com. For customers outside the 50 United States, email international_cs@mcgraw-hill.com.

LearnKey Technical Support

For technical problems with the software (installation, operation, removing installation), please visit www.learnkey.com, email techsupport@learnkey.com, or call toll free 1-800-482-8244.

INDEX

X